The Ministers Manual for 1981

FIFTY-SIXTH ANNUAL ISSUE

The
MINISTERS
MANUAL
(Doran's)

1981 EDITION

Edited by
CHARLES L. WALLIS

HARPER & ROW, PUBLISHERS

SAN FRANCISCO

Cambridge
Hagerstown
Philadelphia
New York

1817

London
Mexico City
São Paulo
Sydney

Editors of THE MINISTERS MANUAL

G.B.F. Hallock, D.D., 1926–1958
M.K.W. Heicher, Ph.D., 1943–1968
Charles L. Wallis, M.A., M.Div., 1969–

THE MINISTERS MANUAL FOR 1981
Copyright © 1980 by Charles L. Wallis. All rights reserved.
Printed in the United States of America. For information
address Harper & Row, Publishers, Inc., 10 East 53rd Street,
New York, N.Y. 10022. Published simultaneously in Canada
by Fitzhenry & Whiteside Limited, Toronto.

FIRST EDITION

Library of Congress Cataloging in Publication Data
The ministers manual; a study and pulpit guide.
   1. Sermons—Outlines. 2. Homiletical illustrations.
I. Hallock, Gerard Benjamin Fleet, 1856– ed.
  BV4223.M5   251.058   25–21658 rev*
  ISBN 0–06–069026–7

80 81 82 83 84 10 9 8 7 6 5 4 3 2 1

PREFACE

Readers of various annual issues of *The Ministers Manual* seem particularly generous in their comments on those parts which for them are suggestive, stimulating, or helpful. Their letters are encouraging and add pleasure to the routine chores required in editing an annual publication.

But the editor disclaims any credit, being only an editorial channel between the contributors and readers—pastors, church leaders, missionaries, youth- and church-school workers, and others.

The less conspicuous an editor's role, the more persuasive the communication between writer and reader and the stronger the testimony to the redemptive life, teaching, death, and resurrection of the Lord Jesus, which is the only justification of this publication.

More than 500 contributors are represented in this fifty-sixth annual issue of *The Ministers Manual.* Included are the words and witness of Christian writers of twenty centuries. Most of the sermon extracts, homiletic and illustrative resources, and worship aids have not previously been published in book form, and much of the material was prepared specially for this issue, either in response to a specific request or on an author's own initiative. A conscientious effort has been made to include only materials not found in earlier volumes of *The Ministers Manual.*

A graduate student, writing a dissertation on homiletic resources, wrote that he had surveyed issues of *The Ministers Manual* covering more than a half century. He found, he said, a family resemblance from first to last, adding that the social implications of the gospel had changed with the passing years but the theological emphases had remained unchanged and showed an evangelical thrust.

He further noted what he considered to be a high quality of thought and expression on the part of the contributors, who, he felt, wrote with biblical insight, vigor, and clarity.

But, he continued in a series of questions as long as a shopping list, Who uses *The Ministers Manual*? How is it used? Where is it used?

A pastor, recently retired, writes that he sent thirty back issues to the library of a Bible school in a developing country.

A military chaplain, assigned to a Pacific outpost where his wife is making a translation of the New Testament, secured eighty copies for distribution to native Christian leaders.

A large urban church provides a copy for each member of the Sunday school staff.

A Congressman says he keeps a copy at his bedside and turns to it each night.

And a copy of *The Ministers Manual* has been placed in the cornerstone repository of a newly constructed church. Perhaps it will be read by a spiritual descendant a hundred years from now, who may discern that the church in 1981 was faithful to him who is the same yesterday, today, and forever.

Rev. Charles L. Wallis
Keuka College
Keuka Park, N.Y. 14478

CONTENTS

SECTION I. GENERAL AIDS AND RESOURCES   1

Civil Year Calendars for 1981 and 1982   1

Church and Civil Calendar for 1981   1

Lectionary for 1981   3

Four-Year Church Calendar   5

Forty-Year Easter Calendar   5

Traditional Wedding Anniversary Identifications   5

Colors Appropriate for Days and Seasons   5

Flowers in Season Appropriate for Church Use   6

Historical, Cultural, and Religious Anniversaries in 1981   6

Anniversaries of Hymns, Hymn Writers, and Composers in
1981   7

Quotable Quotations   8

Questions of Life and Religion   11

Biblical Benedictions and Blessings   12

SECTION II. VITAL THEMES FOR VITAL PREACHING   14

SECTION III. RESOURCES FOR COMMUNION SERVICES   32

SECTION IV. RESOURCES FOR FUNERAL SERVICES   40

SECTION V. RESOURCES FOR LENTEN AND EASTER PREACHING   47

SECTION VI. RESOURCES FOR ADVENT AND CHRISTMAS
PREACHING   55

SECTION VII. EVANGELISM AND WORLD MISSIONS   62

SECTION VIII. CHILDREN'S STORIES AND SERMONS   68

CONTENTS

SECTION IX. SERMON OUTLINES AND HOMILETIC AND WORSHIP
AIDS FOR FIFTY-TWO WEEKS   82

SECTION X. IDEAS AND SUGGESTIONS FOR PULPIT AND PARISH   233

SECTION XI. A LITTLE TREASURY OF ILLUSTRATIONS   237

INDEX OF CONTRIBUTORS   266

SERMON TITLE INDEX   270

SCRIPTURAL INDEX   273

INDEX OF PRAYERS   275

INDEX OF MATERIALS USEFUL AS CHILDREN'S STORIES AND
SERMONS   276

INDEX OF MATERIALS USEFUL FOR SMALL GROUPS   276

INDEX OF SPECIAL DAYS AND SEASONS   277

TOPICAL INDEX   277

SECTION I. *General Aids and Resources*

Civil Year Calendars

1981

JANUARY	FEBRUARY	MARCH	APRIL
S M T W T F S	S M T W T F S	S M T W T F S	S M T W T F S
1 2 3	1 2 3 4 5 6 7	1 2 3 4 5 6 7	1 2 3 4
4 5 6 7 8 9 10	8 9 10 11 12 13 14	8 9 10 11 12 13 14	5 6 7 8 9 10 11
11 12 13 14 15 16 17	15 16 17 18 19 20 21	15 16 17 18 19 20 21	12 13 14 15 16 17 18
18 19 20 21 22 23 24	22 23 24 25 26 27 28	22 23 24 25 26 27 28	19 20 21 22 23 24 25
25 26 27 28 29 30 31		29 30 31	26 27 28 29 30

MAY	JUNE	JULY	AUGUST
S M T W T F S	S M T W T F S	S M T W T F S	S M T W T F S
1 2	1 2 3 4 5 6	1 2 3 4	1
3 4 5 6 7 8 9	7 8 9 10 11 12 13	5 6 7 8 9 10 11	2 3 4 5 6 7 8
10 11 12 13 14 15 16	14 15 16 17 18 19 20	12 13 14 15 16 17 18	9 10 11 12 13 14 15
17 18 19 20 21 22 23	21 22 23 24 25 26 27	19 20 21 22 23 24 25	16 17 18 19 20 21 22
24 25 26 27 28 29 30	28 29 30	26 27 28 29 30 31	23 24 25 26 27 28 29
31			30 31

SEPTEMBER	OCTOBER	NOVEMBER	DECEMBER
S M T W T F S	S M T W T F S	S M T W T F S	S M T W T F S
1 2 3 4 5	1 2 3	1 2 3 4 5 6 7	1 2 3 4 5
6 7 8 9 10 11 12	4 5 6 7 8 9 10	8 9 10 11 12 13 14	6 7 8 9 10 11 12
13 14 15 16 17 18 19	11 12 13 14 15 16 17	15 16 17 18 19 20 21	13 14 15 16 17 18 19
20 21 22 23 24 25 26	18 19 20 21 22 23 24	22 23 24 25 26 27 28	20 21 22 23 24 25 26
27 28 29 30	25 26 27 28 29 30 31	29 30	27 28 29 30 31

1982

JANUARY	FEBRUARY	MARCH	APRIL
S M T W T F S	S M T W T F S	S M T W T F S	S M T W T F S
1 2	1 2 3 4 5 6	1 2 3 4 5 6	1 2 3
3 4 5 6 7 8 9	7 8 9 10 11 12 13	7 8 9 10 11 12 13	4 5 6 7 8 9 10
10 11 12 13 14 15 16	14 15 16 17 18 19 20	14 15 16 17 18 19 20	11 12 13 14 15 16 17
17 18 19 20 21 22 23	21 22 23 24 25 26 27	21 22 23 24 25 26 27	18 19 20 21 22 23 24
24 25 26 27 28 29 30	28	28 29 30 31	25 26 27 28 29 30
31			

MAY	JUNE	JULY	AUGUST
S M T W T F S	S M T W T F S	S M T W T F S	S M T W T F S
1	1 2 3 4 5	1 2 3	1 2 3 4 5 6 7
2 3 4 5 6 7 8	6 7 8 9 10 11 12	4 5 6 7 8 9 10	8 9 10 11 12 13 14
9 10 11 12 13 14 15	13 14 15 16 17 18 19	11 12 13 14 15 16 17	15 16 17 18 19 20 21
16 17 18 19 20 21 22	20 21 22 23 24 25 26	18 19 20 21 22 23 24	22 23 24 25 26 27 28
23 24 25 26 27 28 29	27 28 29 30	25 26 27 28 29 30 31	29 30 31
30 31			

SEPTEMBER	OCTOBER	NOVEMBER	DECEMBER
S M T W T F S	S M T W T F S	S M T W T F S	S M T W T F S
1 2 3 4	1 2	1 2 3 4 5 6	1 2 3 4
5 6 7 8 9 10 11	3 4 5 6 7 8 9	7 8 9 10 11 12 13	5 6 7 8 9 10 11
12 13 14 15 16 17 18	10 11 12 13 14 15 16	14 15 16 17 18 19 20	12 13 14 15 16 17 18
19 20 21 22 23 24 25	17 18 19 20 21 22 23	21 22 23 24 25 26 27	19 20 21 22 23 24 25
26 27 28 29 30	24 25 26 27 28 29 30	28 29 30	26 27 28 29 30 31
	31		

Church and Civil Calendar for 1981

JANUARY

1 New Year's Day
  The Name of Jesus
5 Twelfth Night
6 Epiphany
13 Baptism of Jesus
15 Martin Luther King, Jr. Birthday
18 Conversion of St. Peter
  Missionary Day
18-25 Week of Prayer for Christian Unity
19 Robert E. Lee Birthday
20 Inauguration Day
25 Conversion of St. Paul

FEBRUARY

1 National Freedom Day
2 Presentation of Jesus in the Temple
  Groundhog Day
3 Four Chaplains Memorial Day
8 Race Relations Sunday
12 Abraham Lincoln Birthday
14 St. Valentine's Day
15 Susan B. Anthony Day
15-24 Brotherhood Week
16 George Washington Birthday
  Presidents' Day
24 St. Matthias, Apostle

MARCH

1 The Transfiguration
3 Shrove Tuesday
4 Ash Wednesday
6 World Day of Prayer
8 First Sunday in Lent
15 Second Sunday in Lent
17 St. Patrick's Day
20 Purim
22 Third Sunday in Lent
25 The Annunciation
29 Fourth Sunday in Lent

APRIL

5 Fifth Sunday in Lent
  Passion Sunday
12-18 Holy Week
12 Palm Sunday
  Passion Sunday (alternate)
14 Pan American Day
16 Maundy Thursday
17 Good Friday
18 Easter Eve
19 Easter
  First Day of Passover
24 Arbor Day
25 St. Mark, Evangelist
26 Easter (Orthodox)
  Low Sunday

MAY

1 Law Day
  Loyalty Day
  May Fellowship Day
  St. Philip and St. James, Apostles
3-10 National Family Week
10 Festival of the Christian Home
  Mother's Day
16 Armed Forces Day
18 Victoria Day (Canada)
22 National Maritime Day
24 Rural Life Sunday
25 Memorial Day
28 Ascension Day

JUNE

7 Pentecost (Whitsunday)
8 First Day of Shavuot
11 St. Barnabas, Apostle
14 Children's Sunday
  Flag Day
  Trinity Sunday
18 Corpus Christi Day
21 Father's Day
24 Nativity of St. John the Baptist
29 St. Peter and St. Paul, Apostles

JULY

1 Dominion Day (Canada)
4 Independence Day
22 St. Mary Magdalene
25 St. James the Elder, Apostle

AUGUST

3 Civic Holiday (Canada)
6 The Transfiguration (alternate)
15 Mary, Mother of Jesus

19 National Aviation Day
24 St. Bartholomew, Apostle

SEPTEMBER

6 Labor Sunday
7 Labor Day
14 Holy Cross Day
17 Citizenship Day
21 St. Matthew, Apostle and Evangelist
25 American Indian Day
28 Frances Willard Day
29 First day of Rosh Hashanah
    St. Michael and All Angels

OCTOBER

4 World Communion Sunday
5 Child Health Day
8 Yom Kipper
11 Laity Sunday
12 Columbus Day
    Thanksgiving Day (Canada)
13 First day of Sukkoth
18 St. Luke, Evangelist
20 Shemini Atzeret
21 Simhat Torah
24 United Nations Day
25 Reformation Day
29 St. Simon and St. Jude, Apostles
31 Halloween
    National UNICEF Day
    Reformation Sunday

NOVEMBER

1 All Saints' Day
   World Temperance Day
2 All Soul's Day
3 Election Day
6 World Community Day
8 Stewardship Day
11 Veterans Day
12 Elizabeth Cady Stanton Day
15 Bible Sunday
22 Christ the King
    Thanksgiving Sunday
26 Thanksgiving Day
29 First Sunday in Advent
30 St. Andrew, Apostle

DECEMBER

6 Second Sunday in Advent
   Human Rights Day
13 Third Sunday in Advent
15 Bill of Rights Day
20 Fourth Sunday in Advent
21 First day of Hanukkah
    St. Thomas, Apostle
25 Christmas
26 Boxing Day (Canada)
    St. Stephen, Deacon and Martyr
27 St. John, Apostle and Evangelist
28 The Holy Innocents, Martyrs
31 New Year's Eve
    Watch Night

Lectionary for 1981

The following scripture lessons, with occasional alterations according to denominational preferences, are commended for use in public worship by various Protestant churches and the Roman Catholic Church and include first, second, and gospel readings according to Cycle A from January 1 to November 26 and according to Cycle B from November 29 to December 31.

CHRISTMASTIDE

January 1 (New Year's Day): Deut. 8:1–10; Rev. 21:1–7; Matt. 25:31–46.
January 4: Prov. 8:22–31; Eph. 1:15–23; John 1:1–5, 9–14.

EPIPHANY

January 6 (Epiphany): Isa. 60:1–6; Eph. 3: 1–6; Matt. 2:1–12.
January 11: Isa. 42:1–7; Acts 10:34–43; Matt. 3:13–17.
January 18: Isa. 49:3–6; I Cor. 1:1–9; John 1:29–34.
January 18–25 (Week of Prayer for Christian Unity): Isa. 11:1–9; Eph. 4:1–16; John 15:1–8.
January 25: Isa. 9:1–4; I Cor. 1:10–17; Matt. 4:12–23.
February 1: Zeph. 2:3, 3:11–13; I Cor. 1: 26–31; Matt. 5:1–12.
February 8: Isa. 58:7–10; I Cor. 2:1–5; Matt. 5:13–16.

February 15: Deut. 30:15–20; I Cor. 2: 6–
10; Matt. 5:27–37.
February 22: Lev. 19:1–2, 17–18; I Cor.
3:16–23; Matt. 5:38–48.
March 1: Isa. 49:14–18; I Cor. 4:1–5; Matt.
6:24–34.

LENT

March 4 (Ash Wednesday): Joel 2:12–18;
II Cor. 5:20 to 6:2; Matt. 6:1–6, 16–18.
March 8: Gen. 2:7–9, 3:1–7; Rom. 5:12–
19; Matt. 4:1–11.
March 15: Gen. 12:1–7; II Tim. 1:8–14;
Matt. 17:1–9.
March 22: Exod. 24:12–18; Rom. 5:1–5;
John 4:5–15.
March 29: II Sam. 5:1–5; Eph. 5:8–14;
John 9:1–11.
April 5: Ezek. 37:11–14; Rom. 8:6–11;
John 11:1–4, 17, 34–44.

HOLY WEEK

April 12 (Palm Sunday): Isa. 50:4–7; Phil.
2:5–11; Matt. 21:1–11.
April 13 (Monday): Isa. 50:4–10; Heb. 9:
11–15; Luke 19:41–48.
April 14 (Tuesday): Isa. 42:1–9; I Tim. 6:
11–16; John 12:37–50.
April 15 (Wednesday): Isa. 52:13 to 53:12;
Rom. 5:6–11; Luke 22:1–16.
April 16 (Maundy Thursday): Exod. 12:
1–8, 11–14; I Cor. 11:23–32; John 13:
1–15.
April 17 (Good Friday): Isa. 52:13 to 53:
12; Heb. 4:14–16, 5:7–9; John 19:17–
30.

EASTERTIDE

April 19: Acts 10:34–43; Col. 3:1–11; John
20:1–9.
April 26: Acts 2:42–47; I Pet. 1:3–9; John
20:19–31.
May 3: Acts 2:22–28; I Pet. 1:17–21; Luke
24:13–35.
Mary 10: Acts 2:36–41; I Pet. 2:19–25;
John 10:1–10.
May 17: Acts 6:1–7; I Pet. 2:4–10; John
14:1–12.
May 24: Acts 8:4–8, 14–17; I Pet. 3:13–18;
John 14:15–21.
May 28 (Ascension Day): Acts 1:1–11;

Eph. 1:16–23; Luke 24:44–53.
May 31: Acts 1:12–14; I Pet. 4:12–19; John
17:1–11.

PENTECOST

June 7 (Pentecost): I Cor. 12:4–13; Acts
2:1–13; John 14:15–26.
June 14 (Trinity Sunday): Ezek. 37:1–4; II
Cor. 13:5–13; Matt. 28:16–20.
June 21: Deut. 11:18–21; Rom. 3:21–28;
Matt. 7:21–29.
June 28: Hos. 6:1–6; Rom. 4:13–25; Matt.
9:9–13.
July 4 (Independence Day): Deut. 28: 1–9;
Rom. 13:1–8; Luke 1:68–79.
July 5: Exod. 19:2–6; Rom. 5:6–11; Matt.
9:36 to 10:8.
July 12: Jer. 20:10–13; Rom. 5:12–15;
Matt. 10:26–33.
July 19: II Kings 4:8–16; Rom. 6:1–11;
Matt. 10:37–42.
July 26: Zech. 9:9–13; Rom. 8:6–11; Matt.
11:25–30.
August 2: Isa. 55:10–13; Rom. 8:12–17;
Matt. 13:1–17.
August 9: II Sam. 7:18–22; Rom. 8:18–25;
Matt. 13:24–35.
August 16: I Kings 3:5–12; Rom. 8:26–30;
Matt. 13:44–52.
August 23: Isa. 55:1–3; Rom. 8:31–39;
Matt. 14:13–21.
August 30: I Kings 19:9–16; Rom. 9:1–5;
Matt. 14:22–33.
September 6: Isa. 56:1–7; Rom. 11:13–16,
29–32; Matt. 15:21–28.
September 13: Isa. 22:19–23; Rom. 11:
33–36; Matt. 16:13–20.
September 20: Jer. 20:7–9; Rom. 12:1–7;
Matt. 16:21–28.
September 27: Ezek. 33:7–9; Rom. 13:8–
10; Matt. 18:15–20.
October 4: Gen. 4:13–16; Rom. 14:5–9;
Matt. 18:21–35; (World Communion
Sunday) Isa. 49:18–23; Rev. 3:17–22;
John 10: 11–18.
October 11: Isa. 55:6–11; Phil. 1:21–27;
Matt. 20:1–16.
October 18: Ezek. 18:25–29; Phil. 2:1–11;
Matt. 21:28–32.
October 25: Isa. 5:1–7; Phil 4:4–9; Matt.
21:33–43; (Reformation Sunday) Heb.
2:1–4; Rom. 3:21–28; John 8:31–36.

November 1: Isa. 25:6–9; Phil. 4:12–20; Matt. 22:1–14.
November 8: Isa. 45:1–6; I Thess. 1:1–5; Matt. 22:15–22.
November 15: Exod. 22:21–27; I Thess. 1:2–10; Matt. 22:34–40.
November 22: Mal. 2:1–10; I Thess. 2: 7–13; Matt. 23:1–12.
November 26 (Thanksgiving Day): Isa. 61:10–11; I Tim. 2:1–8; Luke 12:22–31.

ADVENT

November 29: Isa. 63:16 to 64:4; I Cor. 1:3–9; Mark 13:32–37.

December 6: Isa. 40:1–5, 9–11. II Pet. 3: 8–14; Mark 1:1–8.
December 13: Isa. 61:1–4, 8–11; I Thess. 5:16–24; John 1:6–8, 19–28.
December 20: II Sam. 7:8–16; Rom. 16: 25–27; Luke 1:26–38.
December 24 (Christmas Eve): Isa. 52:7–10; Heb. 1:1–9; John 1:1–14.

CHRISTMASTIDE

December 25: Isa. 62:6–12; Col. 1:15–20; Matt. 1:18–25.
December 27: Jer. 31:10–13; Heb. 2:10–18; Luke 2:25–35.

Four-Year Church Calendar

	1981	1982	1983	1984
Ash Wednesday	March 4	February 24	February 16	March 7
Palm Sunday	April 12	April 4	March 27	April 15
Good Friday	April 17	April 9	April 3	April 20
Easter	April 19	April 11	May 12	April 22
Ascension Day	May 28	May 20	May 22	May 31
Pentecost	June 7	May 30	May 29	June 10
Trinity Sunday	June 14	June 6	May 29	June 17
Thanksgiving	November 26	November 25	November 24	November 23
Advent Sunday	November 29	November 28	November 27	December 2

Forty-Year Easter Calendar

1981 April 19	1991 March 31	2001 April 14	2011 April 24
1982 April 11	1992 April 19	2002 March 31	2012 April 8
1983 April 3	1993 April 11	2003 April 20	2013 March 31
1984 April 22	1994 April 3	2004 April 11	2014 April 20
1985 April 7	1995 April 16	2005 March 27	2015 April 5
1986 March 30	1996 April 7	2006 April 16	2016 March 27
1987 April 19	1997 March 30	2007 April 8	2017 April 16
1988 April 3	1998 April 12	2008 March 23	2018 April 1
1989 March 26	1999 April 4	2009 April 12	2019 April 21
1990 April 15	2000 April 23	2010 April 4	2020 April 12

Traditional Wedding Anniversary Identifications

1 Paper	7 Wool	13 Lace	35 Coral
2 Cotton	8 Bronze	14 Ivory	40 Ruby
3 Leather	9 Pottery	15 Crystal	45 Sapphire
4 Linen	10 Tin	20 China	50 Gold
5 Wood	11 Steel	25 Silver	55 Emerald
6 Iron	12 Silk	30 Pearl	60 Diamond

Colors Appropriate for Days and Seasons

White. Symbolizes purity, perfection, and joy and identifies festivals marking events, except Good Friday, in the life of Jesus: Christmas, Easter, Eastertide, Ascension Day, Trinity Sunday, All Saints' Day, weddings, funerals.

Red. Symbolizes the Holy Spirit, martyrdom, and the love of God: Pentecost and Sundays following.

Violet. Symbolizes penitence: Advent, Lent.
Green. Symbolizes mission to the world, hope, regeneration, nurture, and growth: Epiphany season, Kingdomtide, Rural Life Sunday, Labor Sunday, Thanksgiving Sunday.
Black. Symbolizes mourning: Good Friday.

Flowers in Season Appropriate for Church Use

January. Carnation or snowdrop.	**August.** Gladiolus or poppy.
February. Violet or primrose.	**September.** Aster or morning glory.
March. Jonquil or daffodil.	**October.** Calendula or cosmos.
April. Lily, sweet pea, or daisy.	**November.** Chrysanthemum.
May. Lily of the valley or hawthorn.	**December.** Narcissus, holly, or poinsettia.
June. Rose or honeysuckle.	
July. Larkspur or water lily.	

Historical, Cultural, and Religious Anniversaries in 1981

10 years (1971). *January 30–February 2:* two astronauts on lunar surface for thirty-three hours. *April 20:* Supreme Court upholds busing to achieve racial balance in public schools. *May 3:* antiwar militants attempt to disrupt government operations. *June 13:* classified Pentagon Papers published. *July 5:* voting age lowered to eighteen. *July 26–August 7:* three-day landing on lunar surface. *September 13:* Attica prison rebellion ends. *October 25:* Communist China admitted to United Nations.

20 years (1961). *January 3:* U.S. severs diplomatic relations with Cuba. *March 1:* Peace Corps created. *March 13:* Alliance for Progress proposed. *April 12:* cosmonaut first man to orbit Earth in space. *April 17:* invasion of Bay of Pigs in Cuba fails. *May 1:* first U.S. manned suborbital space flight. *August 13:* Berlin Wall built. *September 18:* Dag Hammarskjold killed in plane crash. *November 20:* Russian Orthodox Church joins World Council of Churches.

25 years (1956). *May 21:* first aerial H-bomb tested. *July 26:* Egypt seizes Suez Canal. *September 25:* first transatlantic telephone cable in operation. *October 23–November 4:* Hungarian Revolution. *October 29–November 6:* Second Arab-Israeli War.

50 years (1931). Pearl Buck publishes *The Good Earth. March 4:* Gandhi ends civil disobedience campaign. *April 14:* Spanish Revolution begins. *May 1:* Empire State Building in New York City opened. *December 31:* British Commonwealth of Nations established.

75 years (1906). Galsworthy publishes *Man of Property* and Sinclair publishes *The Jungle. April 18:* earthquake devastates portions of San Francisco. *June 29:* construction of Panama Canal authorized. *June 30:* Pure Food and Drug Act passed.

100 years (1881). Clara Barton organizes American Red Cross. Booker T. Washington founds Tuskegee Institute. Rockefeller founds Standard Oil Company. Persecution of Jews begins in Russia. Revised Version of the New Testament published. Ibsen publishes *Ghosts* and James publishes *Portrait of a Lady. February 1:* de Lesseps undertakes and later abandons construction of Panama Canal. *March 4:* Garfield inaugurated U.S. president, shot by an assassin on *July 2,* and dies on *September 19.*

150 years (1831). Faraday discovers electro-magnetism. Garrison begins publication of abolition periodical, *The Liberator.* McCormick demonstrates mechanical reaper. *August 13–23:* Nat Turner leads slave uprising in Virginia.

200 years (1781). *March 1:* Articles of Confederation ratified. *October 19:* Cornwallis surrenders at Yorktown, Virginia.

250 years (1731). Kant publishes *Critique of Pure Reason* and Rousseau publishes *Confessions. March 13:* Herschel discovers Uranus. *April 26:* Defoe dies.

300 years (1681). William Penn receives royal charter for Pennsylvania.

400 years (1581). *January 28:* James VI signs second Scottish Confession of Faith.

450 years (1531). *October 11:* Zwingli killed at the battle of Kappel.
500 years (1481). Botticelli and others begin frescoes in the Sistine Chapel.
550 years (1431). *May 30:* Joan of Arc condemned and burned at the stake.
600 years (1381). *June-July:* Peasants' Revolt led by Wat Tyler.

750 years (1231). Cambridge University founded.
900 years (1081). Construction of the Tower of London begun.
1250 years (731). Bede completes his *Historia.*
1600 years (381). First Council of Constantinople formalizes the Nicene Creed.

Anniversaries of Hymns, Hymn Writers, and Composers in 1981

25 years (1956). Death of William R. Newell (b. 1868), author of "At Calvary"; J. Edgar Park (b. 1879), author of "We would see Jesus"; Douglas LeTell Rights (b. 1891), author of "Veiled in darkness Judah lay."

50 years (1931). Publication of "Christ is the world's true light" by George W. Briggs; "O God, in restless living" by Harry Emerson Fosdick; "O young and fearless prophet" by S. Ralph Harlow; hymn-tune PURPOSE ("God is working his purpose out"); "Remember all the people" by Percy Dearmer; hymn-tune WATCHMAN ("High o'er the lonely hills") by T. H. Ingham; hymn-tune WELLINGTON SQUARE ("Eternal God, whose purpose upholds") by Guy Warrack; "When restless crowds are thronging" by Thomas Curtis Clark. Death of George W. Chadwick (b. 1854), composer of hymn-tune PEACE ("I sought the Lord, and afterward I knew"); Ozora S. Davis (b. 1866), author of "At length there dawns the glorious day" and "We bear the strain of earthly care"; Harry W. Farrington (b. 1880), author of "I know not how that Bethlehem's babe"; Peter C. Lutkin (b. 1858), composer of hymn-tune LANIER ("Into the woods my master went"); Walter J. Mathams (b. 1853), author of "Christ of the upward way," "Jesus, friend of little children," and "Now in the days of youth"; Kristian Ostergaard (b. 1855), author of "That cause can neither be lost nor stayed."

75 years (1906). Publication of hymn-tunes DOWN AMPNEY ("Come down, O Lord divine") and SINE NOMINE ("For all the saints who from their labors rest") by R. Vaughan Williams; "O God of earth and altar" by G. K. Chesterton; "Father in heaven, who lovest all" by Rudyard Kipling. Death of Edward H. Bickersteth (b. 1825), author of "O God, the rock of ages" and "Peace, perfect peace"; Thomas H. Gill (b. 1819), author of "We come unto our fathers' God" and 200 other hymns; Jemina T. Luke (b. 1813), author of "I think when I read that sweet story of old"; George Matheson (b. 1842), author of "Gather us in," "Jesus, fountain of my days," "Make me a captive, Lord," and "O love that wilt not let me go."

100 years (1881). Publication of hymn-tune ANGEL'S STORY ("O Jesus, I have promised") by Arthur H. Mann; hymn-tunes INVITATION ("Come to the Savior now") and ST. CHRISTOPHER ("Beneath the cross of Jesus") by Frederick C. Maker; "Let the whole creation cry" by Stopford A. Brooke; "Lift up your hearts" by Henry M. Butler; "Lord, thy mercy now entreating" by Mary A. Sidebotham; "Sooner or later" by Christina Rossetti. Birth of Harry S. Mason (d. 1964), composer of hymn-tune BEACON ("Are ye able?"); W. R. Waghorne (d. 1942), composer of hymn-tune GREYSTONE ("All things bright and beautiful"). Death of Leonard Bacon (b. 1802), author of "O God, beneath thy guiding hand"; Josiah G. Holland (b. 1819), author of "There's a song in the air"; Sidney Lanier (b. 1842), author of "Into the woods my master went"; Jane E. Leeson (b. 1807), author of "Savior, teach me day by day."

150 years (1831). Birth of Phillips Brooks (d. 1908), author of "O little town of Bethlehem"; Arthur H. Messiter (d. 1863), composer of hymn-tune MARION ("Rejoice, ye pure in heart"). Death of Ignace J. Pleyel (b. 1757), composer of hymn-tunes GRACE CHURCH ("O thou to whose all-searching sight") and PLEYEL'S HYMN ("Children of the heavenly king.")

200 years (1781). Birth of Ebenezer Elli-

ott (d. 1849), author of "When wilt thou save the people"; Garrett Wellesley (b. 1735), composer of hymn-tune MORNING-TON ("Teach me, my God and king"). 250 years (1731). Birth of William Cooper (d. 1800), author of "God moves in a mysterious way," "Hark, my soul, it is the Lord," "Jesus, where'er thy people meet," "O for a closer walk with God," "Sometimes a light surprises," and "There is a fountain filled with blood"; Aaron Williams (d. 1776), composer of hymn-tune ST. THOMAS ("Come, we that love the Lord," "I love thy kingdom, Lord," and "Send down thy truth, O God").

Quotable Quotations

1. Kindness in ourselves is the honey that blunts the sting of unkindness in another.—Walter Savage Landor.

2. Hope is faith with regard to the future.—Ray W. Wallace.

3. Prayer enlarges the heart until it is capable of containing God's gift of himself.—Mother Teresa of Calcutta.

4. Nothing would be done at all if a man waited till he could do it so well that no one could find fault with it.—John Henry Newman.

5. What a man is on his knees before God, that he is and nothing more.—Robert Murray McCheyne.

6. You've got to say goodbye to some things you know in order to say hello to some things you don't.—William Faulkner.

7. When you say "Our Father," draw the "O" big enough to include all God's children.—Jesse Jackson.

8. Faith is the bird that sings when the dawn is still dark.—Tagore.

9. The world is now too dangerous for anything but the truth and too small for anything but brotherhood.—A. Powell Davies.

10. He who is plenteously provided for from within needs but little from without. —Goethe.

11. God often visits us, but most of the time we are not at home.—Polish proverb.

12. God has many faces; no man can see them all.

13. A God who filled all the prayers of people whose wills were not his own would be no God at all. He would be a heavenly vending machine.—Malcolm Nygren.

14. Love means that I want you to be.— St. Augustine.

15. Never dig up in unbelief what you have sown in faith.

16. Ideas in the head set hands about their several tasks.—Bronson Alcott.

17. The Christian does not have to wait until he suffers himself; the sufferings of his brethren for whom Christ died are enough to awaken his compassion.—Dietrich Bonhoeffer.

18. Tears are a language that God understands.

19. Patient waiting is often the highest way of doing God's will.—Jeremy Collier.

20. The church must be reminded that it is not the master of the state but rather the conscience of the state.—Martin Luther King, Jr.

21. One of America's biggest problems is not simply bad people who do wrong but good people who do nothing.—Ted Lindman.

22. Troubles are often the tools by which God fashions us for better things.— Henry Ward Beecher.

23. Domestic happiness depends upon the ability to overlook.—Roy L. Smith.

24. Every blade of grass has its angel that bends over it and whispers, "Grow, grow."—Talmud.

25. The first most fundamental right of children is the right to be loved.—Paul Hanly Furfey.

26. Man knows how often I've failed; only God knows how often I've tried.

27. Nothing is so terrible as ignorance with spurs on.—Goethe.

28. Hardening of the heart ages more people than hardening of the arteries.

29. The most important use of the word "and" is in "God and man."—Karl Barth.

30. Drink of the chalice of thy Lord lovingly if thou desirest to be his friend and

to have part with him.—Thomas a Kempis.

31. I pray not only, "God help John Smith"; I also pray, "God help me to help John Smith."—Henry B. Wright.

32. Behavior is a mirror in which everyone displays his image.—Goethe.

33. There must be so much in the world around us which is real but of which we in our finitude are not aware.—Elton Trueblood.

34. The quality of life is more important than life itself.—Alexis Carrel.

35. We make a living by what we get, but we make a life by what we give.—Winston S. Churchill.

36. Speak your own word and I shall know you.—Ralph Waldo Emerson.

37. When our relationship with God is continually unhindered and uninterrupted, when all distractions have withered in the warmth of God's love, when our fellowship with God is our only thought—that is heaven.—*Gospel Herald.*

38. The tongue is but three inches long, yet it can kill a man six feet high.—Japanese proverb.

39. The local church is the perennial frontier.—Joseph McCabe.

40. The best way to lengthen out our days is to walk steadily and with a purpose. —Charles Dickens.

41. In sport, in courage, and in the sight of heaven, all men meet on equal terms.— Winston S. Churchill.

42. God's favorite word is "come."— Robert L. Sterner.

43. Man is the only creature who refuses to be what he is.—Albert Camus.

44. Sometimes an open mind is one that is too porous to hold a conviction.—W. Norman MacFarlane.

45. A keen sense of humor helps us overlook the unbecoming, understand the unconventional, tolerate the unpleasant, overcome the unexpected, and outlast the unbearable.—William Arthur Ward.

46. There are people who go on indefinitely preparing for life rather than living it.—Paul Tournier.

47. The evening of a well-spent life brings its lamps with it.—Joseph Joubert.

48. The true Christian practices being God.—Clement of Alexandria.

49. When God is dead, people do not believe in nothing; they believe in anything.—G. K. Chesterton.

50. Nothing can make a man truly great but being truly good and partaking of God's holiness.—Matthew Henry.

51. Some people are so afraid to die that they never begin to live.—Henry van Dyke.

52. When one door is shut, another opens.—Miguel de Cervantes.

53. Hold to Christ, and for the rest be totally uncommitted.—Herbert Butterfield.

54. It is often easier to act oneself into a new way of thinking than to think oneself into a new way of acting.—Eric Fromm.

55. The meaning of my life does not consist in knowledge or art but simply in being human and doing some little thing in the spirit of Jesus.—Albert Schweitzer.

56. It is not enough to possess a truth; it is essential that the truth should possess us.—Maurice Maeterlinck.

57. The holy scriptures are sun by day and stars by night in every era of man's pilgrimage.—George A. Buttrick.

58. Time, sooner or later, is the one commodity we all run short of.—Bill Morgan, Jr.

59. No great thing is created suddenly. —Epictetus.

60. Before religion can be known as sweet communion it must first be known as an answered summons.—John Baillie.

61. When love binds our hearts to work and work to home, we are bound in love to one another and to God.—Elbert Hubbard.

62. All the glorified technological achievements of progress, including the conquest of outer space, do not redeem the twentieth century's moral poverty.— Aleksandr I. Solzhenitsyn.

63. The very act of prayer honors God and gives glory to God, for it confesses that God is what he is.—Charles Kingsley.

64. Too many are waiting for God to do something for them rather than with them. —Ralph W. Sockman.

65. What the heart has once owned and

had it shall never lose.—Henry Ward Beecher.

66. How much pain have cost us the things which have never happened.—Thomas Jefferson.

67. Every human soul has a complete and perfect plan cherished for it in the heart of God—a divine biography which it enters into life to live.—Horace Bushnell.

68. Before you can help make the world right, you must be made right within.—John Miller.

69. The true believer knows how to hoist the sail of his own spirit to catch the winds of God.—Ralph W. Sockman.

70. To understand is hard. Once one understands, action is easy.—Sun Yat Sen.

71. Conversion is conversion from perversion.—E. Stanley Jones.

72. A ship in a harbor is safe, but that is not what ships are built for.—Charlie W. Shedd.

73. He should not preach about hell who can do it without tears.—Dwight L. Moody.

74. Greatness in life consists not so much in doing so-called great things but in doing small things greatly.

75. God whispers to us in our pleasures, speaks to us in our conscience, but shouts to us in our pains.—C. S. Lewis.

76. The three essentials of happiness are something to do, something to love, and something to hope for.

77. The world is a looking glass and gives back to every man the reflection of his own face.—William Makepeace Thackeray.

78. Never answer an angry word with an angry word. It's the second one that makes the quarrel.—W. A. Nance.

79. All truth casts a shadow.—Carl Jung.

80. Men of prayer must knock and knock—sometimes with bleeding knuckles in the dark.—George A. Buttrick.

81. If wrinkles must be written on our brows, let them not be written on our hearts. The spirit should never grow old.—James A. Garfield.

82. Saints are persons who make it easier for others to believe in God.—Nathan Soderblom.

83. In dreams begin responsibilities.—Delmore Schwartz.

84. Prayer is not overcoming God's reluctance; it is laying hold of God's willingness.—Georgia Harkness.

85. It is better to have shallow understanding of profound issues than to have profound understanding of shallow issues.—St. Thomas Aquinas.

86. You have not fulfilled every duty unless you have fulfilled that of being pleasant.—Charles Buxton.

87. We are all here with measured tasks for a measured time.

88. God would sooner we did wrong in loving than never love for fear we should do wrong.

89. A willing helper does not wait to be called.—Danish Proverb.

90. Forgiving the unforgivable is hard. So was the cross: hard words, hard wood, and hard nails.—William S. Stoddard.

91. Let us learn upon earth those things which can prepare us for heaven.—St. Jerome.

92. The coming of the Lord is sometimes like the rushing of a mighty wind and sometimes like the raging of a great fire. But it is also like the sound of silence or one hand clapping.—John Killinger.

93. Grace is the incomprehensible fact that God is well pleased with a man and that a man may rejoice in God.—Karl Barth.

94. Take all of the Bible upon reason that you can, and the balance on faith.—Abraham Lincoln.

95. In the New Testament religion is grace and ethics is gratitude.—Thomas Erskine.

96. We are not children of the moment but pilgrims of eternity.—William Barclay.

97. Jesus is God's idea of man and man's idea of God.—J. S. Whale.

98. There are no hopeless situations; there are only men who have grown hopeless about them.—Clare Booth Luce.

99. In these troubled times, who has enough faith in the future to plant an apple tree?—Martin Luther.

100. Time does not become sacred to us until we have lived it.—John Burroughs.

Questions of Life and Religion

These questions may be useful to prime homiletic pumps, as discussion starters, or for study groups.

1. Is the church adequately preparing its young people for marriage?
2. What are the bases for Christian hope?
3. What contributions has Christianity made to human freedom?
4. Is doubt a contradiction to faith?
5. How may I express my individualism?
6. Are there Christian teachings in non-Christian religions?
7. What is a call to the ministry?
8. How may stress be overcome?
9. In what ways may Christ be said to be the messiah?
10. Is it too easy to get a divorce?
11. What does the word "redemption" mean?
12. Is the sermon a part of worship or separate from it?
13. Are Christians less Christian in their behavior than were their forefathers?
14. In what ways do we benefit from the singing of hymns?
15. Why does St. Paul say that love is greater than faith and hope?
16. How frequently should the Lord's Supper be observed?
17. In what ways may the earth be described as "my Father's world"?
18. What is the single most important topic for pulpit preaching?
19. What does the New Testament say about grace?
20. Is the cross an appropriate symbol for twentieth-century Christianity?
21. What arguments can be found in the Bible to support or refute the practice of abortion?
22. Is the problem of world hunger mostly a problem of distribution of food?
23. What is meant by "death with dignity"?
24. Where in the world is the need for missionaries the greatest?
25. What does the growth of cults say about our society?

26. How may prayer mean more to me?
27. What do scientists say about the biblical story of creation?
28. What does moral living involve?
29. Is it true that "the greater the education the smaller the faith"?
30. What teachings of Christ are most difficult for us?
31. Why was Jesus said to have been born in the fullness of time?
32. Tell me what I can expect to find in the afterlife.
33. What Bible verses mean most to Christians and why?
34. What are good and evil?
35. How may I know I am saved?
36. How can I learn to love people I don't even like?
37. How should I make a choice of a career?
38. Are there spiritual benefits to be derived from humor?
39. Is there a cure for loneliness?
40. Please tell me about faith healing.
41. Should we expect others to agree with us?
42. Are there alternatives to the cocktail party?
43. What reasonable goals should I have in my life?
44. Why does God permit so many people to suffer in circumstances over which they have no control?
45. What does it mean to let Jesus come into my heart?
46. How can I be guided by the Holy Spirit?
47. Did the apostles write the Apostles' Creed?
48. What are the ministries of pain?
49. Why is the word "reverend" used as a title for the ordained clergy?
50. How did the resurrection of Christ influence his disciples?
51. How would our lives change if suddenly the church was taken from us?
52. What is the appeal of gambling to so many people?
53. How much of my life should I give to others?

54. Are we born with consciences or are they acquired?

55. If Jesus were living today as in Galilee what would he find most praiseworthy and most blameworthy in our churches?

56. Will the so-called electronic church make the local church unnecessary?

57. How may we experience the beauty of holiness?

58. Are Americans too materialistic?

59. Are young people more idealistic than older people?

60. Isn't every day the Lord's Day?

61. Why do we worship God?

62. Why does the church emphasize tithing?

63. Is God a loving father or a just judge? Can he be both?

64. What is liberation theology?

65. Were Jesus' greatest miracles of a physical or spiritual nature?

66. What are the levels of prayer?

67. How can I learn to control my temper?

68. What is inspiration?

69. How can truth be determined?

70. Who am I?

71. How can I be freed from nagging fears?

72. Does our survival as a nation depend on military spending?

73. Why do we talk so much about sin and so little about goodness?

74. How can I know God cares?

75. What happened at Pentecost?

76. What can I say and do to help those who are in grief?

77. Why does God seem so far away?

78. In what ways is the Bible our authority for life and belief?

79. Can anger ever be a virtue?

80. What is the body of Christ?

81. What makes a home Christian?

82. What values to the church are offered by the Sunday school?

83. When will Christ return?

84. Does God know me?

85. Why do so many people go to church?

86. Who are the saints?

87. Are angels real or merely symbolic?

88. Can we believe in the final victory of Christ?

89. Explain biblical revelation.

90. How can I keep up with the rapidity of change?

91. Will God right all wrongs?

92. When should I pray?

93. How can I clear my mind of lustful thoughts?

94. Will I know my loved ones in the next world?

95. Are there sins God will not forgive?

96. Does God have favorite children?

97. What do we know about God?

98. What's right with the church?

99. What does Christ expect me to do and be?

100. How can I know the will of God for my life?

Biblical Benedictions and Blessings

The Lord watch between me and thee, when we are absent one from another.—Gen. 31:49.

The Lord bless thee, and keep thee; the Lord make his face shine upon thee, and be gracious unto thee; the Lord lift up his countenance upon thee, and give thee peace.—Num. 6:24–26.

The Lord our God be with us, as he was with our fathers: let him not leave us, nor forsake us: that he may incline our hearts unto him, to walk in all his ways, and to keep his commandments, and his statutes,

and his judgments, which he commanded our fathers.—I Kings 8:57–58.

Let the words of my mouth, and the meditation of my heart, be acceptable in thy sight, O Lord, my strength, and my redeemer.—Ps. 19:14.

Now the God of patience and consolation grant you to be likeminded one toward another according to Christ Jesus: that ye may with one mind and one mouth glorify God, even the Father of our Lord Jesus Christ. Now the God of hope fill you with all joy and peace in believing, that ye may abound in hope, through the power of the Holy Ghost. Now the God of peace be with you all.—Rom. 15:5–6, 13, 33.

Now to him that is of power to establish you according to my gospel, and the preaching of Jesus Christ, according to the revelation of the mystery, which was kept secret since the world began, but now is manifest, and by the scriptures of the prophets, according to the commandment of the everlasting God, made known to all nations for the obedience of faith: to God only wise, be glory through Jesus Christ for ever.—Rom. 16:25–27.

Grace be unto you, and peace, from God our Father, and from the Lord Jesus Christ.—I Cor. 1:3.

The grace of the Lord Jesus Christ and the love of God, and the communion of the Holy Ghost, be with you all.—II Cor. 13:14.

Peace be to the brethren, and love with faith, from God the Father and the Lord Jesus Christ. Grace be with all them that love our Lord Jesus Christ in sincerity.—Eph. 6:23–24.

And the peace of God, which passeth all understanding, shall keep your hearts and minds through Christ Jesus. Finally, brethren, whatsoever things are true, whatsoever things are honest, whatsoever things are just, whatsoever things are pure, whatsoever things are lovely, whatsoever things are of good report; if there be any virtue, and if there be any praise, think on these things. Those things, which ye have both learned, and received, and heard, and seen in me, do: and the God of peace shall be with you.—Phil. 4:7–9.

Wherefore also we pray always for you, that our God would count you worthy of this calling, and fulfill all the good pleasure of his goodness, and the work of faith with power: that the name of our Lord Jesus Christ may be glorified in you, and ye in him, according to the grace of our God and the Lord Jesus Christ.—II Thess. 1:11–12.

Now the Lord of peace himself give you peace always by all means. The Lord be with you all. The grace of our Lord Jesus Christ be with you all.—II Thess. 3:16, 18.

Grace, mercy, and peace, from God our Father and Jesus Christ our Lord.—I Tim. 1:2.

Now the God of peace, that brought again from the dead our Lord Jesus, that great shepherd of the sheep, through the blood of the everlasting covenant, make you perfect in every good work to do his will, working in you that which is well-pleasing in his sight, through Jesus Christ, to whom be glory for ever and ever.—Heb. 13:20–21.

The God of all grace, who hath called us unto his eternal glory by Christ Jesus, after that ye have suffered a while, make you perfect, stablish, strengthen, settle you. To him be glory and dominion for ever and ever. Greet ye one another with a kiss of charity. Peace be with you all that are in Christ Jesus.—I Pet. 5:10–11, 14.

Grace be with you, mercy, and peace, from God the Father, and from the Lord Jesus Christ, the Son of the Father, in truth and love.—II John 3.

Now unto him that is able to keep you from falling, and to present you faultless before the presence of his glory with exceeding joy, to the only wise God our Savior, be glory and majesty, dominion and power, both now and ever. —Jude 2:24–25.

Grace be unto you, and peace, from him which was, and which is to come; and from the seven Spirits which are before his throne; and from Jesus Christ, who is the faithful witness, and the first begotten of the dead, and the prince of the kings of the earth. Unto him that loved us, and washed us from our sins in his own blood, and hath made us kings and priests unto God and his Father; to him be glory and dominion for ever and ever.—Rev. 1:4–6.

SECTION II. *Vital Themes for Vital Preaching*

January 4. The Word for the World
TEXT: Eccl. 3:11.

I. No permanent progress in the spread of the gospel has ever been achieved where the people do not have the Bible in their hands in the language of their heart and home. By the same token the most notable progress has marked those missionary enterprises where successful translations have been widely circulated.

II. The nations of men can never attain a brotherhood until they are all taught the same philosophy of life.

III. The Bible is the only book that demonstrates the qualities needed in a book for all the world.

(a) It is already available in the languages that most of the world speaks.

(b) In every language into which it has been successfully translated men come to feel that it is their book because God speaks to men from its pages.

(c) The machinery for its translation, production, distribution, and encouragement of use has been a matter of earnest study and is today demonstrating its capacity to succeed to the limit of its resources and was never so efficient as at this moment.

IV. In spite of the unprecedented tensions that divide the world of these years, there has never been such a longing among free peoples, if indeed not all peoples, for unity and brotherhood. What an hour it is to make it possible to confront every confused and troubled soul with the book of life.—F. C. Stifler.

January 11. What Does God Have to Say?
SCRIPTURE: Exod. 3:1–12.

Moses was quietly and routinely shepherding Jethro's flock near Horeb, the mountain of God. His isolation was arrested by an expression of God as "the angel of the Lord." The strange phenomenon of a "continuously burning" bush that "was not eaten" was enough to capture the "resolute purpose" of investigation, to use J. Hardee Kennedy's words. What did God have to say?

I. To Moses he said, "Answer me!" When God saw that one turned aside to "see," he called him by name. From Genesis to Revelation, scripture reveals that God is trying to get man to answer him. He truly has something to say.

II. God said, "Respect me!" Every person who has been ushered into the presence of royalty can attest to the consciousness of extraordinary power. God said, "You must not approach me as the ordinary." Acknowledge "my presence" with preparation to worship.

III. God said, "Know me! I am the God of thy Father, the God of Abraham, the God of Isaac, and the God of Jacob." This same covenant initiating, miracle working, consistently leading God says to all in Jesus Christ, "Know who I am!" (John 1: 1–18).

IV. God said, "Follow me!" A plan of deliverance includes you because "I have seen the affliction of my people." Moses protested, magnifying his own failures and inabilities and minimizing the power of

14

God.—Kermit McGregor in *The Baptist Record.*

January 18. When Is Religion Healthy?
SCRIPTURE: II Tim. 1:1–7.
I. A healthy religion accents love and not hate.
II. A healthy religion accents faith and not fear.
III. A healthy religion points beyond individuals and institutions to God.
IV. A healthy religion enables us to accept reality without trying to escape.
V. A healthy religion knows that a church is both for coming in and going out, and more time should be spent out than in.
VI. A healthy religion sees the body as good and does not try to abuse it, sees the mind as a gift from God and tries to fill it with understanding and wisdom, and sees the spirit of a person as sacred and thus surrenders it to God.—Jerry Hayner.

January 25. That Helpful Feeling
TEXT: Matt. 9:36 (RSV).
Acknowledging that all of us at one time or another and to varying degrees are acquainted with a feeling of helplessness, and recognizing its dangerous potential if it gets out of hand, where do we go from here?
I. The pattern of failures has to be broken. We are all creatures of habit, and if we have repeated failures they begin to form a habit pattern. When this happens, and it happens more frequently than we might guess, failure is added upon failure until a feeling of helplessness settles over a person. The only way to break this destructive process is to break up the pattern of failures and introduce some success, no matter how small.
II. We must not be afraid to fail. The only way to avoid failures is to never try anything, and never to try anything is to stop living. Accept failure as part of the life experience, and don't be afraid of it. We learn by our failures. Acknowledge the fact of failure as part of the normal human experience, and in so doing you will not allow it to give you a feeling of helplessness.

III. When the helpless become helpful to others, they help not only them but themselves.
IV. To get out of those dark corners of a feeling of helplessness, we shall have to find and follow a light that is not our own. There is a light that is faithful to our need.
(a) It is the light proclaimed in Isa. 9:2 and declared in Matt. 4:16.
(b) It is the light of God through Jesus Christ that lifts the darkest of clouds and dispels the deepest of fogs. That light, which is not our own, scatters the awful sense of feeling helpless.—Charles L. Copenhaver.

February 1. God's Gift of Peace
TEXT: John 14:27 (LB).
I. The individuality of the gift. "I am leaving you with a gift—peace of mind and heart."
II. The identity of the gift. "Peace of mind and heart."
III. The immeasurability of the gift. "Peace of mind and heart."
IV. The indestructibility of the gift. "And the peace I give isn't fragile like the peace the world gives."
V. The invitation of the gift. "So don't be troubled or afraid."—C. Neil Strait.

February 8. Falling in Love (Lent)
TEXT: Eph. 6:24.
I. Fall in love with the Lord. (a) God is already in love with us (John 3:16). (b) Loving is following (Luke 5:11). (c) Loving is giving (John 12:3).
II. Fall in love with his word. (a) The word was God (John 1:1). (b) God's word is nourishing (John 6:35). (c) "If ye love me, keep my commandments" (John 14:-15).
III. Fall in love with his Spirit. (a) It is the spirit of truth (John 16:13). (b) His spirit is holy (I Pet. 1:16). (c) His spirit is mighty (Zech. 4:6).
IV. Fall in love with his children. (a) We are members of one family (John 1:12). (b) Brothers should not hate one another (I John 4:20). (c) "Beloved, let us love one another" (I John 4:8).—Thomson K. Mathew.

Rowle 2/5/81

February 15. Love and Demand
TEXT: I John 1:5.

The Christian religion tends to boil down to a mixture of two rather antithetical elements—love and demand.

I. It all begins with the fact that God first loved us "while we were yet sinners" (Rom. 5:8). Christ revealed the extent of God's love in his coming and in dying for sinners. (See John 3:16; 15:13.)

(a) Our discipleship is a response to his call of love. He loved us and called us, and we love him in return and follow him. We love him enough to obey him and enough to heed his command.

(b) There it is, the word "command." It includes "demand." The same Christ who loved us enough to die for us, whom we love enough to serve and obey now, becomes the one whose power of command we have recognized and to whom we have pledged ourselves. The continuing relationship is still loving, but it also is demanding.

II. The Christ we serve demands that a man "deny himself and take up his cross, and follow" (Matt. 16:24). (See Luke 14: 27, 33; II Cor. 16:17.)

(a) The Christian religion is love all right, but it is also living up to the demands of Christ in a loving relationship— like living up to the demands of a fair yet firm parent.

(b) We are in an era that puts nearly all the emphasis on love. You don't hear much about demand and less and less about personal purity and the paying of a price. We could get love sick.

(c) The world has to be loved and the call of love must be loud and clear, but we must remember that the Christ who calls in love also makes strong demands. People of character and courage may be as inspired to respond to a proper emphasis on demand as on love.—Frank Owen.

February 22. A Steward's Temptations
TEXT: I Cor. 4:2.

One of the most common metaphors used in the New Testament to describe the relation of the church to the gospel is that of stewardship. The church, and especially those called to any kind of leadership in the church, are servants entrusted with that which is not their property but is the property of their Lord. A steward can fall into several kinds of temptation. All of them are illustrated in the history of the church and in the parables of Jesus.

I. He can forget that he is only the steward and imagine that he is the proprietor. When this happens the church supposes itself to be the saved while the nations ("the heathen") are the lost.

II. He can be lazy, drowsy, and slack, and so allow the treasure to be stolen. When this happens the church falls into a worldly slumber and the world is left without the sound of the gospel.

III. He may forget the purpose for which the treasure was entrusted to him and keep it wrapped up or buried in the ground. It is to such an unprofitable servant that the master in Jesus' parable says: "You wicked and slothful servant . . . You ought to have invested my money with the bankers, and at my coming I should have received what was my own with interest."

(a) To invest the money with a view to a high rate of interest is to risk the capital. The church has often been afraid to do this, thinking that the faith once delivered to the saints is to be preserved inviolate and without the change of a comma.

(b) The mystery of the gospel is not entrusted to the church to be buried in the ground. It is entrusted to the church in order to be risked in the change and interchange of the spiritual commerce of humanity.—Lesslie Newbigin.

March 1. The Church That Makes a Difference
SCRIPTURE: Phil 1:3–11.

I. A church that makes a difference is a church that has a sense of divine mission.

II. A church that makes a difference is a church whose members are growing in fellowship.

III. A church that makes a difference is a church that is constantly being renewed by prayer.

IV. The church that makes a difference is a church that is demonstrating the power of the gospel.—C. Richard Broome.

March 8. Lent: A Second Honeymoon
SCRIPTURE: Hos. 2:16–20.

I. The prophets of Israel were unpopular because they consistently reminded the people of their failures to live up to the covenant with Yahweh. Still they preached their message and, although that message was hard-hitting, it had a tender and essential element—God loves his people and wants them to know and love him.

II. In Hebrew the verb "know" means an intimate awareness of another person. Hosea was telling the Israelites that, in spite of their sinfulness, God still loved them and wanted them to really understand him. The image of God we get here is of a hurt lover who is trying to restore a relationship to a former peak moment.

III. Lent is the church's annual time to be a prophetic voice in a forceful and dramatic kind of way, challenging her people to live up to the demands of the covenant.

(a) Lent requires not a surface housecleaning but a complete job, so that we can get to know both ourselves and our Lord much better.

(b) Lent is an opportunity to get acquainted with God again, to rekindle some of that lost fervor of love and devotion through more frequent prayer, study, and sacrifice.

(c) Lent is giving God the opportunity to speak to our hearts.

IV. Throughout this season we examine our conduct to see if we have been faithful lovers. If not, we try to patch things up and start all over again. We will have to ask ourselves if we want to get to know God better—really know him, not just about him. If so, we need this coming time of covenant renewal which can have all the charm, excitement, prospects, and hopes of a second honeymoon.—Peter Stravinskas in *Pastoral Life.*

March 15. Buried with Christ (Lent)
SCRIPTURE: I Cor. 15:1–4.

I. Baptism is not only the symbol of the cross, the burial of Christ in the new tomb of Joseph of Arimathaea, and the resurrection on the third day. It is also the symbol or picture of the gospel. The whole gospel is set forth in this glorious act of obedience to Christ.

II. In our faith in the son of God and in our repentance of our sins in which we actually die to them, we come to the glorious act in which we have the absolute promise of our forgiveness and the gift of eternal life. When? How? When we are buried with Christ in the waters of baptism. As Christ dies upon the cross, so we have died. We bury that which is dead. In baptism, as a burial in water, the old life is buried. We are forgiven, for as Paul says, "We have been baptized into his death." We have been buried into all his death accomplished for us.

III. Christ did not remain in the tomb. God raised him. And so we in this supreme act of obedience to his will are raised to a new and eternal life. This is what the apostle meant when he said that our old man of sin was crucified with him that the dead body of sin might be done away and that we should no longer be in bondage to sin. (See Rom. 6:11.)—Jesse R. Kellems.

March 22. Christian Loyalty (Lent)
TEXT: Phil. 3:12 (PHILLIPS).

I. Loyalty begins with open commitment—wearing the colors, participating in the ritual acts. Citizens pledge allegiance; fans wear the team colors. And Christians make public confession, receive baptism, celebrate the Holy Sacrament. *Sacramentum* originally meant the oath of loyalty taken by a Roman soldier.

II. Loyalty transcends demonstration. Latin *lex* (law) is the source, for one who is loyal keeps the law. To obey Christ is loyalty. He commands us to follow, pray, learn, love, go, baptize, and teach. And he says, "You are my friends if you do what I command you."

III. Loyalty is working for the cause. Christ's cause becomes clearer as time passes. He wants more than spectators, even cheering ones. He wants workers: "Blessed are those who hear the word of God and do it." How much labor have we done for him.?

IV. Loyalty means seeking to know Christ better and understand his cause more fully in order to give ourselves more fully to it. We must continually learn more of Christ's mind, his spirit, and his hopes. We learn more in order to serve better.—Turner N. Clinard in *The Cumberland Presbyterian.*

March 29. The Cross as Judgment (Lent)
TEXT: John 9:39.

At the heart of Christianity there is a cross, and on that cross the son of God died and thus wrought man's salvation.

I. *Judgment made necessary.* Sin is no mirage and no figment of the imagination of man. It is a dark living reality in the lives of men. The Bible teaches that man is a creature of sin, and experience validates that truth. Man is a sinner by choice as he rejects the will of God for his life and rebels against his son. Man may sin against himself, against another, or against society, but all sin is against the righteousness of a thrice holy God. Thus man's sin brings him under the judgment of God. The greatest sin and the one that ultimately brings us into the wrath of God's judgment is the failure to receive Jesus as our savior.

II. *Judgment pronounced.* In that nighttime conversation with Nicodemus, our Lord sought to give emphasis to the present reality of judgment. It is not solely reserved for some uncertain time in the future but is even now decreed upon those who "hath not believed in the name of the only begotten son of God" (John 3:18). The scriptures reveal the nature of this judgment to be destruction and everlasting separation from God.

III. *Judgment averted.* Does not the Bible teach that all men are sinners and thus under the wrath of God's judgment? Is all hopeless then? Is there any way in which the judgment of God may be averted? Let the word of God speak: "There is therefore now no condemnation (judgment) for those who are in Christ Jesus. Who is the one who condemns (judges)? Christ Jesus is he who died, yes, rather who was raised, who is at the right hand of God, who also intercedes for us" (Rom. 8:1, 34). The cross is judgment for sin to all those who by faith receive the Lord Jesus

Christ as their savior.—Eugene H. Dobbs.

April 5. What Is Faith? (Lent)
TEXT: Matt. 9:29.

I. Faith is the foundation for rational thought. It is acting upon the assumption that truth exists, that our mind has ability to apprehend it, and that knowledge thus gained is worth the effort. It is daring to love God with all our mind.

II. Faith is the fulfillment of reason. It is for the mind what wings and motors are to an airplane. It makes possible the attainment and use of all that reason intimates.

III. Faith is a quality of persistence and courage. It is honoring truth when truth is scorned. It is serving the right when evil is on the throne. It is giving one's best for the highest when the wages may be neglect and abuse. It is Christ setting his face to go toward Jerusalem and from his cross saying, "Father, forgive them."

IV. Faith is a set of the soul. It is belief that issues in trust, venture, and self-surrender. It is commitment to God that is expressed in action and that gives hands and feet to the prayer, "Thy kingdom come, and thy will be done, on earth as it is in heaven."—Everett W. Palmer.

April 12. Day of Decision (Palm Sunday)
TEXT: Luke 9:51.

Palm Sunday could have been called the day of decision for Jesus. The road which Jesus took had no U-Turn signs. Once the direction had been set, that was that. From then on it was straight ahead. When the issue had to be resolved, Jesus did not shirk from making a decision.

I. How is it with us? Are we making the really important decisions in life? Or are we more likely to postpone, yes, even deliberately to avoid making major decisions?

II. How about us in the business of living? How long is our personal list of "somedays"?

(a) Someday I will get around to studying the Bible.

(b) Someday I will make prayer a natural part of my daily life.

(c) Someday I will cheerfully accept a

responsible role in the life of the church.

(d) Someday I'll spend more time with my children.

(e) Someday I'll find more ways of expressing my love for my spouse.

(f) Someday I will get around to doing what I know I should do about my life— diminishing those things I don't like about myself and strengthening those things which I think are good and worthy in myself.

III. The large world of our somedays, the world of our never-realized tomorrows! The postponements which plague our days and enable time to become a thief robbing us of our tomorrows! How right was Horace, "He who postpones the hour of living rightly is like the rustic who waits for the river to run out before he crosses."

(a) What are you waiting for? There comes a point in one's life when the waitingtime has run out and the store of somedays has been exhausted. You know that, do you not? Jesus knew this too. This is why he saw the first Palm Sunday as a day of decision. "He set his face toward Jerusalem."

(b) In doing so he showed us the way. His necessary decision and the necessity of our decision—are they related? I think so.—Charles L. Copenhaver.

April 19. The New Life of Easter

TEXT: Matt. 28:7.

The miracle of Easter is the miracle of personal encounters with the living Christ.

I. *A new belief.* Out of the encounter with the risen Christ came a new belief, the belief we now call Christianity.

(a) For Christians ever since, the words of Jesus have become the words of God. The acts of Jesus, acts of God. The suffering of Jesus, the suffering of God. The love of Jesus, the love of God. The victory of Jesus has become the victory of God.

(b) From the vindication that Easter brings to Jesus comes his great authority. There are no less than fifty names ascribed to Jesus in the Bible. None is so tremendous as "Jesus Christ is Lord." Here was a title to live for and to die for. Out of the

experience of a living Christ came a new belief. Christianity was launched into history.

II. *A new community.* Out of the encounter with the risen Christ came a new community called the church.

(a) The risen Christ created a new community of people with its own form of worship and its own life-style. Soon it was spreading throughout the world. As Bishop Newbigin says, "Jesus left behind him not a book, nor a creed, nor a system of thought, nor a rule of life, but a visible community."

(b) What a community it was! It has survived empires, lived through upheavals like the Renaissance and modern revolutions. Today that community is a global reality.

III. *A new cause.* Out of the Easter encounter with the living Christ came a new cause, the kingdom of God on earth.

(a) Professor Küng says, "For the apostles and Paul appearance and vocation, encounter and mission go together." Dr. Küng is claiming that the experiences of Christ and the call to take up his tasks in the world go together.

(b) We face today the unfinished task which Jesus gave to his disciples in the world. He is calling all to live a truly human existence.

IV. *A new future.* Out of the experience of the risen Christ comes a new future.

(a) Good Friday meant that Jesus had a past but no future. The early disciples on that day faced the terrible finality of death. Once death comes all is frozen. When a leader dies there are no new words from his mind, no new acts which inspire, and no new relationships established. From that moment there is only yesterday. There is no tomorrow.

(b) Suddenly there was a future. Suddenly the disciples realized hope, and they could think of what would yet happen in the future with Jesus. Life indeed was beginning again.

(c) Easter brings hope to everyone of us. There is a new future here for us and for all people. Death itself is not the end. There is eternal life beyond it. Since the first century the stories have been repeated in countless lives. Suddenly there is a new future.—Alan Walker.

April 26. What Do Christians Celebrate?
TEXT: Luke 15:32.
Celebration, for the Christian, is—
I. Opening ourselves to God's life-giving Spirit that is all about us, as a rose opens to the warmth of sunlight.
II. Finding in the eyes of another the light of sympathy and understanding.
III. Offering a cup of cold water to a thirsty child and the chalice of concern to an anxious person advancing in years.
IV. Taking steady steps toward an unknown future instead of standing taut on tip-toe.
V. Seeing the sun shine on distant fields beyond a misty landscape.
VI. Giving yourself to a cause that will live in the world when the days of your years are no more.
VII. Feeling the wholeness—holiness—that comes when we carry our own burdens and take time to share another's.
IX. Seeing the double rainbow after the cloudburst and actually finding in the crucible of experience that all things do work together for good when we love God.—Christopher Garriott in *The Disciple.*

May 3. Myth of Pornography
TEXT: Ps. 24:3–4.
I. Pornography has created a mythical woman. She really doesn't exist.
II. Family life is undermined by pornography. It ignores the importance of human relationships.
III. Sex is divorced from love in pornographic presentations. Sex without love is mere animal coupling.
IV. In its portrayals of sexuality pornography presents the wrong models. Most pornography sets out distorted views of sexuality.
V. The world of pornography is completely fictional and unreal. Anyone who lives for these types of sexual experiences will be bitterly disappointed.—John W. Drakeford in *Baptist Standard.*

May 10. Steps in Prayer
TEXT: Ps. 88:9.
I. *Adoration.* Praise and adore God—his greatness and his holiness.
II. *Thanksgiving.* Specifically name the things for which you are grateful.
III. *Confession.* Admit the wrongs that you have done or the good you have failed to do.
IV. *Petition.* Desire God and spiritual reality. Pray for the needs of others.
V. *Dedication.* Renew your personal consecration to Christ.
VI. *Meditation.* Hold the glory of God in your mind and listen carefully to what he might be saying to you.—Myron J. Taylor.

May 17. How to Live with Uncongenial Saints
TEXT: Rom. 12:18.
I. We need to acknowledge that every mother's son and daughter of us is difficult at times. We all sin against God and one another in different ways.
II. It helps to remember that we can learn from our critics when they are not completely ignorant or misinformed.
III. Sometimes we manage to live and work with uncongenial saints by standing up to them and refuting their unfair charges.
IV. Here is another key to living with uncongenial, even unfriendly persons in the same company, community, and church—remember that the unfair attacks made on your behavior, even upon your reputation and character, are not believed by too many if there is no basis for the charges.
V. Even more helpful in managing difficult people—"saints," that is professing Christians or others—is to remember that all of us are at different stages of maturity.
VI. All of this leads to the center of the matter: Let Christ and his grace enable you to take the uncongenial saints, the unfair sinners' criticism and even enmity, as our master would take it.—David A. MacLennan.

May 24. The Assumptions of Contemporary Culture
TEXT: Eph. 3:17–19.
I. The assumption that someone else is guilty. Someone else is made to bear the

blame for what all of us should shoulder as our sin. We always look for scapegoats and ask who's to blame.

II. The assumption of narcissistic adoration of the self.

III. The assumption that acceptance is our goal—acceptance by the self and conformity to others. The adjusted American so modifies behavior as to make it acceptable enough to be accepted.

IV. The fourth assumption is that there are no absolutes.—Richard M. Cromie.

May 31. My Dream for Our Church
Text: Gen. 37:19.

I. I dream of a church of openness and honesty, tempered with tolerance and respect for other persons as children of God.

II. I dream of a church which reaches out to the hungers and hurts of humankind.

III. I dream of a church with a climate of understanding and love.

IV. I dream of a church whose members practice a dedicated Christian stewardship.—Hoover Rupert.

June 7. Churches as Communities (Pentecost)
Text: I Tim. 3:15.

I. They are communities of faith. They are evangelized. They have a joyous and knowledgeable and obedient faith in Jesus Christ as set forth in the scriptures. They are wedded to the truth as revealed by God.

II. They are communities of love. Persons are important. The law of love is practiced so that members love each other as Christ loves them. This is a costly love. It is love demonstrated in the cross of Jesus Christ. It resolves conflicts which destroy community. It can rebuke and reprove as well as encourage, yet with grace, with long-suffering, and with gentleness.

III. They are communities of hope. Christ is risen! All things are possible. We are called by God to a living hope. Nothing is locked in. In the worst of human circumstances, we are expectant. Hope is dynamic and produces continual excitement even on the most sobering occasions.

IV. They are communities of worship.

There is awe, reverence, joy and jubilation, the power of the Holy Spirit, the drama of the sacraments, singing, and the sober hearing of the word of God.—Robert Henderson.

June 14. The Church and Our Families (Children's Day)
Text: Eph. 3:14–15.

I. Churches can be support systems for the family. The family is essential. Concern for the family needs to be continuously woven into the fabric of church life. It needs natural emphasis in preaching, in the thrust of the prayers, in the nature of worship, in the content of teaching, and in the warmth of the fellowship.

II. Members within congregations can supplement the family. They have excellent opportunities to enhance and enrich family life.

(a) All parents have limitations. Other close relationships can often complement what parents do, particularly in trust-learning, faith-building, and conflict-resolution. They can also provide a cushion between the family and the world.

(b) Many persons within our congregations have no family and need supplemental family relationships. Mobility has separated many from loved ones. Older members have lost family and friends.

III. The Christian community can compensate in some measure for ineffective families. Many persons remain afflicted by emotional malnutrition from childhood years. Some people's needs are so great that they will require special attention. There are innumerable people who simply need strong doses of Christlike understanding, compassion, and helpfulness. They need acceptance instead of rejection, consideration instead of indifference, tenderness instead of harshness, and hope to diffuse hopelessness.—Earl A. Laman in *The Church Herald.*

June 21. A Credo for the Family (Father's Day)
Text: Ps. 68:6.

I. I do not believe that the Christian view of marriage is contractual.

II. I do not believe that one has to work at one's marriage in order to maintain it.

III. I do not believe that men should find their primary satisfaction in their careers, nor that women should find their only gratification in raising children.

IV. I do not believe that the greatest thing a man can do for his children is to love their mother.

V. I do not believe that it is the quality of time rather than the quantity of time that one spends either with one's children or with one's spouse that makes the critical difference in family living.

VI. I believe that the Christian family ought to be the body of Christ in miniature.

VII. I believe that biblical priorities place God first, family second, and vocation third in life.

VIII. I believe that a richer understanding of the love of God the Father, the grace of our Lord Jesus Christ, and the fellowship and communion of the Holy Spirit would considerably enhance our Christian families. (See II Cor. 13:14.)

IX. I believe that each generation of Christian parents should rethink and revise its understanding of the Christian home.

X. I believe that children need to learn that parents need them just as much as they need parents.—Lewis Bird.

June 28. On Loving Oneself

TEXT: Mark 12:31.

Self-love, we think, is the enemy. We believe we must hate ourselves to love God aright. But this is wrong and an un-Christian idea. Jesus showed this in the great commandment: "Thou shalt love the Lord thy God . . . and thou shalt love thy neighbor as thyself." Bernard of Clairvaux unscrambled this seeming conflict 800 years ago. There are, he said, four steps in our development.

I. *Loving self for the sake of self.* Every baby shows this—and some immature adults.

II. *Loving God for the sake of self.* If we examined ourselves carefully, we'd admit that much of our love for God is for our own sakes—for salvation, mental benefits, or to impress others.

III. *Loving God for the sake of God.* God loves us for our sakes. And we find happiness when we respond to God's love by loving him for his own self. This step is as high as we have thought to attain.

IV. *Loving ourselves for God's sake.* This is self-love with no selfishness in it. One who is really happy in God doesn't dislike himself. He is on good terms with himself. St. Paul saw his life as "a constant pageant of triumph." I am God's child. Christ died for me. And I am his right arm. How can I despise myself? When I love myself for God's sake, then I can love my neighbor as myself.—Turner N. Clinard in *The Cumberland Presbyterian.*

July 5. The Christian Citizen (Independence Sunday)

TEXT: Tit. 3:1–2.

I. He is law-abiding. God has ordained that men be governed. This does not mean that all or any governments are absolute. But man must have some authority over him.

II. He is active in service. Responsible and active participation in service is important. When we are called for jury duty, we should serve though we might rather be doing something else. It is much easier to criticize our judicial system than to help reform it.

III. He is careful is speech. Measured words go further and accomplish far greater good than careless speech. We need to make sure our mind is in gear before we speak and that what is to be said will help rather than hurt.

IV. He is tolerant. A good citizen can stand disagreement without being disagreeable. Intolerance is a sign of weakness rather than strength. It is natural for conflicts to arise where there are people. That's par for the course. The tolerant spirit with integrity always wins over bigotry and conniving.

V. He is kind. Kind does not mean weak or cowardly. One can be kind and yet firm. Kindness springs from a right spirit. Kindness is a recognition of the needs of others. Kindness places others above self.

VI. He is gentle. Gentleness does not negate righteous indignation. One can be gentle and at the same time be angry over a wrong. Christian citizenship calls forth the highest and best in us. We should constantly strive to so live that our life-style will enrich the community in which we live.—William Barclay.

July 12. Guidelines for Constructive Criticism

TEXT: Rom. 12:3.

I. Be sure of the facts.

II. Ask yourself, "Would Jesus also think that this warrants criticism?"

III. Consider whether your own conduct gives you a stable platform from which to criticize.

IV. Consider whether you can make your point by commending what you like rather than condemning what you dislike.

V. Focus your criticism on ideas and issues; do not attack persons.

VI. Honor the distinction between testifying to your own feelings and pronouncing judgment.

VII. Credit others with good intentions until there is compelling evidence to the contrary.

VIII. Attempt to add constructive suggestions to your criticism.

IV. Exercise some restraint in sharing your criticisms with friends.

X. Express your criticism clearly, promptly, and directly but without venom to the person who evoked it.—William C. Sanford.

July 19. How Does God Spend His Time?

TEXT: Matt. 28:20.

I. God walks with his people in their garden of failure.

II. God walks with his people in their wilderness of testing.

III. God walks with his people through their valley of uncertainty.

IV. God walks with his people in their sea of extremity.

V. God walks with his people in their fire of trial.

VI. God walks with his people on their road of discouragement.—F. Gene Kordick in *Decision.*

July 26. Guidelines for Boat Rockers

TEXT: III John 8.

I. There are times and circumstances that demand our involvement.

II. Heroes are made, not born.

III. Search diligently for the facts.

IV. Share your known facts and interpretations with others.

V. There could be Christians on both sides.

VI. We need to listen to differences of opinion and to keep our minds open and ready to grow.

VII. Spend energy on facing the issues, not in fighting persons.

VIII. Am I getting involved because of the issues or because of my own psychological needs?

IX. Make your search for facts and involvement in issues the subject of regular, earnest prayer.

X. Be willing to pay the price.—William W. DesAutels.

August 2. A Tender Heart for a Tough World

SCRIPTURE: Luke 10:29–37.

I. How does the parable relate to our world? What does it have to say to us today? The parable points to the condition of the world. Both then and now it is a world of violence. In the parable a man was traveling the seventeen miles between Jerusalem and Jericho and was attacked by robbers. There is a case of out-and-out violence by men who did not care and who used physical violence to get some money regardless of the harm done to the victim.

II. This parable speaks to our world by showing us the care-free religious people who have no interest nor concern for the victims of violence. This is the case in the parable. There was a religious person, a priest, who when he saw the victim passed by on the other side. Another religious person, a Levite, did the same thing. Apparently they were too busy about church work to help. Maybe they were hurrying to pray. Maybe they were on their way to a meeting to make the roads safe for travelers. One thing is sure: they had no sense of responsibility to help a man bleeding to death.

III. The parable is relevant to our age by showing us the compassion of lovers. In the parable we are told about another traveler, a Samaritan, who looked upon the injured man and "he had compassion." He cared, sympathized, and was merciful.

IV. As a follower of Jesus, every one of us needs and wants to be a good Samaritan as a good disciple of Jesus. What does it take to be a good Samaritan? (a) The good Samaritan did not ask any questions of the victim. (b) The good Samaritan did not ask for any reward for helping. (c) The good Samaritan did not count the cost of helping.—John R. Brokhoff.

August 9. The Christian's Leisure Time
TEXT: Ps. 55:6.

The word "leisure" comes from a Latin root, *laetere*. As a verb it means "to be permitted." In its noun form it means "the absence of coercion or constraint." The root meaning is freedom.

I. Leisure means the freedom God gives people to share in his creative and redemptive work.

II. Leisure includes the freedom to explore and to understand the creation, traveling as a pilgrim and child of God rather than simply as a tourist.

III. Leisure brings the freedom to become a new person in Jesus Christ, the freedom to rejoice in the new age, and the freedom to celebrate the new creation within.

IV. Leisure includes the freedom for loving, serving, and enjoying one another.

V. In Jesus Christ we have a model for the use of our leisure because he was totally free. He was free to work, free to play, free to teach his disciples, free to accept little children, free to break bread and pass the cup, and free to give himself to us in love. Jesus used his leisure for physical rest and for spiritual re-creation, for private prayer and for group fellowship, for reflection on recent events in his life, and for preparation for those events yet to come.—Fred R. Doidge in *The Church Herald*.

August 16. Questions for Questionables
TEXT: Heb. 13:20–21.

I. Will it glorify God? (See I Cor. 10:31.)

II. Can it be done for the Lord? (See Col. 3:23.)

III. Can it be done in Jesus' name? (See Col. 3:17.)

IV. How about its appearance? (See I Thess. 5:22.)

V. Would it hinder another Christian? (See Rom. 14:21.)

VI. Does it involve the wrong company? (See I Cor. 6:14.)

VII. Does it compromise my Christian position? (See I Cor. 6:12.)

VIII. Is it God's will for my life? (See James 4:15.)

IX. Am I willing to pay the consequences it might bring? (See Gal. 6:7.)

X. Am I willing to face it in the final judgment? (See II Cor. 5:10.)

August 23. The Two Sacraments of Life
TEXTS: Luke 22:19; John 13:14–15.

Jesus gave to the world two sacraments of life: bread and wine, towel and basin. In the amazing balance and wholeness of the ministry of Jesus, he tied both together. Worship and work, receiving and giving, withdrawal and involvement, communion and service were presented at one and the same time.

I. Jesus in the Last Supper room placed first the symbol of the love of God. He put at the center the call for right relationships with God. A religious rite is the first sacrament of life.

II. Jesus in the Last Supper room made service the inescapable call of the Christian. Into the hands of all who would follow him he places a towel and a basin.

III. Jesus calls us to a double obedience to be faithful to the two sacraments of life. Into all our hands he places bread and wine and towel and basin. In the person of Christ the twofold emphasis of his gospel comes to focus. It is in obedience to him that we become faithful to the two sacraments in life.—Alan Walker.

August 30. Handling Jealousy
TEXT: Prov. 14:30.

I. Recognize the fears which underlie

your jealousy. Ferret out the cause.

II. Learn to rejoice in the successes of others. Share their joys as though they are your own.

III. Hold your judgment until all the facts are in. If you are becoming intolerant, suspect yourself of jealousy and look for hidden motives.

IV. Learn to trust people more. There are no truer words than these: "There is no fear in love; but perfect love casteth out fear." To love is to trust, and to trust is to engender trust and faithfulness in another.—W. Wallace Fridy.

September 6. Your Church Is What You Make It

TEXT: Rev. 2:19.

I. If it is a growing church, it is because you come regularly with your children, together to learn.

II. If it is an active church, it is because you give your time to promote its programs and activities.

III. If it is a scriptural church, it is because you will settle for nothing less.

IV. If it is a friendly church, it is because you are a friendly Christian and make it so.

V. If it is a giving church, it is because you freely give of the fruits of your labor.

VI. If it is a missionary-minded church, it is because you believe that the church is responsible to send forth the message of Christ to others.

VII. If it is a Christian education church, it is because your pastor and leaders have taught that Christian education is important for the training of ministers and laity.

VIII. If it is a soul-winning church, it is because you are a soul winner in your daily life.

September 13. What Is Christian Education? (Rally Day)

TEXT: Matt. 11:29.

I. Christian education is having models and being models—human channels of communication to reach an ever-widening group of children and adults with love, truth, and faith.

II. Christian education is to have an awareness and an expectation so that

meaning can be found in that which God means for us to learn.

III. Christian education is to help each discover and respond to God's Holy Spirit so that all can have a meaningful understanding of themselves in the world.

IV. Christian education is the Bible confronting us in our humanity and opening to us the secret of how we can be at one with God and others.

V. Christian education is seeing for yourself, believing with your own soul, knowing with your own mind, and choosing with your own free action so that faith and obedience are your own.

VI. Christian education is being real in our relationships and responses to others. It is aliveness to truth and to the problems of life with which truth confronts us.—John W. Gaeddert.

September 20. The Fear of Failure

TEXT: Luke 15:18.

How do you overcome the fear of failure?

I. Realize that cowardice is more shameful than failure. It is a self-disgracing and self-dishonoring experience to give in to fear and not strive to succeed. Remember: "I'd rather attempt to do something great and fail than to attempt to do nothing and succeed."

II. Understand that good people never abandon the courageous, honest, and enterprising loser.

III. People accept or reject you not for what you do but for what you are.

IV. If you are going to conquer the neurotic fear of failure, eliminate perfectionism. Think realistically. Nobody is perfect.

V. Remember, if you fail, admit it and start over again. All the world loves an honest and truly repentant person. In the Bible only one man is called "a man after God's own heart." Strangely enough, that man was David and he committed the sins of murder and adultery. But he knew how to repent for his failures openly, honestly, and sincerely. Good people never abandon someone who admits he failed and honestly wants to begin over again. Genuine friends will come to his side and try to help him start over again.—Bill Duncan.

September 27. Authentic Faith

TEXT: Heb. 11:6.

I. Authentic faith is sensitive to the needs of everyone, not just to those who have obvious needs but also to the unnoticed, the nobodies, the language groups, the deaf, the down-and-outs, and the up-and-outs.

II. Authentic faith is limitless. It cannot be fenced in by church fields and state lines, but it reaches to every kindred, tongue, and nation. It must not be stifled by traditionalism or formalism.

III. Authentic faith accomplishes the impossible. It expects an answer from on high.

IV. Authentic faith is faith in Jesus as the only savior and coming Lord.

V. Authentic faith accepts the Bible as God's holy, inspired, infallible word.

VI. Authentic faith says, "Not by might, nor by power, but by my Spirit, saith the Lord" (Zech. 4:6).

VII. Authentic faith looks to the church as the body of Christ and sees it as God's plan for worldwide redemption until Jesus comes back.

VIII. Authentic faith expresses itself in the winning of souls, the tithing of income, and the discipleship of believers.

IX. Authentic faith manifests the spirit of love and cooperation. It means a tough mind concerning matters of doctrine but a big heart concerning needs of others.

X. Authentic faith is the faith our Lord displayed. It is the faith to which he calls us today.—Gerald Stow.

October 4. The Family of God (World Communion Sunday)

TEXT: I Cor. 10:16.

I. This is World Communion Sunday. It surely is an inspiring thought that as we share in the body and blood of Christ in our own church, many thousands of Christians in every nation are one with us in the communion of Christ's body, the holy catholic and apostolic church. It is the family of God partaking of the food of God.

II. In a true family relationship there are no cliques or distinctions among its members. Unhappily this was not the situation in the church at Corinth. The scandal of the Lord's table was real in the divisions and disparagings of one another. There was much self-righteousness at the Lord's Supper.

III. Unfortunately the scandal sometimes remains today. The communion of the body of Christ unites us and divides us. At times some of us still quibble and question each other's interpretation of our Lord's words and actions at his holy table. But on World Communion Sunday we forget our differences as we concentrate on our oneness in the Christ whose body we are.—John Forbes.

October 11. A Christian's Life-Style

TEXT: Col. 2:6.

I. A sense of reserve or reticence in our dealings with others—a closeness and a distance between one and the other, both of which an authentic love must have.

II. A combination of tolerance and anger. God shows both to us. His toleration of us is extreme. It leads even to forgiveness. But his anger with us is real, for we easily turn our backs on him and make a mockery of both his name and his demands.

III. Room in our world of noise and movement for the silence, the waiting, and the withdrawal of the life of prayer and communion.

IV. A recovery of goodness, gentleness, and sensitivity to the needs and claims of others, a willingness to be counted with the underdog in our society, opposition to all coercion, to all pompousness, and to all injustice, and a refusal to call attention to one's own goodness, such as it is.—William Hamilton.

October 18. Love and Hostility

TEXT: Prov. 10:12.

I. Hostility hurts the one who hates and the one who is hated. Love helps the one who is loved and the one who loves.

II. Hostility destroys. Love builds.

III. Hostility produces suffering and

pain. Love produces health and wholeness.

IV. Hostility rejects. Love accepts.

V. Hostility separates, estranges. Love unites and joins.

VI. Hostility is vindictive. Love is great spirited.

VII. Hostility is revengeful. Love is understanding and helpful.

VIII. Hostility stresses the faults and flaws. Love stresses one's good points and continues in spite of the flaws.

IX. Hostility hopes for the worst. Love expects the best.

X. Hostility separates from God. Love opens the way for God.—Myron J. Taylor.

October 25. The Church in Work and Witness (Reformation Sunday)
TEXT: Eph. 5:27.

I. The church is a place of prayer. Through worship we commune with God, and all of the beauty of the sanctuary and all of the liturgy of the service serve to remind us of this great fact.

II. The church is a place for preaching. This is the prophetic ministry of the church and the proclamation of the word. This is why the pulpit still stands at the center of many sanctuaries.

III. The church serves a priestly function. It is the place where the sacraments are observed and where many of life's most sacred events are symbolized. Before the altars of the church, babies are baptized, young people married, and the dead are memorialized.

IV. The church is a place of study. It is that group where the word of God is made relevant to the needs of man. It is that place where the word of truth is rightly divided.

V. The church is a program of service. All the worship and all of the study are of no avail unless the result is a deed that changes a person and thereby helps change a community. The church is the gospel made relevant to our day and time through a group of believers in Jesus Christ who come together for worship, study, the observance of the sacraments, and the doing of God's will.—William M. Holt.

November 1. The Inner Struggle
TEXT: Eph. 6:10–24.

I. The inner life is where the decisive battles are fought. That is where the individual is conquered or defeated. A general can get beaten in a battle through not knowing where the enemy is. The battle with the devil is not an easy fight. If you can't beat the devil inside, you are not likely to succeed in beating devils outside.

II. It is not a fight you win without battle armor. It is a fight against a very clever fighter. It is a dangerous struggle. It is not an exhibition show like a demonstration of karate at the local gymnasium.

III. It is a desperate struggle. There are times when we almost lose hope. The Bible has many psalms revealing the darkness that falls on the bravest and the best of men. The prospect is always grim. We need armor. We must remember that no amount of armor will help a coward.

IV. We must remember that it is a divine war going on within those of us who are Christians. We are caught up in a spiritual whirlwind we did not start and cannot by ourselves stop. What is the lesson? Depend totally in faith and prayer on God.—James H. Landes.

November 8. When Faith Takes Hold
SCRIPTURE: Gen. 15:1–11.

Gen. 15:1–11 records the great dialogue between Abraham and God. It marks the turning point in Abraham's life where faith took hold.

I. Abraham is seen as a listener. Seen throughout this dialogue is the substance of what God is saying. The first requirement for a vital relationship with God is that we listen to what he says.

II. Abraham is seen as a learner. To listen is good, but to learn from the conversation is a plus. Abraham calculated in his mind and in his heart what God was saying and who God promised to be in his life. Vital relationships and faith grow only where one is learning the walk of trust.

III. Abraham is seen taking the leap of faith—"And Abram believed God" (v. 6, LB). Kierkegaard spoke of that moment when man casts himself upon what he believes to be true as the "leap of faith." And every man must launch out upon what he believes if his relationship with God is to be victorious and vital.—C. Neil Strait.

November 15. Keeping Men on Their Feet

TEXT: Dan. 10:11.

What must we do to enable God to keep us on our feet?

I. If God is to keep us on our feet or set us on our feet, we must put ourselves in his hands. Daniel and his three friends were committed Jews. They were men of faith who had committed themselves to the God of Israel and were trusting in his grace. It is the same with us. God can only keep us on our feet as we are committed to him, as we acknowledge our need and accept his provision, and as we put our faith in him. There must be commitment, there must be surrender, and there must be faith.

II. If we want God to keep us on our feet or to set us on our feet, we must obey his commandments. Daniel, like Paul, was not disobedient to the heavenly vision. He kept the lines of communication open between his soul and God. He sought to do God's will so that sin would not break the contact between him and God, and he cultivated the forms of religion—worship, prayer, and fellowship—so that he might be open and sensitive to God's guidance.

III. If God is to keep us on our feet, there must be continuance—not only a good beginning but a good continuing. We must continue in the way. That was certainly a quality which Daniel possessed. Nothing turned him aside. When Daniel was told not to worship any god save the king for thirty days, the record says "he went to his house where he had windows in his upper chamber open toward Jerusalem; and he got down upon his knees three times a day and prayed and gave thanks before his God as he had done previously" (6:10).—S. Robert Weaver.

November 22. What Is Gratitude? (Thanksgiving Sunday)

TEXT: Eph. 5:20.

Gratitude is a characteristic Christian response as we reflect on the natural world from which we derive food and drink, warmth and shelter, and space in which to live and breathe. It is a response we share with our Jewish and Moslem brothers and sisters who also worship, as we do, the God of Abraham who is the creator of heaven and earth. But what is gratitude?

I. It is not easily defined. It is quite possible to recognize that good things exist without being grateful for them. There are countless pieces of ancient statuary beneath the sands of Egypt. I assume that the vast mountain landscapes of Northern India are breathtakingly beautiful. So too must be the coral reefs and their fascinating inhabitants off the coasts of Australia. I do not, however, feel any gratitude for them. I have never seem them, nor have I conversed about them with anyone who has.

II. It is not difficult to be grateful even for a small thing that is directed toward me or toward those whom I love.

(a) Thankfulness is not simply the recognition that something is good but rather that it does good and that it is beneficent toward a perceiving person. Gifts and good deeds toward persons convey meaning, they express favor and benificence, and this often means much more than the actual object or deed.

(b) The warmth of the sun, the air and the water, and the fertility of the soil were all here long before you and me. Yet as we perceive the goodness and beauty of things, they do become gifts to us, they do convey meaning to us, and we give thanks.

(c) Ps. 8 is a reflection on the astonishing fact that the God who made everything is personally concerned with you and me. Simply to think of it is so amazing as to defy belief. Yet when one sees an autumn full moon rise like a ball of burning gold above the eastern horizon, one knows that there is indeed personal meaning in this vast universe, and one gives thanks.

III. Gratitude is both a response to reality and a way of discovery. It is something which Americans speak of a good deal at this time of year, but at a deeper level it is something "meet and right" at all times and in all places.—Boone H. Porter, Jr., in *The Living Church.*

November 29. Preparers of the Way (Advent)

TEXT: John 1:23.

I. John the Baptist was the forerunner of Jesus. His testimony of Jesus is vital for our estimates of the son of man.

(a) John was related to our Lord as cousin, and to some extent he must have lived a life not unlike our Lord's in the days of his youth.

(b) His understanding of the function of the messiah's spiritual powers and liberating work shows a mind in close sympathy with the mind of Jesus.

(c) There seems to be little doubt that in their studies John was supremely influenced by the personality of Elijah, while Jesus took special delight in the writings of Isaiah.

(d) When "the voice of one crying in the wilderness" calling people to repent was silenced because of imprisonment, the tender voice of Jesus was heard to say, "Come unto me all ye that are weary and heavy laden, and I will give you rest."

II. John was to arouse expectation in the heart of a people spiritually dead and by his fierceness to smite and awaken their conscience. He was to pierce dull minds with shafts of fear in the hope of getting them to respond to a new gospel and a brighter hope. John's was the last voice of the old dispensation. His was the great call to repentance. Soon the dawn would break, and the bright day of faith and love would take the place of fear.

(a) Are we not also way-makers for the Christ? Is it not our duty and privilege to be forerunners of the redeeming messiah? Could there be any greater privilege in life for any one of us than to find our own personalities becoming a highway for Christ into other hearts?

(b) This does not mean that we should go out into the wilderness, live on wild honey and dress in the skin of forest beasts, and call with bellowing voices to people to repent.

(c) It is the unconscious heralding of Christ that is always the most powerful.

Before we utter witnessing words, our characters speak silently and powerfully, and these in turn give reliability to the words we declare.

(d) The best way to approach Christmas is to determine to herald the advent of Christ in some other life. By bearing witness to him who is the center and theme of Christmas, we shall join with the Baptist.—Ernest Edward Smith.

December 6. The Light of the World (Advent)

TEXT: John 12:46.

Jesus is called the light of the world because he exemplifies all that light symbolizes and stands for. We associate light with everything that is good—beauty, justice, truth, and innocence. On the other hand, we associate darkness with such things as greed, ignorance, lust, fear, and sin. What does light do?

I. It guides. It shows the way. Jesus is our great guide showing us the way, leading us ever onward to the highest and best.

II. Light reveals. It puts things in a proper perspective. It gets into all the corners. Jesus by his radiant and illuminating life lifts us up out of the dark abysmal cave of human existence with all its terrors of the unknown and fear of the future. He reveals God as a loving father and the source of all love.

III. We associate light with healing, warmth, and growth. In the light of Christ the human soul grows, matures, and expands.—Gardner A. Johnson.

December 13. Light from Bethlehem's Star (Advent)

TEXT: Rom. 5:5.

Wherever the spirit of God has found expression in a life, you can believe that the star of Bethlehem paused over a cradle.

I. November 13, 354, the star stood over a baby lying in a cradle in Tagaste, North Africa. He was named Aureluis Augustinus, and he was to become St. Augustine. Born to Monica and Patricius, he was one who was to speak of the things of God and later was to point to the coming city of God even as the vandals battered down the gates of his home city of Hippo in North Africa.

II. In 1091 that star shone over a cradle in Fonatines in Burgundy. The baby therein was named Bernard by his parents Tescelin and Aletta. Later the word of God sounded through the voice of Bernard of Clairvaux as he sought to carry the light of the gospel to the darkening continent of Europe. Here was the word made flesh in the form of a man of brilliant mind and steady faith.

III. A century later the star hovered over the little village of Assisi in the Umbrian hills of Italy. Bernadone and Pica were the wealthy parents of the baby Francis. The name of Francis of Assisi became associated with purity of motive and deed and with absolute love of God and mankind.

IV. Follow the star to Eisleben, Germany, where on November 10, 1483, the home of Hans and Margaret Luther was gladdened with the arrival of a baby whom they named Martin because the next day was St. Martin's Day. Here was a life that was to be lived for the word and a voice that was to proclaim that the just shall live by faith and that every man is his own priest before God in that inner shrine where he comes face to face with the heavenly Father. From his pen came the Reformation hymn, "A mighty fortress is our God." At Christmas we sing his "Cradle Hymn."

V. The star moves on and stops over the rectory in the little village of Epworth in Lincolnshire, England. There on June 17, 1703, their fifteenth child was born to Samuel and Susannah Wesley. They named him John. And John Wesley was to be the life and the voice that saved England from moral disaster. His was the witness that established the Methodist church.

VI. On March 19, 1813, the star paused over a little cottage in Blantyre on the river Clyde in the Scottish Highlands. There David Livingstone was born. The star and the faith he found in its light were to lead him into darkest Africa. There he gave his life to bring the light of the gospel

of God who has come to earth in Jesus Christ.

VII. The star sought out a log cabin on Sloan's Creek near Hodgenville, Kentucky, and on February 12, 1809, Abraham Lincoln entered the world where he was to become God's man in bringing freedom to a slave people.

VIII. In the humble home of John and Sarah Addams in Cedarville, Illinois, on September 6, 1860, a baby, Jane, was born. In 1889 Jane Addams opened Hull House in Chicago where for forty-six years she personally led the fight against slums, sweatshops, and disease.

IX. In 1875 the village of Gunsbach in Alsace, Albert was the name given to the newest member of the Schweitzer family. He was destined to become famous as a theologian, musician, and medical scientist. He was the first missionary ever to receive the Nobel prize. As today's greatest personality, Albert Schweitzer represented this word made flesh in Lambarene in Africa where he dispensed health and faith, love and peace, in Jesus' name.

X. During this year, scores of homes in our community have been gladdened with the arrival of a baby. Can we dare to believe that these children as they grow in wisdom and stature will also grow in favor with God and man because there is something of God in each of these precious lives? Here is the eternal drama of creative hopefulness forever reenacted. How can you tell but that outside one of these nurseries today the star shines to signify the coming of one whose maturity will see him or her as the leader who brings permanent peace to our struggling world? And who will refuse to hope when his hope is in God?—Hoover Rupert.

December 20. Christmas Gift List (Advent)

TEXT: John 14:27.

I am relieved that the annual shopping spree is over. And yet I may have forgotten something. I think I know what it is. I would like to give gifts that cannot be purchased anywhere. With this in mind I have made a second Christmas gift list.

I. To the person who feels especially

lonely when Christmas comes, I would say that in the gift of Christ to us we can never be wholly alone again. "Lo, I am with you always, even unto the end of the world," Jesus said.

II. To the person who is wrestling with some physical disease or infirmity, what God did for St. Paul has been done for us through Christ. "My grace is sufficient for thee: for my strength is made perfect in weakness," said God.

III. To the persons whose hearts have been chilled by the knowledge that where once love warmed the home only cold ashes remain, may the gift of love's warmth be rekindled. "Beloved, let us love one another: for love is of God; and everyone that loveth is born of God, and knoweth God," wrote St. John.

IV. To the person who feels bitter about another person, may the spirit of forgiveness bring healing reconciliation. "If you have a grievance against anyone, forgive him, so that your Father in heaven may forgive you the wrongs you have done," said Jesus.

V. To the person who confronts death with fear, may the assurances of the Christian faith bring hope and strength. "I am the resurrection and the life: he that believeth in me, though he were dead, yet shall he live: and whosoever liveth and believeth in me, shall never die," promised Jesus.

VI. To the person who is insecure because of the changing circumstances of life, may there come a new stability in the belief that this is God's world. "The eternal God is your dwelling place and underneath are the everlasting arms," declares the Bible.

VII. To the person who has not found true happiness, may the spiritual gifts of Christmas be yours. "I am come that they might have life, and that they might have it more abundantly," declared Jesus.

VIII. To the person who is not at peace with God, himself, or others, may he know anew the blessing of the New Testament: "The peace of God which passeth all understanding, shall keep your hearts and minds through Jesus Christ."—Charles L. Copenhaver.

December 27. The Way (Watch Night)
Text: John 14:6.

I. Christ is the true and living way to God the Father. If we are to travel through life with meaning, we shall need to do so in the company with our God. We know this. Few of us are atheists. We sense we cannot travel successfully through life without dependence on a power not our own that gives strength and purpose to our living.

II. Christ is the way to live as we travel through life. Christ's way is the way of love. In the same conversation with the disciples in which he said he is the way, Jesus also says to them, "A new commandment I give to you, that you love one another; even as I have loved you, that you also love one another" (John 13:34, RSV). If the nature of God is love, then the way for his children is love. Living in the father's love, we share that love with others.

III. Christ is the way to eternal life. In the middle of his discussion with the disciples in the upper room about his leaving them, he speaks of eternal life. (See John 14:2–4.) Christ does not argue about eternal life. He just says that there is a father's home for his children beyond the grave. It is a home where Jesus can be with his friends. Whatever life beyond the grave may be, it is a life lived in love, in the power of the love of God, in the love for others which the Father sheds abroad in our hearts, and life in communion with God and therefore in communion with others. It is a fulfillment of the life that Christ kindles for those who travel the way of love for God and love for others. Indeed, as Jesus says, we do know the way he has gone. It is the way of love he has shown us.—Colbert S. Cartwright.

SECTION III. Resources for Communion Services

SERMON SUGGESTIONS

Topic: This Table Talks
TEXT: I Cor. 11:26.

I. This table talks. It proclaims the Lord's death. And according to the New Testament those of us who belong to Christ have to identify with Jesus' death. We have to die to self. We are to lay ourselves with time, energy, talents, and strength on the table as Abraham laid Isaac on the altar of sacrifice. We must die in service to Christ. The table tells us that when we receive the total offering of Christ in the supper, it is then that we can respond with ourselves in terms of body and soul.

II. The table talks to us of Christ's return. (a) It is in identifying with Christ's death that we become eligible to participate in his resurrection. And we participate in his resurrection not only at some future date but now. We rise with him now in newness of life and as a new creature.

(b) This is more than a memorial feast to a past resurrection. In and through this communion we have direct fellowship with the living, resurrected Christ.

III. The table tells us that Christ is coming to us at the end of time. The ground of our hope is the return of Christ. The New Testament teaches that there will be an end to chaos and anarchy and an end to suffering and man's inhumanity to man. Out of the dark shall come light, truth will prevail over falsehood, and love will con-

quer hatred. In Christ we are on the winning side of life. His return will be for our good and victory.—Donald Caperton.

Topic: Media of Grace
Since Christ is the center of all worship, all the media of the past, which sought to restore the bond of unity between God and sinful man—purificatory rites, washings, baptism of John—are replaced by the media of grace in which Christ as agent communicates himself in the fullness of the community's possession of the Spirit in the sacraments of baptism and the Lord's Supper, which are the indispensable expressions of the Christian service of worship.

I. Both have this in common that Christ employs material realities which point to the Christ event to disclose his presence in the Spirit (water, bread, and wine). Although these elements are not in themselves efficacious, they are as necessary as the body of flesh was necessary for the work of the incarnate logos.

II. Both sacraments have this in common that in the time after the resurrection they take the place of the miracles performed by the incarnate Christ.

III. Both have this in common that they are bound in the closest way to the death of Jesus both chronologically and in the work of grace, which consists of the forgiveness of sins through Christ's atonement.

IV. Both have this in common that they

32

are related to the ascension of Christ since Christ communicates his presence in the Spirit and mediates through the Spirit the anticipatory participation in his resurrection.

V. Both have this in common that they foreshadow what will happen at the end of the day.

VI. Both presuppose the necessity of faith.

VII. The difference between baptism and the Lord's Supper, according to John's gospel, consists in this that it belongs to the essence of baptism that it is once-for-all and unrepeatable, whereas it belongs to the essence of the Lord's Supper that it is repeated.

VIII. Each has a particular work of its own. For baptism this is the work of regeneration. For the Lord's Supper it is the creation of the fellowship of love among the brethren. In baptism the individual receives once-for-all part with Christ; in the Lord's Supper the community as such receives part and that again and again.—Oscar Cullmann.

Meditation: Hands That Break the Bread

Nowhere do we feel the mystery of our most holy faith as when we meet at the table of the Lord. We have his promise that he is here spiritually present. We feel his nearness. Across the table we can almost hear the beating of his loving heart. His hands reach out to us in benediction. Yes, he is here. When the bread is broken, it is his dear hands that break it. When the fragments are passed to the worshipers, it is he who transforms them into living bread.

Lauchlan Maclean Watt tells of an incident in the history of the MacGregor clan. The chieftain was struck down in battle and for a moment his followers wavered. Rising on an elbow, he cried: "I am not dead, my clansmen. My eyes are looking on you to see that you are true." Quickened by his words and his brave gaze, his followers pressed on to victory.

There is one with us today far greater than the chieftain of a Highland clan. He too says: "My eyes are looking on you, my children, to see that you are true. Lo, I am

with you alway, even unto the end of the world." His searching eyes are reading the innermost secrets of our hearts. May God grant us strength to commit our lives wholly to him in surrender and utter devotion. Then from this supper of the Lord we shall go out again to meet life's responsibilities, knowing that it is his hand that rests upon us and his Spirit that inspires us with courage and faith.—John Sutherland Bonnell.

Topic: Wesley's Counsel

TEXT: Luke 22:19.

It is the duty of every Christian to receive the Lord's Supper as often as he can.

I. The first reason why it is the duty of every Christian so to do is because it is a plain command of Christ. That this is his command appears from the words of the text—"Do this in remembrance of me"—by which, as the apostles were obliged to bless, break, and give the bread to all that joined with them in these holy things, so were all Christians obliged to receive those signs of Christ's body and blood. Here therefore the bread and wine are commanded to be received in remembrance of his death to the end of the world. Observe too that this command was given by our Lord when he was just laying down his life for our sakes. They are therefore, as it were, his dying words to all his followers.

II. A second reason why every Christian should do this as often as he can is because the benefits of doing it are so great to all that do it in obedience to him—namely, the forgiveness of our past sins and the present strengthening and refreshing of our souls. In this world we are never free from temptations. Whatever way of life we are in, whatever our condition be, whether we are sick or well, in trouble or at ease, the enemies of our souls are watching to lead us into sin. And too often they prevail over us. Now, when we are convinced of having sinned against God, what surer way have we of procuring pardon from him than the "showing forth the Lord's death" and beseeching him for the sake of his son's sufferings, to blot out all our sins?—John Wesley.

Topic: Their Hymn of Praise (Maundy Thursday)

TEXT: Mark 14:26.

I. The hymn they sang was Ps. 136, a hymn of passionate praise to God. And with that the Last Supper ended. But when you look at that scene with twelve men and their master gathered in a small room singing the praises of God, isn't it somehow astonishing? What on earth was the cause of their thankfulness? What reason did they have to praise God?

II. What of Jesus of Nazareth on that night when he shared the last meal with the twelve? Why the hymn of praise?

(a) There was no successful career for which to give thanks. Already the darkness of the end was approaching, and his path led through the valley of the shadow.

(b) There wasn't even the satisfaction of achievement—only the remembrance of odd moments along the way when the crowds had surged forward and God had seemed to open their eyes for an instant so that, hushed and still, they listened to his words, cleansed and refreshed for a while by the power of God.

(c) There were not even steady, reliable friends and followers for whom to give thanks. By their own confession the disciples proved that, when the storm struck at last, they wavered and broke, unable to take even the first buffeting blows staunchly.

III. The praise was not for things easily touched, quickly seen, and promptly valued as blessings.

(a) That's the kind of mistaken praise you and I are always tempted to offer. We equate thanksgiving with gifts heaped upon us and things freely given by God. We tend to think of the praise of God in terms of gratitude for pleasures peacefully enjoyed and the number of days we've managed to live free of worry and in tranquility.

(b) Thanksgiving for these is right and proper, but the deepest reason for praise is not the gifts but the giver—God himself. Praise God not for blessings but because God is God.

(c) That's not senseless optimism or thoughtless ignorance of life's deeper shades and somber tones. That's the true song of every Christian, the battle hymn of every believer. For at the heart of it is the confident affirmation that, while we are in God's hands, nothing can really blight us or spoil us or destroy us. We know and we trust the God who made us and the world in which we live. We know that, though mountains be moved and the seas run dry, we are ever in his care.—*Pulpit Digest.*

Topic: Where All Meet Together (World Communion Sunday)

TEXT: Prov. 22:2.

I. The sanctuary of the church is an outstandingly happy meeting place where Christians meet God and each other. In the sanctuary we forget our several distinctions, and in the name that is above every name we enjoy sweet and united fellowship. Of all places the sanctuary is the place where all men may gather in a common unity on grounds of real equality.

II. In a port on the Mediterranean Sea, it is reported, there is a little mission room where sailors of every nationality gather together to worship the Christ. One of the hymns they sing is "When I survey the wondrous cross." The Englishman sings it in English, the German in German, and the Spaniard in Spanish, but they sing it in the same spirit and to the same tune. That is an illustration of the unity of the table of the Lord which draws not only men of various tongues and color but also men of all ranks and clans, all singing and acclaiming a common savior's love and sacrifice. The table of the Lord gives a sense of oneness in Jesus Christ as the savior of those who put their trust in him.

III. The cross of Christ is a common meeting place. For it is there also that all men are made equal, where barriers of social class and clique break down, and all are included in common fellowship. Before that cross we stand in need of the same common grace from the same common Lord. That is where sin levels us. That is where grace finds us. The cross, like the sanctuary and the table of our Lord, brings us together into a common unity and a common equality.

IV. Why do the rich and poor meet together? The Lord is the maker of them all. They owe their common origin in him. They have their common need of him. And he blesses all who are of a contrite heart.—Ernest Edward Smith.

INVITATIONS TO COMMUNION

Is there any danger that you and I are not worthy to partake of the Lord's Supper? Often people refuse to participate because they think they are not good enough. We come because we are not good enough and want to be better. If you have sinned, ask for forgiveness. If you are perplexed, seek God's guidance. If you are in sorrow, accept God's peace and comfort. Only if you are insincere, have no appreciation of the cost of God's love, no reverence for the meaning of the Lord's Supper, and no intention of pleasing God do you partake unworthily. "Let a man examine himself, and so eat of the bread and drink of the cup."

We sometimes wish that it had been given to us to see the Lord Jesus in the days of his flesh, to walk with him through the fields, and to hear him teach. Yet it is possible for Jesus to be with his people in a very real sense. While in the flesh he was "the prisoner of an hour and place." Only when he was no longer present as a man among men could his presence be manifested to all men in every place through the power of the Holy Spirit. That was the reason Jesus said that it was "expedient" for him to go away (John 16:7). As we open our hearts to him, he will come and live in us. "Behold I stand at the door and knock: if any man hear my voice and open the door, I will come in to him, and will sup with him, and he with me."

The Lord's Supper is effective. It does something. This is strange language to most of us. We understand how we do something—take the bread and break it and the cup and drink it—but we may not see how God does anything. We do not come to the table to learn something with our minds. We come to meet God. God and man meet here and something happens. Here we touch eternity. Here God gives love, forgiveness, and acceptance—and we receive. He acts and we adore. In prayer we go to God. In the Lord's Supper he comes to us. We are not learning something or remembering something but doing something. We are meeting God.

When we speak of Jesus being present in the observance of the Lord's Supper, what do we mean? The risen Lord is universally present. He is not present in the Lord's Supper any more than he is present anywhere else. Brother Lawrence felt the Lord very near when he was washing the greasy dishes in the monastery kitchen. But what happens in the Lord's Supper is that everything is designed to make us aware of his presence. He is not especially present, but we are specially aware of his presence. The purpose of the Lord's Supper is to make us specially aware of the Lord's presence in all of life.

In the New Testament a sacrament is a mystery. This is the only word in the New Testament that is actually used in reference to both baptism and the Lord's Supper. As used in scripture mystery is not something complicated and complex and hard to understand, as in the modern sense of the term. In the Bible a mystery is something, usually in itself quite simple, which is completely obscure to the outsider but completely meaningful to the initiated. To the uninstructed it is meaningless; to the instructed it is the vehicle of grace and truth. So the action of the Lord's Supper, in which we eat a little piece of bread and swallow a sip of wine, often seems to the outsider incomprehensible and even ridiculous or amusing, while to the instructed Christian it is one of the supreme experiences.

There is a social aspect to the Lord's Supper which we must never forget. From the very beginning the disciples met together for a service in memory of our Lord which they called the breaking of bread (Acts 2:45; 20:7). At first apparently this was an ordinary meal, which was called the love feast, and at the end of this meal the

Lord's Supper was observed. Gradually the communion became a separate service. It was celebrated every Sunday and came to be recognized as the distinguishing mark of the Christian community. In this respect communion is a constant reminder that Christian discipleship is not a solitary life but one in which we are united in a great fellowship with others. Appreciate your Christian brothers and sisters as you commune today.

"This do in remembrance of me." But we are not remembering someone who is dead and gone, someone who lived and who died and who left a memory. We remember the risen Lord who is gloriously alive. In the Lord's Supper we remember Jesus Christ in order that we might encounter him. As the hymn writer puts it: "Here, O my Lord, I see thee face to face." The memory turns into an experience and an encounter. Something happens in the Lord's Supper. We meet our crucified and risen savior. This enables memory to become a present reality.

The Lord's table is a place of proclamation. Here we proclaim that Jesus is our Lord and that it is he who feeds us spiritually and upon whom we depend in our hunger. Here the benefits of Christ's death are made real to us. Here we proclaim to the world our unity in Christ. Our unity is declared by our common need, our common prayer, and our common food. This is a unity not of our own creation but of God. He makes us one. Here we proclaim our thanksgiving. "Eucharist" means thanksgiving. The first communion was a thanksgiving to God, and so is our feast today. Join us in our proclamation.

The Lord's Supper summons us to look away from the dreary frustrations of wrecked vows and broken dreams and away to a cross towering o'er the wrecks of time, to a love that has borne our own sins in its body on the tree, and to the living Lord who still comes back to his friends on the first day of the week and communes with them and is known in the breaking of bread. It is on Jesus, crucified and risen, that all our thoughts this day are focused. Beyond our futile striving shines his sufficient grace and beyond our perplexities, his peace. Come aside with us and look away from self to the savior.

As we examine ourselves at the time of communion we honestly face up to our sins and failures. Having faced our sins, we offer them to God in penitent confession. We believe in the forgiveness of sins, but God can forgive us only as we are forgivable. We make ourselves forgivable by acknowledging, confessing, detesting, and resolving to part company with our sins. As you do this be absolutely simple and direct. Offer your sins to God and ask him to take them away from you. One Christmas night Jerome wanted to give a special present to Jesus. First he offered Christ his monumental works on the scriptures, then his labors for the conversion of souls, then his own virtues. Christ is said to have answered him by saying: "It is your sins I wish for. Give them to me that I may pardon them." Christ asks the same of you.

When we come to the holy table we come into a presence of Jesus as truly as did the people who went to him in Galilee. It is with him that we keep this holy tryst. The bread and the wine speak to us in the first person. "This is my body." "This cup is the new covenant in my blood." These elements speak to us with the voice of Jesus—"This means me." This is the first great truth for which the Lord's Supper stands. It was something given to the disciples which should bring to them not the words nor the example of their master so much as his own person. "Where two or three are gathered together in my name, there am I in the midst of them." So may your experience at this table today be a meeting with the master.—Myron J. Taylor.

ILLUSTRATIONS

AT THE ALTAR.   During the celebration of the Lord's Supper in a little mission church in New Zealand a line of worshipers had just knelt at the altar rail when suddenly from among them a young native arose and returned to his pew. Some minutes later he returned to his place at the rail. Afterward a friend inquired why he had done this. He replied: "When I went forward and knelt, I found myself side by side with a man who some years ago had slain my father and whom I had vowed to kill. I felt I could not partake with him, so I returned to my pew. But as I sat there my mind went back to a picture of the upper room, with its table set, and I heard a voice saying, 'By this shall all men know that ye are my disciples, if ye have love one to another.' And then I saw a cross with a man nailed on it, and the same voice saying, 'Father, forgive them; for they know not what they do.' It was then I arose and returned to the altar rail."—G. A. Johnston Ross.

FACES IN THE CUP.   When you look into the communion cup, you see the wine as the light falls upon it and is reflected in many purplish hues. From the quiet surface the royal color is caught up in widening circles and mirrored in the silver bowl. The mere physical aspects and beauty of it intrigue you, but as you look there is something that rivets your attention. There are faces in the cup. Perhaps in this matter-of-fact age, it is hard for you to see them. Perhaps in the busyness of life you never have time to see them. Perhaps in this materialistic world, they are so obscured you cannot see them.—Roy F. Miller.

CHORDS OF RENEWAL.   How many are the chords struck in a communion service —memory, consecration, hope! We follow the group to the cross. We associate with the early Christians. We have fellowship with many of many lands and many who have gone on before. God comes to us, and a new purpose forms in our wills. As we feed our souls on the living bread we grow in strength, in insight, and in courage, and we are renewed from day to day. The presence of the creating, living, and loving God and the purpose to lead a new life—the human spirit in these ex-

periences knows renewal.—Ivan Lee Holt.

FIRST COMMUNION.   In a London slum a doctor was examining the children in a Catholic day school. One of the sisters, seeing a puny lad leave the doctor's room, asked, "Well, Jim, what did the doctor say to you?" The boy replied: "He took one look at me and said, 'What a miserable specimen you are.' But he didn't know that I'd had my first communion, did he, sister?" He was no longer insignificant, for he had heard the words, "This is my body which is broken for you."—John Bishop.

THE FLAME HE LIT.   On the night before Calvary, our Lord met with his disciples in the upper room for the passover supper, and he kindled a flame in the hearts of those gathered round the table—a flame which would be passed on to succeeding generations who would spread out through the entire known world and set it ablaze for Jesus Christ. Every time we come to the holy table we receive anew that power, that spiritual energy which will rekindle the flame within us, which will guide us, heal us, and illuminate our lives. Communion means fellowship or partnership. It is now up to us to do our part to give to others this light which is given to us. The disciples went forth from the upper room, and from subsequent events it would seem that the flame which our Lord lit within each one of them became extinguished, especially with such incidents as St. Peter's denial. But just like those novelty birthday candles which one blows out and then after a few seconds the flame miraculously reappears, so it was with the disciples, and set aflame by the wondrous experience at Pentecost and filled with an urgent sense of mission, enthusiastically they spread out through Asia Minor and the Mediterranean area determined to bring the whole world to the light of Christ. And others followed in their train, like the apostle Paul, who was converted amidst a blaze of light. The light was carried throughout the wilds of Europe at the cost of tremendous hardship and sacrifice by those great pioneers

who were men of adventurous faith.—
Gardner A. Johnson.

TRADITION.   It is a long-standing tradition in the Church of Scotland that the elders carry the bread and wine in procession to the communion table as the congregation sings Ps. 24:7–10. In some churches the elders carry the elements high above their heads to signify that Christ by his cross has triumphed over all the powers of evil and the forces of spiritual wickedness.—John Forbes.

EMBRACED.   One of the most charming stories in the life of Jesus is that of our Lord taking a little child into his arms. The apostles had been arguing as to which of them was the greatest. Jesus told them, "If any man wishes to be first, he shall be last of all, and servant of all." Then he took a little child, and set it in the midst of them, and taking it into his arms, he said to them, "Whoever receives one such child for my sake, receives me; and whoever receives me, receives not me but him who sent me" (Mark 9:36).

According to tradition, this little boy became the great St. Ignatius of Antioch who gave his life for Christ in the year 107. While still a boy, Ignatius often took his companions to the spot where Jesus held him and told his friends, "Look, here is the place the Lord Jesus took me in his arms and embraced me."

Call this a legend, a medieval fiction, if you will, we do know positively that Jesus did embrace a little child. In Holy Communion we not only embrace Jesus, but Jesus also embraces us.—Arthur Tonne.

COMPANY OF HEAVEN.   A young minister in a small village church invited the congregation to wait for a communion service after the regular service was over. Only two waited and he was tempted to cancel the service, but he did not. Following the ancient ritual he came to the passage, "Therefore, with angels and archangels and all the company of heaven, we worship and adore thy glorious name." He stopped as the wonder of it gripped him. He repeated, "Angels and archangels and

all the company of heaven," and then he said: "God forgive me. I did not know that I was in that company."—Alan Walker.

HELD.   Martin Luther, who stood at his first celebration of communion with trembling hands and feet, said, "I could not hold the host, but the host held me."

SPIRITUAL POWER.   A sacrament is a material object endowed with spiritual significance and power, a material object which possesses and conveys spiritual value. A wedding ring, in this sense, is sacramental in nature. It is a material object. It may have great, little, or no value in the marketplace, and yet it will be a man or a woman's most precious possession because it has been infused with spiritual meaning and power by the giver and the receiver within the context of Christian commitment. The bread and wine of the communion service are physical objects, but through their association with the life and the death of Christ they are given spiritual power and significance so that when we receive them in remembrance of him we know the real presence of Christ. —Roger W. Blanchard.

FARTHING BREAKFASTS.   The Salvation Army observed no sacraments, though they denied they were against them. Perhaps the wranglings these had caused in other churches did not encourage William Booth to change his mind. "Your people do not have the Lord's Supper," said a school inspector once to a Salvationist pupil. "No, sir." "Then what do they put in its place?" "Farthing breakfasts for starving children, sir."—J. C. Douglas.

INVITATION.   There is no better place to find true joy than at God's altar on a Sunday morning at corporate worship in the Holy Eucharist. In the midst of all the ugliness of the world, it is always refreshing to find that joy is really present in the world, especially in the eucharistic presence of Christ.

In each Eucharist, Christ by the power of his Holy Spirit opens a window for us joyously to see, touch, taste, and feel him.

In the Eucharist, he touches us with his presence—and it is always a touch of love and joy.

The best way to overcome the gloom and depression that creep into our lives is to participate in the Sunday Eucharist. There is something about coming together at God's table that is uplifting and that points us toward those matters that are truly important in this life and for the life to come.

Come, let us enter into the joy of the Lord.—*The Anglican Digest.*

LIVING PRESENCE.   To remember something in Hebrew fashion is not merely to entertain a pale and static idea of it; it is to make the past event present again. To remember Christ and his death at the supper is to make the living Lord present again in the power of his accepted sacrifice.—A. M. Hunter.

COMMUNION MEDITATION.   Each of us comes to this communion table with different needs.

Some of us are in pain, some of us have fears, and some of us have sorrows in our hearts.

The Lord said, "Come to me, all of you who are tired from carrying your heavy loads, and I will give you rest."

He also said, "Let not your hearts be troubled."

We also bring other needs to share.

We have much thankfulness in our hearts, for we have uncountable blessings —the joy of a new baby safely welcomed into the world, an evening spent quietly enjoying a fire, and a happy and noisy dinner with all of the family gathered.

Let us praise the Lord!

Praise the Lord! Yes, let us indeed praise the Lord!

Let us be thankful that we may share this communion, symbolizing the sacrifice of Christ, and also share our calling as true disciples of Christ.

Help us to reach out to our neighbors and our community, encircling all with love and care.

Put on love, which binds everything together in perfect harmony.

And let the peace of Christ rule in our hearts.—Sara Humphrey.

ANALOGY.   If we allege as a pretext for not coming to the Supper that we are still weak in faith or in integrity of life, it is as if a man excuses himself from taking medicine because he is sick.—John Calvin.

PREPARATIONS.   Our life is one of rhythm from the battle of life in the world back into the sanctuary where vision may be renewed by the preaching of the word, our bodies fed by the sacrament and our courage renewed in the community of fellow soldiers. What we do within the life of the church are not pious exercises but rather preparations directed toward our mission in the world.—George Webber.

SECTION IV. Resources for Funeral Services

SERMON SUGGESTIONS

Meditation: The Greater Light

Everything wears a new face in the light of our Lord's resurrection. I once watched the dawn on the east coast of England. Before there was a gray streak in the sky everything was held in deepest gloom. The toil of the two fishing boats seemed very somber. The sleeping houses on the shore looked like the abodes of death. Then came gray light and then the sun, and everything was transfigured. Every window in every cottage caught the reflected glory, and fishing boats glittered in morning radiance. And everything is transfigured in the risen Christ. Everything is lit up when the sun of righteousness arises with healing in his wings. Life is lit up, and so is death.—John Henry Jowett.

Topic: Life Triumphant

TEXT: John 11:25.

I. My reasons for a life after this one go back to the very character of God, what he is and what he has done for man, a God of love and justice who has endowed man with such unlimited powers of knowledge, advancement, and self-betterment which he cannot fully and adequately complete in this earthly life. God has given man an innate religious faculty whereby he can love and be loved by God and others.

(a) God is primarily a God of love and justice which qualities involve the very integrity of the created universe. I do not believe in a capricious and cruel God who

created man as a joke—that human life is, as Shakespeare puts it, "a tale told by an idiot, full of sound and fury, signifying nothing."

(b) I believe that life does have meaning and that this earthly life of ours is but a segment in God's great master plan for his children.

(c) I believe in a God who is just. All of us look forward to a time when good is ultimately rewarded and evil punished and when there will be a balancing of the scales.

(d) I believe there must be some extension of this life where an opportunity will be afforded for the fruition of one's latent possibilities.

II. All human beings have a strong feeling or intuitive conviction that points to a life beyond this one. We are not content with life as it is, and we long for the heavenly Jerusalem where the evils and misfortunes of this present life will no longer exist and where there will be no grief, no pain, and no sorrow. I don't think that this intuition within us can be classified as wishful thinking.

(a) We know that this life of ours is not our real home. We know that this world does not satisfy. We feel at home on this earth, yet something tells us that we are not of this world, and that this is not our real home.

(b) The human soul does not want to be hemmed in, to be restricted to a lower level of existence, or to live always in the valley. It wants to be free to soar, to expand, and to rise to heights unknown. It

40

seeks something higher and better. It is not content with things as they are but is firmly convinced that there is something better to be sought after and attained.

III. I believe in an extension of this earthly life because of what Jesus was, what he did, and what he said and taught.

(a) He gave a new meaning and dimension to life. He takes the whole business of eternal life out of the future and brings it down to the past and present. Life in the future is but a part of life. The church teaches that our life in the future depends upon the manner in which we conduct ourselves in this present life. Life has eternal significance, so what we do in this life affects our future. For the Christian, true life is life in the risen Christ, here and now, as well as forever. The life that we now lead matters immensely.

(b) The Christian life begins at baptism when we are grafted into Christ's body and become one with him. We become members of the kingdom where God's rule is obeyed. As members of Christ's body we have been buried with him in his death, and we also share in his resurrection. Our physical death is but an incident —a transition, a transformation from one form of life to another. We shall be given a new spiritual body, and our personality or selfness will continue.

(c) Jesus does not tell us much about the life beyond. Perhaps he knew that our finite minds simply could not comprehend it. We do know that the life in the future will be a life of quality where there is recognition of each other, a place where mutual love and fellowship abound, where there will be fellowship with God and others, and where there will be peace and fullness of life. It will be a heavenly home. —Gardner A. Johnson.

Topic: An Attitude Toward Death
Text: I Cor. 15:54–55.

I. The first element in the Christian attitude toward death is faith and trust in God's keeping.

II. The second element in the Christian attitude toward death is the conviction that we shall survive the experience of dying.

III. Christian faith with respect to death includes the conviction that in the life to come our highest powers shall find creative and zestful employment.

IV. From Bible hints and suggestions it is clear that heaven will include fellowship with God in Jesus Christ, fellowship with the spirits of just men made perfect and especially with those whom we have loved long since in Christ and lost awhile, and satisfying labor akin to the creative activity of an artist.—Norman Victor Hope.

Topic: Handling Grief
Text: Matt. 5:4.

I. We must be willing to face our loss.

(a) Psychiatrists point out that after dealing with hundreds of grief-stricken people they have concluded that we can overcome our grief only as we give expression to it. Joshua L. Liebman wrote: "Express all of the grief which you actually feel. Do not be ashamed of your emotions. Do not be afraid of breaking down under the strain of your loss. The pain you now feel will be the tool and the instrument of your later healing."

(b) As we as friends of the bereaved can help them by being a sounding board for their grief. Friends should offer the opportunity and encouragement to the man who has lost a loved one to talk about his loss, to dwell on his sorrow, and to rehearse the beauties and virtues of the departed one.

(c) To talk out our problem with a trusted friend, with our minister perhaps, or with someone who can share our problem is to lift a burden from our hearts.

II. We must accept our loss. We must consider death not as a calamity sent to us but as an event which comes to us.

(a) Many get so mixed up on this issue they say with a note of defeat in their voices, "Well, it was God's will." It is not the will of our Father in heaven that anyone should perish. The God whom Jesus revealed does not send suffering as punishment for sin. Those who sin do suffer and some of them die simply because this is a law-abiding universe, and it is impossible for us to escape the results of our follies.

(b) Life is so constituted that the edges

of our lives touch the lives of those about us, and many times the innocent suffer and die, but Jesus would have us know that while sin brings suffering, sin does not always preclude suffering or death. God wills only life and joy for his children.

(c) We must explain death as a part of the life of earth in which disease, accident, old age, and other free causes play significant roles.

(d) When death comes to our homes, we will not say so much that "God has taken our loved one" as we will say that "life became too difficult for the body and God received him." So accept death as a part of the on-going process of life.

III. We will handle our grief only as we make our way through and beyond it.

(a) Some say that time heals. That is not always true. Time can make us more lonely; it can even make us bitter. Only when we put our hand into the hand of him who is the master of both time and eternity will healing come. He will give us insights into the deeper meaning of life.

(b) God will help us make our way through and beyond our grief by giving us great tasks and responsibilities. Young parents resolve to become parents again if not to one of their own flesh and blood then to some who have been orphaned. Widows find themselves absorbed in caring for their children. Others find tasks through which they may channel their talents, energy, and resources into something creative.

IV. The ultimate secret is to reaffirm our faith in the indestructibility of life.

(a) The Christian accepts and lives by the verdict of Jesus that life is spiritual and divine. And being spiritual and divine, even as God is spiritual and divine, life is eternal and not bound by time or space.

(b) Victor Hugo wrote: "The tomb is not a blind alley but a thoroughfare. It closes on the twilight and opens on the dawn."—Homer J. R. Elford.

Topic: The Image of the Heavenly
TEXT: I Cor. 15:49.

I. The image of the heavenly will be the image of great strength and power.

II. The image of the heavenly will be the image of holiness.

III. The image of the heavenly will be the image of high achievement.

IV. The image of the heavenly will be the image of great joy.—Clarence Edward Macartney.

Topic: Good Grief
TEXT: I Thess. 4:13.

I. Bad grief is harmful.

(a) It bottles up its sorrows. Mary Jane Blank's husband died suddenly with a heart attack. But she put on a bold front, never shedding a tear. Friends remarked how brave she was. But a couple of weeks later she was taken to a mental ward of a hospital. She had smothered her grief within herself, and it produced a complete inner breakdown. She eventually emerged from the experience healthy and happy but at a terrible emotional cost.

(b) Bad grief causes self-pity. Why did this happen to me? Why was my beloved taken? Why must I be left to carry on alone? This is a sad preoccupation with self which only leads to deeper sadness. The end is a morose and bitter spirit.

(c) Bad grief lives in the past. Often people who suffer grief turn in on themselves and live in a shell. They retreat from the active pursuits of life and dwell on their past memories. They live immersed in their regrets and become sadder with the passing of time.

II. Good grief is helpful. Grief can actually be beneficial when handled in the right way. This is especially true of believing Christians. They can draw on the sustaining resources of their faith in times of sorrow. Several practical steps can serve to derive help out of grief.

(a) Express your grief. Pour it out freely in tears. Jesus wept quite unashamedly at the tomb of his beloved friend Lazarus. Talk freely of your beloved, remembering and treasuring the good and glad experiences shared together.

(b) Be grateful for life. Be thankful for the privileges of having known and loved the departed. Be glad for the chance to take on and further the interests and causes of your beloved. That life can have continuation through you.

(c) Affirm your faith. Within yourself, as well as with others, vocalize your faith, despite your sorrow. The Christian gospel is God's promise of life eternal for your loved one and for you. This means the assurance of a shared life in the future and the glad hope of a reunion.

(d) Share yourself with others. Share your time and strength and faith with those around you—family, friends, and associates. As you love and serve others you will find healing for yourself. In helping others you will be helping yourself.—Emil Kontz.

Meditation: Where the Rainbow Never Fades

It cannot be that the earth is man's only abiding place. It cannot be that our life is a mere bubble cast up by eternity to float a moment on its waves and then sink into nothingness. Else why is it that the glorious aspirations which leap like angels from the temple of our hearts are forever wandering unsatisfied? Why is it that all the stars that hold their festival around the midnight throne are set above the grasp of our limited faculties, forever mocking us with their unapproachable glory? And why is it that the bright forms of human beauty presented to our view are taken from us, leaving the thousand streams of our affections to flow back in Alpine torrents upon our hearts? There is a realm where the rainbow never fades, where the stars will spread out before us like islands that slumber in the ocean, and where the beautiful beings who now pass before us like shadows will stay in our presence forever.—George D. Prentice.

ILLUSTRATIONS

NEW OPPORTUNITY.   A few years ago I had to face personal loss in a way that I had never anticipated. My wife of nearly twenty-five years died of cancer. The greatest difficulty I had was dealing with the feeling of being guilty to be alive, for I still had the gift of life while my wife and the mother of my children had it taken away. When I was able to realize that it was no honor to her for me to waste away any day, not to make it more fruitful in the commitment which was mine to our Lord, that I could not hold onto that which was past, then it became clear that God was giving me a new day, a new life, and a new opportunity to bear witness to his love and to the victory which he has made possible for each one of us in Jesus Christ.—Donald G. Lester.

STRENGTH IN SORROW.   Exod. 14 records the miracle of the dividing of the Red Sea. In 1873, Horatio G. Spafford planned a European trip for his wife and four daughters. At the last moment because of business problems he decided to remain in the States. He sent his family on ahead as scheduled on the *S. S. Ville du Haver.*

A few days later the *Ville du Haver* was struck by another ship and sank. Mrs. Spafford was rescued, but her four daughters drowned. Upon reaching England, she cabled her husband a simple message: "Saved alone."

Immediately Spafford left by ship for England. While en route he asked the ship's captain to inform him when they reached the approximate place where his daughters had drowned. As requested, the captain informed Spafford when they reached the approximate place of the tragedy. Spafford walked on the deck of the ship and gazed out to sea. After some time passed, he reached into his pocket, pulled out pen and paper, and wrote these words: "When peace, like a river, attendeth my way,

When sorrows like sea billows roll;

Whatever my lot, thou hast taught me to say,

It is well, it is well with my soul."

Spafford's experience reminds us that, if God does not divide the waters as we would wish, he will give us the strength to stand on the shore.—Larry Kennedy in *The Baptist Record.*

HOMING INSTINCT.   The Lord is faithful to the homing instinct of the lower forms of life. The robin will fly to the mild climate during winter season. But the next spring it will return to the same tree in the same backyard to build its nest. The salmon will leave the Columbia or some other river and go thousands of miles to its secret feeding flats in the Pacific. Then when its life cycle is about ended, it returns to the same river it left, fights its way up the falls and through rocky shoals, and refuses to stop until it is at the same bend in the river where it hatched. If the Lord is faithful to these homing instincts, he will be faithful to our desire to live and love and learn forever.—Taylor Mendell.

TRYST.   Can anyone name a single normal desire which does not have over against it a corresponding satisfaction? If men hunger, there is food for them. If they want breath, there is air in abundance. The desire to live on after death is normal, widespread, and persistent. Why not trust the integrity of the universe to keep tryst also with the demand of human nature.—Charles R. Brown.

INSTINCTIVE.   My belief in immortality is instinctive. I feel I was not born to die. I had it when a boy, and it does not become less with the passing of the years. There is something down deep in me which rebels against the idea of personal extinction. I feel the revulsion most keenly on the death of a man both great and good. This instinctive recoil reaches its climax at the suggestion that Jesus of Nazareth is no more.—Charles F. Jefferson.

VALUING LIFE.   It is chic in some circles to say, "When I am gone, I want no mourning and no sadness and no memorial." Chic it may be, but it only serves further to diminish the value of life. To mourn, to remember, and to memorialize one who was precious to us in the company of others says more than a Kaddish and more than a prayer. It says: "Life is of supreme value, and I value the life that was led."—Harry K. Danziger.

TREASURES OF DARKNESS.   Like all men, I love and prefer the sunny uplands of ex-

perience where health, happiness, and success abound, but I have learned far more about God and life and myself in the darkness of fear and failure than I have ever learned in the sunshine. There are such things as the treasures of darkness. The darkness, thank God, passes. But what one learns in the darkness one possesses forever.—Leslie D. Weatherhead.

DESIGN.   As a knot appears unexpectedly in a thread, so disappointment blocks the smoothness of life. If a few deft strokes can untangle the skein, life continues evenly; but if it cannot be corrected, then it must be quietly woven into the design. Thus the finished piece can still be beautiful, though not as perfect as planned.—Christian Herald.

BOND OF SORROW.   Several years ago Helen Hayes' daughter Mary died of polio. While her daughter was still sick, Helen Hayes used to go early each morning to a little church near the hospital to pray for help in facing the terrible ordeal of her sorrow. As she looked around, she saw the tired and troubled looks on the faces of those around her. Life had not been kind to them, but they unmistakably were drawing spiritual refreshment from these moments of worship. Said Helen Hayes: "It seemed, as they prayed, their worn faces lighted up and they became the very vessels of God. In my need I gained strength from the knowledge that they too had needs, and I felt an interdependence with them." From this experience she learned the meaning of Christian compassion and fellowship.

MIGNONETTE.   In a lonely farmhouse a woman was slowly dying. The doctor, who had known her all her life, stood by her bed. "Doctor," said the dying woman, "how much time have I?" "About a week, Sarah," he replied. "Only a week and then this body will be decaying up there on the hillside. But I, oh, where will I be?" The doctor stepped to the window and took from the sill a flower crock in which mignonette was growing. Carrying it to the bedside, he quietly said: "Sarah, a few weeks ago I saw you planting the seeds of this mignonette in this crock. Now the hulls of the seeds are rotting in the ground, but what beauty and fragrance have come from them! 'If God so clothe the grass of the field, shall he not much more clothe you?' " Sarah's eyes were full of sudden tears. "Give it to me," she said. The doctor placed the silent comforter in her hands and quietly left the room.—Eva M. Wallace.

BUOYANCY. In my earlier ministry in Newfoundland I had occasion to travel a number of times by coastal steamer. These boats supplied the more isolated settlements along the coast with the necessities of life. Many of the smaller fishing villages had no wharf, so the steamer had to anchor off shore. Small boats came to transfer the cargo to land. Boxes and bales, sacks, barrels and casks were lowered into the small boat until you would think it must surely sink. But the sea opened its broad arms a little wider to hold it up, and by a miracle of buoyancy is chugged safely to shore. Even so, as life adds to the responsibilities and burdens we must bear, the buoyancy of the power and strength of God is about us and beneath us, and we will be sustained. Our God is that great.—Guy Case in *The United Church Observer*.

EMERGENCE. Cecil B. DeMille, having been commissioned to write a play, was drifting on a lake in a small boat in order to think and take notes without being interrupted. Making no effort to direct the little vessel, he drifted toward shore, the prow of the boat plowing gently into the soft mud. The writer made no effort to move from the place but continued his work. Later he glanced up to see a clumsy water beetle perched on the gunwale. It had come up out of the mud, set its sharp claws, and died.

With his eyes on the beetle drying in the warm sun, he saw a split start and run the full length of the back. Then out of the crevice poked a wet head that was followed by an equally wet body. For a few moments it dried itself in the sun. The texture changed. Color emerged. Wings began to move. And in a moment a beautiful dragonfly circled above him.

DeMille said after seeing the transformation, "If God does that for a water beetle, don't you believe he will do it for me?" —W. Morris Ford in *The Beam*.

COMFORT. When Calvin Coolidge was in the White House one of his sons died. The president read a book which was of great comfort to him and then gave it to a friend who was similarly bereaved. He wrote in the book an inscription that ran like this: "To my friend, in memory of his son and my son, who have the privilege of remaining boys throughout eternity."—*The Living Church*.

IDENTITY. The very heart of the Christian faith rests on the notion that individuals are what count. If we were to have mere immortality in the sense that each spirit is reunited with a general spirit, thus losing its identity like a drop of water when it flows back into the ocean, this would not represent the saving of what is most precious to us.—Elton Trueblood.

BEYOND THE SHELL. Sadhu Sundar Singh compared man's life to the life of a baby chick in a shell. In imaginary conversation the chick says: "I don't think there is anything beyond this shell. This world is all there is." The mother hen tries to stretch the mind of the baby chick by describing the world of trees, shrubs, and flowers. The chick cannot comprehend until one day it breaks through the soft part of the shell and sees a vast new world beyond the rim of its former existence. He suggests that in the great adventure our eyes will see and our ears will hear the wonderful things God has prepared.—Friedrich Rest.

SOMETHING BETTER. Then the new earth and sky, the same yet not the same, will rise in us as we have risen in Christ. And once again, after who knows what aeons of silence and the dark, the birds will sing and the waters flow, and lights and shadows move across the hills and the faces of our friends laugh upon us with amazed recognition. Guesses, of course, only guesses. If they are not true, something better will be. For we know that we shall be like him for we shall see him as he is.—C. S. Lewis.

THE CHOICE.   An ancient Greek legend tells of a woman who came to the River Styx to be ferried across to the region of departed spirits. There she found the kindly ferryman Charon. He reminded her that it was her privilege to drink of the waters of Lethe and thus forget the life she was leaving. Eagerly she said, "I will forget how I suffered." "Yes," replied Charon, "but remember too that you will forget how you have rejoiced." The woman said, "I will forget my failures." "And also your victories," the ferryman added. But she continued, "I will forget how I have been hated." "And also how you have been loved," added Charon. Then she paused to consider the whole matter. The story ends with her leaving the waters of Lethe untasted. She preferred to retain the memory even of sorrow and failure rather than to give up the memory of life's loves and joys.—Hoover Rupert.

JOHN'S LETTER.   In October 1800 a boy named John Todd was born in Rutland, Vermont. Shortly afterward his family moved to Connecticut and settled in the little community of Killingworth. There, when John was only six years old, both his parents died. The children in the family had to be parceled out to the kind-hearted relatives, and John was assigned to an aunt who lived ten miles away in the village of North Killingworth. He lived with her until he went away to study at Yale College for the ministry. When he was in his early forties and minister of the Congregational Church in Pittsfield, Massachusetts, his aunt, now a woman of advanced years, fell seriously ill. In great distress of mind she

wrote to her beloved nephew. Suppose she died. What would death be like? Would it mean agony, terror, maybe annihilation?

Here is the letter John sent in reply: "It is now nearly thirty-five years since I, a little boy of six, was left quite alone in the world. You sent me word you would give me a home and be a kind mother to me. I have never forgotten the day when I made the long journey of ten miles to your house in North Killingworth. I can still recall my disappointment when, instead of coming for me yourself, you sent Caesar to fetch me. I can still remember my tears and my anxiety as, perched on your horse and clinging tight to Caesar, I started for my new home. Night fell before we finished our journey, and as the darkness deepened I became more and more afraid. Finally I said anxiously to Caesar, 'Do you think she'll go to bed before we get there?' 'Oh, no!' he answered reassuringly. 'She'll stay up for you. When we get out of these here woods, you'll see her candle shining in her window.' Presently we did ride out into a clearing, and there, sure enough, was your candle. I remember that you were waiting at the door of your house, that you put your arms around me, that you lifted me, a tired and frightened little boy, down from the horse. There was a fire on your hearth and a warm supper on your stove. Then after supper you took me up to my room, heard me say my prayers, and sat beside me till I dropped off to sleep. You undoubtedly realize why I am now recalling all these things to your mind. Some day soon God may send to take you to a new home. Don't fear the summons, the strange journey, and the dark messenger of death. At the end of the road you will find love and a welcome. You will be safe, there as here, in God's love and care. Surely he can be trusted to be as kind to you as you were years ago to me!"—S. Robert Weaver.

SECTION V. Resources for Lenten and Easter Preaching

SERMON SUGGESTIONS

Topic: The Lenten Emphasis
TEXT: Phil. 3:13–14.

Lent is a period of going into training for serious Christian living and for getting some needed practice in putting first things first. It is a time for consciously profiting by Dean Inge's warning that, if out of the sixteen waking hours of the ordinary day we spend fifteen hours and fifty-five minutes in dealing with material things and give only five minutes to spiritual things, the material things are likely to seem to hundred times as real. Three notes are especially appropriate for Lenten accent.

I. *Self-examination.* Here is a time for taking an honest look at ourselves instead of drifting along in the ruts of everyday routine. Socrates' remark that "the unexamined life is not worth living" is doubly true for those for whom the life of Christ is the standard.

II. *Self-discipline.* This is something that runs counter to the current mood of America. There is little around us to suggest that true self-realization always involves self-denial. The popular prescription is to relieve tension, to conform, and to avoid conflict. "Relax!" is the magic word. There are tensions that are hurtful, but there is also a kind of tension that is creative. Our Lord's word, as Halford Luccock commented, is not "If any man

would come after me, let him relax" but "let him take up his cross."

III. *Self-commitment.* It is a time for renewed dedication. In the light of the completeness of Christ's self-giving, how marginal our devotion seems! In Shakespeare's *Hamlet*, when footsteps are heard, the question is asked, "Is Horatio there?" To which Horatio replied, "A piece of him." A piece of ourselves is what we are ordinarily offering to God. Lent is a reminder, as we contemplate the cross, that "Love so amazing, so divine, demands my life, my soul, my all."—Samuel McCrea Cavert.

Topic: Why the Cross?
TEXT: I Cor. 15:3.

I. Christ died because under the conditions of the time it was inevitable, as it had been inevitable historically that John the Baptist and other martyrs should die. Not only because tyrants now governed the nation but because men are what they are. "It is impossible that a prophet should perish away from Jerusalem" (Luke 13: 33).

II. He died because in a world like this, which always destroys its best, the political, social, and religious conditions always continue to make Christ a martyr and lead to the murder of the prophets.

III. He died because it was so written in Isa. 53, in Ps. 22, and elsewhere—the scriptures themselves reflecting and in a

47

measure interpreting this fatal trait in human nature and in the world's history.

IV. He died because God permitted it, and since God is absolutely sovereign he must will what he permits. God's purpose is evident from the later consequences, the removal of sin, the breaking down of the barrier between himself and the world, the whole new life in grace, the new creation, and the new being in Christ.

V. He died because he himself willed to die in taking the risk involved in going to Jerusalem, of which anyone could have warned him. This was the acceptance of God's way for him to go. And out of it came and have ever come the blessings of a new life for all who accept his way, take up his cross, and live in him.—Frederick C. Grant.

Topic: Christ of the Gospels
TEXT: Matt. 20:28.

I. The touch of his hand and spirit upon the sick somehow released hidden powers of healing.

II. The appeal of his love brought men back to God through forgiveness.

III. The coming of his peace restored disturbed minds and souls to their own peace.

IV. The power of his faith set men free from death's dark prison.

V. The allure of going with him, being with him, and doing his will put to flight even the demons of selfishness and pride.
—*Pulpit Digest.*

Topic: The Crucial Hour
TEXT: Luke 22:53 (RSV).

Thus far in Jesus' life it had always been "my hour." Once he spoke with caution and reserve: "Mine hour is not yet come." Another time the gospel writer called it "his hour." But now everything seemed to be in reverse; the tables were turned, as we are apt to say. Jesus faced these temple officials and the other rabble and said, "This is your hour."

I. It was their hour because they were about to be seen for what they were. For three years Jesus' work among his people had been marked by kindness, mercy, and sympathetic concern for all, especially the helpless. Yet his overtures of love and the sincerity of his motives were met with ignorant superstition, cold indifference, or the heated opposition of religious respectability. And so as the days passed, it was clear that the rolling momentum of this wave of passion had to break sometime. Or, to change the metaphor, inevitably the festering sore must discharge. Things were mounting toward a climax. Jesus had done everything for these people—he had taught, healed, blessed, and pleaded with them—everything short of making the ultimate sacrifice. Now it was their move.

II. It was their hour because they were forced to fight him on their own ground. The mob in Gethsemane in their moral impotence could contest Jesus on no other ground than their own. They were grasping at anything and everything to prove their case, to justify their actions, and to whitewash themselves, but their only weapons were lies, trumped up charges, and false witnesses who had been bribed to speak their piece. These were the features of the battle on their ground. This was their hour.

III. It was their hour because their old order was about to be shattered by the new. What was uppermost in their minds in this hour? This Jesus had been a thorn in their flesh. He flouted the Jewish law, he accused religious people of hypocrisy, he was too fond of sinners and social outcasts, and he made church folk feel uncomfortable and gave them an uneasy conscience. The most expedient thing to do was to get rid of him. After all, their God was safely institutionalized within the framework of a law, but this man had let God loose and was upsetting things in a sweeping fashion. Put him to death, and then all will be over and done with, they hoped.

IV. "This is your hour," said Jesus. But we are lost and are in for disaster if we keep it so. But when we accept the love of God which yearns over us, the hour of darkness becomes the hour promise from Jesus: "And I, if I be lifted up from the earth, will draw all men unto me." A new order takes over. And what was a dark hour of man's sin and shame near Gethsemane becomes new life higher up on God's everlasting hills.—Donald Macleod.

Topic: What Happened at Calvary?
TEXT: Luke 23:33.
I. God's nature was revealed to the world. Look at the cross and see revelation.
II. God redeemed a lost world. Look at the cross and see redemption.
III. God restored men to the kingdom. Look at the cross and see reconciliation.—John R. Brokhoff.

Topic: How to Hear the Easter Story
TEXT: John 20:26.
I. Millions in our days have slammed a door of solid skepticism. If they listen at all to the story of the resurrection, it is with total disbelief—the same disbelief, by the way, that we read of in the New Testament.
II. There are probably more today who are not so much sheer skeptics as nostalgic half-believers. They would like to accept the story as they hear it in the Bible. They rejoice in the signs of returning faith and are happy when the churches show signs of new vitality. But they find themselves swivelling between belief and unbelief.
(a) It is very tempting to settle for the symbolic resurrection story. Whatever happened at the tomb that morning, surely we can say that Easter means that life will triumph over death and that hope is the true posture of the human spirit. Not for a moment would I belittle this way of accepting the Easter story or attempt to rob the half-believer of the Easter joy. Some of the greatest spirits of our time have been men and women of intellectual integrity who could not profess what they did not believe but want to throw their weight on what Disraeli once called "the side of the angels."
(b) Whatever sense it makes, the symbolic hearing of the Easter story was not the hearing of the apostles, was not the hearing of the first Christians, was not the faith that swept across the world, and is not normally the kind of hearing today that brings about that reorientation we call rebirth.

(c) How thin that door of half-belief really is and at any moment the living Jesus walks right through it and says, "Happy are they who never saw me and yet have found faith."
III. It is possible to hear the Easter story out of sheer habit. We church-goers are so often locked in the narrow room of religious routine. The doors are closed not by unbelief or half-belief but by use and wont.
(a) This could be the thickest door of all. Jesus believed in religious routine. The people Jesus found hardest to reach were not the skeptics, the half-believers, the scoffers, the down-and-outs, and the up-and-outs, but the believers who were so encrusted with inherited convictions that the spirit of life could find no entrance.
(b) It was to one of them, Saul of Tarsus, that he suddenly appeared on the Damascus road, the door of his heart being shut. At any moment it can happen to any of us for whom the story lies dead and unexamined in the back of our minds.
IV. How then do we hear?
(a) With minds alert to what is being reported by the eye-witnesses.
(b) With minds open to the possibility that this was no ancient legend of someone being brought to life again but the supreme miracle in which, as C. S. Lewis put it, God leaned against the fly-wheel of history and reversed its direction.
(c) And with the realization that we are not alone but surrounded by the church catholic in every land and by the great company of heaven who respond to our whisper of "He is risen" with the eternal chorus: "Hallelujah! He is risen indeed." —David H. C. Read.

Topic: Getting a Rise Out of Resurrection
TEXT: I Tim. 4:8.
If the reality of Christ's mastery over death doesn't make us glow, our congregations will leave their lily-decked sanctuaries on Easter Sunday with more lethargy than vivacity, more torpor than tonic. And this will be a disaster.
I. We should get a rise out of the realiza-

tion that it is Christ's resurrection that shapes history.

II. We should get a rise out of the realization that Christ's resurrection shatters failure.

III. We should get a rise out of the realization that Christ's resurrection hangs a death sentence on death itself.

IV. We should get a rise out of the realization that Christ's resurrection shines on the life that now is.—Paul S. Rees in *World Vision.*

Topic: The Difference Easter Makes
TEXT: I Cor. 15:58.

I. Paul says that faith in the resurrection makes us steadfast.

II. Paul says that a Christian is unmovable.

III. As a result of the resurrection there is an abounding in the work of the Lord.

IV. Paul speaks of the assurance that comes to believers in the resurrection.—Gerald Kennedy.

Meditation: Easter Confidence
Easter faith carries us into each moment with confidence, a confidence we may only have if we believe God will be in that moment to meet us when we get there, regardless of what else the moment may bring. This gives us reason to move on with courage. This assures us that life takes its direction and purpose from God. God is in history working out his purposes, and we may choose to be or not to be a part of that process. It gives us cause to stand firm for what we believe God stands for without equivocation. It was this conviction that took Christ to the cross. He dared to confront those who defied the purposes and love of God. He suffered death upon the cross. But he was certain, when the moment came and he committed his Spirit to the Father, that the Father was there even ahead of the moment and that he was adequate.—Dwight E. Loder.

Topic: Suddenly It's Easter
TEXT: Phil. 3:10.

Easter came unexpectedly—suddenly—and found even the closest followers of Jesus unbelieving.

I. *Suddenly—Christ returns in power.* Some miss this because they leave Jesus as "one of earth's greatest men," "a perfect pattern and example for human achievement." Easter proclaims that Christ is a living person among us to help us live in the power of divine love. Easter, which changed life and history, is visible only to the eyes of faith.

II. *Suddenly—life has meaning and purpose.* For many pre-Easter persons, life is absurd and without meaning. The disciples had lost their purpose and were drifting back to the status quo life as it was before Christ. Then came that flash of recognition with its accompanying amazement and astonishment. "They recognized Jesus!"

III. *Suddenly—we see Jesus as living presence in our lives.* Where do we see him? Right where we live—in the storm of emotional despair; at the depth of our being; in great literature, music, and the arts; in the beauty of nature; in sorrow, despair, loneliness, and fear. He comes to us and brings God's redeeming love to guide, to cleanse, and to empower us for life that is eternal. —Hoover Rupert.

ILLUSTRATIONS

CALL FOR REPENTANCE.   Repentance is essential to the receiving of the gospel. Repentance calls for action, a turning around, a re-orientation of outlook and life-style. During this Lenten season, contemporary Christians must examine their lives to see if their repentance leads them to obedience to Jesus Christ, concern for the less fortunate, a willingness to become involved and seeing that equity and justice occur in our common life. Repentance is meaningless if it does not reveal itself in lives that become more sensitive to the cries of pain in the world about them.—J. Metz Rollins, Jr.

CRUCIFIXION.   Crucifixion was the most terrible means of execution ever devised. It was invented by the Phoenicians. Roman law forbade it for Roman citizens. Paul, a Roman citizen, was beheaded. Jesus, a Roman subject, was crucified.

The gospels do not record the gruesome details, but from other sources we know what was done to Jesus. He was stripped naked. The upright pole of the cross was placed erect in a hole in the ground. The crossbeam was laid on the ground. Jesus was made to lie down. To render him helpless, his arms and legs were jerked out of joint. With his arms stretched out along the crossbeam, his hands were nailed to it. Then the beam was fastened to the upright pole. Jesus' feet were crossed on a small shelf about two feet above the ground, and spikes were driven through his feet into the pole. There he hung for six hours. Because of his outstretched body, his ribs could be counted.

The slightest body movement tore at the gashes in hands and feet. Due to his position, blood collected in his abdomen causing excruciating pain. Every sunbeam became a leech sucking out his vital body fluid. His lips became cracked and parched. His mouth was as dry as dust, and his tongue swelled. Due to inflamed vocal cords, his voice became raspy. Fever mounted so as to cause a terrible headache. The soaring temperature was burning out his life. His joints were wracked with agony. Every nerve throbbed with pain. Gradually his body grew stiff and his strength ebbed away. And his physical suffering was enhanced beyond measure by his mental and spiritual agony.

We cannot enter into his suffering. We can only describe it and imagine it. And remember that he did it for you and me.—Herschel H. Hobbs.

THE ONE WE REMEMBER.   The busy Londoner and the bemused tourist may not stop to wonder why Charing Cross is so called. They do not remember that once Charing Cross was a little green village on the outskirts of Westminster.

It was one of the many stopping places of the entourage which bore the body of a greatly loved queen from the place of her death in the north to Westminster Abbey where she now lies buried. Wherever her body paused on that long journey, they set up a cross, known first as Eleanor's Cross.

She was the wife of Edward I of England and lived during the latter half of the thirteenth century. For 300 years after her death she was remembered, as candles burned without dimming around her tomb in the abbey. But she became forgotten. Today not one of her crosses survives and no candles flicker at her tomb. Eleanor of Castile—a lovely name, a generous and thoughtful queen, loving and loved but long forgotten.

Nearly 2,000 years ago there came out of a small town in the Near East a young man who had only a short time to live. He lived the life of a wandering teacher. He wrote no books. He moved among the rich and poor, the great and the less with equal grace. He was joyously welcomed at feasts and weddings. He was urgently summoned to the house of sickness and death. He was loved and maligned, sought after and rejected.

Finally he was arrested, accused of heresy and treason, scourged, tried, and executed by crucifixion, as was the Roman custom.

He had no lasting tomb; no epitaph was ever written for him; no memorial ever set up. But for nineteen centuries he has been remembered as no man has ever been in the world's long history.—Christine McMillan in *The War Cry.*

GOD WAS THERE.   A little girl who was looking at a picture of the crucifixion asked what it meant and why this good man was nailed there. Suddenly it dawned on the little girl what was happening. She burst into tears and said, "If God had been there, he wouldn't have let it happen!" But he was and he did. And aren't you grateful?—Alton M. McEachern.

ADVOCATE.   There is a popular question that has been going the rounds for a number of years: If you were on trial for being a Christian, would there be enough evidence to convict you? That question challenges your Christian witness. I have suggested a quite different question: If Jesus Christ were on trial today (and he still is!), would he want you for his lawyer? That question challenges your ability as an advocate.—Richard S. Armstrong.

MAN IN A WELL.   After falling down the deep shaft into the slimy, cold water at the bottom of the well, his first thought was to cry for help. But after hoarse calls led only to silence he began to try to climb. Again and again he tried to inch up the slippery, algae-covered brick, only to slide back into the water. His nails bloodied from his attempts to get a grip in the cracks. He simply couldn't make it to the top before slipping back. Despairing, he called out again.

A passerby appeared above. "Well, I can't get you out of the well, but I can make it better for you," said the passerby. "Here, have a fifth of whiskey." And so he drank the fifth, and being quite drunk, the well didn't seem so bad. But as sobriety returned, he was still in the well and miserable.

A woman appeared. "Well, I can't get you out of the well, but things could be much worse for you. You must accept your situation and make the best of it." So he tried not to feel sorry for himself and to be grateful to be alive, but it didn't work. He was still miserable and alone, and despair maintained its grip upon him.

He started to climb. He had always been able to take care of himself. But bloody, cold, and hungry, now he slid back into the water again. And then another man appeared above. "I can get you out of the well, but you must trust me. Do you?"

The man in the well had never known before his need for another's rescue, and how this man would get him out he didn't know, but he said, "Yes, I'll trust you." And Jesus Christ dropped into that well. Upon his shoulders the man climbed out. Jesus remained in his place.—Arthur McPhee.

GATE OF HEAVEN.   The cross is the abyss of wonders, the center of desires, the school of virtues, the house of wisdom, the throne of love, the theater of joys, and the place of sorrows; it is the root of happiness and the gate of heaven.—Thomas Traherne.

YOKE AND BURDEN.   We can of course shake off the burden which is laid upon us, but only find that we have a still heavier burden to carry—a yoke of our own choosing, the yoke of our self. But Jesus invites all who travail and are heavy laden to throw off their yoke and take his yoke upon them—and his yoke is easy and his burden light. The yoke and burden of Christ are his cross.—Dietrich Bonhoeffer.

RESOLUTION.   How may we believe and declare that God loves and forgives without thereby making light of sin? How can the holiness which must exclude saying, "Depart from me," be at the same time and in the same situation the love which must include saying, "Come unto me?" It is this contradiction between condemnation and forgiveness, between Depart and Come, between No and Yes, between Justice and Mercy, between Law and Grace, irresolvable in logic, which was not only expressed but also resolved finally and forever in the action and passion of the eternal Son upon the cross.—J. S. Whale.

BEYOND FAILURE.   Christ did not have to face failure in himself, but he did have to face it in respect to the hopes and desires he had formed for mankind. One of the chief elements in the agony of Gethsemane was the terrific and final adjustment of his spirit to the fact of the almost total failure of his call to his own beloved people. It is one of the grandest things in Jesus that he accepted this failure and went on to the cross with love and faith undiminished, so turning the failure, as we believe, into victory.—H. H. Farmer.

LEGEND.   A group of martyrs arrived at the gates of eternity. The guardian of the gate said to them: "God has given much to you. Have you brought any gift for him?" "Only our pain," said the martyrs, "and that is nothing compared with Christ's suffering for us." "Yet it is a good gift," said the guardian, "and you are doubly welcome as comrades of the cross."

PASSERBY.   Stainer many years ago painted a picture of Christ on a cross that is not pictured on top of a hill between two thieves. Instead he painted the crucifixion as occurring in the midst of a busy and throbbing marketplace. All the people are passing by. There are business men scurrying past, busily thinking of the next deal. Doctors hurry by, minds occupied with the newest medicines. Lawyers hurry past, minds saturated with legal procedure. Housewives, secretaries, nurses, and people from all walks of life walk past the crucified Jesus. Nobody pays any attention to the rejected, pale figure on the cross except one person. A little woman, amazed and bewildered by the fleeting crowds, turns to them and cries pleadingly, "Is it nothing to you, all ye that pass by?"—Bernie Wiebe.

THE FATHER'S FACE.   In the National Gallery in London there is a painting in which one sees Christ on the cross against a black background. Darkness wraps him in loneliness and apparent God-abandonment. He alone loves men enough to suffer and die for us. The universe is uncaring. But if one looks at that canvas intently, there emerges from the blackness the dim outline of another crucified sufferer—the Father sharing Golgotha with his son. "God was in Christ reconciling the world unto himself"; "God commendeth his own love towards us." In taking on himself the confusion and doubt of a sinful world, Christ took away the shrouding darkness sufficiently to let a Father's face shine through. On that cruel cross where the combination of the forces which bedevil every human society and every man's own heart brought Jesus of Nazareth to a death of agony and shame, he did most in those brief hours to set afoot counter forces which down the ages continue to defeat them.—Henry Sloane Coffin.

DISCOVERY.   R. W. Dale had preached many years in his famous pulpit at Carr's Lane, Birmingham, England, but one Easter morning the truth of Christ's resurrection came alive to him. He walked up and down his study, saying: "Christ is living! Christ is living!" He said: "At first it seemed strange and hardly true, but at last it came upon me as a burst of sudden glory. Yes, Christ is living. It was to me a new discovery. I thought all along I had believed it, but not until that moment did I feel sure about it."

EASTER MESSAGE.   In William Faulkner's novel, *The Sound and the Fury,* one frame of time concerns Dilsey, the black woman who cares for Ben, the idiot child of the Compson family. Dilsey, Ben, and Frony (Dilsey's son) attend the Easter service in her own church. The visiting minister, undersized, in "a shabby black coat," at first evokes disappointment and then astonishment. Gathering up the motifs from crucifixion to resurrection, the preacher fixes their attention with the words, "I got the recollection of the Lamb!" As he tramped steadily back and forth he poured out the stark reality of "a serene, tortured crucifix," and a woman's voice cried, "Yes, Jesus!" Dilsey sat upright, tears streaming down her face, as the preacher pointed to the children and the suffering of humanity. He led that congregation, step by step, through the saving event of Jesus Christ. Later Dilsey, walking home with the children, still tearful but with her head up, spoke softly, "I seed de first en de last . . . I seed de beginnin', en now I sees the endin'."—Charles R. Stinnette, Jr.

THE KEY.   The gospels cannot explain the resurrection; it is the resurrection alone which explains the gospels. Here is the mightiest of the mighty acts of God, foreign to the common experience of man, inscrutable to all his science, astounding to believer and unbeliever alike. But here and here only is an activity of God, wrought out in this world of pain, sin, and death, which is the key pattern for the world's true life. Here is the sure promise that life according to this pattern is eternal. This and this alone is the key to the Christian doctrine of history.—J. S. Whale.

IN THE WAKE OF HIS APPEARING.   The essential fact is that Jesus came back and was personally present with his disciples. He was able to make his presence known and his will understood. Nothing but such a real appearance, which the disciples naturally apprehended in forms conditioned by their past experience with Jesus, will explain the new start, the amazing vigor, the continued life and growth, and the intensive theological development of the church. The Christian faith is essentially a resurrection faith. Christian theology is essentially resurrection theology. The resurrection was the climax of the apostolic preaching, and when the center is moved to other events in order to provide a more easily acceptable message or a more common ground of faith, the Christian faith and message cannot but begin to disintegrate. It can only be what it has always been from the first day of the apostolic church by remaining the good news of the risen Christ.—Floyd V. Filson.

BROKEN EGGS.   Can it be Easter without Easter eggs? The egg seems to be part and parcel of the Easter celebration. No doubt you have a nest of colored eggs in your home for this Easter day. Did you ever notice that an egg is perfectly enclosed? It has no opening, not even a crack. If you were inside that egg you would not have any light or air. It is a self-contained world. After proper incubation a chick takes its beak and starts pecking on the shell until it is broken open. Then a whole new world begins for the baby chick. You and I can live in a similar self-contained world of selfishness and unbelief. It can be only a physical, materialistic world without spiritual reality. What we need to do is to take our beaks of faith and peck, peck, peck until the shell is broken. Then a whole new world of spiritual reality opens up. Faith opens us up to life in and with Christ. Christ is now a reality in our lives. And that life in Christ is truly liberating and everlasting.—John R. Brokhoff.

WHAT THE BELIEVER SEES.   While even the unbeliever must see what the life and death of Jesus have effected in the world, to the believer that life and death are something deeper still. To him they are nothing less than a resurrection from the dead. He sees in the cross of Christ something which far transcends its historical significance. He sees in it the fulfillment of all prophecy as well as the consummation of all history. He sees in it the explanation of the mystery of birth and the conquest over the mystery of the grave. In that life he finds a perfect example and in that death an infinite redemption. As he contemplates the incarnation and the crucifixion, he no longer feels that God is far away and that this earth is but a disregarded speck in the infinite azure and he himself but an insignificant atom chance-thrown amid the thousand million living souls of an innumerable race, but he exclaims in faith and hope and love, "Ye are the temple of the living God; as God hath said, I will dwell in them, and walk in them."— Frederick W. Farrar.

SECTION VI. *Resources for Advent and Christmas Preaching*

SERMON SUGGESTIONS

Topic: Season for Preparing
TEXT: Luke 1:17.

Advent is not just an extension of Christmas so that we can sing Christmas carols for several weeks instead of just one day. Advent is the season of the preparation for the coming of Jesus Christ.

I. In Advent we prepare ourselves for his coming as the child of Bethlehem, the savior of the world.

II. In Advent we prepare ourselves for his coming into our lives as lord of all our living.

III. In Advent we prepare ourselves for the final coming of his kingdom which is triumphant over all sin and evil and which is forever.—Charles L. Seasholes.

Topic: This Hallowed Season
TEXT: Matt. 1:21.

I. How desperate is the urgency that Christ's friends redeem the meaning and experience of this season. It is a hallowed time but not because of Santa and a spirit of generosity that moves us to send gifts and extend greetings. There is nothing essentially Christian about that. The season is hallowed because it marks the dawning of new hope in the lives of men.

II. It is hallowed because in the fullness of time, out of his compassion and mercy, God thrust himself into the physical presence of men that they might see and hear and know him—and knowing, turn to him

in repentance; and turning, experience again the reality of meaning and purpose of life, the joy of peace, and the wonder of hope.

III. Christmas is hallowed because God in Christ came as a man to dwell among men. He came to show the way through the truth to life. He came to redeem mankind, and in his dying took from every heart who would accept him in faith the burden of guilt and the stain of sin. In his victory over death he held out to all humanity the power of his resurrection that man might never see death but live in the sustaining, exhilarating hope of eternal life in the power of his spirit.—Glenn B. Ogden.

Meditation: The Day of God's Visitation
TEXT: Gal. 4:4.

In this advent of the redeemer there was nothing outwardly remarkable to the men of that day. It was almost nothing. Of all the historians of that period few indeed are found to mention it. This is a thing which we at this day can scarcely understand. To us the blessed advent of our Lord is the brightest page in the world's history, but to them it was far otherwise.

Remember what the advent of our Lord was to all outward appearance. He seemed —let it be said reverently—to the rulers of those days a fanatical free-thinker. They heard of his miracles, but they appeared nothing remarkable to them. There was nothing there on which to fasten their attention. They heard that some of the populace had been led away, and now and then, it may be, some of his words reached their ears, but to them they were hard to be understood—full of mystery or else they roused every evil passion in their hearts, so stern and uncompromising was the morality they taught. They put aside these words in that brief period, and the day of grace passed.

Just such as this is God's visitation to us today. Generally the day of God's visitation is not a day very remarkable outwardly. Bereavement and sorrows no doubt, in these God speaks—but there are other occasions far more quiet and unobtrusive which are yet days of grace. A scruple which others do not see, a doubt coming into the mind respecting some views held sacred by the popular creed, a sense of heart loneliness and solitariness, a feeling of awful misgiving when the future lies open before us, the dread feeling of an eternal godlessness for men who are living godless lives now—these silent moments unmarked are the moments in which the eternal is speaking to our souls.—Frederick W. Robertson.

Topic: Deeper Meanings of Christmas
Text: Luke 2:7.

Perhaps those of us who are neither saints nor poets cannot realize any moment of life to its fullest or tell what Christmas truly means, but we can, if we pause for a moment, say some of its meaning to ourselves.

I. We can say love—love in its widest sense, love that is the touch of young lips together and love that grows, love that is of human bondage and part courage to bear the burdens of love. We can say love, as the youngster carrying a crippled child said it: "He ain't heavy. He's my brother." Love has many faces but all are kind, from that of the madonna to the love behind a smile for a friend or a smile of thanks or welcome to a stranger. A mother's love is largely working love, as is a father's, and their love for each other. All love is a part of what Christmas means, we believe.

II. We can say quiet—yes, just quiet. Let our Christmas mean some quietude, dear Lord—quiet in the sense of the absence of sound as well as in tranquillity of mind, for we know communication is impossible among those who talk all the time. Christmas is a time for moments of silence, like this one, for how else can we speak to our God and hear him?

III. Christmas to us means simplicity—simplicity of worship and of hospitality and of gifts. Simple things, like love, are unencumbered by pretense. Children often put aside the complex, costly toys and spend hours happily playing with the boxes they came in. St. Luke's account of Christ's birth is an unexcelled model of simplicity—so simple in fact and in the telling but so divinely magnificent in meaning. May we remember especially on Christmas Day that expensive gifts and all the gaudy blaze of the Christmas celebration have no meaning except as tokens of love.—*Ladies' Home Journal.*

Topic: Why Did Jesus Come?
Text: John 1:9–30.

I. He came to give God a new visibility (v. 18).

II. He came to give people a new possibility (v. 12).

III. He came to give grace a new immensity (v. 16).

IV. He came to give truth a new vitality (v. 14).

V. He came to give glory a new identity (v. 14).—Paul S. Rees.

Meditation: Prophetic Day
Christmas is the theology of civilization yet to be. The time has come when man must take a step into a higher range of being or else lose and slip back. Christmas is a prophetic day, looking not so much backward as forward. It is a song out of the heart of the world. It is not a mortal melody but a divine symphony. Because it is far off we know that it is not our own music but was sent into the souls of man by one who is as far above us as the stars are above the mists. the world will fill up with men of goodwill who keep step to its music and live by its law—men who know that man was made for love because God is love and that love and joy will blend in the

final note of the great world song.—Joseph Fort Newton.

Topic: The Consolation of God
TEXTS: Job 15:11; Luke 2:25.
Job's comforters could not bring him comfort. They could talk about the consolations of God, but something was lacking. Simeon's comfort sprang out of the promise that he would see the Christ before he died. He awaited eagerly the coming of the one who would redeem Israel and bring hope to the people.
I. Christmas is God's consolation of concern. We do not have any easy answer to the problem of suffering, but we have this ultimate experience which carries us through it. We learn that in Jesus Christ God is telling us that no man suffers alone. In the darkest hour God suffers with us.
II. Christmas is God's consolation of love. Salvation does not lie in our being protected but in the assurance that we are loved. If you are seeking a unique thing about Jesus Christ, find it here in the fact that without him men dared not believe in the love of God, but with him they never could deny it.
III. Christmas is God's consolation of power. We may turn the birthday of Jesus into a sentimental, passing experience, but that is only when we substitute worldly glitter for spiritual reality. He is the power to become, the power to conquer evil, and the power to wait. Down through the years ordinary people like us have been overcoming the world in his strength.—Gerald Kennedy.

Meditation: The Luminous Christ
TEXT: II Cor. 4:6.
The real Christmas experience for any one is the turning on of the light within which comes from the spirit of the indwelling Christ. It is still his incoming that makes the difference between a darkened inn and a glorified stable. Before we go on with our Christmas preparation, let us ask ourselves whether the real Christmas has come to us, whether what we are going through is just a form, a bartering of gifts, a forced holiday, or whether we have the real experience that makes Christmas a joy

and not a bore. Christ taken in and then given out makes it a genuine Christmas for us and for others, for God shined in our hearts that the light might be passed on. All about us are those who wait for our coming and lonely people, discouraged people, and heart-sick people living starved lives with so little of love and joy. Christmas opens our eyes and challenges us to let our light shine outside our own little circle and give cheer where it is needed most—to the cheerless, the lonely, and the destitute.—Albert W. Beaven.

Meditation: When the Shepherds Returned
TEXT: Luke 2:20.
What happened to the shepherds? They didn't become seers or priests or ministers or prophets. They remained shepherds. They went back to their work. They went back to the common round. They went back to their duties and responsibilities. But when they returned, everything was different because there was a glory upon their lives. They returned glorifying and praising God. The shepherds are singing now; they are shouting; they are happy. They return to their work, but their work is no longer common for God has made it uncommon with his presence and with his good news. They are praising God for all the things that have been made known to them. We have to ask ourselves if we've had things made known to us so great and so glorious that life becomes a continual pageant of praise and giving glory to God who has made known such great things to us.—Lowell M. Atkinson.

ILLUSTRATIONS

SEASON OF PREPARATION.   Advent is the near approach of the son of God in the flesh for which one must prepare oneself with greater watchfulness and by the practice of works of charity; it is the voice of the prophets announcing the messiah who comes; it is the world awaiting its redeemer, sighing as the parched ground for the dew of heaven; it is St. Paul exhorting the faithful, awakening them from their sleep upon the vigil of the coming of

Christ; it is John the Baptist, the last of the long line of prophets, who cries in the wilderness, "Prepare ye the way of the Lord!"—Fernand Cabrol.

MESSAGE OF ADVENT.   The word "advent" is derived from the Latin verb *advenio*, "to come," and in the Christian year it refers to the coming of Jesus Christ. Advent reflects a double significance: this season of joy looks backward and forward. It recalls the coming of Christ as God's love broke in on the earth, never to fade away. It anticipates Christ coming again to judge mankind in awesome power and victory.

Advent's stirring message challenges us to fulfill John the Baptist's plea, "Prepare the way of the Lord" (Matt. 3:3). This call implies self-examination on our part. Are we ready to receive Christ our Lord?

This Advent mood of self-examination embraces the four Sundays prior to Christmas day. It culminates in the joyful festivities of Christmas. It is our prayer that the expansive heart, the note of joy, and the awe of the Bethlehem birth should spread over the whole year.—Jack R. Van Ens.

ADVENT PURPLE.   The people of Tyre at the eastern end of the Mediterranean Sea used to extract from certain fish (the purpura) a dye which they used in coloring fabrics. The color was more crimson than blue and so accounts for the contradictions of colors in the gospel accounts of our Lord's passion. The gospel for Good Friday says, "They put on him a purple robe"; the gospel for Tuesday before Easter says, "and they clothed him with purple"; the gospel for Palm Sunday says, "Put on him a scarlet robe."

Because Tyrians dipped their fabrics twice, the color was much stronger and lasted much longer. Consequently it was so expensive that only the rich and powerful could afford it. Eventually Tyrian purple became the symbol of power and authority and was worn only by emperors and other royal persons. It is from this custom that we have the phrase "born to the purple."

We should think that Tyrian purple ought to be the color symbolic of our Lord's kingship and the color used in Advent, but because he humbled himself and took upon himself our sins, his purple took on a tainted or darker hue. And so the purple we see on altars and the eucharistic vestments which our priests wear during Advent is of the darker or tainted purple. We are thereby reminded not only of our Lord's majesty but of his revelation of the love of God and consequent redemption of mankind.—*St. Andrew Herald.*

BURNING STAR.   During an Advent service the children presented a Christmas pageant, complete with blue and purple bathrobes and white cotton beards. A three year old was the eastern star. After he had led the wise men to Jesus' cradle, pointing the way with his starlike wand, he stood there like a good star—beaming!—until he noticed the candles. He reached out with his wand and extinguished one. Every eye in church watched him. He was working on the second candle when his papier-mâché wand burst into flames. Suddenly, before us stood a burning star, crying and calling, "Mama!"

God surprised a number of us that day with a fresh insight. Shouldn't the star that leads the way to Christ put out other lesser lights? The glory of his star causes all others to pale. The real light of Christmas is Jesus, the light of the world.—Joseph E. Galle III in *Proclaim.*

FOUR MIRACLES.   Martin Luther pointed out that there were three miracles at Bethlehem. One, that God became man; two, that a virgin conceived; three, that Mary believed. Luther thought that the third one was the greatest of the three. A fourth could be added—that God believed in humanity.—John A. Holt.

GIFTS AND THE GIVER.   The gifts are no more than the shining rays of the Spirit who is himself the gift par excellence, the gift who contains all other gifts within him. We must abide with this Spirit, as a person, in his living and radiant reality. The manifestations of the Spirit are the workings of the Holy Spirit. This action or movement of God is infinitely subtle, discreet, and supremely free. The Spirit blows how, when, and where he wills. The gifts are related to the giver as are its rays to the sun. They are not to be identified with him, but neither have they substance apart from him.—Leo Cardinal Suenens.

LIGHTED CANDLE. A six year old was sitting on his father's lap on Christmas night and looking at his Christmas tree. He had been permitted to stay up until the unheard-of hour of nine as a special concession.

Suddenly he dropped off to sleep and dreamed that an angel came down from heaven. Starting at the top of the beautiful Christmas tree, the angel snuffed out every candle on it but the one at the top. That candle the angel carried over to the little boy. Handing it to him, she said: "Here is the candle of Christmas light and love. Never let it go out!"

The little boy stirred uneasily in his daddy's lap as he dreamed and muttered aloud something about candles, trees, and an angel.

The father took the little fellow up to bed and tucked him in. Just before he turned to go he kissed the boy good night. Then the boy aroused, put his arms around his daddy, and said: "Don't let the angel go away, daddy. And don't let the candle go out!"

In that child's Christmas dream lies all the hope of the world. If we could keep the Christmas spirit of light and love alive, this would be a kindlier world.—William L. Stidger.

GREATER THAN RICHES. Among the most valuable paintings in all the art galleries of the world is Raphael's glorification of the Christ Child and his mother. Millions of dollars could not purchase this picture. If you receive and believe God's Christmas gift and have Christ imprinted in the fibers of your heart, you have a blessing that makes millions of dollars seem paltry. One of the most costly pieces of property in the world is the site of the Church of the Nativity in Bethlehem. No amount of money could purchase this reputed spot of our savior's birth. Streams of blood have flown from ten thousand wounds as many have tried to seize or to protect this place. Yet if you have God's Christmas gift and kneel in spirit at the Christ Child's manger, you are richer than if you held the title to that church at Bethlehem. When Christ is born in your hearts, you have a living, victorious assurance that can never come from any disputed traditional spot of the savior's birth.—Walter A. Maier.

MOMENT IN TIME. A moment out of time, but in time, in what we call history; transecting, bisecting the world of time, a moment in time but not like a moment of time. A moment in time but time was made through that moment: for without the meaning there is no time; and that moment of time gave the meaning.—T. S. Eliot.

WINTER WITHOUT CHRISTMAS. Preparations were being made for a great feast. Things seemed to be going very well. There was every evidence that a great throng would be at the festive occasion. When the night came, a great group of people gathered together. All the preparations had been made, and the feast was about to begin. Someone said, "But where is the guest of honor?" And it developed that in the midst of all the expensive and busy preparations everybody had forgotten to invite the guest of honor. The feast was there and the people were there, but the guest of honor had not even been invited to come.

It is a parable of the kind of activity that characterizes many people at this season of the year. There is ample activity, there is much busyness, there is a crowded schedule, and there are festivities and feasts, but the guest of honor has not been invited. And he is not there. At the very center of all of this vital energy there is a tragic emptiness, an ironic vacancy where the guest of honor should have been.

The mission of the church is to see to it that our people invite the guest of honor into their Christmas festivities so that

Jesus Christ gives meaning to the season in our church and in our community, in our homes and in our hearts. Otherwise we are simply going through a nerve-racking routine for nothing. This is the tragedy of winter without Christmas.—Lowell M. Atkinson.

THE LIVING TREE. There are many legends as to the origin of the Christmas tree as an element of the day's celebration. One of the oldest is the legend of St. Bonifice, that the first Christmas tree grew miraculously out of the ruins of Thunder Oak, sacred to the pagan god Thor. Warriors, women, and children were gathered there for the annual sacrifice of a child, and the hammer was raised to strike when the saint appeared with the cross, which turned the blow aside and wrecked the tree.

With his arm about the rescued boy, the saint told the story of Jesus, and as he spoke his eyes fell on a young fir tree, straight and green amid the branches of the fallen oak, pointing to the stars.

"Here is the living tree," he said, "with no stains of blood upon it, that shall be the sign of your new worship. Let us call it the tree of the Christ Child. You shall go no more into the shadows of the forest to keep your secret rites of shame. You shall keep them at home with laughter and song and rites of love."

COMMENTARY ON JOHN 1:11. When he came to his own people, they received him not. Such is the tragic motto one of the gospels sets over his story. There is little reason to believe that the story had greatly changed. "He is too common." We know his folks. Is he any different from them? Is he not a man such as we? "He is too usual." When the messiah comes, doesn't he come in power and glory, as lightning in the storm clouds? Can the infinite take form in the finite? "He is too demanding." He bids us leave parents, friends, and property and follow him. We thought he would come to give us more possessions, not take from us what we have. "He doesn't look or act like a God." Where is

his power? What can he command? Why does he suffer resistance and not call on legions of angels to clear his way? Is not God able to do all he wills? "God is a God of power and of glory." We can admire this man's courage, sincerity, and purity, but he isn't our idea of what God should be. We know what God ought to be. This one is not his image.—Conrad Bergendoff.

REPRESENTATIVE. Simeon is in many ways a symbolic and representative figure. The world has never been without men of his type, men with a forward look, men in whom there burned a great hope, men on tiptoe, the flame of freedom in their souls and the light of knowledge in their eyes, living in the expectation that a great day was coming when wrong would be righted, when justice would be done, and when God would make bare his arm and bring salvation to all mankind.—Robert J. McCracken.

HIS BUSINESS. In Dickens' *Christmas Carol* the miserly Scrooge is confronted in a dream by the ghost of his dead partner Jacob Marley. Marley, like Scrooge, had been hard and stingy during life. And now from the realm of the departed appears the spirit of Marley, condemning himself and warning Scrooge against the fate that had befallen him. As the ghost wrings his hands and bemoans his shortcomings, Scrooge tries to console him with the remark, "But you were always a good man of business, Jacob." Whereupon Marley's ghost cries: "Business! Mankind was my business. The common welfare was my business: charity mercy, forbearance, benevolence were all my business." Too late Marley discovered what his real business in life was.

CHANGED HEART. Did Charles Dickens know the historical meaning and deliberately choose the name Ebenezer for his Ebenezer Scrooge? I'm inclined to believe he did. For the Israelites, though well off, abandoned God, then received his strong judgment, repented, and changed their hearts to one of gratitude. That's also what happened to Dicken's Ebenezer. So he becomes for us a symbol of the difference a changed heart can make, especially when we let our gratitude be transformed into ministries of generosity, goodwill, and peace.—Robert P. Bunch.

RULED BY LOVE.   King Herod wants to know if Jesus will be a warrior king? One of the wise men answers, "He will rule his people in love." Herod responds: "You cannot rule man by love. When you find your king, tell him so. Only three things will govern a people —fear and greed and the promise of security. Do I not know it? Have I not loved? But whenever I loved, I found treachery—wife, children, brother, all of them. Love is a traitor; it has betrayed me; it betrays all kinds; it will betray your Christ."—Dorothy L. Sayers.

HEAR THE BELLS.   Today the bells call you to the Christmas of mankind. For it has begun, and we shall not falter nor turn back until every man and woman and child has a chance to live happily and develop his mind and do the best of which he is capable. Hear the Christmas bells! How they answer one another from end to end of the country, chime upon chime! From every spire and tower they utter the good tidings of great joy, the tidings of the great change, the cry that no human heart can resist: "Brotherhood! Brotherhood! Brotherhood!"—Helen Keller.

THE CHRISTMAS GOSPEL.   This is the Christmas gospel—that we are to be worldly people as God made himself a worldly person and that we are to get into the world and use the world and enjoy the world and that with no sheepish, hang-dog reluctance, no pitiful Christians-can-have-fun-too bravado but honestly, wholeheartedly, and robustly. The ethics of the incarnation is the ethics of involvement. It bids us get into the world to claim it for God as he claimed it for himself. The Christmas gospel is the platform for politics and education and homemaking and painting and acting and exploring and every other activity which makes room in the world for its Lord.—The Christian Century.

LINGERING MOMENTS.   Another Christmas has moved within our ken. Our minds linger over moments unique against the background of the year.

Moments of awareness when our landscape was washed by the light of the spirit of God.

Moments of joy when some act of grace in the midst of the commonplace filled our cup of living to the brim.

Moments of hope when the flickering light was extinguished and the despair of the spirit did not prevail.

Moments of strength when the right word was said and the courage to dare invaded the spirit.

Moments of thanksgiving when in one vast sweep the sheer wonder and beauty of living overwhelmed us.—Howard Thurman.

SECTION VII. *Evangelism and World Missions*

SERMON SUGGESTIONS

Topic: Commissioned Christians
TEXT: Matt. 28:18–20.
Jesus has given Christians a compelling commission. It is set forth in varying forms in the New Testament, but it is characterized by four distinct factors.

I. "To preach" or literally "to herald the gospel to every creature." "Gospel" means "good news." Christians are to herald the good news that God has broken into our sin-sick, harassed world to make himself known and to redeem men from the power and eternal aftermath of their sins.

II. To teach. "Teach all nations . . . to observe whatsoever I have commanded you." An inscription on a fresco at the eastern entrance of Rockefeller Center reads: "Man's ultimate destiny depends not on whether he can learn new lessons or make new discoveries and conquests but on his acceptance of the lesson taught him close upon two thousand years ago." This is still true. But it was to his disciples that Jesus gave the commission to teach men that lesson.

III. To witness. "Ye shall be witness unto me"—witnessing to the fact and the teachings of Christ.

IV. To make disciples—"baptizing them in the name of the Father, and of the Son, and of the Holy Spirit." The reference is not merely to the sacramental sign but to all for which it stands. Christians are to enable men to discover God and his forgiving love, to follow Christ, and to possess his Spirit.—Harry A. Fifield.

Topic: What Is Evangelism?
TEXT: I Cor. 15:1.
Our understanding of New Testament evangelism will always be helped if three things are kept in mind.

I. There is the central fact and figure of Jesus Christ.

(a) For the purpose of reconciling his rebellious human creatures to himself, God has come to them fully and finally in the loving life, the atoning death, and the victorious resurrection of Jesus Christ. Through him—and through no other—can humans be released from their sins and, more radically, from their self-centeredness.

(b) All persons need Christ. All persons may have Christ. All persons must be confronted with the tremendous claims and offers of Christ. Nothing is more basic to evangelism than these straightforward, central facts.

II. In evangelism there is not only the central place of Christ but also the functional place of the church. New Testament congregations are communities of people who, having been evangelized, are now evangelizers. Those who have heard and believed the good news are summoned to be communicators of the glad tidings. The Bible knows no evangelism that is not somehow church related.

III. There is the optional place of method in evangelism.

(a) On the same evening, somewhere in

62

the world a Billy Graham may be heralding the gospel to 75,000 people in an amphitheater, while Mr. John Q. Christian, unknown and unpublicized, is sitting down in the home of a neighbor to talk to him quietly about the meaning of faith and the significance of new life in Christ and two Christian citizens—one a pastor and one a layman—are preparing to stand up in court as witnesses in defense of a powerless man who is about to be railroaded to prison. They thereby give to the gospel a credibility it would not otherwise have. God sees our motivation. If that is worthy, our methods can vary widely.

(b) It was not a finicky methodologist, hung up on formalized expertise, but an impassioned evangelist who said, "I have become all things to all men, that I might by all means save some" (I Cor. 9:22).—Paul S. Rees.

Topic: Seeking and Saving
TEXT: Luke 19:10.
What is the main purpose of the church?
I. *To be aware of the lost*—"the lost." (a) What does it mean to be lost? The lost is one who is estranged, isolated, or separated.

(b) Zaccheus was a lost person. His condition was symbolized by his climbing a tree, separating himself from the people. Because he was a chief publican, he was despised by his fellowmen as a traitor working for the enemy, the Romans. His wealth separated him from the mass of poor folks. Since he got his wealth unjustly by gouging people for taxes, he was hated. Nobody liked him. He lived in solitary confinement.

(c) A sinner is lost because sin separates him from God. He is estranged from God and a lonely outcast.
II. *To seek the lost*—"to seek." (a) Jesus saw Zaccheus in the tree and approached him, saying, "Make haste and come down: for I must stay at your house today." Jesus invited himself to Zaccheus' home. This is grace in action. We do not invite Jesus into our lives; he invites us. We do not make a decision for Christ; Christ chooses us. C. G. Montefiore, a Jewish scholar, claimed that the one absolutely new thing Jesus

had to say was that God is a seeking God.

(b) The practical application is that the non-Christian is not going to seek the church. The church must go out and seek the lost. Since we are the body of Christ, we are to go anywhere and everywhere to seek, to bring, and to win the unchurched. This is the primary task of each organization and each member.
III. *To save the lost*—"to save." (a) By our bringing people to Christ, they receive salvation from him. The church saves by preaching the word and administering the sacraments. Through the word, faith in Christ is born.

(b) What does it mean to be saved? Jesus said that salvation came to Zaccheus. When Jesus entered his home, Jesus had forgiven and accepted him when the rest of society excluded him as a sinner. This absolution aroused Zaccheus to repent. The fruits of his repentance were giving half of his wealth to the poor and returning four-fold any money he may have received by fraud.—John R. Brokhoff.

Topic: What a Difference!
TEXT: Acts 5:20.
If we can accept the role of ministry for every Christian as being one of helping and serving others and a sense of being a personal representative of the person and mission of Jesus Christ, what new dynamism can be released within each of us and through us!
I. What a difference that would make in evangelism as every Christian would sense the privilege and imperative to represent and share the good news in Jesus Christ.
II. What a difference that would make as persons would see themselves as personally responsible for the upbuilding and maintenance of the good health of the church, the body of Christ.
III. What a deep difference that would make in the caring, compassionate responses to the needs of one another and to the needs of the world.
IV. What a difference that would make when every follower of Jesus Christ would sense his or her opportunity to be an advertisement for hope, uplift, wholeness, and direction.

V. What a difference that would make in all sectors of our society and culture if we all sensed the power and the imperative of being salt and leaven—change agents—through the power of the Spirit.

VI. What a difference that would make to those who are in special Christian callings to know that they are in vital partnership with a vast cadre of people who understand their role as ministers in the biblical sense.—Robert Shaw.

Topic: The Gospel We Proclaim
TEXT: I Cor. 15:1–2.

I. The comfort of Christ who said, "Come unto me all ye that labor and are heavy-laden, and I will give you rest."

II. The healing of Christ the physician who came to cure the ills of mind and body.

III. The vision of Christ the poet and seer who shows us stars we never saw before.

IV. The challenge of Christ who, in the words of H. G. Wells, sweeps like a mighty huntsman across the landscape of history, digging men out of the little burrows of respectability in which they have ensconced themselves.

V. The peace of Christ which the world cannot give or take away.

VI. The power of Christ which is "able to do exceeding abundantly above all that we ask or think."

ILLUSTRATIONS

FROM AN INDIAN CHRISTIAN. In my country, if you were going to hold an outdoor evangelistic meeting, you would announce to the Christians in the village that you were going to hold a service. There would be the speaker in the center, seated in front of him would be the Christians, and standing on the fringes behind the Christians would be the Hindus. The speaker would announce that Jesus Christ is the light of the world. The Hindus would not look at the speaker. They would look at the Christians seated in the front of the speaker. What would they be trying to see? They would be looking to see what difference Jesus Christ, the light of the world, made in the lives of those who professed to be his followers. The Christian is to be holy. He is to be different from other men in spite of the pressure of society to conform. He is to be different in his attitudes and different in his conduct in human relationships. He is not to be led around by the capricious whims of an unregenerate society. The Christian is God's man by God's choice. He is chosen for a task in the world and for a destiny in eternity. He is chosen to live for God in time and with God in eternity. It is our privilege and responsibility to reflect in the world the nature and the character of the God who has redeemed us.—D. T. Niles.

MOTIVATION IN EVANGELISM. We need always to understand our motivation in evangelism. Never must we merely seek new members or become victims of the statistics game or simply work in order to keep the institution alive and growing. Genuine evangelism is sharing the love of God in Christ with people whose lives are banal, meaningless, and empty. A lot of people have lost their purpose in living. Our call in evangelism is to identify for them the source of joy, purpose, and faith which alone will make their lives vibrant. As we evangelize let us be moved by a sense of thanksgiving—gratitude to God for all he has done for us and all he can do for others.—Finis A. Crutchfield.

THE WHITEFIELD WITNESS. The real thrust of revival that affected America's move toward independence came with the arrival of George Whitefield, a 24-year-old English evangelist, in 1738. Within two years this amazing young man had stirred and revitalized churches all the way from Georgia to Maine and had preached to crowds of up to 30,000 persons. Whitefield spent ten years of his ministry in America, during which he accomplished more than most men do in a lifetime.

Whitefield was an ordained priest of the Church of England, yet it was said of him that he did not have a denominational hair on his head. Often he preached fifty or sixty hours in a week. He spent a total of two years at sea traveling thirteen times between Britain and America. Always his journeys involved physical discomfort, yet his journals speak of little but praise. Whitefield was a torch who burned himself out in the cause of evangelism. "God forbid," he said, "that I should travel with anybody a quarter of an hour without speaking of Christ to him. Believe me, I am willing to go to prison and to death for you, but I am not willing to go to heaven without you."—Sherwood E. Wirt in *Christian Herald*.

PATH OF DUTY. David Brainerd, as a missionary to the American Indians, came to a point when he thought of himself as a failure. Convinced he was wasting the money of his supporters, he was about to give up and return home. He had begun to see his work accomplishing only a superficial civilizing of the natives and bringing them to a mere profession of Christianity.

But God's ways are not man's ways. A tribe in New Jersey came under the influence of Brainerd's preaching. They sensed his love for them, and God mightily moved upon them. Converts were won. A church was organized. Brainerd's diary records: "It is good to follow the path of duty—though in the midst of darkness and discouragement." Although his ministry was ended at age 29 by tuberculosis, his legacy remains, as John Wesley said, "Absolute self-devotion, total deafness to the world, and fervent love to God and man." —Randolph Lanier.

MISSION. In the world—a world of uncertainty and fear, of revolution and violence, complacency, chaos, and yet God's world—where he is at work creating new persons, new situations, judging, and redeeming, the future we cannot know. We only know who holds the future. Given to us is the now—this moment, this particular place in history—to live as forgiven people in grateful obedience, turning ourselves outward to all around us, responding and responsible, wherever we are, one people of God engaged in one mission to the ends of the earth and to the end of time.

TESTIMONY. When Russell Conwell left Yale to be captain of a Massachusetts regiment in the war between the South and the North, he considered himself an atheist. As he left for the front there was given to him a sword which he prized very highly. A neighbor lad named John Ring, only sixteen, too young and too undersized to enlist, went as Conwell's orderly. Ring was very religious and was often twitted by Conwell about it. At the battle of New Berne, Ring was killed while rescuing his captain's prized sword. When Conwell learned that a Christian friend had died for him, he was deeply moved. Then at the battle of Kenesaw Mountain he himself was wounded and left for dead. He heard footsteps of men searching for him, but he was too weak to call for help. Finally rescued and taken to a hospital, he was led to Christ by a chaplain. Later Conwell gave this testimony: "Decision must go with conversion. It is not only a matter of emotion. One must do something. Merely getting excited and doing nothing is not conversion. Decision and action must go with the change of thought or it is not real. True conversion changes the main purpose of life from selfishness to unselfishness, from the desire to have one's way to a willingness to do whatever God commands, no matter what the consequences."

WHOM GOD LOVES. Fort Hancock is on the farthest tip of Sandy Hook, which reaches out into the Atlantic on the New Jersey coast. During World War II it was a military training center. A civilian of the area was eager to bring the good news of Christ to the thousands of young men stationed there. The military authorities would not permit him to enter in person. Not to be denied, he asked a firm that specialized in novelties to make several thousand mirrors about three inches in diameter. On the back of each mirror he had printed the words of John 3:16. Beneath these words he had this direction, "If you want to see who it is that God loves, look on the other side." As each soldier looked at himself he saw the person whom God loved.—Arthur Tonne.

RESPONSES. Albert Schweitzer, who looked on Jesus as the great unknown, in response to his call forsook a distinguished career in Europe to take medicine to Africa.

A missionary in China during the Japanese occupation relates how, during the persecution of the church, a man in a neighboring town had been beaten by the Japanese police and was in dire need of medical help. No doctor in the city dared go. The missionary called on his own doctor, told him the story without a hint that he should go. He responded: "Of course I'll go. Jesus meant it."

John Macmurray suffered a shipwreck of faith in our civilization as a result of World War I. "As I brooded over this experience I suddenly saw it in the light of what I knew of the life and teaching of Jesus and both were transformed. Jesus himself came alive for me as a real person whom I knew, and what had seemed the meaninglessness of life took on a new meaning."

Lincoln Steffens tells of his first encounter with the New Testament. "The experience was an adventure so startling that I wanted everybody else to have it. It is news. Jesus had discovered that he could not save the righteous, only sinners. Christianity, unpreached, untaught, unlearned among the righteous, works wonders still among sinners."—Roland H. Bainton.

GLITTERING DIAMONDS. Princess Eugenie of Sweden sold her diamonds so money could be available to build a home for incurables.

On one of her visits to the home she met a sick woman who was very wicked. The princess talked about Christ, but the wicked lady did not seem interested. Before leaving the home, Princess Eugenie told the matron that she hoped special attention would be given the woman. The princess expressed how anxious she was for the lady to find Christ before she died.

While visiting the home on a later occasion, Princess Eugenie was pleased to hear that her friend had accepted Christ. The invalid now had a bright face, and it radiated with her newfound hope.

When the princess returned to the palace, she said to her husband, "I saw the glitter of my diamonds today." Then she explained how a life had been changed and made new. Diamonds that had been sold to build a home for incurables were now glittering in the eyes of changed lives. —C. Neil Strait.

LIFE'S MEANING. Leo Tolstoy at the age of 50 felt life growing stale, and for two years he endured mental anguish and torture. He hid the rope lest he hang himself. He would carry no gun into the forest lest he shoot himself. Life had no meaning for him.

Then one day, while walking alone in the forest, he began thinking about God and found himself wondering, "Why should the thought of God keep popping into my head?" He noticed that every time he did think of God, his despondency seemed to leave. He felt an upsurge of hope and a feeling of certainty and stability.

"So then," he said, "why look I further? This is it. The reason I can't help thinking of God is because God is here. And the reason life takes on meaning when I think of God is simply because it is God who gives life meaning. This is what I'm looking for. This is it. I will seek God and live." —Jerry Hayner.

MISSIONARY INSTINCT. The Christian church is of necessity—because of its very origin and nature—a missionary body. The missionary impulse is of its very essence. This is so not primarily because the true follower of the master must believe passionately that Christ is the supreme need of all men everywhere and that his church is under a solemn obligation to urge upon everyone the claims of his discipleship and to offer to everyone the supreme good of the Christian life. This we must do in no spirit of smugness or superiority but that we may freely offer to all the opportunity to accept what we believe to be and in our own experience have found to be the richest blessing that can come to any individual or nation.—Hermann N. Morse.

REACHING OUT.   By evangelism I mean reaching out to others in Christian love, identifying with them, caring for them, listening to them, and sharing one's faith with them in such a way that they will freely respond and want to commit themselves to trust, love, and obey God as a disciple of Jesus Christ and a member of his servant community, the church.—Richard S. Armstrong.

SYMBOL OF LIFE.   On one of the islands in the Fijis is a white chapel with a typical thatched roof. Most of the islanders are members of the church, but that has not always been the case. Before missionaries arrived more than a hundred years ago, the natives were pagans who practiced human sacrifice. The baptismal font in the chapel has a most unusual history. At one time it was the stone altar upon which the human victims were sacrificed. Now, instead of being a symbol of death, it serves as a symbol of the new life.—John Wade.

PLEDGE CARD.   Years ago in the First Baptist Church of Richmond, Virginia, a collection was taken following a missionary address. In one of the plates was a card. The pastor picked it up and found written on it these words: "Myself. John Lewis Shuck." That was the beginning of a great missionary career, as he became the first Baptist missionary appointed to China, sailing for Hong Kong in 1835.

SECTION VIII. Children's Stories and Sermons

January 4. Late Christmas

A gentleman and his wife thought they were hearing things as they watched television in late January. Out on the lawn there arose the solo clatter of a young boy singing Christmas carols slightly off key. He finally rang the bell, and when the man of the house opened the door, the little boy started to sing, "Hark! the herald angels sing, 'Glory to the newborn king.'" He had a little basket to collect for the poor children of the city. The man could hardly believe his ears, and he was so surprised he waited until the song was over and finally said, "Thank you, lad, but didn't anyone tell you that Christmas was a month ago?" To which the boy replied, "Yes, sir, but you see I had the measles then, and my mother wouldn't let me go out caroling till now."—Richard M. Cromie.

January 11. Joey's Friend

Joey Oliver was a third-grade school boy from a poor family. Attending a one-room school, he often came without lunch. On one occasion his hunger got the best of him, and he stole a classmate's lunch. He was discovered and punishment was imminent.

The rule was that if anyone were caught stealing he would be whipped severely. Joey was taken to the front of the room and told to take off his shirt. As his frail body was exposed, the teacher and children gasped. The teacher knew that, no matter what, the punishment would have to be given. It was the rule.

As the teacher raised the switch, a voice from the back said, "Wait!" It was Jimmy-John Turner, the biggest boy in the school. "Let me take his whipping."

"Why?" questioned the teacher. Jimmy-John's answer was short. "'Cause he's my friend."

Love for one another gives us strength to suffer with and for one another.—Mic Morrow in *Home Life*.

January 18. Reaching Out in Love (Missionary Day)

She rises at 4:30 each morning, prays, eats a simple meal, and goes to the city to work. It is some of the most difficult and heartbreaking work in the world, but she does it gladly. Her name is Teresa; the city is Calcutta.

Although the work Mother Teresa began many years ago has spread all over the world, the heart of it is still in Calcutta, a city where thousands live in the streets—malnourished, clothed in little more than rags, consumed with the one task of somehow surviving until tomorrow. For thirty years Mother Teresa and her friends have sought out these destitute ones, providing what food and clothing and shelter they could. They have carried on a ministry to the dying too, bringing them to shelter where they can die in dignity and peace among friends who have genuine love for them.

The world needs more Mother Teresas —persons, who because they have known the love of Christ, feel compelled to reach out in love to the lost, the hungry, the destitute, and the dying. But where do you find such persons? Where do the Mother Teresas of the world come from? When you reflect upon it, you are amazed at the answer. Albert Schweitzer, St. Francis of Assisi—make your own list of these great and selfless characters—most of them seem to have one common denominator. They have experienced and want to share the love of Jesus.

Jesus said his disciples would be known by their love. Jesus' ministry on earth was a ministry of spiritual and physical healing. He wanted to make people whole again, and he still does—in part by reaching out in love through those who seek to follow him.—Arthur McPhee.

January 25. Saying Thanks

A little boy had been invited to a friend's house for dinner. And when the mother of the household called out, "Come and get it," the entire family raced to the table and began to compete with each other for the food—grabbing and gulping as rapidly as they could. They were hungry, the food was good, and there was lots of it.

However, after the initial bedlam of grabbing and getting and gulping and passing had subsided and some semblance of quiet had returned, the young guest said: "Why, you people are just like my dog. He doesn't say 'Thank you' for his food either."

How easy it is to assume that we deserve what we have—to think that life and health and food are things that we have coming to us. The bill was paid at the hospital when we were delivered into the world. We pay the doctor to keep us healthy. And our food budget is sufficient to enable us to lay a sumptuous table.

But must we be like the little boy's dog? Have we no reason to thank God for all the blessings of this life?—Gilbert Runkel.

February 1. Holding the Rope

Through the quiet streets of a fishing village that lay at the mouth of a turbulent river, a cry rang out, "Boy overboard!" Quickly a crowd gathered, and anxious eyes looked out over the rushing water to the figure of the drowning boy. Each anxious mother's heart was asking, "Is he my boy?"

A rope was brought, and the strongest swimmer in the village volunteered to rescue the drowning lad. Tying one end of the rope to his waist, he threw the other among the crowd and plunged in. Eagerly they watched him breast the tide with strong, sure strokes, and a cheer went up when he reached the boy and grasped him safely in his powerful arms. "Pull in the rope!" he shouted over the swirling waters.

The villagers looked from one to another. "Who is holding the rope?" they asked. But no one was holding the rope. In the excitement of watching the rescue, the end of the rope had slipped into the water. Powerless to help, they watched two precious lives go down because no one had made it his business to hold the shore end of the rope.

February 8. God's Valentine

A little boy was a member of the four-year-old's class of a church-related school. This little tyke did a beautiful thing. He came to school carrying a long envelope and proudly announced, "Teacher, this is a valentine for God!" And sure enough, on the outside of the envelope in childlike printing was one word, "God." The teacher opened the envelope and found a heart-shaped valentine with pictures of little boys and girls and angels on it. To this little four year old, Valentine's Day was a time to remember those he loved. And he decided that if anyone deserved to have a valentine, it was God.—Edith Brock.

February 15. Accepting One Another (Brotherhood Week)

A neighbor gave us a little kitten to help us with our "mouse in the house" problem. When we brought her home, Rocky, our Irish setter, scowled at her, and Little Frisky hissed back. They had nothing in common apart from sharing the same new home.

Soon we noticed Rocky proudly strutting about the yard with the kitten's head in his mouth. My family thought this would be injurious to the little kitten and tried repeatedly to separate them. We discovered Little Frisky actually liked this treatment and would hurry back to Rocky's side when we separated them. They seemed to enjoy their relationship without much ado when they began to accept each other.

Sometimes acceptance of others is much more difficult for human beings. We tend to be judgmental and irritated if others are not like us. Sometimes we do not even like ourselves, and this makes us prone to find fault with others. Someone said, "The greatest stumbling block for most Christians today is not what they believe or think about God but what they feel about themselves."—Donna Roberts Ewell.

February 22. Dare to Be a Daniel

There is an interesting story in the Old Testament about a man named Daniel. He lived in Babylon when Darius was king. Darius liked Daniel because he was so bright, industrious, and faithful. He liked Daniel so much that he gave him a very important position. He made Daniel next to himself in power, a sort of assistant, to rule over the land.

This made many of the other officers of the king jealous. Daniel was a Jew, and they didn't want a Jew in such an important position. They made plans to get rid of Daniel. They knew that he worshiped God and prayed to him every day, so they went to the king and had him sign a decree saying, "Whosoever shall pray to any God or to man for thirty days, save to thee, O king, he shall be cast into a den of lions."

It pleased the king to think that everyone would be worshiping him. So he signed the law. He did not realize that when he signed it Daniel would be the first to disobey it.

Daniel went to his home at noonday, opened wide the window facing his temple in Jerusalem, and prayed to God. He could have pulled down the shades or waited until it was dark so that no one could see him, but Daniel was a brave man and wanted to save his people.

The king's officers had spies watching him, and when they saw him praying they arrested him. When King Darius heard of it he was very sorry because he liked Daniel, but since he had signed the decree it had to be obeyed. Daniel was put in a cave or den filled with lions, and you know the rest of the story as well as I do. The lions didn't touch him. When the king came the next day, he found Daniel alive and still praying to his God. When the king saw how his friend's life had been spared, he issued a decree saying that everyone should worship Daniel's God.

The wicked men who plotted against Daniel's life—what happened to them? They were put in the den with the lions. As they didn't know how to pray, it was a sad ending for them, and I won't tell you about it. I'll just say, whenever you are tempted to do wrong or to deny your God or your religion, I hope that you will dare to be a Daniel.—Ralph Conover Lankler.

March 1. Brother Little

There was a preacher. He was a little preacher. His name was Little. He was pastor of a little church that met in a little building. It could only pay him a little salary. He was married to a little woman with whom he lived in a little house, and to this union was born seven little Littles.

Brother Little was highly respected by his congregation for numerous reasons, not the least of which was the fact that he was a good manager of his family's finances. Despite having only a little salary, the Littles seemed to keep things going pretty well with the large family that Brother and Mrs. Little had to support.

One day a parishioner of the little church said, "Brother Little, you are just a little preacher, a pastor of such a little church that can only pay you a little salary and you and Mrs. Little live together in that little house with seven little Littles with only a little income. How is it that you manage and get along so well?"

Brother Little replied, "The answer is very simple. Every Little helps."—Frank Owen.

March 8. A Gift of Love (Lent)

For years the English archaeologist Howard Carter had painstakingly excavated a huge area of desert. At last in

1922 he discovered an ancient wall behind which he hoped was the untouched tomb of King Tutankhamun. He drilled a small hole in the wall. At first he saw nothing. Later Carter wrote, "But presently, as my eyes grew accustomed to the light, details of the room within emerged slowly."

His colleague and patron, Lord Carnarvon, standing behind him, anxiously demanded, "Can you see anything?" Carter's reply has become legendary: "Yes, wonderful things." He had discovered King Tut's tomb.

As they slowly removed the ancient rocks that had sealed the tomb, they uncovered the entrance. And there on the threshold of the doorway was a bouquet of flowers preserved as if new in the dry sands of eternity. They were given by a loving admirer just before the tomb was enclosed for what was thought to be forever. More precious on a truly human level than all the gold of King Tut. Suddenly the ancient was made present, love was rekindled, love could touch us over the span of 5,000 years.—Craig Biddle III.

March 15. God's Daily Blessings (Lent)

We should take a lesson from our hearts! The human heart, about which we think very little unless it is sick or damaged, reflects the daily blessings of God. Your heart and mine pump 80 strokes every minute, 4,800 strokes every hour, 115,200 every day, 806,400 every week, 3,225,600 every month, and 38,707,200 every year. If we live three score and ten, our faithful hearts will have each beat well over three billion times. Working against 120mm of mercury, a heart pumps a lake of 7,300,00 gallons in an eighty-year lifetime. Such prodigious labor is accomplished by a fist-sized bundle of nerves, muscle, and gristle weighing perhaps two-thirds of a pound. Should a skeptic question the daily mercies of God, take a lesson from your heart.—John H. Townsend.

March 22. What Is Love? (Lent)

Helen Keller, who lost her sight and hearing at nineteen months from a severe infection, tells how she learned the meaning of love from Ann Sullivan, her teacher, who was half blind herself. Helen tells about their first meeting three months before she was seven years old. "The morning after my teacher came she led me into her room and gave me a doll. When I had played with it a little while, Miss Sullivan slowly spelled into my hand the word D-O-L-L. I was excited when I finally spelled out the word myself. And I ran down stairs to show my mother." Helen tells how (several days later) Miss Sullivan pumped cold water on her hand and spelled out W-A-T-E-R. After learning to spell hundreds of words, one day Miss Sullivan spelled out the word L-O-V-E in Helen's hand. Perplexed, she spelled back, "W-H-A-T IS L-O-V-E?"—Robert McEniry.

March 29. What He Remembered (Lent)

When Edward VII was crowned king of the British Empire, the most notable leaders from all over the world attended the splendid affair. Alfred Deakin was prime minister of New Zealand and was one of the honored guests. When he returned home, he was asked by newsmen what impressed him most about the coronation. He said that he was on his way back to his hotel one night and passed by a dark alley in a slum section of London. A little boy about twelve years old was sitting on a doorstep with his arm around a little girl about six years old. It was late and cold, and the boy had draped his jacket around the little girl's shoulders. He had put his cap over her bare feet. And that was the sight that had impressed him most at the coronation.—A. Daniel Freeman.

April 5. Easter Blossom of the Poor (Passion Sunday)

"Flowers for your holiday? Only a penny a bunch!"

The pudgy figure of the country woman cried her wares amid the din of Jerusalem's market. Coins jangled in the deep pockets of her sturdy black apron tied over a clean print dress. It was nearing the feast of the Passover. The Christians called it Easter. People were hurrying to finish last minute shopping for the festive season.

The woman's stall was stacked with tied bunches of a scarlet flower. They were everywhere—filling her table, crowding the floor about her, and hanging from the walls of her small cubicle. The mass of red blooms told of much plucking nearby, for they were a wild flower from the hills of Judea.

"What kind of flower is it?" tourists asked her, examining closely the flat-topped, clustered heads set upon long gray-green stems. The narrow furry leaves, like lacy fingers, stretched out to be claimed.

"We call them passion everlastings," she answered. "They grow on our hill-sides. The children pick them. They won't fade, you know," she hurried to explain. "We call them flowers that never die!"

Another stand across the narrow marketway had magnificent potted lilies on sale. People sniffed their fragrance and feasted their eyes on the bloom.

The little countrywoman did not seem worried when the people left her to stare at the lilies.

"Only the well-to-do will buy them," she foretold cheerfully. "They'll come back to me. You'll see. Mine are the Easter blossoms of the poor!"

Down through the years the passion everlasting has come to speak of Christ to the Christians of Jerusalem, for it too is lowly and of patient endurance. Its scarlet, never-dying bloom is a symbol of his triumph on the cross.

While the white lily speaks of Christ's resurrection glory, the blood-red passion everlasting whispers: "Remember him? All this he did for you."—Helen Ross in *The War Cry*.

April 12. Messengers (Lent)

Every red-blooded American thrills to the story of our pony express. Daring and rugged riders carried United States mail horseback between St. Joseph, Missouri, and Sacramento, California, through Nebraska, Wyoming, Utah, and Nevada. The young riders galloped at top speed from one station to the next, about fifteen miles, jumped on a fresh horse, and were on their way in two minutes. Generally each man covered seventy-five miles in a day. There were about 190 stations, four hundred station keepers, more than four hundred horses, and eighty riders, who earned from $100 to $150 a month, high wages in those days. Usually they carried two revolvers and a knife to fight off Indians and bandits. They rode day and night in every kind of weather, completing the 2,000 miles in anywhere from eight to ten days. At first the postage rate was $5 a half ounce, later $1.

With the completion of telephone connections between the East and West coasts the pony express came to an end in October, 1861, after a year and a half existence, but the story of those sturdy and fearless riders still thrills us.

We think of these mounted messengers when we hear God declare: "I send my messenger before thy face, who shall prepare the way; the voice of one crying in the wilderness. Prepare the way of the Lord."

That messenger was St. John the Baptist, the immediate announcer of our savior, Jesus Christ. The Baptist, a rugged and daring messenger in his own way, announced to the world: "He is here. The one we have been waiting for is here."—Arthur Tonne.

April 19. An Easter Candle (Easter)

Leo Tolstoy, the Russian writer, told of a peasant who was forced to plow in the fields on Easter and could not attend church to praise the risen Lord and to light a votive candle, as was the custom of his people, to celebrate the resurrection of Jesus Christ. So the peasant fastened a candle to the plow handle and kept it lighted while he labored. We show our love and loyalty to Christ not only by worshiping him in church on Easter but also by remembering when we work and play that he is the light of the world.

April 26. The Shortest Prayer

"Goodbye!" This is the shortest and most common prayer of all. We say it so often that we have forgotten it is a prayer. Spoken in full, it is, "God be with you." In church we call it a benediction from the Latin meaning, "to say well." In most of the places I have worshiped, when the minister raises his hand to bless us, he usually looks down at the floor as though he were talking to his shoes and the people bow their heads. But a benediction is one prayer that is really addressed not only to God but to the earthly folk who hear it as well. "God be with you!" You ought to look the preacher in the eye as he asks God to bless you. It is his way of saying "goodbye" to you after church, and you ought to be saying it back to him. Indeed, we ought all to be saying it to each other.—Pat McGeachy.

May 3. Companions

Oliver Wendell Holmes was one day strolling on the beach near his summer home when he began chatting with a little girl who was playing in the sand. The child soon slipped her hand in his and walked with him. By and by she said, "I'll have to go home now." "Goodbye, my dear," said Dr. Holmes, "and when mother asks you where you have been, tell her you have been walking with Oliver Wendell Holmes." "And when your folks ask you where you have been," said the child, "tell them you were walking with Mary Susanna Brown."—Charles L. Allen.

May 10. The Mother Hen (Mother's Day)

A poultry owner in eastern Oregon has a mother hen of whom she is proud. One day a chicken hawk swooped down upon the band of baby fowls of which the old hen was the mother. The hen didn't squawk and run, calling upon her offspring to follow her; she faced the hawk to fight, and so fierce was her onslaught as she buried her bill beneath the hawk's left wing that the hawk seemed surprised and dazed. It feebly rose, flew aimlessly against a clothesline, and then dropped into the garden, stone dead. Ordinarily the hen was timid. It was the "mother" in her that rose to the great emergency. How much it means when God says, "As one whom his mother comforteth, so will I comfort you" (Isa. 66:13).—Louis Albert Banks.

May 17. One Tick at a Time

A clock pendulum began to calculate how long it would be expected to tick so many times a minute, sixty times every hour, twenty-four times every day, and three hundred and sixty-five times every year. It was awful! Enough to stagger the mind. Millions of ticks!

"I can never do it," said the poor pendulum.

But the clockmaster encouraged it. "Do just one tick at a time," he said. "That is all that will be required of you."

So the pendulum went to work, one tick at a time, and it is ticking yet.—Dwight L. Moody.

May 24. Beauty Everywhere

Robert Haven Schauffler told of a shop assistant in Zurich whose hobby was painting and who lived in resentment because his artistic soul was assaulted by all the ugliness he had to pass on his way to work. One day illumination came. A taste for art, he reasoned, was not given to him to resent ugliness but to see beauty where others were blind to it. He resolved to find ten pictures he could paint every time he did that familiar walk. It became fun finding them. A youth helping his mother from a red bus. A ragged boy aping a pompous policeman. A burst of sunlight making a halo round the head of a frizzy blonde. Pictures everywhere.

May 31. Possibilities

A few weeks ago I planted some seeds. The seeds were shriveled up and ugly. I put them in the earth and watered them. Something happened to those seeds. The husk cracked. They started to sprout. The water, the soil, the sunshine—and the miracle of growth. Now those little plants came up the ugliest, gangliest plants you have ever seen. Down at the end of the row I put on a stake the empty seed packet with the picture on it. Some gardeners do this so they can remember what they planted where. I did it so those little ugly plants could see the possibilities of the future. Right now they are weak and awkward and fragile. I want them to look down at the end of the row and say: "Wow! That's beautiful. That's what we are created to be! That's what, with God's help, we are going to be!"—Joe A. Harding.

June 7. Learning Experiences

We do not know much about Jesus' boyhood. From the time of his birth and infancy there is virtually no recorded biblical material. Scholars have speculated and theorized on his youth, but we have no written record apart from one episode, recalled in the book of Luke, which tells of Jesus' encounters with the teachers in the temple of Jerusalem.

From his dialogue with the learned men in the temple, it seems obvious to us that the boy Jesus knew what course his life was destined to take. After all, didn't he say to his surprised parents: "How is it that you sought me? Did you not know that I must be in my father's house?" And yet, even with his special calling from his father God, Jesus was eager to learn. He quickly and easily engaged in theological dialogue with the Jewish scholars and astonished them with his understanding of scripture. Certainly God must have been there with Jesus at that meeting, guiding and encouraging him.

Many of our personal encounters with God take place in the educational setting of our churches, where formal and informal dialogue between students and teachers takes place. As with the boy Jesus, these opportunities for learning help us grow in understanding of and commitment to our faith.—Jameth Kaplar in *Family Devotions.*

June 14. The Mountain's Complaint

One day Mount Hermon, the northernmost of all the mountains in the holy land, appeared before the Lord God in heaven with a complaint. Mount Hermon said to the Lord God: "Now there are many great and wonderful mountains in the holy land and many things of great importance occurred on them. On Mount Horeb, Moses encountered the burning bush and was called to become the leader of God's people. On Mount Sinai he received the law from the hand of God not only for the Jews but for all mankind. From Mount Nebo, Moses viewed the land of promise, died, and was buried. On Mount Moriah, Abraham went to sacrifice Isaac, and there later Solomon built his magnificent tem-

ple. And on Mount Zion, King David is buried. But," said Mt. Hermon, "nothing of importance ever happened here." And the Lord God said to Mount Hermon, "I will give you a mantle of snow, and from your tears I will make the Jordan River." —Adapted by Alton H. McEachern.

June 21. Life with Father (Father's Day)

A little boy took a trip deep into a coal mine with his dad. They were lowered down the pitch-black shaft in a barrel, and the only assurance the little boy had was his father's hand. When at last they reached the bottom of the shaft, someone in the mine asked the boy if he was afraid. "No," he said, "but I would be if my father weren't with me." Then the boy's father said to him, "Son, you will never have to be afraid because no matter what you have to face in life a greater Father than I will always be with you."—Arthur McPhee.

June 28. The Part God Made

In a Sunday school class a little girl was asked, "Who made you?" And she said, "Well, God made part of me." "What do you mean, God made part of you?" asked the teacher. "God made me real little," she said, "and I just growed the rest myself."—Jerry Hayner.

July 5. In God We Trust (Independence Sunday)

There is a word that we seldom hear. It is "numismatist." If someone should call you a numismatist, you might be insulted and ready to fight. But it is not a name of which you need to be ashamed, and there is usually at least one numismatist in every group of boys. It means "one who collects coins." Some of you collect stamps, others insects like butterflies, still others stones, and I hope that in your midst is a numismatist.

A coin collector learns much about metals and history. The earliest known coins were used by the Greeks about seven hundred years before Christ. By studying the coins of the different nations since that time we can learn much about the history, manners, religion, and art of the people who used them.

Let us suppose that five thousand years from now someone should dig up a coin that we are using today. What could they learn from our twenty-five-cent piece that would interest them? They would know that we loved freedom because written over the top of the coin is the word "liberty." Farther down they would read these words: "In God We Trust." That would tell them that the people of the United States depended upon God for the freedom they enjoyed. We are a strong nation, but our trust is not in our military might as much as it is in the power of God.

Most of the people who established this country were very religious. Many of them left their homes in Europe because they desired to worship God according to their particular views of religion. Some were persecuted and driven from their homes, and they came to America believing that God would help them to do his will. Is it any wonder that they should have made the motto of this great nation? "In God We Trust."—Ralph Conover Lankler.

July 12. He Saved Others

More than forty years ago a brilliant young black doctor named Charles Drew discovered the use of blood plasma in saving human lives. His discoveries saved millions of lives in World War II, Korea, and Vietnam. At Pearl Harbor 96 percent of those who received plasma survived. He was named director of the National Blood-bank Program. Many of us are indebted to Dr. Drew for the plasma that sustained and strengthened us after accidents or surgery. Dr. Drew devoted himself to teaching future doctors at Howard University Medical School. Then on April 1, 1950, as he was driving some young doctors to a conference, he was involved in an accident at Burlington, North Carolina. They took him to the hospital. His life might have been saved by a transfusion of plasma, but he was denied admission because of the color of his skin. He died on the way to a hospital that would have received him.—Joe A. Harding.

July 19. My Face

A second grader made a good start toward a sense of self-esteem when he submitted an essay entitled "My Face" to his teacher. "My face has two brown eyes," the seven year old began. "It has a nose and two cheeks. And two ears and a mouth. I like my face. I'm glad my face is just like it is. It is not bad, it is not good, but just right." Liking ourselves is essential to a healthy love of self which is the basis for loving others. Take a good look at yourself. Discover and accept what has been given you. It may not be as much as you'd like to see. But growth depends on acceptance of what you have and where you're starting from.—A. Dudley Dennison, Jr.

July 26. The Hidden Beauty

A traveler in Honolulu saw an old wood-carver roughing out a block of monkeypod wood, preparatory to shaping it into an exquisite tray. The visitor could see little promise in the rough block and said so

"Come tomorrow when I have it polished, and you will see," said the old man. "You can't judge a thing like this until it is finished."

A few days later the old wood-carver displayed his finished product. He said proudly, "I knew there was beauty in it, but I had to have time to bring it out. You judged it before it was finished."—*Herald of Holiness.*

August 2. The Wren and the Cowbird

One morning in my backyard I saw a large bird being fed by a wren. I thought, how strange that a large bird was being fed so lovingly and carefully by a small wren, and then I remembered something I had learned years before—a cowbird lays its eggs in the nest of other birds. What had happened was that a cowbird had laid its egg in the nest of a wren, and the wren had cared for those eggs, and from that egg had come a chick which matured to the point that it was three or four times the size of a wren. Yet the wren was caring for that bird as though it was her own.—Donald L. Germain.

August 9. Forty Martyrs of Sebaste

Forty soldiers, all Christians, were members of the famed Twelfth Legion of Rome's imperial army.

One day their captain told them Emperor Licinius had sent out an edict that all soldiers were to offer sacrifice to the pagan gods. These Christians replied, "You can have our armor and even our bodies, but our hearts' allegiance belongs to Jesus Christ."

It was midwinter of A.D. 320, and the captain had them marched onto a nearby frozen lake. He stripped them of their clothes and said they would either die or renounce Christ. Throughout the night these men huddled together and sang their song, "Forty martyrs for Christ." The temperature took its toll, and one by one they fell to the ice.

At last only one man was left. He lost courage and stumbled to the shore where he renounced Christ. The officer of the guards had been watching all this. Unknown to the others, he had secretly come to believe in Christ. When he saw this last man break rank, he walked out onto the ice, threw off his clothes, and confessed that he also was a Christian.

When the sun rose the next morning, there were forty bodies on the ice.—Leighton Ford.

August 16. The Longest Shadow

One of the longest shadows in the world stretches more than two hundred miles off the Canary Islands. El Tition Peak, a mountain that rises more than 12,000 feet over Tenerife Island, casts the shadow.

Every person casts a shadow. It is a shadow of influence that touches those who are our neighbors. If we do not love, our shadow will be a short one. If we love others as we love ourselves, then our shadows will be long.

Jesus spoke a great deal about love. His emphasis was on serving others. He attempted to instill within his followers a compassion for others.—Mic Morrow in *Home Life.*

August 23. The Straight Line

Bobbie was working away at his drawing lesson. Presently the teacher came around to see what progress he was making with it.

"Look here, Bobbie," she said: "That line isn't straight." "No, it isn't quite straight," answered Bobbie, "but I can fix that up later."

"A straight line never needs to be straightened," said the teacher quietly, as she turned away to look at the work of another pupil.

That simple remark the teacher made set Bobbie to thinking. A straight line never needs straightening. How much better to make the line straight rather than to draw a crooked line which would have to be straightened afterward. Besides, a line that has been partly rubbed out and then made straight never looks quite as good as one that is drawn perfectly straight and true the first time.

When we speak the truth, we do not have to stop and correct what we have said.—*Sunshine Magazine.*

August 30. Two Reflections

Ramakrishna tells the fable of a motherless tiger cub who was adopted by goats and raised to eat grass and bleat as they did. At last the cub came to think of himself as a goat. But one day a magnificent King Tiger came along and asked the cub what he meant by all this masquerade. All the cub could do was bleat nervously and nibble the grass.

So the King Tiger carried the cub to a pool where he forced the cub to look at their two reflections side by side. Then he gave him a piece of raw meat to eat. At first the cub recoiled from this strange taste, but as he ate more his blood warmed and the truth dawned. Lashing his tail and digging his claws into the earth, the young tiger raised his head with great dignity and let out a roar. He was a tiger—a real tiger.

Isn't that what Christ does for us? He tells us we don't have to nibble the grass like goats. Rather we are created by God and made in his image. There is something great and grand about us. We were made to lift up our heads and sing our own songs.—Robert C. Brubaker.

September 6. A Lifelong Work (Labor Sunday)

A magnificent new Gothic cathedral has been completed in Liverpool, England. This church has been under construction for three-quarters of a century. After nearly seventy-five years of painstaking labor, this vast hall of red sandstone reached its moment of completion. This fifty largest cathedral in the world has the highest vaulting of any cathedral in the world, the highest Gothic arches, the heaviest ringing peal of bells, and many other amazing features. Pictures reveal it to be a breathtaking center of inspiration.

Tom Murphy is representative of a cadre of skilled craftsmen whose entire working lives have been spent on this one project. For forty years Murphy and others have carved the sandstone and lettered the inscriptions and shaped the structure which today is Liverpool Cathedral. This man has known no other calling and no other vocation than to help to complete a house of worship where people will be drawn to God.—John H. Townsend.

September 13. What He Left Behind

A controversy involved a busing issue. One man who was particularly hostile and abrasive had risen on several occasions to speak against the issue. During these times he attacked the integrity of several of the other speakers and made vehement comments against the chairman. Finally he was called down by the chairman and ruled out of order. The man turned and stormed out of the meeting.

As he was about to leave through the rear exit, a little lady sitting in the back row looked up and sweetly said, "Sir, you left something behind."

The man snapped back, "What did I leave?"

"A very bad impression."—G. Roger Schoenhals in *The Lookout.*

September 20. Forgiving One Another

Two little children were prone to getting into arguments just before bedtime. One evening the brother and sister had a particularly vigorous disagreement and had gone to bed especially angry at each other. About two o'clock in the morning an earth-shattering thunderstorm began, awaking the entire family. Between the gigantic thunderblasts and lightning flashes, their father heard an unusual noise down the hall near the children's bedroom. Listening carefully he overheard his two children whispering in a bedroom closet. He called out: "What are you doing in there? Is everything all right?" A terrified little voice answered, "We are in the closet forgiving each other."—Craig Biddle III.

September 27. His Father's Voice

John Sutherland Bonnell was fifteen at the time. One Friday night, as was his occasional practice, he set out to meet his father who worked at a hospital three miles across fields and countryside. The moon was shining brightly as he began, but he had gone scarcely a mile when the skies clouded and the moon disappeared. Time and again young John found himself off the pathway. But he was encouraged by the thought that at the end of what they called the "green road" there would be a light burning at the gateway to the hospital.

As he looked far ahead, trying to pierce the darkness, he determined to his dismay that no light was burning. Listening intently, he could hear the snap of twigs in the woods and with the vivid imagination of boyhood pictured some vast terror of the night on the prowl. He broke into a run, but the more he hurried the more frightened he became. Suddenly out of the darkness a voice was heard—a familiar voice—saying, "Is that you, son?" It was his father! Then came the explanation, "I just discovered that the light was out at the gate, so I came to meet you." Dr. Bonnell wrote: "In that moment a miracle happened. The night was no longer dark, for I was now walking with my father."—John H. Townsend.

October 4. They Knew Jesus (World Communion Sunday)

A missionary in China told a group of people about Jesus for the first time. When he finished, someone said: "Oh,

yes, we've met him. He used to live here."
"No, that would be impossible," said the missionary. "Jesus lived many centuries ago in Palestine." But the people insisted he had lived there and to prove it took the missionary to the grave of a former medical missionary who had lived, served, healed, and died in that community. When, because of the love of Christ, we share our bounty with others, Jesus Christ is with us.—Arthur McPhee.

October 11. Spelling Lesson
A girl spelled out the word *good* on wooden blocks for her younger sister. A few minutes later the child excitedly showed her mother the two words she had made from the one. "Look mommie, *good* became *go* and *do!*"—Raymond L. Cox.

October 18. Going to Bed
There's an art in going to bed. One just doesn't tumble in any old way. How do you do it?

The greatest way is to go to bed thankful for what the day has brought, conscious that you've hurt no one, that you've done what you should, and that you've made someone happy.

Going to bed like that is going to bed to sleep dreamlessly and to wake up the next morning with a gallant spirit and a brave heart, ready for whatever the day may bring.—*Sunshine Magazine.*

October 25. The Prince and the Fisherman
A kind fisherman lived with his wife in a pigsty adjoining the sea. They were very poor but very happy. And then one morning while at sea he caught an enchanted prince, disguised as a large flounder.

The fish said to him: "I am a prince. You may have anything you ask if you will only throw me back into the sea."

"That my wife and I might forever be together," said the fisherman. "It shall be as you say," said the fish.

After hearing her husband's story, the fisherman's wife said, "Oh, kind fisherman, go back to the sea and ask for one more request—that we might have a cottage rather than this pigsty." This he did

and the request was granted.

Only now his wife asked, "If the fish can give us this cottage, let's ask for a palace." The fisherman was reluctant, but he loved his wife, so he went and it was granted. Only now he saw less and less of his wife, they being occupied with the affairs of the palace.

And then the wife said, "Fisherman, ask if I might not rule the kingdom." And the fisherman worried, for his wife seemed not herself. But he loved her, so he asked and she became ruler.

Then one morning she was awakened by the sun in her eyes, and she flew into a rage. "Go ask that I be given authority over the sun and moon," she cried. But this time the heavens roared and the wind blew and the fish replied, "Kind fisherman, return to your pigsty." And when he arrived, there was his wife, clad in rags but herself again, and his heart was glad.

November 1. Love Letter
An eight-year-old girl in an orphanage was so painfully unattractive that she was shunned by other children and ignored or disliked by her teachers. Two institutions managed to get rid of her, and the officials of her current home were seeking a pretext for freeing themselves of her. One day they thought their opportunity had arrived. An ironclad rule had been broken. No communication from a child in the orphanage could be mailed or distributed before it had been approved by the director. And the girl had been observed stealing down to the gate where she carefully placed an envelope in the branches of a tree overhanging the fence. The director and his assistant eagerly rushed down to the tree to intercept the letter. The director tore open the envelope. He read it and silently passed the note to his assistant. It read, "To anybody who finds this, I love you."—James M. Dodson.

November 8. Diamonds Where You Are
Among the most beautiful crowns ever fashioned was one designed for a princess of Iran. The incredibly beautiful diamonds that are a part of that crown defy

description. Many of the diamonds in that crown came from the famous Golconda mine, the same mine from which came the famous diamonds of the crown jewels of England and Russia. Golconda is also the source of the well-known story by Russell H. Conwell called "Acres of Diamonds."

According to Conwell, a farmer who lived in Persia had a wife, children, some sheep, camels, and raised wheat on his land. He was contented and happy and, according to his standards, very rich. His contentment with his lot in life ended one day when a priest told him about a strange stone that sparkled like a million suns. He had never heard of diamonds, but now that he had learned about these beautiful gems he was determined to have some for himself. "Where can I find diamonds?" he asked the priest. "Look for a stream that flows through white sands surrounded by high mountains," the priest told him.

So the farmer sold his farm, left his wife and children, and set out on a journey to find diamonds. He traveled for many years, searching for a stream that flowed through white sands surrounded by high mountains. With passing years he one day found himself broke and destitute, on the lonely coast of Spain. Utterly defeated, he plunged into the sea and died.

Meanwhile the man who had bought the farm found one day, while watering his camel, an old black rock. He took it home and thought no more about it until one day the priest came by to visit. The priest examined the black rock and suddenly saw a flash of color in it. "A diamond! Where did you get it?" the priest asked. "By the cool sands and white stream near the high mountains where I water my camel," the man responded. Together they ran to the stream, where they scratched and dug with their hands. They found more diamonds. Their discovery today is known as the Golconda mine, one of the greatest diamond mines in the world.

Diamonds were in the farmer's backyard. Yet he spent a lifetime in a fruitless search. We can spend our life in all kinds of travels and pursuits of pleasure, fame, and wealth, when all the time what we are looking for can be found right where we are.—Donald L. Germain.

November 15. Life's Handbook (Bible Sunday)

There are two books that every boy and girl should read. They are the handbook for scouting and the Bible.

In the handbook for scouts you may read how to become a tenderfoot, a second-class scout, a first-class scout, a star, a life, and an eagle scout. You may also read the scout oath, the scout law, the scout motto, the sign, the hand-clasp, the salute, and many other requirements for scouting. No one would think of becoming a scout without reading the handbook and learning the requirements.

How about the handbook for Christians? Do you think that anyone should become a Christian without reading the Bible and learning how to become a follower of Jesus? We should learn the law, the oath, the motto, and the salute of the Christian. We are doing it every Sunday that we go to Sunday school, and when we are old enough and learn enough, we are eligible to unite with the church.

Some boys who join the scouts never become more than tenderfoot scouts. It takes skill and hard work to become a second-class, and then a first-class, and finally an eagle scout. Many boys have starting power, but they do not have staying power. They are good beginners but poor finishers.

The same may be said for many people who join the church. They become tenderfoot Christians, but they never develop into first-class Christians. What is a tenderfoot Christian? A tenderfoot Christian is one who wants to belong—who wants his name on the church roll, who wants to be married and buried and have his children baptized in the Christian religion—but that is as far as he goes. His feet are too tender to walk him to church every Sunday. They are too tender for him to stand upon long enough to declare himself for righteousness and against evil.

A real scout is a first-class scout and a real Christian is a first-class Christian. The scout must study his handbook, and the

Christian must study his Bible.—Ralph Conover Lankler.

November 22. The Boy Who Kept Sunday

A boy in his early teens was working for a New York newspaper as a printer's devil or apprentice. Everything went fine until one Saturday when he was handed a job that had to be finished before Monday morning. That meant he would have to work on Sunday. The lad approached the composing-room manager and stammered, "I will work until twelve tonight, sir." "You can't finish by tonight," growled the boss.

The young fellow tried his best, but when midnight came the job was unfinished. With the papers trembling in his hand, he told the manager: "I must resign, sir, as I cannot work on Sunday. I can't break God's law."

The manager tried to convince the boy that a few hours work on the Lord's day would not be so wrong, but the boy, who was the main support of his mother, stood firm and was about to accept his paycheck when the manager slapped him on the back and smiled: "Say, you've got real stuff in you, son. You're just the kind of boy I need here. You can finish that job Monday. Go to church and worship God. God bless you, John."

That young fellow advanced steadily in the printing business. His name was John Harper, founder of Harper & Row, whose publications are known around the world. —Arthur Tonne.

November 29. Love Never Fails (Advent)

A lad was told by his mother not to go near an iron grating in the street where they lived. The mother knew that the grating was loose. But the lad, disobeying his mother's instructions, played on the grating, fell through, and broke his leg. Things went wrong in the hospital, and for a time it was thought that he would never be able to walk again. One of the nurses was careless enough to let the lad hear this report.

When his mother came to see him, the little boy wound his arms around her neck. Tears welled up in his eyes, and he said:

"Mummy, I know it was my fault and I disobeyed you. But if I can never walk or run again, will you go on loving me?" You can imagine what the answer was. "Then," said the boy, smiling through his tears, "I can bear anything."

That little chap taught me a lesson. We ask of God a great many things, and some of them cannot be answered. Yet the richest thing in the world is an experience of his love which is open to us all. If we are quite sure he goes on loving us, we can bear anything.—Leslie D. Weatherhead.

December 6. The Man Who Wrote "Silent Night" (Advent)

On the afternoon of Christmas Eve in 1818 a humble priest named Father Joseph Mohr scrawled three six-line stanzas of a simple verse and asked his friend and fellow-worker, the organist at the St. Nicholas Church in Salzburg, Franz Gruber, to set the words to music for the service that evening.

The only problem was that the organ was not working. At times of high water, St. Nicholas was flooded by the Salzach River. The organ was damp and rusted, and all possibility of a good inspiring service was dampened as much.

At midnight mass around the carved nativity scene, Father Mohr, a tenor, sang melody, and Gruber sang the second part. The choir sang with them both, and Mohr accompanied on his old guitar.

At that disappointing moment "Silent Night" was born. Father Mohr was accused by the church hierarchy of what were called "musical inclinations" and the heinous sin of bringing a guitar into the church. He was transferred twelve times in eight short years, was banished to a minor vicarship, and was buried in a papuer's grave before his time. But his little hymn lived on to comfort friend and foe alike on every Christmas Eve since then.—Richard M. Cromie.

December 13. The Christmas Apple

In a town in Holland everyone would bring a gift to the church, offering it to the statue of the virgin and child. It was commonly believed that one Christmas a miracle would happen. The infant Jesus would reach out and select one of the gifts.

The town clockmaster worked all year, building an expensive clock which he intended to offer the Christ Child. However, he sold the clock to help feed and house a poor old woman. He kept only enough to buy an apple for his Christmas meal. The clockmaster was sad for he had no gift to offer. He walked to the church and saw all of the marvelous gifts that the mayor, merchants, and princes had brought. With lowered eyes he placed his apple next to their rich gifts near the statue.

The people whispered, "Did you see the cheap gift he placed there?"

"An apple!" they exclaimed. "Giving a common apple!"

Then the miracle happened. The Christ Child picked up the apple. God continually surprises us, doesn't he?—Diogenes Allen.

December 20. A Christmas in Greece (Advent)

One of our navy destroyers was tied up in Hong Kong. It was late fall. As the men began to look forward to Christmas, they wondered just where they might be on that day and what they might do to celebrate.

When they learned that they would be in Greece on Christmas Day, they wrote to a Greek orphanage in the port city and asked if they might have the pleasure of entertaining thirty of the children between the ages of six and fourteen. And then they took up a rather sizable collection from among the crew. One of the sailors sent the money to his mother who worked in a department store in a midwestern city and asked her to purchase presents, Christmas wrap them, and send them to Greece in care of the ship. The department store, moved by this demonstration of Christmas spirit on the part of the sailors, added several hundred dollars more of gifts.

On Christmas Day the men went to the orphanage, collected the children, took them back to the ship, and gave them a Christmas dinner and party that they would never forget. When it came time to return the children to the orphanage, the thing the sailors dreaded most was meeting the other children who had no presents, no dinner, and no party. But they need not have worried, for the moment that the children entered the gates of the orphanage, they immediately began to share all the good things they had received and all the presents with all the other children.—Roger W. Blanchard.

December 27. Commitment

In 1918 an engineer named Joseph Strauss stood on a windswept cliff overlooking the Golden Gate and the city of San Francisco. He pictured in his imagination a bridge spanning that wide and often stormy strait.

Most people said it couldn't be done. The winds were too strong. The tide too powerful. The waves too devastating. The distance too great. No major harbor entrance had ever been bridged. The vertical clearance would have to be greater than any other bridge over navigable water.

Strauss believed it was possible. He made a great commitment to his dream.

He sketched a daring plan with a suspension span of more than 4,000 feet—far longer than anything yet attempted.

People laughed at his plan, but he refused to give up. Finally years later on January 5, 1933, work began. The pier at the Marin end created few problems. But the San Francisco pier, 1,125 feet off shore, was totally unprotected from the open sea. It was rammed by a ship and partially carried away by a storm. Finally the piers were completed, the great towers rose, and the cables were suspended.

The Golden Gate Bridge was completed and ready for traffic on May 28, 1937. On the day before it was opened for pedestrians and 200,000 walked across the new bridge.

Strauss believed it would be done and made that bridge the great commitment of his life.—Joe A. Harding.

SECTION IX. *Sermon Outlines and Homiletic and Worship Aids for Fifty-Two Weeks*

SUNDAY: JANUARY FOURTH

MORNING SERVICE

Topic: A Life Full of New Beginnings
TEXT: Isa. 43:18–19 (NEB).

Let us think about new beginnings for our lives, the resources that are available, and the way we move creatively forward in newness of life.

I. If we are to find our way toward new beginnings, we shall need to cease dwelling on days gone by. Brooding over the past is an escape from the issues of the present.

(a) When we begin to recall those past events as the good old days when life was simple and cares were free, then something has gone wrong. We have escaped into a never-never land of make-believe, forgetting there were heartaches in every period of our past. We have abdicated the possibilities of the present for the rosy reveries of a time beyond recall.

(b) Perhaps our brooding over the past has to do with those dark things we have done or which have been done to us.

(1) Who does not have an ample storehouse of regrets and resentments? You did something back there that you would give anything to have undone. You were younger, less mature, and you know that "what's ended can't be mended." But the memory keeps haunting you like some gray ghost.

(2) There are those incomprehensible things that others have done to you which continue to sting at their very thought. They are done and over, and whatever harm they did cannot be changed, no matter how long we dwell on them. Life must go on, but our minds gravitate back to them again and again like faithful homing pigeons. Somehow we feel helpless to get beyond them into dealing with the real problems of the here and now.

(c) The Lord tells us to cease dwelling on days gone by. We need to let him have the past in the knowledge that only he can deal with it. Let him take care of those who have hurt you in the infinite wisdom of his loving righteousness. Let him accept your past by the power of his loving forgiveness shining in Jesus. Let him heal your memories so as to liberate you into the present of where you now exist.

II. If we are to move beyond our discouragements and defeats, we need to hear the Lord speaking to us of his present power to help.

(a) To us, as to Isreal of old, the Lord says: "Here and now I will do a new thing; this moment it will break from the bud." For Israel it meant a new exodus, this time not from Egyptian bondage but from their present captivity in Babylon. It is easier to rejoice in the ancient stories of God's power than to believe in his present power to help. The Israelites were called to believe not simply in exodus past but exodus present. God was at that very moment preparing their exodus.

(b) We never face a situation in life devoid of God's presence. He is always opening up fresh possibilities in the face of every difficulty. With him there is always a way out. Believe in the adequacy of God creatively to meet you in every circumstance of your life.

(c) We are still in the process of being created. We are still becoming. God is growing us, and he is not yet finished with his work. Often our discouragement comes because we do not understand what is required if we are to grow.

III. Our need is to become aware of the many new beginnings God offers us as we enter the new year.

(a) By God's grace opportunities abound for us if we can only see them. "Can you not perceive it?" Isaiah asks the Israelites, as he speaks of God's doing a new thing here and now for them. "This moment," he says, "it will break from the bud." We need to sharpen our perception of God's new ways in our lives.

(b) There is no place where God cannot be encountered in a life-transforming way. (1) Rabbi Moshe of Kobryn affirmed: "God says to man, as he said to Moses, 'Put off thy shoes from thy feet.' Put off the habitual which encloses your feet, and you will know that the place on which you are now standing is holy ground. For there is no rung of human life on which we cannot find the holiness of God everywhere and at all times." (2) That is true of those parched wilderness places in your life in which you find no sense of direction for new beginnings. The need is to perceive God's liberating presence at work here and now.

(c) Often on Jesus' lips were the words "watch and pray." "Watch" literally means "be awake," as if most of the time we go around walking in our sleep. To watch does not mean to go off in some kind of retreat from life but to see God's help at work right where you are. Watchful prayer is the secret of becoming aware of God's living presence.

(d) Slowly, possibly not at the pace you would wish but at God's pace, you shall begin to see dimly the tiny bud of a hope that may blossom with God's purpose. The new beginnings are there as surely as God is present to us in prayer.—Colbert S. Cartwright.

Illustration

STEP BY STEP. A friend who flew his plane in the first airmail route across the Andes one day was caught in the down draft between two mountain peaks, and he crashed in the snow. For five days he walked against the blizzard, his feet frozen, and he was tempted to lie down and give in to sleep and death. But by instinct he walked on, knowing that his wife believed that if he were alive he would be on his feet. On and on he went until he was rescued. "What saves a man," he said, "is to take a step. Then another step. It is always the same step, but you have to take it."—Antoine de Saint-Exupery.

Sermon Suggestions

ONE DAY AT A TIME. Texts: Matt. 6:34 (NEB); Lam. 3:22–23 (NEB). (1) Jesus warns against disabling anxiety and not against common sense foresight: "So do not be anxious about tomorrow." (2) Jesus gives the assurance that tomorrow will bring its own resources for the meeting of its problems and troubles: "tomorrow will look after itself." (3) Jesus calls persons to face up to responsible living today in this manageable slice of time: "every day has troubles of its own."—J. A. Davidson.

GOD OUR DWELLING PLACE. Text: Ps. 90:1. (1) God is our security. (2) God is our safety. (3) God is our adequacy. (4) God is our continuity.—David L. Larsen.

Worship Aids

CALL TO WORSHIP. "Great is the Lord, and greatly to be praised: and his greatness is unsearchable. One generation shall praise thy works to another, and shall declare thy mighty works." Ps. 145:3–4.

INVOCATION. Most holy and gracious God, who turnest the shadow of night into morning: satisfy us early with thy mercy that we may rejoice and be glad all the day. Lift the light of thy countenance upon us, calm every troubled thought, and guide our feet into the way of peace. Perfect thy strength in our weakness and help us to worship thee in the spirit of Jesus Christ our Lord.

OFFERTORY SENTENCE. "Give unto the Lord the glory due unto his name: bring an offering, and come before him." I Chron. 16:29.

OFFERTORY PRAYER. Our Father, we bow in humble gratitude that as a new year dawns we may call on thee to guide, strengthen, bless, and forgive and that through these gifts we may share thy love with all who call upon us and thee.

PRAYER. Our Father, amid the fears and frustrations that haunt us at this year's beginning, let us hear thy counsel and let us feel thy comfort. May there be inroads of thy strength in our lives to make us conquerors in the times of crisis. May there be wells of spiritual reserve in our souls for the valleys through which we will surely walk. And may there be deposits of divine guidance firmly planted in our minds for the times of decision that will be ours.

Help us, Father, to face the future with definite courage and with deep commitment. Grant to each of us a sensitive heart —a heart of true concern and a heart that will respond to the hurts and ills of those about us.

We ask, Father, for wisdom in the hour of opportunity and for patience in the moment of failure. May we ever remember that thou art the craftsman of life and that we are thy tools. Help us to be ready instruments of thy Spirit. May we be assured of the prodding of thy Spirit when we choose the path of indifference.—C. Neil Strait.

EVENING SERVICE

Topic: Ten Commandments for 1981
TEXT: Ps. 71:16.

I. I will mind my own business and not gossip nor believe anything discouraging about any person until I know it to be absolutely true, and even then I will not repeat it to anybody unless I mean to help that person.

II. I will not wear my feelings on my sleeve nor be so sensitive as to look for personal offenses or slights or be envious and suspicious of anyone.

III. I will wear a smile. When I am gloomy, I will go away and hide rather than inflict myself on others who have troubles enough of their own.

IV. I will be kind to others and severe toward myself and do nothing to either another or myself which may become a bitter memory in after years.

V. I will not be headstrong and will remember that other people with different ideas from mine may be right.

VI. I will play the game of life on the square, doing nothing to discourage an honest man, offend a good woman, or cause a child to weep or go astray.

VII. I will hold my temper and each night ask God to forgive me as I have forgiven my neighbors.

VIII. I will face the world each morning with confidence, determined to be as true, happy, clean, and brave as I can. Believing in myself, I will not make excuses. I will strive at all times to be progressive, positive, and practical.

IX. I will move out into some battle for a worthy cause. I will get under some load of human need and help life, realizing that my personality will break down and my soul shrivel up to dryness if I do not give of myself in some unselfish service.

X. I will not be too proud or pagan to pray. Realizing I cannot accomplish these resolutions in my own strength, I will make God a partner in everything I do.— Carl J. Sanders.

SUNDAY: JANUARY ELEVENTH

MORNING SERVICE

Topic: A Close Encounter with God

TEXT: John 14:8.

I. A close encounter with God is a universal experience. From the ancient to the modern world, within primitive cultures and sophisticated Western society the claim comes: I know God.

(a) Here is a vast area of human experience which cannot be lightly dismissed. How are we to explain the claim of millions, among them many of the finest the human race has produced, that they have met God?

(b) What if there is a reality you are completely missing? It is said there are colors and sounds beyond the power of the naked eye and ear to record. But they are there. What if others are thrilling to the love and power of God and these experiences are passing you by? What if, through blind secular prejudice, you are missing the obvious?

II. How do we come to a close encounter with God? It is by opening our lives in sincerity to God who in his son Jesus Christ proved he is ever seeking to come to us.

(a) There are three clear guidelines for a personal encounter with God. (1) There must be a yearning, a desire to experience the presence of God. "If with all your heart you truly seek him, you shall surely find him."

(2) There must be the courage of repentance, the simple, sincere confession to God, "I'm sorry, for my selfishness, my moral failure, and my sin."

(3) There must be a full trust in God's accepting love and power. We must discover what it means to accept the fact that we are accepted by God.

(b) How and where does the presence of God break into our lives? It is different for every life. There are lives into which God has come slowly, imperceptibly. There are

others to whom a dramatic first experience of God has come. It was the day when life was transformed and when vividly there was a passing from darkness to light, from death to life.

III. A close encounter with God is a disturbing, even a dangerous experience.

(a) In the early part of the Bible the belief is held: "No man can look on the face of God and live." Certainly no man or woman can truly see God and ever be the same again. An experience of God stirs us to the depth of our being, bringing to us revolutionary changes in thinking and living.

(b) To come near to God is in many ways a fearful experience. It is much more comfortable to keep away from a close encounter with the eternal.

(1) To come near to God is to know that his purity all our lusts condemns.

(2) His integrity makes us ask whether what we think and what we say really match.

(3) To touch God is to be suddenly forced to examine how we make and hoard and spend our money.

(4) To know God is to see our neighbors in a new light and to realize there is no one who is not our neighbor.

(5) To realize the unbelievable love of God is to know compassion, and generosity must flow out from us to others.

IV. A close encounter with God brings an enduring satisfaction found nowhere else on earth. "Show us the Father and we will be satisfied."

(a) Religious joy and peace and satisfaction are strangely ignored today. We live in a generation which is frantically searching for happiness. Through sex and speed and sport and travel the search for personal satisfaction goes on. Yet how many miss the secret, seeking but never really finding inner serenity and happiness.

(b) There is no satisfaction on earth to equal being in right relationship with God.

Millions worship Sunday by Sunday because the experience which comes in the presence of God is real. The church abides because what it offers is true. Human beings are made in the image of God, and it is only as we are in relationship with him that we can be satisfied.

(c) Living close to God gives so deep and abiding a satisfaction because of the amazing self-giving of God. All rests on this one fact. If God were not willing to show himself and if God were not full of tenderness and patience and love, our reaching out to him would be useless.

(d) God poured out his creative strength in the making of this universe. He held nothing back in his fashioning of the human family. He offered his all in the gift of Jesus as the savior of the world.—Alan Walker.

Illustrations

REPORT TO THE EMPEROR.   Governor Pliny was frustrated. These stubborn Christians simply could not be stopped. Their worship was against the law, but they kept right on doing it. "But," he wrote the emperor in about A.D. 110, "they declared the sum of their guilt or error had amounted only to this, that on an appointed day they had been accustomed to meet before daybreak, and to recite a hymn antiphonally to Christ, as to a god, and to bind themselves by an oath *(sacramentum),* for the commission of any crime but to abstain from theft, robbery, adultery, and breach of faith, and not to deny a deposit when it was claimed. After the conclusion of this ceremony it was their custom to depart and meet again to take food."

MICROCOSM.   In Hugh Walpole's *Rogue Herries,* Francis Herries rides into a desolate village in the north of England. It is the early eighteenth century. Casting his eye about, he declares, "This village is cut off from the world." But the local clergyman responds to him: "It is the world, sir. Here within these hills, in this space of ground, is all the world. In every village through which I have passed, I have found

the complete world—all anger and vanity and covetousness and lust; yes, and all charity and goodness and sweetness of soul. In this valley I have found the whole world. God and the devil both walk on these fields."

Sermon Suggestions

GOD OUR REFUGE.   Text: Deut. 33:27. (1) The eternal God is the refuge from the unsoluble mysteries of life. (2) The eternal God is the refuge from all the illusions of life. (3) The eternal God is the refuge from all human limitations and the sense of insignificance. (4) The eternal God is the refuge from the sense of sin and loneliness. (5) The eternal God is the refuge in the last great adventure into the future life.—Thomas W. Davidson.

THE ROADS WE TRAVEL.   Text: Job 23: 10. (1) On the road (Luke 24:35). (2) The road of witnessing (Acts 8:38). (3) The road of neighborliness (Luke 10:37). (4) The road of vision (Acts 9:3). (5) The road of friendship (John 12:1). (6) The road of the burning heart (Luke 24:32).—Josephine E. Seymour.

Worship Aids

CALL TO WORSHIP.   "Bless the Lord, O my soul: and all that is with me, bless his holy name." Ps. 103:1.

INVOCATION.   O thou who art the light of the minds that know thee, the life of the souls that love thee, and the strength of the wills that serve thee, help us so to know thee that we may truly love thee and so to love thee that we may fully serve thee, whom to serve is perfect freedom.

OFFERTORY SENTENCE.   "And they came every one whose heart stirred him up, and every one whom his spirit made willing, and they brought the Lord's offering to the work of the tabernacle of the congregation, and for all his service." Exod. 35: 21.

OFFERTORY PRAYER. Our Father, help us this day to remember that we do not live in our own strength but that thou art our help and that from thee cometh even these gifts which we consecrate in Christ's name.

PRAYER. God our Father, giver of every grace, clothe our lives with those simple graces of the everyday which will make life lovely.

Grant us the grace of courtesy, that we may live as always at the court of the king and that we may treat all men as sons of the king.

Grant us the grace of reliability, so that when we make a promise we may always keep it, so that others will be able to depend on us.

Help us to be ready to welcome people, even when we are busy, and help us never to make anyone who comes to see us feel a nuisance.

Give us the grace of generosity and save us from giving so grudgingly, so condescendingly, and so humiliatingly that it would have been better not to give at all.

Help us always to be interested in other people, and so to be more ready to listen to them and less eager to talk about ourselves.

Give us the grace of gratitude that we may always speak the word of thanks which means so much to others.

Give us the appreciative spirit that we may ever speak the word of praise and of congratulation, which makes such a difference to others.

Help us to do faithfully the things we do not like doing and to meet graciously the people we do not like meeting.

Help us not to grow irritable even when we are tired and not to grow impatient even when everything goes wrong.

Help us never to be angry at criticism, never to be indifferent to advice, and never to be resentful at lack of appreciation.

Help us ever to remember the feelings of others and ever to think less of our own.

Give us the grace of an even temper which can meet upsetting things with calm serenity.

O God, our Father, we know so well how very difficult these things can be. Help us to make some time each day to be with Jesus that we may go out from his presence to meet the world with the strength and the peace and the beauty upon us which only he can give.—William Barclay.

EVENING SERVICE

Topic: In the Direction of Perfection
TEXT: Phil. 3:13–16.

Paul offers some practical advice gleaned from his own experiences as well as observations on how an individual might move most effectively in the direction of Christian perfection.

I. Be sensitive to where you are in relation to where you want to go. Paul shows this awareness by saying, "Brethren, I do not consider that I have made it (perfection) my own." People whose judgment is clouded by pride, cockiness, and overconfidence usually discover the prize they thought was in their grasp has slipped away. The same applies to individuals filled with empty talk and wishful thinking. You won't reach your goal if you close your eyes to reality, and the reality is that making a decision for Christ or joining a church does not immediately erase all your imperfections and sins.

II. Don't dwell on what you can't do anything about. Paul calls this "forgetting what lies behind." The hesitation, distraction, and wasted effort involved in gazing backward hinder advancement. That is especially true when you're concentrating on past failures.

III. Strive for the goal with everything you've got. This "straining forward to what lies ahead" is vital, says Paul. That is why life's successes are not always those you'd expect—namely, the ones with the most going for them—but rather those who make up for their lack of "natural equipment" with above average drive, desire, and determination.

IV. Retain whatever gains you've made and whatever goodness and virtue you possess. "Let us hold true to what we have attained," writes Paul. Life is dynamic. So those who quit a task are apt to find taking it up again either difficult because they've lost ground or impossible because circumstances have changed and the opportunity is gone.—David A. Spieler.

SUNDAY: JANUARY EIGHTEENTH

MORNING SERVICE

Topic: **Partnership in Service (Missionary Day)**

Scripture: Luke 5:1–11.

I. *How partnership in service is established.* Jesus said to Simon Peter, "Launch out into the deep, and let down your nets for a draught."

(a) All true partnership in service must be based upon the word of Christ. Those fishermen could have refused his word and disagreed among themselves. After all, they had toiled all night and taken nothing. Fishing conditions and the state of their own minds and bodies all argued against having another try, but happily the authority of the Lord prevailed, and at his word they "let down the net."

(b) Partnership begins with what Jesus directly says.

(1) When he gave the great commission, he did not address his words to any one individual but to the church. (See Matt. 28:19–20.)

(2) As we think through the implications and ramifications of this commission we could raise all manner of objections, but the work would never be done. To enjoy partnership in service we must say with Peter, "Nevertheless at thy word I will let down the net."

(c) Partnership begins with what Jesus divinely sees.

(1) While Peter and his colleagues were experienced fishermen, they had demonstrated over a period of hours that the fish were just not there. But Jesus saw beyond the pessimism and faithlessness of these tired men.

(2) Nothing unifies Christian people in service like a divine vision. Solomon reminds us that "where there is no vision, the people perish" (Prov. 29:18).

(3) When Helen Keller was asked what she considered to be the greatest tragedy that could ever befall a person, she instinctively replied, "To have sight but lack vision."

(4) It was to the shortsighted disciples that the Lord said, "Lift up your eyes, and look on the fields; for they are white already to harvest" (John 4:35).

II. *How partnership in service is encouraged.* We read that Peter and his colleagues "beckoned unto their partners, which were in the other ship, that they should come and help them."

(a) Once we are launched on a course of divine service God always has a way of encouraging us. As the nets were cast in obedience to the master's commands, there were two things that encouraged the disciples—and disciples ever since.

(1) There is the blessing of oneness. Adam Clarke observed that "had not the other disciples been called in to assist, the net would doubtlessly have broken, and all the fish would have been lost. What a pity that there should be such envious separation among the different sects that profess to believe in Christ Jesus! Some will rather leave souls to perish than admit partners in the sacred work."

(2) The emphasis throughout the New Testament is on body life both in our unity and ministry. No member of the body can say to the other, "I have no need of you" (I Cor. 12:21). This sense of oneness is our strength. It is one of the most convincing evidences of Christ's redemptive work.

(b) Imagine what would have happened if there had been no partnership in this fishing venture. In the Greek the verb in v. 6 reads that "the net began to break." This disaster was obviated by united action. Not only was the net saved from breaking but two boats were also filled to capacity with the miraculous haul of fish.

III. *How partnership in service is extended.* After the miracle, it is recorded that "when . . . Peter saw it, he fell down at Jesus' knees, saying, Depart from me; for I am a sinful man, O Lord . . . And Jesus said unto Simon, Fear not; from henceforth thou shalt catch men."

(a) Because of our sinfulness and selfishness, we are limited in our vision and lacking in our passion for souls. This is what happened to these disciples. Though called by the savior to follow him, it is obvious from this passage that they had returned to their fishing. Their perspective of service had narrowed down to personal interests and gain. But what happened on this memorable day altered everything.

(b) When Peter exclaimed, "Depart from me; for I am a sinful man, O Lord," he admitted his defective view of Jesus.

(1) He acknowledged the deity of Christ, for he knelt at Jesus' feet.

(2) He acknowledged the sovereignty of Christ, for he called him "Lord."

(3) He acknowledged the purity of Christ as he sensed his unworthiness and sinfulness before the presence of the son of God.

(4) He discovered, as did the others, that Jesus was God, the lord of all creation —including the fish—and the savior of men.

(c) As a result, Jesus elevated and extended their partnership in service. From catching fish they were now to catch men. God's redemptive mission is nothing less than worldwide evangelization. This is the priority work of the church. Anything else is peripheral and unimportant.—Stephen F. Olford.

Illustration

COMMENT ON PHILLIPS BROOKS. I remember his vast, benevolent bulk filling my study like Gulliver in Lilliput. In the pulpit his torrential eloquence was all that tradition says, but after talking with him I remember wondering whether he did not love everybody too dearly to care especially for anybody.—Ellery Sedgwick.

Sermon Suggestions

THE CHURCH ON A MISSION. Text: Matt. 28:19–20. (1) The church is on a mission if it has vision. (2) The church is on a mis-

sion if it loves. (3) The church is on a mission if it gives. (4) The church is on a mission if it is selfless.—Jerry B. Hopkins.

HOW GOD WOULD FINANCE A CHURCH. Text: Exod. 35:29. (1) God calls for unanimous giving: "All the men and women." (2) God calls for systematic giving: "whose heart moved them." (3) God calls for voluntary giving: "their freewill offering to the Lord."—John R. Brokhoff.

Worship Aids

CALL TO WORSHIP. "Thou wilt keep him in perfect peace, whose mind is stayed on thee: because he trusteth in thee. Trust ye in the Lord for ever: for in the Lord Jehovah is everlasting strength." Isa. 26: 3–4.

INVOCATION. O Lord of light, in this hour of worship in thy house make pure our hearts, and we shall see thee; reveal thyself to us, and we shall love thee. Strengthen our wills, and we shall choose the good from the evil, and day by day manifest in the world the glory and power of thy blessed gospel, which thou hast made known to us through thy son Jesus Christ.

OFFERTORY SENTENCE. "Prepare ye the way of the Lord, make straight in the desert a highway for our God." Isa. 40:3.

OFFERTORY PRAYER. O God, in whose sight a contrite heart is more than whole burnt offerings: help us with these our gifts to dedicate ourselves, body, soul, and spirit, unto thee, which is our reasonable service.

PRAYER. Lord God Almighty, maker of heaven and earth, creator of man in thine own image, and giver of the covenant of faithfulness to them who honor thee, we bless thee that thou hast not left us solely to our own resources to live for thee, witness to thee, and work for the needy of this earth. In the sending of thy son, Jesus Christ our Lord, heaven lent its best to the sons of men. How grateful we are for his sense of such oneness with thee that he dared to call thee "my Father." Yet this was not something to be cherished but to share, and when his disciples asked to be taught to pray, he responded, "When you pray, say 'Our Father. . . .' " For Jesus, the fatherhood of God, the righteousness of God, and the mercy of God were things to be shared with the sons of men, and so he commanded his disciples to go into all the world and preach the gospel to every creature. O God, help us to go, help us to live, and help us to tell men that they may know that thou hast so loved the world that the sending of thine only begotten son that men might believe is the only response that thou couldst make and we can make. —Hillyer H. Straton.

EVENING SERVICE

Topic: Steps Toward Health of Mind and Spirit

TEXT: Ps. 27:1.

I. *Evaluate your time.* Time is a precious gift, one of man's most sacred possessions. It is in time that one finds happiness, renders service, and fulfills his stewardship. We live in a culture that demands time and often clutters time with many things. The result is confusion, tension, frustration, and fatigue. Periodically one needs to evaluate time and to establish priorities, so that there is adequate time for rest, relaxation, spiritual growth, and communion.

II. *Recognize and accept your responsibilities.* There can be no health without this. Some attempt too much and try to carry the weight of the world on their shoulders. Some attempt too little and through laziness, fear of failure, or making of excuses fail to see or to face their responsibilities. The mature person recognizes that he is accountable for his behavior and acts accordingly.

III. *Find time to relax.* The healthy person not only accepts responsibility, but he can also withdraw from it, relax, let down, rest, and enjoy himself. Relaxation is the opposite of tension. If one would work well, he must be able to rest and relax.

IV. *Seek help if it is needed.* There are people, pastors, counselors, doctors, psychologists, and social workers who are trained to help. To seek help when it is needed is not a sign of weakness. It is a sign of strength. It is the realization that we are human and that there are other humans who are both able and willing to help.

V. *Focus your attention on strengths.* In every situation there is a positive and a negative aspect. Both must be recognized and taken into account. One can find causes for complaint anywhere. One can also find things for which to be grateful in most situations. To focus on the negative is to become negative. To focus on the positive is a step toward health.

VI. *Help someone else.* "He who finds his life will lose it." The neurotic is inevitably self-centered. He cannot concentrate on the needs of others because of his own concerns and worries. The healthy person has anxieties and concerns too—everybody does. But he is also able to lay them aside and think of others. The more we are able to help others, the stronger we become. The path of service is a road to health.

VII. *Pray and trust.* (a) A basic trust is a road to health and strength. Some find this difficult because there is so much uncertainty and confusion in religion. There are many differing points of view and quarrels among scholars. This will always be so. One should attempt to understand to the best of his ability. There is no virtue in ignorance; credulity is not faith.

(b) One need not wait until the questions have been answered and all the problems solved to live by faith. There are many areas one simply marks "unresolved" and continues to live by faith and trust. As he does so, his knowledge increases, his faith becomes confirmed, and he increases in spiritual health and strength.—Adapted by Myron J. Taylor.

SUNDAY: JANUARY TWENTY-FIFTH

MORNING SERVICE

Topic: Praying as Jesus Prayed (Week of Prayer)

TEXT: Luke 11:1.

I. Jesus assumed that God is all-knowing. One does not have to describe his situation to God in boring detail, though there is value in reviewing for our own good what the situation is that confronts us. God could not be the God of Jesus if he is dependent on our individual wire-services to bring him the latest bulletin from our particular part of the battle-line of life. Jesus believed that God was aware of the sparrow's fall, the lily's growth, and the life and death of the natural process in grass and trees. If you believe, as Jesus did, in this all-knowingness of God—called in theological circles "omniscience" —then you are moving into the first basic assumption required of Jesus' disciples who would learn to pray as he prayed.

II. A second assumption underlying the prayer life of Jesus was that God loves us, cares for us as individual persons, and wants only the best for us. If you have had a loving and mature parent, this could be the easiest phase of Christian faith to accept. Your parents love you and cared for you when literally you could not care for yourself, and on into your adult years you have been aware of their love and their desire for only the best for you. If your human parents could effect this, why is it difficult to believe that the one whom Jesus called Father could not similarly, albeit with an added divine dimension, thus care for you and love you and will only your good? There is not much effective prayer unless we can accept this assumption of Jesus.

III. Jesus' third assumption was that God's concern is unlimited. Here he broke with his tradition which believed that Judaism was a special case with God. God had an exclusive covenant with the Mosaic tradition, and while he was the one God, yet his concern was primarily to the "chosen people." There is no doubt of our indebtedness to our Judaistic forebears for preserving the religious tradition of the Hebrew faith in God. But Jesus said God is no respecter of persons. He loves us all. He cares for us all. He accepts us all even though we fail to accept each other. God is the eternal contemporary of every age— at all times, in all places, and with all peoples. If you believe that, then it makes a difference how you pray.

IV. A final assumption is God's willingness to do good for his children. That there is evil in the world, none can deny. That there is sin in our natures, no honest human can ignore. But Jesus believed that the will of God was a will for good. He wills health for us though there is ill health among us. He wills peace for mankind though we are always fighting somewhere on his earth. He wills equality of opportunity for all his children though our greed and selfishness prevent many of God's children from their God-given rights. The kingdom of God can come, but it will come only when we become so Godlike in our lives and our relationships that God's will to do good for his children is never thwarted by our human sin.

V. How did Jesus so pray that his disciples wanted him to teach them the secret?

(a) He prayed in trust and confidence that he need only learn God's will and purpose, surrender his own will and purpose to that divine will, and God would provide the power for him to meet whatever came in life.

(b) Jesus prayed receptively. He opened the channels to his mind and heart and made them clear channels without interference of other voices that he might listen to God.

(c) Jesus prayed affirmatively. His was positive prayer. He knew his weaknesses as we know our sins. But these he cast upon God in the confidence that there would come a positive affirmation of him as a person and an answer that would affirm God's will.

(d) Jesus prayed dangerously. There is real peril in answered prayer. A successful businessman prayed to God about whether or not he should become a missionary. So many conditions developed in that direction that he was certain God was calling him to give up his business and go to Africa. There he is today. It was a dangerous prayer. God heard it and provided him the courage and power to answer it for himself. Jesus prayed to be delivered from the cross. But he was crucified. He prayed to live. But he died and was buried. Yet God answered his prayer and gave him, and through him gave us, life that is eternal. To pray for God's will in your life is to risk being called to a duty that becomes the compelling will of God.

(e) Jesus prayed undiscourageably. Think of the many times Jesus was disappointed in his hopes and expectations. The disciple, who had asked him to teach them to pray, deserted and denied him in that bitter hour of testing. His idea of God's love as the basis for man's living hardly got off the ground with his disciples, let alone the people. But the final recorded words of Jesus are the confident and prayerful declaration of the trust which had underlain his whole ministry— "Father, I commit my soul into your hands."—Hoover Rupert.

Illustrations

MAN OF PRAYER.   Christ prayed and prayed—in the great congregation of the temple and the local friendship of the synagogue, in the circle of his friends, on the housetop under Syrian stars, in the fields outside Jerusalem, on the lonely mountainside, and in the inner chamber—until prayer became the climate of his days.—George A. Buttrick.

RENEWAL.   I had the privilege of spending two days with Albert Schweitzer at his hospital in Lambarene. It was a wonderful experience to follow him about during the day and join the staff for dinner in the evening. Schweitzer was eighty-four years old, and he was active from morning until night. He climbed the hills as agile as a goat, and he kept his eye on everything from the repairing of a boat to the performing of an operation. At night he was tired and he looked tired. He ate without much conversation. Then he walked across the floor to the piano, and he walked like a weary man. We sang a hymn together, and he returned to his place. After the Lord's Prayer he opened the Bible and read from the scriptures. Then, behold, a kind of miracle! The weariness dropped away, the eyes sparkled, and the face was alight with the excitement of a child. The Bible seemed to have renewed his youth like the eagle's.—Gerald Kennedy.

Sermon Suggestion

WHAT DOES PRAYER ACCOMPLISH?   Text: Jas. 5:16. (1) What does prayer accomplish in one's own experience? (2) What does prayer accomplish in the family circle? (3) What does prayer accomplish in the local church? (4) What does prayer accomplish in the work of missions? (5) What can prayer accomplish in a world cursed by war?—Andrew W. Blackwood.

Worship Aids

CALL TO WORSHIP.   "They that wait upon the Lord shall renew their strength; they shall mount up with wings as eagles; they shall run, and not be weary; and they shall walk, and not faint." Isa. 40:31.

INVOCATION.   Grant, O God, that because we meet together this day life may grow greater for some who have contempt for it, simpler for some who are confused by it, happier for some who are tasting the bitterness of it, safer for some who are feeling the peril of it, more friendly for some who are feeling the loneliness of it, serener for some who are throbbing with the fire of it, and holier for some to whom life has lost all dignity, beauty, and meaning.

OFFERTORY SENTENCE. "It is God who is at work within you, giving you the will and the power to achieve his purpose." Phil. 2:13 (PHILLIPS).

OFFERTORY PRAYER. Our heavenly Father, may thy kingdom be uppermost in our minds, our hearts, and our lives. Accept our gifts and with them the rededication of all that we are and have to thy greater glory.

PRAYER. O God, Father of all mercies, whose love reaches across the expanse of our universe to care for the least of us even more than we care for ourselves, you alone are worthy of our praise and adoration. Your presence supports all of life, and creation mirrors your majesty and your power.

We confess that we have carelessly marred the beauty of the earth. We have broken the unity of man with man. Our human achievements too often have become our Babels. We have refused to accept our creatureliness and have played God—standing in judgment, condemning, destroying, and killing. You are merciful, but we are lacking in mercy; you are patient, but we are often rude and intolerant; you are forgiving, but we often harbor our resentments and nurse our angers. For this, O God, forgive us.

O God, help us not to be conformed to worldly ways, but let us be renewed until we can love the unlovely, forgive even the unforgiving, plant and not uproot, build and not tear down, disagree without being disagreeable, listen more and talk less, remain serene when others lose their cool, and keep the faith when life crashes in.

We commit ourselves anew to the work of Christ and his church. Use our lives that some good may come to others and that your kingdom may be hastened.—James O. Bradford, Jr.

EVENING SERVICE

Topic: The Faith That Pleases God
TEXT: Heb. 11:5.
I. The faith that pleases God manifests itself in one's personal walk. This was the most noticeable fact of Enoch's life—he "walked with God" (Gen. 5:22, 24).

(a) The word "walk" is used frequently in scripture to indicate faithfulness to and fellowship with God. God is not some austere tyrant detached from the cares and concerns of his creatures. He is a loving person who desires communion with his people.

(b) Walking with God is a private experience which must be practiced by faith. It is only through faith that man can please God and have fellowship with him. (See Heb. 11:6.)

II. The faith that pleases God manifests itself in one's practical work.

(a) Enoch lived a normal life, and his family and social relationships were no handicap to his devotion. He had all the duties, distractions, and complications of such responsibilities, but he hallowed them all with the sense of divine fellowship.

(b) Some people never understand that God wants their fellowship in the midst of their everyday concerns. It is said that in the Middle Ages, Angela of Foligbo was glad when her husband and children died so that she could spend all her time contemplating the love of God. Spirituality is always in danger of passing into empty sentimentality. If our faith beckons us to escape from the commonplace, it is dangerous and false. God calls upon us to serve him in the discharge of our daily duties.

III. The faith that is pleasing to God manifests itself in one's public witness.

(a) From the Bible's description of the age in which Enoch lived, we know that humanity had reached the peak of pride and had plumbed the depths of godlessness, scorn, and violence. It was to this type of society that Enoch witnessed. "Enoch . . . prophesied . . . Behold, the Lord cometh . . . to execute judgment" (Jude 14–15).

(b) Enoch witnessed for God during a nightmare of moral and spiritual darkness. It was a period approaching a climax when, in mercy to unborn generations, God would wipe out the entire human race except for Noah and his family. Enoch didn't compromise with the world, but he didn't withdraw from it either. He maintained and proclaimed his faith in God when almost everyone else was forsaking him.

(c) Although one's faith in God is personal, one cannot hold it long without either sharing it or losing it. Jesus prayed that his people would be preserved from the contamination of the world, but he did not pray that they should be removed from the earth.—Mervin L. Chapin in *The Preacher's Magazine.*

SUNDAY: FEBRUARY FIRST

MORNING SERVICE

Topic: Going to Church
Text: Ps. 84:2.

I. The first thing that I like about going to church is that it is an exercise in honesty.

(a) I spend my week, as you do, in a world of false values—a world that would have me believe that the only thing that matters in the long run is material success, measured by the amount of money I can get for myself and the degree of power over other people I can wield.

(b) Then on Sunday I come to church. What is the first thing I do? I stand and sing a hymn of praise to God that acknowledges that this dreary, stale world is not the be-all and the end-all of reality. Over and above it, in the bright light above the clouds, there is a living God who stands for truth and justice, integrity and helpfulness, and kindness and consideration and human decency—things that the weekday world seems pretty largely to have forgotten.

(c) Then do you know what I do? I get down on my knees and admit in a voice loud enough to be heard that I have erred and strayed from God's ways like a lost sheep, that I have followed too much the devices and desires of my own heart, that I have left undone the things I ought to have done and done the things I ought not to have done, and that, instead of being congratulated on the success I have achieved in the eyes of the world, I really need to be forgiven for having fallen so far short of the standards that God expects of me. I shouldn't be surprised if church were just about the last place in the world where honesty of that kind is still expected of people.

II. The second thing I like about church is the chance it gives me to rejoice.

(a) Confession over, I rise from my knees and join my fellow worshipers in the ancient song that begins, "O come, let us sing unto the Lord; let us heartily rejoice in the strength of our salvation." Or "O be joyful in the Lord, all ye lands; serve the Lord with gladness and come before his presence with a song."

(b) How little real joy there seems to be in life these days. Then I come to church, and here is joy. Music plays such an important part in the church service because it is the natural expression of joy. Just look at the hymns we sing. These are paeans of joy, songs of celebration and thankfulness and praise. What a lift they give to the spirit!

III. I come to church to learn. (a) That's why I like the custom of calling the scripture readings the lessons. Church is about the last place left where you can hear a lesson from the Bible, the Bible that was the spiritual food and drink of those who laid the foundations of our freedom.

(b) I need to be reminded again and again of what the Bible has to say about the fundamental issues of life—that the world belongs to God and men are not free to abuse it and pollute it and destroy it in the pursuit of their own selfish ends, that there is a difference between right and wrong and that it matters desperately in terms of suffering—often visited on the innocent—when men choose wrong for their own selfish ends, and that individual human life is sacred in the eyes of God and must be treated as an end in itself and not as a means to some other end. I need to be reminded of those truths, and I need to be told the story, over and over, of the one whose life was the incarnation of them.

IV. I go to church because I like sermons. That may sound strange to some of you. Sermons are surely not the most popular form of expression these days.

(a) They deal with spiritual and moral matters, and in the long run those are the most important things there are.

(b) They are or they should be in language that is worthy of the subjects that the sermon deals with, and language—decent language—seems to be in short supply these days.

V. I go to church for the offering, the offering of bread and wine and money, which is the heart of our worship. (a) Jesus came not merely to proclaim the nearness of the kingdom of God but also to demonstrate, in the little community that he formed around himself, the possibilities of a life of righteousness, of forgiveness, and of sharing. The offering is that act of sharing, in which we give ourselves—our souls and bodies—to the life of sharing to which Jesus has called us.

(b) The offering is the high point of our worship, the moment of beauty, surrounded always by the loveliest music in the service, music whose function it is to remind us, by lifting us out of ourselves, that in the act of giving we come closest to God.—Charles H. Buck, Jr.

Illustrations

PLAYING CHURCH.   When father came in he noticed that two little boys were playing store. He said, "If you are playing store, let me buy something." He put a penny on the counter. One of the boys said, "We are not playing store, father. We are playing church."

PERFECT WORSHIP.   As long as you notice and have to count the steps, you are not dancing but only learning to dance. A good shoe is a shoe you don't notice. Good reading becomes possible when you need not consciously think about eyes or light or print or spelling. The perfect church service would be one we were almost unaware of. Our at-

tention would have been on God.—C. S. Lewis.

Sermon Suggestions

THE JOY OF THE LORD.   Scripture: Neh. 8:1–10. (1) The source of our joy (v. 10). (2) The secret of our joy (v. 8). (3) The service of our joy (v. 10).—Stephen F. Olford.

CHRIST'S CHURCH.   Text: Matt. 16:18–19. (1) His church is a strong church: "On this rock I will build my church." (2) His church is a dynamic church: "and the gates of hell shall not prevail against it." (3) His church is a witnessing church: "I will give you the keys of the kingdom of heaven." (4) His church is a revelant church: "and whatever you bind on earth shall be bound in heaven."—J. Randolph Taylor.

Worship Aids

CALL TO WORSHIP.   "He that dwelleth in the secret place of the most High shall abide under the shadow of the Almighty. I will say of the Lord, He is my refuge and my fortress: my God; in him will I trust." Ps. 91:1–2.

OFFERTORY SENTENCE.   "Give unto the Lord, O ye kindreds of the people, give unto the Lord glory and strength. Give unto the Lord the glory due unto his name: bring an offering, and come into his courts." Ps. 96:7–8.

INVOCATION.   Our heavenly Father, who by thy love hast made us, and through thy love hast kept us, and in thy love wouldst make us perfect: we humbly confess that we have not loved thee with all our heart and soul and mind and strength and that we have not loved one another as Christ hath loved us. Thy life is within our souls, but our selfishness has hindered thee. We have not lived by faith. We have resisted thy spirit. We have neglected thy inspirations. Forgive what we have been. Help us to amend what we are, and in thy spirit direct what we shall be that thou mayest come into the full glory of thy creation in us and in all men.

OFFERTORY PRAYER.   Awaken us to the claims of thy holy will, O God, and stir us with a passion for thy kingdom, that we may respond at this time with our gifts and also with our lives.

PRAYER.   O Father, thou who art the ancient of days, yet the ever-new God, we are grateful for thy mercy renewed every morning and thy faithfulness every night. As the dew refreshes the earth morning by morning, so does thy spirit restore our souls to newness of life. We thank thee for Christ in whom all things are becoming new, for in him we have discovered a new life, a new song, and a new hope that nothing in life or in death can dismay.

Eternal Spirit, evermore creating, grant to us discernment to read the signs of the times that we may behold what new thing thou art doing in our day. As a congregation, keep us open, alert, and alive to the movings of thy spirit in all the relationships of our common life. Grant us wisdom to change the tack of our sail—our attitudes—that through faith the sail of our life may be lifted to the wafting of the winds of thy spirit. In all kinds of weather, help us to follow patiently the North Star of thy eternal purpose—even Jesus Christ. As in him thou dost call us out of our cozy harbors to risk life on the open seas, grant us courage for our voyage.—John Thompson.

EVENING SERVICE

Topic: The Church's Calling
TEXT: I Pet. 2:9.
I. The church is called to be a commu-nity. Early Christians were bonded together by mutual concern and sharing and by constant fellowship (Acts 2:44–47). Churches these days are often composed of people little more than casual acquaintances occasionally involved in common projects. No wonder our congregations are in trouble.

II. The church is called to be a missionary community. Having experienced new life in Christ, we're expected to pass on the good news. "Go therefore and make disciples of all nations" (Matt. 28:19). There is also sensitivity to the various needs which persons may have. Our churches don't reach out as they should, particularly when the prospects are different.

III. The church is called to be an enthusiastic, missionary community. First Peter expresses this bubbling joy: "That you may declare the wonderful deeds of him who called you out of darkness into his marvelous light" (2:9). Enthusiasm ought to fairly radiate from every Christian. Churches are filled with individuals who exude gloom, doom, and pessimism. When visitors receive a cold shoulder instead of a cheerful smile, warm handshake, and friendly words, poor performance is predictable. We need the kind of drive exemplified in John 14:12, Matt. 28: 20, and Acts 1:8.

IV. The church is called to be a unique, enthusiastic, missionary community. Christians are not supposed to be indistinguishable from non-Christians. Churches are not supposed to function like every other organization. "You are a chosen race, a royal priesthood, a holy nation, God's own people" (I Pet. 2:9). We're special and we've a vital job to do.—David A. Spieler.

SUNDAY: FEBRUARY EIGHTH

MORNING SERVICE

Topic: When Trouble Comes
Text: Ps. 30:5.
"Weeping may endure for a night." The Hebrew word for "endure" or "tarry" means "spend the night as a lodger." So much for the night, but what happens in the morning?

I. The psalmist says, "Weeping may endure for a night but joy cometh in the morning." What does that mean? When morning comes, trouble goes on his way. So we have understood David, and there is undeniable truth there.

(a) Eventually even the darkest night passes. Clarence Hall tells of a journey he made to Palestine. It was the Easter season, and he very much wished to attend the sunrise service at the Garden Tomb. The night before seemed endless. He was restless and could not sleep. Finally he turned to the Arab who had promised to be his guide and asked him if the night would ever pass. To which the guide replied: "Never fear, my friend. The day will come. You can't hold back the dawn!" Two hours later at the Garden Tomb the service began. The minister read from the Bible with the aid of an electric light, and the choir sang Easter anthems. Then with dramatic suddenness the sun burst over the horizon, dispelling the darkness and flooding the sky with light. Eventually even the darkest night passes. You can't hold back the dawn.

(b) That is true not only of the physical world but also of life. You see that in this story of David. He has been sick, even unto death. He has had his night of sickness, but when he prayed, God healed him and restored him to life. His weeping—his tears and lamentations—endured for a night, but the joy of restored health and strength came in the morning.

(c) If that was true in the life of David, it was also true of the people of God. They have had their dark days of persecution. One thinks of the bondage of the Hebrews

in the land of Egypt. There comes to mind the lot of the exiles languishing and lamenting their situation by the river Chebar. The story of the Maccabees and what they suffered at the hands of Antiochus Epiphanes is well known. And so is the anguish of the church from the days of the Roman Empire to our own time. The people of God have had their seasons of trial and their night of weeping, but the night has passed and a new day has dawned.

(d) Is that not equally true of our individual experience? We all have our nights of frustration and disappointment. We have our problems and difficulties. We have our suffering and our sorrow. But in each case the night passes— things improve, we make adjustments, time heals, a new day dawns, and life goes on.

II. "Weeping may endure for a night but joy cometh in the morning." We have understood that to mean that when morning comes—and it always does—trouble goes on his way. But joy does not always come in the morning. There are experiences in life that we never get over.

(a) There are experiences of sickness that leave us crippled and handicapped so that life is never what it might have been.

(b) It is true of at least some of our experiences of failure. There are experiences of failure that cast a shadow upon all the days that follow.

(c) It is true of our experiences of loss and grief. There are loved ones who can never be replaced, and there are separations from which we never recover.

(d) There is another aspect of our lives where, while weeping may endure for just a night, joy does not come in the morning. I am thinking of the night of our estrangement from God. In God's providence and by God's grace that night may pass, but so often when it passes the joy of the morning is missing.

III. Is it possible that we have misinterpreted David? Is he saying something different from what we have commonly understood? Listen to him again. "Thou hast turned for me my mourning into dancing, thou hast loosed my sackcloth and girded me with gladness!" That hardly suggests the departure of trouble with the coming of the morning but rather that with the dawn of a new day trouble itself is transformed into joy.

(a) In the providence of God sorrow may actually be the instrument God uses to bring a new joy and a greater happiness to our lives. David was brought through trouble—through the visitation of sickness —to the joy of a new spiritual experience. He came to recognize his own insufficiency, the inadequacy of material possessions, and the wonder of God's grace so that he is constrained to praise God, saying in effect: "Everything's grace. We walk upon it, we breathe it, we live and die by it. It makes the nails and axles of the universe."

(b) Weeping may endure for a night, but when trouble is received not with bitterness and resentment but in faith and trust, joy does come in the morning. There is nothing automatic about it. Trouble in itself is neutral. It needs something else— the spirit of God—to make it positive and creative.—S. Robert Weaver.

Illustration

FAMILIAR DARKNESS.   A little girl visiting her grandmother was put to bed in the dark. It was not long before some sobs were heard coming from the little girl's room. The grandmother went to see what was the matter. The little one said, "I'm afraid in the dark." The grandmother replied, "Your mother puts you to bed in the dark at home and you are not afraid." "Yes," answered the child, "but that is *my* dark."

Sermon Suggestions

FORTUNATE MISFORTUNE.   Text: Ps. 119:71 (MOFFATT). (1) Misfortune serves to deepen life. (2) Misfortune is often the means of releasing undreamed of powers. (3) Misfortune brings enlarged capacity to understand and help other people. (4) Misfortune can make real

and vital one's relationship to God.— William M. Elliott.

OUR MINISTRY OF RECONCILIATION. Scripture: Rom. 15. (1) The need for unity in love (vv. 1–13). (2) The need for evangelism (vv. 17–24). (3) The need for material aid (vv. 25–29). (4) The need for prayer (vv. 30–33).—Ernest Trice Thompson.

Worship Aids

CALL TO WORSHIP.   "Lord, who shall abide in thy tabernacle? Who shall dwell in thy holy hill? He that walketh uprightly, and worketh righteousness, and speaketh the truth in his heart." Ps. 15:1–2.

INVOCATION.   O God of mercy, in this hour in thy house have mercy upon us. O God of light, shine into our hearts. O thou eternal goodness, deliver us from evil. O God of power, be thou our refuge and our strength. O God of love, let love flow through us. O God of life, live within us, now and forevermore.

OFFERTORY SENTENCE.   "Verily I say unto you, inasmuch as ye have done it unto one of the least of these my brethren, ye have done it unto me." Matt. 25:40.

OFFERTORY PRAYER.   Accept, O Lord, these offerings thy people make unto thee and grant that the cause to which they are devoted may prosper under thy guidance, to the glory of thy name.

PRAYER.   O God, it is good to be in thy house—away for a few moments from the world and yet somehow closer to all that is real and true and good.

Keep us from using this hour to escape what we know we must finally do, or to hear only what we want to hear, or to expose only the surface of ourselves.

Make us better than we think we are— with courage to try the high hurdles, with humility to do the nasty little jobs without whining, and with the grace to admit we might we wrong.

Help us to see not only the beauty of the

world but also the brooding love of thy spirit that hovers over us, helping us to make our decisions the right ones.

Above all, O God, bring to the surface the goodness dormant deep within us that we may not be good for nothing but of some real help to our family and friends and to the cause of Christ our Lord.— Harry W. Adams.

EVENING SERVICE

Topic: When Life Matters Most
TEXT: Jer. 29:13.

I. "When life matters most." When life is most real, men seek God's presence. This usually happens when young people reach maturity and ask, "What is life all about?" Life, they find, is a gift from God, and each person is on a pilgrimage. The mature young person will seek the church for guidance.

II. "When life matters most." This is when two young people are in love and are confronted with the real meaning of marriage. Reality and religion, respect and love are the ingredients of marriage. At a time like this, young people seek guidance in God's church.

III. "When life matters most." This comes at that great time of parenthood. A father and a mother can rise to spiritual heights together when life's triumphant fulfillment takes place. Good parents seek guidance in God's church.

IV. "When life matters most." This comes when one looks at his life and feels disappointment with himself. Few escape it. True values haunt us in our materialistic world. If we gain things but lose self, we have failed. When one faces this time, one usually comes to the church.

V. "When life matters most." This comes when we lose a loved one—a father, a mother, a mate, or a child. The severance of the cords, woven ever so delicately through years of intimate association, brings strain and suffering. In such a time one turns to God's church.

VI. "When life matters most." This always comes when we stand near the end of our human existence and have but a little time to bid farewell to this earthly world and its cares. Then one comes close to the church. It's a good port from which to embark into eternity.

VII. In times like these we seek God's church not as a crutch but because it is the only place a man can feel at home in moments of supreme reality. It is instinctive; it is irresistible. Man is God's child.—Robert N. DuBose.

SUNDAY: FEBRUARY FIFTEENTH

MORNING SERVICE

Topic: Shalom (Brotherhood Week)
TEXT: Num. 6:24–26.

"Shalom" is both a greeting and a benediction, a salutation and a blessing. Its predominant meaning is peace. The Hebrews from ancient times to the present characteristically have met and departed with the word "shalom" on their lips. When a single word survives so long in the history of language, there must be a reason.

I. "Shalom" is used by the Bible as a way of describing the ideal state of life.

(a) The root meaning is completeness, wholeness, or harmony. One authority defines it this way: "The untrammelled, free growth of the soul." If you were to envision an ideal state of life, could you improve much on these meanings?

(b) "Shalom" is not an unrealistic slogan nor a dreamy-eyed appraisal of life. Its lyrical sound summons us to make of first importance being rather than having. What a man truly is is more significant than what he possesses.

(c) A man can be measured not by the quantity of his possessions but by the largeness of his soul. He is a man as God meant him to be. He is a man of "shalom," a man of inner peace, of completeness, and of wholeness.

II. "Shalom" is descriptive of the normal and proper relationship which ought to exist among men. The apostle Paul meant this when he urged Christians at Rome to "pursue what makes for peace and mutual upbuilding."

(a) The best place to find harmony and mutual upbuilding ought to be the home. How tragic it is when the home is a center of strife and antagonism among its members. Any extension into larger society of the things which make for peace and growth of character really must wait upon what is provided by the home. We have not become so urbanized or so sophisticated that home and family life are incidental to society or somehow unnecessary. The proverb asks, "If kinsmen cannot dwell together in peace, shall the world be free from strife?"

(b) On the desk in my office is a card bearing the Latin words, *Dona nobis pacem,* a prayer meaning simply, "Give us peace." This is not intended as a plea for escape from responsible action nor as a desire to flee from the real world of turmoil and trouble. It is a prayer for wholeness, for singleness of mind, and for perspective in relating my work to those who come through my office door.

(c) In the deepest sense this is a prayer for "shalom." Would that there could be inscribed over the entrances to our homes, the words, "Give us peace"! More importantly, would that this prayer could be written on our hearts! Let us then pursue peace and mutual upbuilding.

III. The peace signified by the word "shalom" ultimately is a gift from God.

(a) God bestows the peace of "shalom," meaning inner wholeness and harmony. It remains for us who have received this gift to implement it in the larger world of human relationships where conflict and antagonism abound. Individuals in whom the "shalom" of God is real are needed desperately for meeting the turbulent national and international issues of our time.

(b) We stand in the heritage and tradition of those ancient congregations. We also stand under the presence of him whom we confess as Lord, the one who said to all of his disciples: "Peace I leave with you; my peace I give to you; not as the world gives do I give to you. Let not your hearts be troubled, neither let them be afraid."

(c) The peace described by Aaron and the peace offered by Christ direct us initially to the ideal state of personal life. From there we are led into the normal and proper ralationship which ought to exist among men. But above all else, we realize that peace is a gift from God, bestowed upon us as we are willing to receive it.—John H. Townsend.

Illustration

WHAT THE BABY NEEDS.   A famous baby doctor examined a feverish and irritable baby and prescribed, "What this baby needs is to be loved." Every baby needs to feel the warmth of someone's arms, the touch of a sympathetic hand, and the sound of a voice that is kind. We could widen the prescription for a sick and irritable world. What this world needs is to be loved. It has had so much of hate. Torn by its hates, saddened by its sorrow, and orphaned by its sins, it must be made to feel again the healing touch of compassion and care.—Carl J. Sanders.

Sermon Suggestions

WHAT IS BROTHERHOOD?   Text: Matt. 23:8. All men are brothers. There is only one race upon earth—the human race. (1) Men are brothers in body. The organs and functions of the body are the same in every race. The blood in the veins of men is everywhere the same. (2) Men are brothers in mind. The great men of all the races think about the basic issues of life—Who am I? Why am I here? Where am I going? (3) Men are brothers in spirit. The high faith of the race is one. God is the father of the human family. Every soul is sacred, justice is the basis of life, love is its saving power, brotherhood its crown, and a beloved community its goal.—Myron J. Taylor.

WHAT CAN WE SAY ABOUT LOVE?   Text: Rom. 5:8. (1) It is of the nature of love, as we know it, to desire the highest good of the one who is loved. (2) It is the nature of love, as we know it, to be willing to give itself to the one who is loved in order to impart the highest good. (3) It is the nature of love, as we know it, to want to possess its object.—John A. Redhead, Jr.

Worship Aids

CALL TO WORSHIP. "Hereby perceive we the love of God, because he laid down his life for us: and we ought to lay down our lives for the brethren. Let us not love in word, neither in tongue; but in deed and in truth." I John 3:16, 18.

INVOCATION. God of all life, we have come here today alone as persons, together in families, all joined in the community of Christian faith. Though we seek your face in the world of life, we ask your blessing in these moments of withdrawal. Take us not from the world, but prepare us for life in the world. Let us not imagine special privilege for ourselves, but let us encourage common opportunity for all. Give us not love for ourselves alone, but make us instruments of your love in the midst of every human place.—Richard D. Bausman.

OFFERTORY SENTENCE. "We then that are strong ought to bear the infirmities of the weak, and not to please ourselves." Rom. 15:1.

OFFERTORY PRAYER. O eternal God, may these gifts represent an inner commitment to love thee above all else and to love our brethren in need because they are loved by thee.

PRAYER. Eternal God, ruler of every nation, we thank thee today for our own land. We are grateful for our American freedom and democracy. May these blessings not keep us from seeing how far short we fall from developing fully the personalities of our citizens nor blind us to the accomplishments of other peoples and different ways of life.

Our land has sinned, O Lord. We have given lip service to equality and denied adequate schooling to some of our children. We have sung of our oneness in Christ and put up the middle wall of partition. Even in our churches we have divided not only color from color but Christian from Christian. Surely thy holiness ought to burn against us in our self-righteousness. Yet thou hast been long-suffering and more plenteous in mercy than we deserve. Forgive us, cleanse us, and heal us of the perversity that makes race and birth and money count for much when thy balances are concerned with righteousness, justice, and brotherhood.—Hillyer H. Straton.

EVENING SERVICE

Topic: How Good Is Good?
TEXT: I Thess. 5:21.

I. *Coerced goodness.* In the average classroom children are pretty good until the teacher leaves the room; then all sorts of things begin to happen. At a more adult level we have all sorts of laws to force people to be good. Coerced goodness, necessary though it is, is not a very high level.

II. *Long-faced goodness.* This describes people who never break the law, and never violate one of the ten commandments. But they are so very negative about it—what one calls "doleful goodness." Jesus went about doing good, but he was never long-faced about it. Rather he talked about a life that was abundant and filled with joy.

III. *Self-righteous goodness.* Jesus wanted men to be good, but he didn't want them to be self-righteous about it.

IV. *Dutiful goodness.* (a) That is, a person does what he or she feels compelled by duty to do. In every home, every church, and every community some fine things have been done because it was one's duty to do it.

(b) A similar form of goodness grows out of a sense of gratitude. Someone does us a favor, someone is kind to us, or someone is good to us, and in fairness we are good to them.

V. To put goodness on the level of Jesus' teaching and example, we have to go higher than this.

(a) Jesus went about doing good not only to those who deserved it but also to those who didn't deserve it. He not only was good to those who were good to him but also to those who opposed him. In the sermon on the mount he said, "If you love those who love you, what reward have you?"

(b) What was significant about the good Samaritan? He did something he didn't have to do. No law could require it. The finest things in history have been done by those people who did more than could have been asked of them.

(c) Our churches have been sustained not only by those who did their duty but also by those who did more than their duty. Psychologically and theologically this is sound. It is those who have forgotten themselves in the welfare of others who have found real meaning in life. It is those who have gone the second mile who have fulfilled the demands of God.— Charles F. Kemp in *The Disciple*.

SUNDAY: FEBRUARY TWENTY-SECOND

MORNING SERVICE

Topic: Keeping the Sabbath

TEXT: Exod. 20:8.

I. The basic faith expressed in this commandment affirms that God the creator is saving love. The ten commandments are listed in Exod. 20 and in Deut. 5.

(a) In the Exodus account this commandment is related to creation. "Remember the Sabbath day to keep it holy . . . in it you shall not do any work . . . for in six days the Lord made heaven and earth" (Exod. 28:8–11). The Sabbath in the book of Exodus is a reminder of God's creative power and activity.

(b) In Deut. 5 this commandment is related to God's redeeming love: "Observe the Sabbath day to keep it holy . . . in it you shall not do any work . . . You shall remember that you were a servant in the land of Egypt and the Lord your God brought you out" (Deut. 5:12–15). The Sabbath in the book of Deuteronomy is a day to remember God's saving love and activity on behalf of his people.

(c) This commandment calls for a day to be kept holy in remembrance of God's creating and saving love. The biblical word "holy" means set apart or consecrated. The Hebrew word "Sabbath" means rest or cessation from labor. Thus this commandment can be accurately paraphrased to read, "Set apart a day of rest as a reminder to you of God the creator whose nature is saving love." This commandment affirms that that one who is the source and ground of our being is saving love.

II. This commandment affirms that our nature as persons is both physical and spiritual.

(a) This ancient law recognizes our physical nature and points out that physical rest and renewal are essential to the health of our physical bodies. This law affirms that every person needs a regular time of rest in the midst of work. Many persons have broken this law and in doing so have broken themselves. All of us know persons who have broken their health because they could not or would not obey this commandment. This law addresses the matter of the stewardship of our physical bodies.

(b) This law recognizes the spiritual dimension to personhood. From the beginning of Israel's life as the covenant people, the Sabbath was a day for worship. The rest and renewal for which the day was set apart included spiritual renewal. The New Testament indicates that Jesus used the Sabbath as a day for synagogue study and worship (Luke 4:16), and his example calls us to be a worshiping community on the day of rest and renewal.

III. If the church would be obedient to this commandment today, Christians must reaffirm the meaning of this commandment.

(a) Let us reaffirm in word and actions the faith expressed in this law, the faith that God, the maker of heaven and earth, is saving love. We reaffirm this truth each time we love others as he has loved us.

(b) Let us become obedient to this commandment as we become better stewards of the physical bodies that God has entrusted to us.

(c) Let us respond to this ancient and yet contemporary law as we affirm the spiritual dimension of our personhood by seeking a closer relationship with God and the Holy Spirit and by sharing in regular joyous Sunday celebration of his power and redeeming love.

IV. This commandment places upon the covenant people a responsibility for the physical and spiritual welfare of others— "your son, your daughter, your manservant, your maidservant . . . or the sojourner . . . that your manservant and your maidservant may rest as well as you" (Deut. 5:14).

(a) This commandment will not let us rest complacently while other persons have physical and spiritual needs that are unmet. We cannot ignore the needs of the hungry, the unemployed, the tired, and the overworked.

(b) This means that a part of the church's Sunday observance will be the planning of some corporate worship experiences at times other than Sunday morning for those who because of job or profession cannot be present at 11 A.M. on Sunday for worship and spiritual renewal. —C. P. Minnick, Jr.

Illustrations

DAY TO REMEMBER.   The social function of the Jewish sabbath and the Christian Sunday is to ensure that, for one day out of seven, a creature who has been cramped and blinkered for six days shall on the seventh remember his creator and live the life of an integral human soul.— Arnold Toynbee.

WHITE RINGS.   In an English coal mine where the water percolates through limestone, interesting stalactites are formed. During the week when the miners are working, coal dust fills the air and it mixes with the minerals that form stalactites, causing that portion of them to be dark gray or black. But on Sunday, when the miners are not working, the dust is not stirred up and that portion of the stalactite is white. These areas appear as white rings on the dark stalactites.—John Wade.

Sermon Suggestions

BEHAVING LIKE CHRISTIANS.   Scripture: Rom. 14:1–15:13. (1) So live that our way of life does not cause our brother to stumble. (2) People are more important than pleasures. (3) Do not tax the conscience of the weak brother. (4) We are to support the weak. (5) There must be full acceptance of one another.—R. Lofton Hudson.

ECHOES IN THE OLD HOUSE.   Text: Isa. 30:21. (1) The echo of memory. (2) The echo of courage. (3) The echo of sacrifice. (4) The echo of faith.—Charles F. Jacobs.

Worship Aids

CALL TO WORSHIP.   "O come, let us sing unto the Lord: let us make a joyful noise to the rock of our salvation. Let us come before his presence with thanksgiving, and make a joyful noise unto him with psalms." Ps. 95:1–2.

INVOCATION.   Almighty and everlasting God, whom the heaven of heavens cannot contain, much less the temples which our hands have built, but who art ever nigh unto the humble and the contrite: grant thy Holy Spirit, we beseech thee, to us who are here assembled; that cleansed and illumined by thy grace, we may worthily show forth thy praise, meekly learn thy word, render due thanks for thy mercies, and obtain a gracious answer to our prayers.

OFFERTORY SENTENCE.   "Remember the words of the Lord Jesus, how he said, It is more blessed to give than to receive." Acts 20:35.

OFFERTORY PRAYER.   Our Father, help us to trust thee more fully and to accept our responsibility toward thy work and thy children who are our brethren in Christ.

PRAYER.   Almighty and everliving God, we thank thee for thy ever-loving presence in our lives. We rejoice in the magnificence of thy purpose, compact of goodness, love, and power. We turn to thee with eager and happy hearts, knowing that we can surely place our reliance in thee, and find in thee the light that never fails, the guidance that never betrays, and the friendship that ever gives us greater strength. Bless our worship this day and all who come here to praise thy name in the sacred fellowship of Christ.

We thank thee for thy presence in our lives through thy Holy Spirit, closer than breathing and nearer than hands or feet, who continually illumines the wonder of thy love as revealed through Jesus Christ, and transforms our human life with the divine glory.

Grant to us, on our part, the faith, the high purpose, and the strong resolve to respond to thy wonderful goodness and to walk in his steps who is our life.—Lowell M. Atkinson.

EVENING SERVICE

Topic: The Door

TEXT: John 10:9.

People go through the wrong doors seeking the meaning and significance of life. Their pursuits end in frustration. Jesus claims to be the access into genuine personhood and being.

I. Jesus is the door to salvation. Jesus opens the way to God. He introduces us to God in a unique manner.

(a) Jesus is the only door to salvation. All others claiming to lead people are "thieves and robbers." Many doors are marked "The Way to God," but Jesus is the right door.

(b) Jesus opens the door of possibilities. The term "saved" in John 10:9 has two ideas. First, it means a rescue from real danger. Second, it means the healing from a disease. Only Jesus can rescue and heal.

II. Jesus is the door of security. Having gone through the door to salvation, the Christian can feel secure. Sheep felt secure because of the faithful, reliable shepherd.

(a) We can feel secure because of the presence of the shepherd. Trials, tribulations, and threats will come our way. The security comes by the continual presence of the good shepherd.

(b) We can feel secure because of the fidelity of the shepherd. He seeks the highest good for his sheep. We can feel secure with a faithful shepherd.

III. Jesus is the door to satisfaction. Jesus said, "I am come that they might have life, and that they might have it more abundantly" (John 10:10). Others promise satisfaction but fail to bring it. Jesus brings genuine satisfaction.

(a) Jesus brings the essence of life. Real life comes with the spiritual birth. Paul said, "For to me to live is Christ, and to die is gain" (Phil. 1:21).

(b) Jesus brings the exuberance of life. The phrase used for "abundant life" means to have life in surplus. The Christian not only has the real life but he also has the superabundance of life.—Harold T. Bryson in *Proclaim.*

SUNDAY: MARCH FIRST

MORNING SERVICE

Topic: From Sin to Salvation

TEXT: Acts 16:30–31.

The Philippian jailer asked Paul and Silas the direct question, "Sirs, what must I do to be saved?" The jailer was asking for information concerning the salvation of his soul. Perhaps Paul had informed him the night before when his feet were locked fast in the stocks, but the man was too occupied to get the message. Paul's response was a direct answer to a definite question. The jailer's response demonstrated the steps to salvation.

I. Conviction of sin is essential. There is

definite evidence that the jailer was deeply convicted of his sin. He was aware of his sin and was under conviction when he "sprang in, and came trembling, and fell down before Paul and Silas" (Acts 16:29). Sinners will not turn from sin until they are under conviction of the presence and the power of sin in their lives.

II. Repentance of sin is required. John the Baptist preached, "Repent ye: for the kingdom of heaven is at hand" (Matt. 3:2). Jesus said, "Except ye repent, ye shall all likewise perish" (Luke 13:3). Paul stated that God "now commandeth all men every where to repent" (Acts 17:30). There is no salvation without repentance. The jailer was penitent as he approached the men of God, and his sins were immediately forgiven.

III. Faith in Christ is necessary. (a) When the jailer said, "Sirs, what must I do to be saved?" the definite reply was given: "Believe on the Lord Jesus Christ, and thou shalt be saved" (Acts 16:31). The answer was simple, direct, and positive.

(b) To "believe on the Lord Jesus Christ" is to leave the case of your sinful soul to him and to completely trust him for your salvation. He is able, anxious, and willing to save the sinner who will trust him. It takes nothing more, nothing less, or nothing else. It requires simple faith in Jesus Christ.

IV. Confession of Christ is demanded. (a) The jailer showed his faith in Christ and his acceptance of him as lord and savior by his attitude toward Christ's servants. He took Paul and Silas into his home, washed their stripes, gave them food, and listened attentively to the word of God.

(b) No true believer will ever be ashamed of Christ. Jesus had something to say on this subject. He said, "Whosoever therefore shall confess me before men, him will I confess also before my Father which is in heaven" (Matt. 10:32–33). When one truly believes in Christ he will confess Christ.

V. Obedience to Christ will follow. When the jailer received Christ, he immediately "was baptized" (Acts 16:33). He followed the Lord in baptism to express his faith in him as lord and master and then "rejoiced, believing in God" (Acts 16:34). Great joy will always follow obedience. It is a great evidence of salvation.—Delbert D. Rose.

Illustrations

TOO FAR AND TOO LATE.   A man started out as a social drinker and ended up as a drunk. He had three little boys at home, and they grew up and followed in his footsteps. One day this man took a good look at himself and decided he wouldn't waste whatever time he had left. He gave his heart to God, became a good member of the church, and soon had the respect of many people. He went to his sons and talked to them about Christ, hoping to persuade them to become Christians. The boys laughed at the old man. They refused to listen. With a feeling of much regret the old man said: "I went too far, stayed too long, and came back too late. My boys followed me into the far country, but they didn't follow me back home."—Pierce Harris.

CHANGE.   A minister went up to an old Jewish rabbi whom he had not seen for many years and said, "Why, you haven't changed a bit since the last time I saw you." The old rabbi looked over his glasses and said: "That's an insult. There are very many ideas within me that have grown since you last saw me." The minister said, "But I mean you look the same." And the old rabbi said: "My son, that still is an insult. There are new wrinkles in my brow and some lines in my face, and every one of them is a symbol of some crisis, and all these crises have deepened my soul. Please acknowledge the lines in my face. Don't tell me I haven't changed."—C. A. McClain, Jr.

Sermon Suggestion

GOD'S PECULIAR TREASURE.   Text: Mal. 3:16–17. (1) What they did for God. (a) They feared God. (b) They spoke with one another. (c) They thought on his name. (2) What God did for them. (a) The Lord gave attention and heard them. (b) God wrote down their deeds in a book of remembrance. (c) God considered these faithful to be his jewels, his peculiar treasure. (d) God spared the righteous as a man spares his son who serves him.—Brian L. Harbour.

Worship Aids

CALL TO WORSHIP. "Oh that men would praise the Lord for his goodness, and for his wonderful works to the children of men! For he satisfieth the longing soul, and filleth the hungry soul with goodness." Ps. 107:8–9.

INVOCATION. Almighty God, who hast given us minds to know thee, hearts to love thee, and voices to show forth thy praise, we would not know thee if thou hadst not already found us. Help us to know thee with pure minds and to praise thee with clear voices.

OFFERTORY SENTENCE. "Let the beauty of the Lord our God be upon us: and establish thou the work of our hands upon us; yea, the work of our hands establish thou it." Ps. 90:17.

OFFERTORY PRAYER. O Christ, may we walk constantly in thy way and work fervently for those causes which are dear to thee.

COMMUNION PRAYER. Our heavenly Father, it is with great and glad thanksgiving unto thee that we meet this hour in this holy place. Here spread before us, poor in spirit and weak in good works as we may be, is the table of thy blessed son, Jesus Christ. Its cleanliness reminds us of a purity of living that we wish were ours. Its simplicity makes us wish our lives were as uncluttered and neat. Its sturdiness bespeaks a strength we wish we felt day in and day out.

In spite of our unworthiness, our frailty, and our sin, thy table stands in our midst, ready, and waiting. O Lord, break through our dullness, our shame, or our cockiness, as the case may be, and let us realize that thy presence is as real as this table which is spread before us. May thy message make its way into our consciousness by the persistent presence of the communion table throughout this service of worship. May it remind us of Jesus, who met with his friends at table, shared a meal with them, blessed the food and gave it to them—to all of them, even to Judas who betrayed him, even to Thomas who doubted him, and even to Peter who failed to understand him—and told them to eat and to drink always in remembrance of him.

Take us, our Father, to the table of our Lord. Tenderly feed us, and then turn us to face once again the demands and opportunities of our daily lives with new faith and fervor.—Jeffery S. Atwater.

EVENING SERVICE

Topic: Why Are You Here?

TEXT: I Kings 19:9.

I. "Why are you here, Elijah?"

(a) Twice that question was asked of the prophet, and twice his conscience was disturbed by it. The first time he was in his dark cave, and he answered it evasively. Then came storm and earthquake and fire —and in the eery silence which followed Elijah heard the "still small voice," the voice of conscience, of inner authenticity, and of personal reality. Then he went out and stood in the cave's entrance. From there he could look out over the world. Again the question came from the Lord: "Why are you here, Elijah?"

(b) Almost as if in a trance, Elijah responded with the same evasive words as before. But immediately the Lord ordered Elijah out on an enterprise of practical service. And Elijah went. In service of God's purposes Elijah found new meaning and fulfillment.

II. What happened to Elijah?

(a) He moved out from his mood of self-pity and morbid self-concern. He stopped feeling sorry for himself. In his cave he was like a woman I read about: "She is blessed with a sympathetic disposition, but she wastes it on herself." Elijah had allowed his sympathies to become poisonously ingrown. The change came when he redirected his sympathies to other persons and their needs.

(b) Elijah found life's deepest meanings not in contemplation but in commitment. Life presents its meanings and purposes to us not in neat intellectual formulas but when we engage in the life of service to which our commitments direct us. Albert Schweitzer said that we should all look for places where we can "invest our humanity."

III. Some of Jesus' contemporaries saw him as Elijah come back to life. I find this very suggestive. It gives me a new perspective on the New Testament, particularly the gospels. Much of Jesus' teaching and activity can be interpreted as exercises in showing persons how they can break out of their dark caves and respond to the great question, "Why are you here?" I find that I can face that question only as I can grasp, and be grasped by, the spirit of Jesus that reaches out to me from the New Testament and in the worship and witness of the church.—J. A. Davidson.

SUNDAY: MARCH EIGHTH

MORNING SERVICE

Topic: Call to Commitment (Lent)
SCRIPTURE: I Tim. 4:1–11.

I. To be a Christian means to be committed to a person—Jesus Christ. Paul tells Timothy there is going to be a time of falling away from the faith. There is going to be a time of discouragement for the church. When that happens, you should "be a good servant of Jesus Christ."

(a) Being a Christian does not mean to be committed to a certain church, to a certain program, to a certain style of music, or to a certain preacher. It means to make Jesus Christ lord over your life.

(b) That is the clarion call which has emanated from the church since the first century. In order to be a Christian you must die to your desires, your will, your feelings, and your ambitions. You must die to yourself and let Jesus not be just your friend, not just your companion, not just your teacher, and not just your savior but your lord.

II. To be a Christian means to be committed to a pattern of living. Paul told Timothy, "Discipline yourself for the purpose of godliness."

(a) The Bible says that the purpose of the Christian life is godliness, holiness, and purity. When you become a Christian, you are not only committing yourself to Jesus Christ but also to the pattern of living which he laid out for you.

(b) This is a word for our day, for all around us immorality is running rampant. There is a point where we Christians take our stand on the matter of morality. There is the world's way, and there is the way of Jesus Christ. We simply cannot have both. We cannot serve the world and Jesus at the same time. We are going to have to make a choice. As a Christian you have already made that choice. The challenge is to follow through on that commitment.

III. To be a Christian means to be committed to a people—to his church. Paul says: "You will be a good servant of Christ Jesus when you are constantly nourished on the words of the faith and of the sound doctrine which you have been following." He adds, "Until I come, give attention to the public reading of scripture, to exhortation and teaching."

(a) Spend time with other believers in the study of God's word is what Paul is saying. Be committed to the people of God, to the body of Christ, to the church.

(b) If you are a Christian, you should be a member of a church, you should be involved in that church, you should be faithful in your attendance at that church, you should support that church, and you should love the church.

IV. To be a Christian means to be committed to a program. That program is called witnessing. Paul says, "Now, prescribe and teach these things."

(a) Share with the world the good news of Jesus Christ. Be a witness about the things that he is doing in his church.

(b) To be committed means to take all

that you have and are and lay it before Jesus and say: "All that I have is yours. Dispose of it as you will."—Brian L. Harbour.

Illustration

EXPERIENCE. A blustering businessman arrived at the eternal gates. He briskly made his way up to the admissions desk and asked for quick service. Whereupon St. Peter asked him what role he would like to play. The question took the busy man by surprise because he had assumed heaven was a place to receive one's rewards and not to be assigned a role. Although he was a church member, he had not given much thought to the nature of the afterlife and the preparation for it. But there flashed into his mind the words of a hymn. It was about the only hymn he knew, and he had learned it in Sunday school. So he gave the line of the old hymn as his answer. It was this: "I want to be an angel and with the angels stand." Whereupon St. Peter after the fashion of a personnel officer took out pen and paper and asked: "Let's see now. What experience have you had?"—Kenneth Foreman.

Sermon Suggestion

MUSTARD SEED FAITH. Text: Matt. 17: 20. (1) A mustard seed is a little thing. It's ever so small, but it is a beginning. (2) The mustard seed has within it the mysterious stuff of growth. The power of a seed to grow and realize its possibilities is almost beyond imagination. (3) The mustard seed does not grow of its own accord but only as it is receptive to the sun and the soil and the rain, only as it is receptive to the powers of the God of all nature.—Robert E. Goodrich, Jr.

Worship Aids

CALL TO WORSHIP. "Worthy is the Lamb that was slain to receive power, and riches, and wisdom, and strength, and honor, and glory, and blessing." Rev. 5: 12.

INVOCATION. Merciful God, forgive the halting nature of our discipleship. We confess that so little of thy love has reached others through us and that we have borne so lightly wrongs and sufferings that were not our own. We confess that we have cherished the things that divide us from others and that we have made it hard for them to live with us. And we confess that we have been thoughtless in our judgments, hasty in condemnation, and grudging in our forgiveness. Forgive us, we beseech thee.

OFFERTORY SENTENCE. "Thy prayers and thine alms are come up for a memorial before God." Acts 10:4.

OFFERTORY PRAYER. O Lord, upon whose constant giving we depend every day, teach us how to spend and be spent for others that we may gain the true good things of life by losing every selfish trait.

PRAYER. It is not thy gift we crave but thee. It is when we lose sight of thee that we have fretful days and sleepless nights; when we forget that thou art our strength and our song that we become anxious for the morrow.

We come to thee because we long for what is real. We have followed the will-o'-the-wisp pleasure to find that it leads to satiety and that nothing makes us so sad as our cheap joys. We have heeded the siren voices of selfish success, and they have mocked and betrayed us. We have made a fetish of security. We are beginning to suspect that our only security is in thee who hast been man's dwelling place in every generation. We have learned to our cost that the things that are seen are transient. We want to stay our souls on the things that are eternal. What is our restlessness and our discontent but the soul's cry for thee?

Strengthen our faith, that we may know that we are not alone in a troubled world; that we may look for the coming of a better world; that, taking firm hold on thee, we may strive to overcome the evil in the world and in ourselves, to do with our might what our hands find to do, to follow more closely in the footsteps of our Lord, upheld by the promise that our labor is not in vain.—Frank Halliday Ferris.

EVENING SERVICE

Topic: Why Go to Church?
TEXT: Neh. 6:10.

I. If you do not attend—and not merely attend but enter into its ongoing life—you are a parasite.

(a) The church is the chief conserver of spiritual values, and it is the institutional embodiment of our Christian heritage.

(1) During the Dark Ages it preserved not only religion but civilization.

(2) It has fostered the spread of education throughout the centuries.

(3) It has nourished the spirit of democracy.

(4) It has built moral attitudes into the lives of millions of persons.

(5) It has made people more humane in their treatment of the weak and underprivileged.

(6) It has goaded consciences to abolish slavery.

(7) It has lifted the position of women and children.

(b) We are the inheritors of this freedom and this humanization in which the church has not been the sole but has been the chief agent. To turn our backs on it is to cast off our cultural heritage.

II. You need to go to church because the church needs you.

(a) Every criticism which can be brought against it is true in some places and in some respects. A very large reason that the church is not in better health is that many persons have shunned it because it was sick.

(b) Its major need is for active and intelligent leadership in congregations as in pulpits. It has done great things; it can do greater. Criticism comes best from those who appreciate its value and who are working from the inside to improve it.

III. The church offers you corporate worship of God in the name of Christ.

(a) Churches are not cinemas, soda fountains, or concert halls and are not to be judged by the amount of entertainment they provide. They are places for worship for the nourishing of the good life and for Christian fellowship.

(b) Conceivably one might maintain a growing religious experience without the church, especially with some other religious organization as a substitute. But not many people do. Among a hundred who say they are going to worship in nature or at home on Sunday morning, there is perhaps one who does.

(c) Instead of asking, "Does one need to go to church to be a Christian?" one might better say, "If one is a Christian, would he want to stay away?"—Georgia Harkness.

SUNDAY: MARCH FIFTEENTH

MORNING SERVICE

Topic: Eternal Life: The Christian's Hope (Lent)
TEXT: I John 3:2.

I. We are sure that there is an eternal life. The confidence which Jesus displayed in life eternal is one of the great assurances of our faith. The life and teachings of Jesus are for us a revelation of the mind of God and our final authority for religious matters.

(a) When he said, "I go to prepare a place for you . . . that where I am there ye may be also" (John 14:3), he proclaimed the reality of the eternal life.

(b) So certain was Jesus of the fact of immortality that he told men as he went voluntarily to his death, "Destroy this temple, and in three days I will raise it up again" (John 2:19).

II. We believe that death sets us free from the limitations of earth.

(a) Because I am limited by flesh and blood, I cannot immediately change my location to some distant place. Because we are of the flesh, we have wrong desires which cramp the fullest expression of the spirit of our spirits.

(b) Jesus must have found the body of

flesh confining for the expression of the spirit of God. He could walk only a few miles a day. He could talk to only a small number of people in an hour. He could use only the language of the people. All of these things limited his activity.

(c) Death set Jesus free. It set the stage for the resurrection. It was the doorway into a new and greater life. The Christian hope is founded on the victory already won by Christ. Death set him free from the limitations of earth. It will set us free.

III. We cherish the Christian hope because of the existence and vitality of the church. The resurrection gave meaning and power to the Christian fellowship, and it continues to do so today.

(a) Central to the thought of the New Testament is the phrase, "That I might know him and the power of his resurrection" (Phil. 3:10).

(1) Think of the scene on that first Good Friday "when from his side the nearest fled and death was close in sight." The loyal eleven had dwindled to a few heart-sick women and a single beloved disciple who witnessed the crucifixion. They all were filled with disillusionment and despair. There were only a weary few who were paying their last respects to a dead leader who was now gone.

(2) Then something happened. From sorrow came joy. From despair came startling hope. From utter disillusionment came great expectation. From helplessness came heroism. Eleven men became heralds of a new era in the world's history.

(b) Jesus had risen from the dead. There were those who disputed this, but men do not find staying power in a fantasy or a lie. The power of Jesus' resurrection led Peter and others to a martyr's death for they were convinced that Jesus lived. They had intimate knowledge of the daily presence of his spirit. And because he lived they were sure that they too would live. The existence of the church bears witness to this conviction.

IV. The Christian hope is that death and frustration are overcome when we live in Christ.

(a) Death becomes an episode by which we are released from bondage of the pre-sent physical body. To the Christian it is a gateway through which the soul of man passes into a nobler life unfettered by the things of earth. Frustration is overcome by confidence in God's eternal care. Sin, sorrow, and weakness are finally defeated.

(b) If we follow the teaching of Jesus, heaven is that eternal condition of spiritual life in which sin is finally overcome and in which fellowship with God and others leads us into an ever richer and fuller life.

V. The Christian hope involves belief in judgment. Our lives are judged at death. While God is merciful and kind, he is also holy and righteous.

(a) There is plenty of evidence in the scripture to indicate that the day of judgment will be a bad day for those who have not responded to God's love but have chosen to live in sin.

(b) The scripture reveals that it will be a happy day for those who have responded to his love and lived for him. It will be their privilege of continuing in fellowship and love with God throughout eternity.

VI. Our Christian hope is founded on confidence in God. The richness of our present experience of his fellowship can be so great that this earthly life is too small to hold it. Our hope of eternal glory is anticipated by the light of his presence now illuminating our lives. In fellowship with God and the people of God we come at last to understand the whole meaning of the Christian faith concerning the never-ceasing love of God.—A. Ray Adams in *Wesleyan Christian Advocate*.

Illustrations

TO WHAT PURPOSE?   In one of the dialogues of Lucian, Charon, who has left the underworld for a day in order to see what human life is like, is talking with Hermes while the two look out on the pageant of humanity from a great height. As he looks upon Milo of Croton, the great athlete who has just picked up a bull and is carrying it along the race course while the Greeks applaud, Charon says: "He is mightily elated. What is one to think? Does it ever occur to him that he must die someday?" Later, still looking down from a great height, Charon says to Hermes: "Now that we are up here, how would it be for me to cry out to them at the top of my voice to abstain from their vain endeavors and to live with the prospect of death before their eyes? 'Fools, I might say, why so much in earnest? Rest from your toils. You will not live forever. Nothing of the pomp of this world will endure nor can any man take anything hence when he dies. He will go naked out of the world, and his name and his lands and his gold will be another's and ever another's.' If I am to call out something of this sort, loud enough for them to hear, would it not do some good? Would not the world be better for it?"—Lynn Harold Hough.

TRANSFORMATION.   Faith can transform doubts into discoveries, obstacles into opportunities, conflicts into challenge, grief into gratitude, sorrows into springboards, and limitations into launching pads.—William Arthur Ward.

Sermon Suggestion

HOW PRAYER CHANGES THINGS.   Text: Rev. 3:20. (1) Prayer changes things by changing a person's conviction of what is important. (2) Prayer changes things by making a person submissive to the will of God. (3) Prayer changes things by exposing a person's life to the presence of God. —Frank B. Fagerburg.

Worship Aids

CALL TO WORSHIP.   "Having therefore, brethren, boldness to enter into the holiest by the blood of Jesus, by a new and living way, which he hath consecrated for us, let us draw near with a true heart in full assurance of faith." Heb. 10:19–20, 22.

INVOCATION.   Almighty God, the giver and lord of life: we bless and praise thee for thy merciful keeping and gracious care, for all the gifts of thy providence and grace, and for all the blessings which manifest thy fatherhood. We thank thee for the faith which sustains us, the hopes which

inspire us, and the light by which we daily walk. We thank thee for Jesus Christ, who, by the life he lived, the temptations he conquered, the gospel he taught, and the cross he bore, has brought us nigh to thee and closer to one another.

OFFERTORY SENTENCE.   "Whatsoever ye would that men should do to you, do ye even so to them: for this is the law and the prophets." Matt. 7:12.

OFFERTORY PRAYER.   O God, who hast given us thy son to be an example and a help to our weakness in following the path that leadeth unto life, grant us so to be his disciples that we may walk in his footsteps.

PRAYER.   O Lord our God, each time we worship thee we are stricken by a consciousness of the poverty of the lives we offer thee. We have not loved thee with all our hearts. We have loved ourselves too much and our neighbors too little. The life we live is not like the life of Jesus, and the mind in us is not the mind of the master. Let the piercing light of thy truth so shine into our lives this day that we shall see ourselves as thou dost see us.

Uncover, we beseech thee, O Lord, all the little falsehoods whereby we lull ourselves into complacency. Prick our consciences awake to the heroic needs of the day in which we live. Set our sights higher so that we may not be satisfied with lives conformed to the standards of this world. We hunger with an appetite that is not eased by anything less than the bread of heaven. Give us, we pray thee, both the wisdom and the strength to live as those who aspire to be thy children.

Be in this fellowship this day, O God, for we have gathered together in thy name. Let this be a fellowship of healing for the downcast, strengthening for the weak, and for all of us one of forgiveness and reconsecration to the great task that is our common mission, even the bringing in of thy kingdom.—Nathanael M. Guptill.

EVENING SERVICE

Topic: What Is Faith?
    TEXT: Heb. 11:1.
    I. What is faith?
    (a) Faith is not blind credulity. It is not believing what isn't so. The queen in *Alice Through a Looking Glass* said to Alice, "I am a hundred and one, five months, and a day." Alice replied, "I can't believe that!" To which the Queen responded in a tone of pity: "Can't you? Try again. Draw a long breath and close your eyes!" Too long some advocates of the Christian religion have said to us: "You can't believe? Try again. Draw a long breath and close your eyes." But faith is not credulity. Faith is not blind.
    (b) Faith is not a substitute for knowledge. There never will come the day when faith can supplant knowledge or knowledge replace faith. The more we know the greater will become our faith. Faith and knowledge walk down the same road together, and we need both if we are to be Christians of stature.
    II. The life of faith is a life of adventure. (See Heb. 11:8–10.) Ask any successful businessman if he has not had to venture out more than once on faith. Ask any college student. He never would have entered college if he had not had faith that he could make good. Ask any physical scientist if he ever made progress without the leap of faith that we call an hypothesis which took him from proven knowledge to a new frontier of knowledge. Intelligent man is so made that he is always venturing beyond the known to the unknown by a leap of faith. What is Christian faith? In a classic definition of Christian faith, the writer of Hebrews says, "Faith is the assurance of things hoped for, a conviction of things not seen."
    (a) Christian faith makes the daring assumption that there is a God and that he is the kind of God whom Jesus revealed him to be.
    (b) Christian faith dares to believe that God continues to be active in the universe that he created.
    (c) Christian faith dares to believe that God is not only powerful but good.
    (d) Christian faith dares to believe that God loves each one of us as if there were only one of us to love and that he is willing to go to any length to forgive and to redeem people like ourselves.
    (e) Christian faith dares to believe that Jesus' death on the cross is God's highest expression of his love and forgiveness and that the Christian interpretation of life, far from being a poetic fancy, is the one stubborn, irrefutable fact on which this mad world has now smashed itself.
    (f) Christian faith dares to believe that any one of us can live a victorious life in this world and face eternity not with fear but with a spirit of eager adventure and profound assurance.—Ivan B. Bell.

SUNDAY: MARCH TWENTY-SECOND

MORNING SERVICE

Topic: The Lordship of Jesus (Lent)
    TEXT: John 13:13.
    Scholars tell us that the first declaration of the church, its earliest creed, was the simple statement "Jesus is lord." And it is for the purpose of repeating this affirmation in word and in life that the church exists today.
    I. He is entitled to be called lord because he has won the allegiance of men and women in all times and places not by satisfying their wishes and desires but by "drawing them," as the New Testament says, to himself.
    (a) The New Testament represents him as saying to his followers, "You did not choose me, but I have chosen you." And that is deeply true. He is not the kind of lord they or we should have chosen.
    (1) The lord we should have chosen according to our natural preferences would have come to assure us that we can find the meaning and goal of life by the enlargement and extension of ourselves, by self-realization and self-affirmation. But this lord comes telling us that the only way to

the central core and substance of life's meaning is by losing ourselves into it.

(2) The lord we should have constructed out of our desires would have been someone to teach us how to do for ourselves everything necessary for happiness, peace of mind, and self-fulfillment. He would show us how to be truly independent, self-sufficient, and autonomous.

(b) The Lord Christ does from the very first something we never can do for ourselves. He comes to offer God's forgiveness not only for what we have done and have left undone but for what we are.

(c) He brings something other than the response to our desires. He comes bringing truth. This is not the way we would like to understand the universe and our own life within it. This is rather how, in the light of Christ, we are obliged to see that things really are.

II. The church affirms that Christ is lord because he has captured and transformed our understanding of our own humanity. He has given a new dimension and a new hope to our vision of what it means to be human. This he has done not merely by being himself a man but by winning our acknowledgement that we have seen in this man what humanity is intended to be.

(a) The church knows from its experience—reaching across nineteen centuries and into every corner of the world—that there is this fact that has been called "the universal appeal of Christ."

(b) His power to awaken reverence, loyalty, and devotion is entirely independent of the boundaries and classifications that divide the human family. There is nothing parochial about it. The appeal of Christ has no relationship to factors of race, geography, social status, or education. In this sense it is universal.

III. The church knows that Christ is lord because it knows that he has taken command of history and has radically changed our human situation.

(a) This was what brought the church into existence. It did not appear because a company of people, mourning a lost leader, decided it would be a good thing to preserve the memory of his teaching and perpetuate his ideals. The church came

into being because they knew that the event of Jesus Christ had transformed their existence and had changed the direction of human life and history.

(b) In him they had met a new kind of life of confidence, joy, and freedom. For they had seen beyond all doubt that the maker and ruler of the universe, the God and Father of the Lord Jesus Christ, was one to be utterly trusted. He could be trusted through suffering, infamy, defeat, and death. In this event had been disclosed to them not only God's power and righteousness but also his mercy and forgiveness.

(c) Because whenever they looked toward Christ in remembrance and faith they came in touch with this power of new life, they were sure that he himself was alive. And wherever he was, there was his church. That is the simplest definition of the church and the most comprehensive.

(d) The church is known not by the magnitude of its own claims for itself nor by its outward splendor and success. It is known by his presence—in truth, in charity, in self-forgetfulness, and in the power of a new life.—Truman B. Douglass.

Illustration

WITH WHOM HE SAILED.   An Englishman had spent his life as a sailor in the British navy, sailing in the fleet of Sir Francis Drake. He had never won any fame nor wealth, and there were not many personal achievements for him to bask in during his old days. One day someone said to him, "You really haven't made much of your life, have you?" "No," the old sailor replied, "I've not made much. I've been cold, hungry, shipwrecked, and desperately frightened at times, but I've been with the greatest captain who ever sailed the seven seas."

Sermon Suggestions

REVOLUTIONARY CHRISTIANITY.   Text: Luke 12:49–50 (NEB). The messiah who came to set fire to the earth heralded a revolutionary Christianity. This revolutionary Christianity as a force of rebirth and renewal was meant to be the dynamic of history. The Christian faith was to be the harbinger of change and progress, constantly exchanging the old decadent order for the new emerging order. (1) A revolutionary Christianity as the dynamic of history cannot be considered apart from its messianic and revolutionary leader, Jesus Christ. (2) A revolutionary Christianity as the dynamic of history has never been lost entirely in the fellowship of believers. These can be found in all countries, in all centuries, and among all races in the form of a revolutionary church. (3) The conversion or the rebirth of personality lies at the heart of a revolutionary Christianity. (4) Revolutionary Christianity is relevant to society and is concerned with the renewal and reconstruction of that society. (5) Revolutionary Christianity needs regenerated men to effect the reform and renewal of society.—Frank H. Epp.

THREE GREAT PROMISES.   Text: I Thess. 1:5 (LB). Paul gave the Thessalonian church three great promises. (1) A promised rest (II Thess. 1:7). (2) A promised reward (II Thess. 1:11). (3) A promised reunion (II Thess. 2:1).—C. Neil Strait.

Worship Aids

CALL TO WORSHIP.   "The kingdoms of this world are become the kingdom of our Lord, and of his Christ; and he shall reign for ever and ever." Rev. 11:15.

INVOCATION.   O Lord, who hast taught us that the love of money is the root of all evil, teach us to care for what money can buy—not security but opportunity, not withdrawal from the world but a full participation within is, and not prestige but use. Help us to handle all the goods of life in the spirit of thy son who out of his poverty made many rich.

OFFERTORY SENTENCE.   "Greater love hath no man than this, that a man lay down his life for his friends." John 15:13.

OFFERTORY PRAYER.   We praise thee, O God, for thy countless blessings and pray that thou wilt accept these gifts in gratitude in Jesus' name.

PRAYER.   Father, make our worship this day worthy of the high company we keep in the Christian fellowship.

Accept our thanks for calling human ministers of genuine goodness. They have opened our eyes, and because of them we know something about redemption. For the ministry of mothers and fathers who make good homes, we are grateful. For friends who help to make life beautiful, we are grateful. For the loved ones close to us who through personal sacrifice have given us a great heritage, we are thankful.

Grant that, in this high company where we have come to worship, your love and their love will transform us. Move us out of here determined to cut ourselves off from the festering grudges we have borne, determined to change the unbrotherliness we have practiced into being "our brother's keeper," and determined to make the unclean in us clean.—Kenneth Watson.

EVENING SERVICE

Topic: His Decision and Ours
Scripture: Phil. 2:4–7.

I. At some point in his life Jesus had to make a decision. Perhaps it was the natural result of several likeminded, similarly directed vows of purpose. Or perhaps it was the first thing recalled from his former glory with the Father—a recollection of a commitment from which all other choices and vows would unveil a progressively realized purpose. But at some point the big decision had to be made.

II. The decision which Jesus had to make is a decision we have to make, and it is the hardest decision to make because it involves a choice between our way and God's. It is a choice that can mean standing against the shifting and often violent tides of public favor and popular opinion and a choice that will always be met by the resistance of candid intimations from well-meaning family and friends and will have to resist scores of candy-coated persuasions to "get with it" and "do your own thing." It is a decision that requires much.

III. The decision to choose God's way over our own is not easy because we must die to self in order to realize it. It is no small matter that Jesus says: "If any man would come after me, let him deny himself and take up his cross and follow me. For whoever would save his life will lose it, and whoever loses his life for my sake will find it." Jesus knew the difficulties of choosing the way of the cross over a present experience of a life full of vitality and all too immediately realized promises.

IV. Apparently God's way is not natural to the characteristics of the flesh. This is why the book of Hebrews speaks of Christ as having shared in our flesh and blood nature, on one hand, and of his having been tempted in every respect as we are, on the other. But that is exactly why we must make a decision, a strong one, to follow God. We won't come to him by the characteristic bent of our nature. We must choose against our natural proclivities as a conscious effort to make God's way our own.

V. We are continually bombarded with choices which will either support or detract from a decision to accept and follow God's way. Sometimes consistency to that decision will lead us to the garden of Gethsemane. Sometimes we will have to shirk comfort for challenge. But whoever said that the way of the cross was an easy path to follow? Certainly not Jesus.—Randal Lee Cummings.

SUNDAY: MARCH TWENTY-NINTH

MORNING SERVICE

Topic: The Uniqueness of Christ (Lent)
Text: Phil. 2:9.

I. His birth was unique. Since there is a baby born every second, what was there about this baby that compels a world of men two millenniums removed from him to stop and take notice of his birthday? Why reckon history and date correspondence from it? Why give presents, prepare feasts, and illuminate cities to celebrate it? Why is the music around the world dominated by songs about his birth? These things are done for no other baby. But there are valid reasons why they are done for him.

(a) Of no other babe could it be affirmed that his birth was not the beginning of his existence. If Jesus had no existence prior to his conception and birth of the virgin Mary, then there was no incarnation of the son of God, only the birth of another human being, remarkable though he might be. And if there was no incarnation, then there is no savior, only another sinful man needing a savior himself.

(b) He was the only babe conceived without a human father. But is this surprising? Is it likely that this unique event for which God had been making preparation for four millenniums would occur in the ordinary course of nature? If science demands that every event must have an adequate cause, the presence of a sinless man in the midst of universally sinful men surely implies some such miracle of origin.

(c) No other babe was born without taint of sin. "That holy thing which shall be born of thee," said the angel. In the case of the birth of one who was to be called the son of God, the entail of sin, the normal transmission of the racial heritage, was interrupted by the direct act of God. Had he himself been tainted with sin, how could he "save his people from their sin"?

(d) He was the only babe of whom it could be claimed that he was more than man, for he called himself both the son of God and son of man—one person but possessing two natures—the God-man. Yet these natures were so really united as to constitute them a single person acting with a single consciousness and will.

(e) He was the only babe of whom it could be said that his death was the supreme purpose of his birth. To all others, death is inevitable and unwelcome, to be escaped for as long as possible. To Christ death was avoidable but deliberately chosen. "No man taketh [my life] from me, but I lay it down of myself. I have power to lay it down, and I have power to take it again." Martin Niemoller said: "The cradle and the cross were hewn from the same wood."

II. His claims and assertions were unique. He claimed to be the only way of approach to God. "I am the way . . . no man cometh unto the Father, but by me." No claim could be more definite and more absolute. Spoken by someone without his moral authority and unsupported by the quality of life Jesus displayed, it would have sounded puerile.

(a) He asserted that he was the full and final revelation of God expressed in terms of human life. He defined his work in terms of God's activity. "He that hath seen me hath seen the Father." "I and my Father are one." In his acts and attitudes he claimed that men could see the acts and attitudes of God. In him was to be found the answer to every problem, the meaning of life, and the solution to the riddle of the universe.

(b) He claimed the power to forgive sin, and the full significance of this fact was not lost on the Pharisees. "Who can forgive sins but God only?" they blustered. And they were right, for he was indeed claiming to be the son of God. For this blasphemy they were more determined than ever to do away with him.

(c) In Rev. 1 the glorified Christ makes five significant assertions which further support his claim to be unique.

(1) "I am Alpha and Omega," a metaphor implying absolute completeness.

(2) "I am the beginning and the ending," the origin and goal of all creation. All things began with him, and all things will end with him.

(3) "I am he that liveth and became dead." Two amazing thoughts are enshrined in this assertion. The one who died was alive before his birth, and the living one became dead and is alive forevermore.

(4) "I am alive for evermore," for death was powerless to hold its prey.

(5) "I have the keys of death and hades," keys wrested from the tyrant who had the power of death—the devil.

III. His character was unique, a fact conceded by athiest and believer, by non-Christian historian and naturalistic philosopher alike.

(a) Christ alone among men possessed a character that was absolutely symmetrical in which there was neither excess nor deficiency.

(b) He was unique in that he was sinless, for scripture everywhere either states or assumes his sinlessness. "In him is no sin," asserted John. "He did no sin," affirmed Peter. "He knew no sin," said Paul. "He was tempted, yet without sin," wrote the author of the letter to the Hebrews.

(c) Unlike the holiest of men, never once did Jesus evince any discontent with himself of his achievements or manifest any sense of sin. Yet he was the humblest of men.

IV. The death of our lord was no less unique than his birth. If the indescribable humility of God is seen in the incarnation, what shall we say of the humility involved in the shameful death of the son of God?

(a) His was the only death which fulfilled millenniums of prophecy. In the details of his death on the cross, no fewer than thirty-three distinct prophecies were fulfilled.

(b) Of no other person could it be claimed that his death was not inevitable. "It is appointed unto men once to die." But for himself Jesus claimed the power to either lay his life down or to take it up again. To him death was no necessity but a deliberate choice. At the end, death did not overcome him. He summoned death as his servant, and by a sublime act of his will, dismissed his spirit—not victim but victor.

(c) He was the only person on whom death had no claim. It is true that "the wages of sin is death," but since he had no sin, his life had not been forfeited and was available to be offered as an atoning sacrifice for the sins of the world.—J. Oswald Sanders.

Illustration

WHAT CHRIST SAYS. What is the best word Confucius has for the man who is sinking? "Profit by your experience." What is the most hopeful message which Buddha has for him? "Struggle." What is the most encouraging teaching of Hinduism for the sinking man? "You may have another opportunity in the next incarnation." What does Mohammed say? "Whether you sink or whether you survive, it is the will of God." And what does Jesus Christ say? "Take my hand."—John R. Mott.

Sermon Suggestions

THE BODY OF CHRIST. Scripture: I Cor. 12:12-31. (1) The unity of the body of Christ. (2) The harmony of the body of Christ. (3) The sympathy of the body of Christ. (4) The ministry of the body of Christ.—Stephen F. Olford.

CHRIST THE PHYSICIAN. Text: Matt. 4: 23. (1) Christ the physician heals the body with the curative force of faith. (2) Christ the physician imparts a power to transcend the body's limitations and passions, making it possible for his followers to say with the apostle Paul, "I keep my body under." (3) Christ the physician imparts a healthy-mindedness which dispels the gloom of darkening thoughts and breaks the vicious circles of fixed ideas. (4) Christ the physician heals the sick in heart when they walk through the valley of the shadow of death.—Ralph W. Sockman.

Worship Aids

CALL TO WORSHIP. "Be strong and of a good courage, fear not: for the Lord thy God, he it is that doth go with thee; he will not fail thee, nor forsake thee." Deut. 31:6.

INVOCATION. Our heavenly Father, we thy humble children invoke thy blessing upon us in this hour of worship. We adore thee, whose nature is compassion, whose presence is joy, whose holiness is beauty, whose will is peace, whose service is perfect freedom, and in knowledge of whom standeth our eternal life. Unto thee be all honor and all glory.

OFFERTORY SENTENCE. "Walk in love, as Christ also hath loved us, and hath given himself for us as an offering and sacrifice to God." Eph. 5:2.

OFFERTORY PRAYER. O God, help us so to practice by our gifts and our lives the divine principle of goodwill that in our homes, our communities, and among all the nations of the earth men may enjoy the boon of peace.

PRAYER. O God, our Father, we thank thee for all the gifts with which thou hast filled our lives; for the daily miracle of light and shadow, work and rest, life and love; for high thoughts which uplift us and for pure hopes which bind and beckon us to thee.

We thank thee for disappointments and failures which have humbled us, for pain and distress which have taught us our need of thee, but most of all for our faith in thee and for the fullness of joy which thy presence brings. Thou hast opened thy heart to us in great mercy. May we open our hearts to thee in penitence and gratitude.

From our meditations here may we learn that our lives, so frail and fallible, may be shaped after a noble pattern. So may we rise to thy expectation of us. So may we endeavor this and every day to be what thou desirest, to do what thou hast commanded, listening to the inner voice of thy spirit, searching the depths of our hearts, leaving no spot uncleansed, and sparing not the sin with which it may cost us most to part.—Charles C. Albertson.

EVENING SERVICE

Topic: The Sources of Joy
Text: Gal. 5:22.

I. Joy comes from knowing that we are safe and secure in God's love. As Christians we ought to be assured of our salvation and security in the love of God. We have sinned, we have rebelled, we have disobeyed, and we have neglected so many opportunities to be kind and to do good. After we have repented and turned to God through faith in his son Jesus, we have the promise of forgiveness.

II. The source of a Christian's joy is being in harmony with God.

(a) Sin produces alienation—alienation on man's part and not God's. The Bible never speaks of God being alienated from man. Always it is man who is separated from God. The Bible depicts sin as a barrier that men have raised between themselves and God. But when we turn to God in faith and accept his love which he revealed in the cross, the Bible says that we are reconciled.

(b) When friends who have been alienated are reconciled there is joy. How much more joy there is in the life of believers who have experienced this harmony with their heavenly Father.

III. A third reason for joy is the knowledge that we have a never-failing friend. Of all life's treasures, few are more valuable than friendships. As long as we hold on to the hand of our divine friend, we shall be able to do things that otherwise we could not do.

IV. Joy comes from the knowledge that all of God's promises will be fulfilled. One of the sources of joy, happiness, and contentment in life is the assurance that when a person makes a promise, it will be kept. All of us have been disappointed, frustrated, disillusioned, and saddened because promises made to us were not kept. But when God makes a promise, he always keeps it. The promises of God are dependable, and that brings joy.

V. Joy comes from the knowledge that we shall eventually triumph over all the troubles, inequalities, and enemies of life including death. That life has its difficulties, its disasters, and its problems no one can deny. And death does invade our homes and take our loved ones. Our friends die and something dies within us. The promise of Jesus is that if we are faithful and if we endure to the end, the ultimate victory shall be God's and God's victory shall be ours, and that brings joy.

VI. Joy comes from being in the company of the saints. When we worship, Jesus is there and all the company of heaven is there.—John C. Middlekauff.

SUNDAY: APRIL FIFTH

MORNING SERVICE

Topic: **What the Cross Shows (Passion Sunday)**

Text: Rom. 5:10.

I. The cross shows us what God is really like. It reveals his very heart, and we see it to be a heart of infinite love.

(a) The New Testament presents the cross as the supreme expression not just of the love of Jesus but also of the love of God. Any theory of the atonement which imperils the unity of the Godhead by depicting a merciful son whose self-sacrifice is a means of placating an angry Father so as to induce the Father to love sinners whom he did not love before, stands condemned at the bar of the New Testament. In everything he did, and supremely in his death on the cross, Jesus acted in perfect obedience to his Father's will. His prayer in Gethsemane is the clearest proof of his obedience "unto death, even death on a cross."

(b) The cross was not an event due to chance or to human violence alone. In some mysterious way it was necessitated by the providential purpose of God. The cross as an event in time is the outcrop on the plane of history of an eternal atonement in the heart of God. "As God was incarnate in Jesus," wrote D. M. Baillie, "so we may say that the divine atonement was incarnate in the passion of Jesus."

(c) No doctrine is adequate that does not see in the cross the extent to which God's love is willing to go to reconcile man to himself. In the New Testament God is always the subject of reconciliation and man the object. It is the love of God that initiates the process of reconciliation.

II. The cross shows us what sin is really like. (a) This means not merely that the crucifixion of Jesus was the blackest deed ever perpetrated by human wickedness, true as that is. It means that the cross reveals—in the words of Anselm—"of what great weight is sin." Its weight is such that to lift and remove it involves the incalculable cost of Calvary.

(b) Only shallowness of thought could ever imagine that to forgive sin is an easy matter for God, almighty ruler of the universe though he be and great as is his yearning desire to reconcile the sinner to himself. A human father who treats his child with good-natured indulgence, condoning all his misdeeds and glossing over his delinquencies, cannot be said to love the child deeply. How much less can the holy love of God for his children treat their sins as a matter of small importance.

(c) It is not a case of God's justice restraining his love. To quote D. M. Baillie again, "God must be inexorable towards our sins; not because he is just but because he is loving; not in spite of his love but because of his love."

(d) In the cross we see the inexorable love of God dealing realistically with sin in a way that enables him to restore the sinner to a right relationship with himself without compromising his own essential character as the just and holy God. (See Rom. 3:25–26.) But this was achieved only by the payment of the greatest price that even God himself could ever pay; he "did not spare his own son." Nothing could reveal more graphically the awful seriousness and the terrible weight of sin.

III. The cross shows us what man is really meant to be like in his relation to God.

(a) Reconciliation, the mending of a broken personal relationship, necessarily makes demands on both parties to the relationship. There must be, on the part of the offended party, a genuine desire for reconciliation and a loving readiness to forgive. But this cannot bring about the reconciliation unless it is met by an equally genuine desire for reconciliation on the part of the offending party. The cross reveals how completely the former requirement is fulfilled by God's attitude towards man. But what of man's responding attitude towards God?

(b) A really genuine desire for reconciliation on the part of a sinner must entail a sincere penitence for his sin and a humble willingness to submit to to the penalty which is its just desert and a steadfast resolve to sin no more. Only as sinful man approaches God with such an offering of penitence, submission, and obedience can he receive God's gracious offer of forgiveness and restoration to fellowship with himself. The tragedy of man's condition is that his captivity to sin renders him utterly incapable of ever making such an offering for himself.

(c) As we look at the cross we see Christ, who by his incarnation identified himself so completely with humanity as to be able to act representatively on behalf of men, offering to God the perfect penitence, submission, and obedience which is their proper response to his grace. Thus Christ has fulfilled the conditions, on the human side, necessary to the reconciliation of sinful men with God. He did this not as man's substitute so as to spare man himself from doing it but as man's representative so as to enable man to participate in his offering by joining himself to Christ by faith. The offering which we could never make for ourselves we may make in Christ by trusting implicitly in his offering made on our behalf and so making it our own.

(d) In the cross all the conditions upon which the reconciliation of God and man depends have been fulfilled. And the fulfillment of the conditions, on the human side no less than the divine, is the work of God himself. "God was in Christ reconciling the world to himself." Owen E. Evans in *The Expository Times*.

Illustrations

PHILOSOPHY. Mother Teresa's philosophy is summed up in the prayer which hangs on the wall of the mother house in Calcutta. "Let each sister see Jesus Christ in the person of the poor; the more repugnant the work on the person, the greater also must be her faith, love, and cheerful devotion in ministering to our lord in this distressing disguise."

GOD'S CONCERN.   The concern which Jesus had for the disinherited is the concern which God has for men. All his sympathy for the downtrodden is God's sympathy for us. All his willingness to suffer and die is the willingness of God to endure sacrificial suffering that we might be saved. Here is the complete revelation that brings us to our knees. Here is the experience which opens our eyes and unstops our ears. Here is all the satisfying fullness of the love of God for men. In Christ we see the goodness and severity, the mercy and the judgment, and the wisdom and the foolishness of God.—Gerald Kennedy.

Sermon Suggestions

CROWN HIM WITH MANY CROWNS. Texts: John 13:13; Rev. 19:12. (1) His revelation of truth. (2) His redemption by atonement. (3) His ritual of remembrance. (4) His rule over life. (5) His return in glory.—Paul S. Rees.

CHRIST AS PHYSICIAN.   Texts: Mark 1: 29–34; Luke 5:31. (1) He believes in God. (2) He is interested in his patient. (3) He is a diagnostician. (4) He listens well. (5) He speaks the truth in love. (6) He accepts hope.—Jerry Hayner.

Worship Aids

CALL TO WORSHIP.   "I will praise thee with my whole heart. I will worship toward thy holy temple, and praise thy name for thy lovingkindness." Ps. 138:1–2.

INVOCATION.   O God our Father, creator of the universe and giver of all good things: we thank thee for our home on earth and for the joy of living. We praise thee for thy love in Jesus Christ who came to set things right, who died rejected on the cross, and who rose triumphantly from the dead. Because he lives, we live to praise thee, Father, Son, and Holy Spirit, our God forever.

OFFERTORY SENTENCE.   "This is the thing which the Lord commanded, saying, Take ye from among you an offering unto the Lord: whosoever is of a willing heart, let him bring it, an offering of the Lord." Exod. 35:4–5.

OFFERTORY PRAYER.   Our Father, forgive our indifference and neglect, and help us to hear thy call to partnership with thee in making a new heaven and new earth.

PRAYER.   O Lord God, most high and yet most close to us in spirit, we enter anew into this experience of meditation and prayer in the sense of offering.

We offer our prayers, our hymns of praise, our participation in the Lord's Supper, our dollars-and-cents, but, even more than these things, we offer ourselves —our bodies, spirits, and minds in humble thanksgiving for life and breathing, for health and vitality, for prosperity and fortune, for opportunity and challenge, for growth, though sometimes difficult, and for change, though sometimes painful. Our Father, we are thankful for your love —your continuing and constant love—so well expressed in the life, death, and resurrection of your son. Lead us to demonstrate that love again and again in our relations with our fellow human beings. We all realize how easy it is for us to neglect, overlook, pass by, or even hate others for any of many reasons. But we earnestly and fervently pray that you would speak to us every day to reinforce our good intentions to put into action that love that dwells within us so that we may feel more a child of your creation and your redemption.— Arthur H. Bishop.

EVENING SERVICE

Topic: Lesson in Geography
Text: Luke 23:33.

If someone were to ask you to name the most important geographical point in our world, would you hesitate? The Christian should not hesitate, for the most important geographical point in the world is Calvary. The hill of Calvary might seem insignificant to most of the world, but the events that took place there changed all of history.

I. At Calvary, God met man. God met man, not man met God. The initiative of the meeting was in God's hands. He chose the way and the place where he would meet man. We learned at Calvary that God meets man in love, grace, and forgiveness. There have been many great meetings of history, but the meeting at Calvary was the most important for the day of the Lord had come, and God came to meet man.

II. Calvary is geographically important because there the savior met sin. This little hill outside the city wall of Jerusalem seems an unlikely place for the savior and sin to meet. Calvary is the place of Roman crucifixions, the place of death. "The wages of sin is death." The savior meets sin and pays the price of death for all men.

III. At Calvary love met hate. It seems unreasonable to think of these meeting in one place, but at Calvary they met. The love of God confronted the hate of men. Throughout the history of Israel God had told his people that he loved them. This love is proven at Calvary where love dies for the unlovely and the unlovable. The love of God is stronger than the hate of men.

IV. At Calvary life meets death. The followers of Jesus are engulfed in the reality and sadness of the death of their Lord. But when Jesus cries, "It is finished," death is conquered and life is assured. The disciples were soon to learn that the lord conquered death and all who would believe in him would live eternally.—James E. Scirratt.

SUNDAY: APRIL TWELFTH

MORNING SERVICE

Topic: His Convictions and Ours (Palm Sunday)

Text: Matt. 20:18.

At the threshold of the greatest week in all time, Holy Week, we try to understand what Jesus was really doing as he rode through the streets of old Jerusalem on a donkey and permitted the people to shout their glad hosannas and cry, "Blessed is he that cometh in the name of the Lord."

I. Whatever else he may have been doing, Jesus was affirming some of his basic convictions.

(a) Seeing the storm clouds gathering and envisioning the cross at the end of this very street through which he now rode in majestic splendor, Jesus knew that he had to make known his stand before it was too late. Knowing full well the consequences, Jesus was of the firm conviction that God had sent him into the world to proclaim some eternal truths.

(b) One of those truths was that he was God's anointed—the messiah. Realizing that probably only a handful of people would catch the full significance of it all, Jesus felt under obligation to make this journey in this way so that in years to come people like ourselves might sing with real conviction, "All glory, laud, and honor, to thee, redeemer, king."

III. Because Jesus had great, compelling convictions, he set "his face steadfastly to go to Jerusalem."

(a) In that act of resolution he was seeking to fulfill what he had become convinced was his life purpose. By speaking out against the corrupt temple practices and by holding fast to his idealism in the face of the cross, Jesus did more to establish real life for mankind than the Roman Empire had accomplished throughout its long history.

(b) Ever afterward when men were to look at the cross, they would be reminded of one who believed so much in truth that he was willing to die rather than deny it. Because of his convictions, Jesus was able to live out his life for a cause which would outlive his life on earth. He succeeded in setting up a standard of life which would lead to life abundant for all men.

IV. We too live in proportion to the convictions which we hold. Just as what a man believes determines the way he lives, so his convictions determine the things to which he will give his best resources.

(a) We are not referring now to the little petty opinions which we often hold in spite of much evidence to the contrary. We are talking about the really great issues which draw forth our best allegiance and command our finest resources of body, mind, and spirit, the things which set our eyes on great goals and direct our hands and feet to tasks which command all of us there is.

(b) As we worship in the presence of the living Christ, singing our hosannas to him, let us resolve that we are going to become people of his quality of conviction about the really important things in life. When we do that, we will be showing that we believe with him that to have convictions is to live.—Homer J. R. Elford.

Illustration

THE BRIDGE.   Here is the high priest, untouched by sin, eternal, who not only stands on the side of men in complete and utter self-identification, representing them to God, but also stands absolutely on the side of God to bring him to men. Thus the veil is rent in twain from the top to the bottom. The unabridgeable gulf is bridged once and for all. The initiative of the divine forgiveness—this too is made actual in Christ. For now—and this is what makes Christianity such a miracle to crown all miracles—the oblation is not man's but God's. It is God who makes the offering in the person of his son. The cross is the one true altar, the defeat of the devil, and the atonement of the world. And the resurrection seals the act of reconciliation.—James S. Stewart.

Sermon Suggestions

SELF-EXAMINATION ON GOOD FRIDAY.
Text: John 19:17–18. When we look deep into ourselves, honestly, we come to understand that (1) if we had been among the disciples, we would have slept as Jesus prayed in the garden; (2) if we had been in Peter's shoes, we would have denied knowing the prisoner; (3) if we had been among Pilate's praetorian guard, we would have helped weave the crown of thorns; (4) if we had been in Pilate's judgment seat, we would have seen the political wisdom of letting one man die to prevent a riot; (5) if we had been among the chief priests, we would have wished this trouble-maker silenced; (6) if we had been among the crowds, we would have shouted, "Crucify him"; and (7) if we had been among the soldiers at the foot of the cross, we would have joined in throwing dice for his garment.—Richard L. Ullman.

DAY OF CONTRASTS.   Text: Matt. 21:5. (1) There is the contrast between a sorrowing Christ and a rejoicing crowd. (2) There is the contrast between a steadfast Christ and a fickle crowd. (3) There is the contrast between a Christ going toward his crown and a crowd going toward a crime.—W. Mackintosh Mackay.

Worship Aids

CALL TO WORSHIP.   "O Zion, that bringeth good tidings, get thee up into the high mountain; O Jerusalem, that bringeth good tidings, lift up thy voice with strength; lift it up, be not afraid; say onto the cities of Judah, Behold your God!" Isa. 40:9.

INVOCATION.   Our Father, thou who wast received amid the shouts of an earlier day, open our hearts and journey into our inward parts. Help us to lay aside all prejudices, forsake all sins, and overcome all biddings that might bar thy entrance. Let thy entrance into our hearts be triumphant. Conquer our fears, silence our unbelief, and quicken our faith. Lead us through thy Spirit to spiritual victory and conquest.

OFFERTORY SENTENCE.   "If any man will come after me [saith Jesus], let him deny himself, and take up his cross daily, and follow me." Luke 9:23.

OFFERTORY PRAYER. As thy faithful disciples blessed thy coming, O Christ, and spread their garments in the way, covering it with palm branches, may we be ready to lay at thy feet all that we have and are and to bless thee, O thou who comest in the name of the lord.

PRAYER. Almighty God, our Father, as we enter this holy week we join the throngs who on this day down through the ages have shouted songs of praise, saying: "Hosanna to the son of David. Blessed is he that cometh in the name of the Lord!" Through long years of half-hearted devotion we have followed many kings. Time was when our delight was in things, our joy was the praise of men, and our security was in arms and in dollars. Lord, God of hosts, be with us yet, lest we forget.

Now, O God, amid the shadows of this latter day, while the sons of perdition strive to build a house on shifting sand and the ashes of former pleasures fly away with the wind, we shout the praise of the only king of men whose empire is everlasting. We remember that he is humble and common, keeping no court, putting on no airs, commanding no armies, and approached at will by the humblest of his subjects. Yet the mightiest rulers of the earth are pygmies beside him, for the citadel of his kingdom is the human heart and his authority is the authority of God.

Give unto us, O Lord, the sense of how great a kingdom it is to which we belong. Open our eyes to the vision of the mighty train of his followers, his unarmed soldiers who have "climbed the steep ascent of heaven through peril, toil, and pain." May the fire in their hearts kindle a like flame in our own souls, that this generation may not be without its witness and that the vindication of the faithful may not much longer be delayed.

Remind us, O our God, of the message of the prophet: "Not by might nor by power, but by my Spirit, saith thy God." So shall our trust be placed where victory is assured. So shall our lives fulfill their holy destiny.—Nathanael M. Guptill.

EVENING SERVICE

Topic: Dimensions of Palm Sunday
Text: Luke 19:37–40.

As Jesus enters Jerusalem we are witnesses to a heroic act, to buoyant enthusiasm among the disciples, and to a majestic faith. Palm Sunday shows Jesus in his heroism and his insurgency, and it shows the disciples in their eagerness and vigor and makes the faith more beautiful and more majestic.

I. The heroism of Jesus is seen most clearly as he turned his face toward Jerusalem.

(a) He knew full well what he was doing as he rode on that donkey, hailed by friends and cursed by Pharisees. The center of his religious and political world lay in Jerusalem—the two centers of power he had by necessity alienated and frustrated as he traveled from village to village. Jesus knew that he must finally face his religious and political enemies.

(b) Clearly his whole ministry would be stymied unless he could settle the issues which caused people to fear and even hate him. So he did what he knew he must. He went to the heart of the problem.

II. Consider the disciples. St. Luke calls them a multitude. Clearly they were more than a mere handful. Consider their rather astonishing behavior.

(a) There they were in the open air, enthusiastically praising God in loud voices. It made a lot of the bystanders feel rather awkward. Some of the Pharisees shouted out over the hosannas: "Teacher! Rebuke your disciples. Tell them they are going too far. Tell them to shut up! Tell them their enthusiasm makes us feel uncomfortable."

(c) Enthusiasm literally means God within—en-theos. It means a passion for the faith, a sense that the heart and not just the head is involved in the faith.

III. Jesus liked enthusiasm, overstatements, and irrationality in the name of God. He indulged in a bit of that himself.

(a) Jesus got rather excited about the disciples' excesses. Their immoderate behavior didn't embarrass him at all. He responded to the Pharisees, "I tell you, if these were silent the very stones would cry out."

(b) The phrase is ambiguous—probably a common saying of the day. But it has the feel of freedom. To the creative Christian the words seem to be a message of salvation. Apparently Jesus thought it so obvious that the disciples should be ecstatically praising God that if the disciples didn't do it the very stones would become animate and shout out to heaven the wonders of God.

(c) The Christian faith is heroism and courage and enthusiasm and majesty and power and glory and peace and mighty works. Palm Sunday is the living out of Christianity.—Craig Biddle III.

SUNDAY: APRIL NINETEENTH

MORNING SERVICE

Topic: The Resurrection and the Life (Easter)

Scripture: John 11:17–27; 20:24–31.

What shall we make of this story and particularly of Jesus' words, "I am the resurrection and the life"? Is there good news for our lives to be found here? What would Christ tell us through this odd resurrection story born out of season?

I. Jesus speaks of the resurrection from the dead in the present tense. Jews in Jesus' day commonly believed that God would raise up his faithful from the dead at the end of time to dwell forever with him. This was what Martha thought Jesus meant when he said to her, "Your brother will rise again." "I know that he will rise again in the resurrection at the last day," she replied. The startling new thought comes as Jesus transports that far-off day into the present, declaring, "I am the resurrection and the life."

(a) In Jesus is the power of life itself. Through him the dead are quickened into life now. One's hope no longer lies in some far-off resurrection day but in the newness of life Christ offers today. Where Christ is there is resurrection from the dead. That is a staggering claim. This is a declaration of his present divine life-giving power to conquer death.

(b) Jesus is shown to be supremely the great battler against death. This is his vocation. He has come that the world may have life—here and now and always. Death is the ultimate enemy to be conquered. Easter proclaims that with Christ's resurrection the last enemy of humankind has been defeated. Death was not defeated at the end of history but in the midst of history. Jesus was raised not on the last day but in our time.

II. If Christ is the resurrection from the dead, then we need to expose to him the places in our lives where death holds reign. We need consciously to think of the way death has a grip on us.

(a) Christ who is the resurrection and the life is ready now to do his resurrection work in you. It is all too true that death's power over our daily living is such that we tend to feel half dead much of the time. Why do you walk around half dead when there is newness of life available here and now? Christ is the resurrection. The resurrection is not a distant event to take place on the last day. The resurrection is a person—Jesus Christ. You can experience resurrection now. Through him new life can grow out of hopelessness and despair, deadened bodies can awake to life, atrophied minds can become alert and sensitive, and hardened hearts can come alive with caring.

(b) There are no situations without hope. Christ is creatively present in every circumstance of life. It is never too late to start over again. We need never to be bound by the death-dealing forces of life that would entrap us and hold us down. With Christ every day is resurrection day. The power that raised Christ from the tomb is sufficient to resurrect you from the daily deaths that now hold you.

III. Christ who is the resurrection cares for us beyond the grave. The new life he gives us here and now is life that persists beyond the grave.

(a) Life is the gift of Christ both now and always. The same power that assures real existence for us in this earthly life will, after the death of the body, raise us up to renewed existence in a world beyond.

(b) Jesus is the resurrection and the life. The judgment of life has been brought against death. That judgment hung in the balance on Good Friday and agonizingly on through Black Saturday. Then the verdict came in. Easter proclaims Christ victor over earth's last enemy—death. Let us bring our death-bound lives to Christ for renewing.—Colbert S. Cartwright.

Illustration

GOD IN ACTION. It is immensely significant that the first Christians never preached the resurrection simply as Jesus' escape from the grave, as the reanimation of one who had died, or as the return of the master to his friends. They always proclaimed it as the living God in omnipotent action. Their insight taught them that it was what lay behind the resurrection that mattered. And what lies behind it is this—God vindicating the dreams for which Christ died, God ratifying righteousness, justice, and truth against the evil powers that hate these things and seek to crush and crucify them, and God announcing his invincible divine determination to make Christ lord of all.—James S. Stewart.

Sermon Suggestion

HOPE OF RESURRECTION. Text: Acts 26:8. (1) Resurrection was the supreme demonstration that all Jesus' words were true. (2) Resurrection was the supreme demonstration that Jesus was more than man. (3) Resurrection was the supreme demonstration that Jesus died for all men. (4) Resurrection was the supreme demonstration that you and I will rise again.— Marcus L. Loane.

Worship Aids

CALL TO WORSHIP. "Blessed be the God and Father of our Lord Jesus Christ, which according to his abundant mercy hath begotten us again unto a lively hope by the resurrection of Jesus Christ from the dead, to an inheritance incorruptible, and undefiled, and that fadeth not away, reserved in heaven for you." I Pet. 1:3–4.

INVOCATION. O God, we thank you this Easter morning for the eternal beauty and everlasting power of the resurrection of Jesus. We pray that these days shall see our Christ emerging from the tomb in which our generation has placed him—a tomb which we have closed with the stone of our selfishness and sealed with our hardness of mind and heart. Fill us this day with the spirit of reverence and humility because we are permitted to sing your praise. Help us to remember that we are your children, living in your divine presence in our human lives. Make us faithful to duty and worthy of your love, through Jesus Christ our risen Lord.

OFFERTORY SENTENCE. "Therefore, as ye abound in everything, in faith, and utterance, and knowledge, and in all diligence, and in your love to us, see that ye abound in this grace also." II Cor. 8:7.

OFFERTORY PRAYER. As we bring our offering today we thank thee, O God, for the happiness of our earthly life, for peaceful homes and healthful days, for our powers of mind and body, for faithful friends, and for the joy of loving and being loved. We pray that these blessings may come to abound throughout all the world and to all people.

PRAYER. Our Father and our God, it is Easter again, and we are gathered in this congregation to worship thee. Give us the will to worship thee in spirit and in truth. Help us to be made ready to be found by thee. Help us to prepare ourselves to be confronted by thee. Thou didst create us, and thou hast given us life and a world in which to live. Thou dost love us with a love we find hard to understand. Thou didst give us the power to determine our own destinies, even the power to reject thee and to rebel against thee.

We have misused the world thou hast

given us. Instead of beautiful gardens, we have too often created slums. Too often we have exploited the resources of thy world for to our own selfish advantage.

We have failed in our relationship with the people in thy world. Instead of creating a climate of love, we have created a climate of bitterness, suspicion, prejudice, and hatred. Instead of building a world of justice for all, we have allowed pockets of injustice to flourish.

As we look upon the cross, help us to realize the pain and agony our waywardness has caused. Help us to know the cost of our separation from thee. Help us to understand the pain and agony thou dost suffer because of our rebellious willfulness.

But as we look at the resurrection and realize that all our sin, selfishness, prejudice, hate, bitterness, and willfulness cannot defeat thy purpose for us, cannot overcome thy love for us, and cannot finally separate us from thee, grant that we may give thanks for thy mighty love that will not let us go.

May we stand tall this day, ready to accept thy love, ready to be renewed, and ready to reach toward our potentialities with thy very real and ever-present help. Lift us up that we may together sing the alleluias—shout, "Christ is risen"—to celebrate the death of our self-centered selves and the birth of our new life in thee. —Lyle V. Newman.

EVENING SERVICE

Topic: Three Roads of Easter
Text: II Tim. 1:10.
I. The road from doubt to faith.
(a) This is expressed in the words of the disciple Thomas, who hearing from the others the accounts that Jesus had risen from the dead said: "This is impossible. Except I see with my own eyes, I cannot believe." Then later on the basis of his own experience with the risen Christ he affirms, "My Lord and my God."
(b) To be human is to have some doubts and to be uncertain. That is the way we are made. More than half the world is Thomas, and half of every human heart is

Thomas too. Many people are sitting in churches this Easter halfway believing, halfway saying with Thomas: "Too good to be true. Unless I see, I cannot believe."

II. The second road is from emptiness to meaning expressed in words from the Easter story: "They saw that the stone was rolled away."
(a) The world's greatest picture of the emptiness of life and the world's greatest picture of the meaning of life have to do with the rolling of a stone. Albert Camus in his essay, "The Myth of Sisyphus," says that our human life is basically absurd, like that of Sisyphus, a character from ancient Greek mythology, who was condemned by the gods to the difficult labor of rolling a huge stone up a mountain to the summit, only to watch it by its own weight roll back down again, whereupon he must return to the lower level and go through the same process again, and after that again and again and again. That absurdity or emptiness is an accurate picture of many lives today.
(b) The meaning of life also comes with the rolling of a stone. From the resurrection faith, symbolized by the stone rolled away from the door of the tomb, comes the faith that our lives can have meaning and can be infinitely rich. This does not simply have to do with the assurance of survival after death. It means also the continual renewal of life here and now so that every day has such quality and meaningfulness that it is worthy of lasting forever.

III. A third road goes from death to life.
(a) *Life After Life* by Raymond Moody tabulates experiences of more than one hundred people who come very close to death or are declared dead by physicians but who come back and record what they went through. One says: "I began to experience the most wonderful feelings. I couldn't feel a thing in the world except peace, comfort, ease, just quietness. I saw a big light. I felt that all my troubles were gone, and I thought to myself how quiet and peaceful and I don't hurt at all." Most of the reports are similar in significant details. There is an unusual light, not blinding but warm and welcoming, seeming to exude love. There is meeting with

friends and loved ones. There is peace.

(b) Our faith in the resurrection and our belief in immortality are based on our faith in God through Jesus Christ, a God who cares for us and a God who is absolutely trustworthy forever.—Winfield S. Haycock.

SUNDAY: APRIL TWENTY-SIXTH

MORNING SERVICE

Topic: What More Can You Say After the Sermon?

Text: II Sam. 7:20.

What more can we say after our preacher's sermon?

I. When we have heard a good sermon, we can say "Hallelujah!" and then go out and live a hallelujah life.

(a) "Hallelujah" means "praise the Lord," and a hallelujah life is one in which everything we do is dedicated to God's praise and glory. Certainly David lived a hallelujah life. He wasn't a perfect man, but he was a man after God's own heart. He tried to live a life that praised God in every way. Hallelujahs and praises echo again and again in the psalms which are attributed to him.

(b) What enables a Christian to live a hallelujah life? He has more reason to be happy than anybody can imagine. He knows that God loves him with a love unending. Like David, he knows that God is for him, not against him. Because of his faith in Jesus, he knows he has been saved. Because he has Jesus Christ as savior and lord, he has no fear about anything. (See Rom. 8:38–39.) When one is a Christian, his whole life becomes a doxology of praise to God.

II. We can say "Amen."

(a) At the conclusion of every worship service, after the benediction, the people are supposed to say, "Amen," which means, "Let it be so." This is what David in II Sam. 7:25–26 after Nathan's sermon. David went on to live in such a way as to make Nathan's sermon a reality in his life and in his nation's life. David said "Amen" and became an "amen" to his people.

(b) To say "Amen" is a biblical way of saying, "I will be responsible." When a fellow Christian says "Amen," he is saying to his pastor, his fellow Christians, and to his God that the words of his pastor's sermon have become the word of God to him and that he intends to let that word become flesh in his own life. A Christian's "amen" tells the world: "I entered this place an hour ago to worship. Now I am ready to go out into the world to serve." When a Christian says "Amen," he is saying to all who can hear: "This is my church, my community, and my world, entrusted to me as a steward by God who created me. Here I am responsible."

III. We can say, "Thanks be to God," and then go out to live a life of thanksgiving.

(a) Most church members appreciate their pastor and the time he spends in preparing and delivering his sermons, and one of the finest gifts they can give him is to express their gratitude to him sincerely at the end of the service.

(b) Even more important is that they thank God for speaking to them through their pastor's words and then seek to make gratitude an integral part of their lives. That was the main theme of David's response to God's word in Nathan's sermon. He was so grateful for what God had said that his whole response was a prayer of thanksgiving to God, ending with the words, "For thou, O Lord God, hast spoken, and with thy blessing shall the house of thy servant be blessed forever" (7:29).—Raymond W. Gibson, Jr.

Illustrations

END OR BEGINNING. Leonard Griffith sometimes at the close of a worship service just before he pronounces the benediction asks the congregation to turn around and face the front door of the church. Then he asks, "Is that door an entrance or an exit?" I did this once at the close of a service. A layman said to me later, "It is both." He was right. There is a time for the church to be the gathered church in worship. We must meet God in his house of worship and hear his word that we may be prepared to go out into the world to witness for him. If our worship ends at the front door of the church as we leave the sanctuary, it is false worship. A lady came to a church one morning as the service was being concluded and asked an usher, "Is the service over?" He wisely replied, "No, madam, the service is just beginning." From the high hours of worship the church scatters out into the community to be God's people in his world.—W. Aubrey Alsobrook.

PARAPHRASE.   Two men went to church to pray. One was a so-called leading citizen, and the other was a teacher. The prominent citizen stood and with his eyes looking upward said: "O Lord, I thank thee that I am not like these professional men, even as this poor teacher. I pay half the teacher's salary. It is my money that built this church. I subscribe literally to foreign missions and to all the work of this church. It is my money that advances this cause." The teacher's prayer was quite different. He simply bowed his head in deep humility and said: "God, be merciful unto me. I was that man's teacher."

Sermon Suggestions

PAUL'S WORD FOR PASTORS.   Text: I Tim. 4:12. (1) In practical life the minister is to be sensible (v. 6). (2) In personal life the minister is to be sociable (v. 12). (3) In pastoral life the minister is to be spiritual (v. 13). (4) In private life the minister is to be scrupulous (v. 16).—Stephen F. Olford.

LYRIC RELIGION.   Text: I Cor. 14:15. What are the tests of a good hymn? (1) Is the content Christian and biblical? (2) Is the spirit of the hymn worshipful? Does it express Christian feeling or or merely impress Christian doctrine? (3) Is the style lyrical? Does the hymn appeal to the imag-ination with words that help a person to see, to feel, and to move?

Worship Aids

CALL TO WORSHIP.   "Ho, every one that thirstest, come ye to the waters. Incline your ear, and come unto me: hear, and your soul shall live; and I will make an everlasting covenant with you, even the sure mercies of David." Isa. 55:1, 3.

INVOCATION.   We turn our minds unto thee, O God, that thou wilt give us deeper insight into the meanings of the life of thy son, our Lord. We turn our hearts unto thee that thy love may flow through them. We turn our wills unto thee that thou mayst guide us in all that we do and in all that we say.

OFFERTORY SENTENCE.   "Give unto the Lord the glory due unto his name: bring an offering, and come before him: worship the Lord in the beauty of holiness." I Chron. 16:29.

OFFERTORY PRAYER.   O Father of our Lord Jesus Christ, we dedicate these offerings to the fellowship of him, whom to know aright is life eternal.

PRAYER.   Almighty God, who canst give the light that in darkness shall make us glad, the life that in gloom shall make us joy, and the peace that amidst discord shall bring us quietness, let us live this day in that light, that life, and that peace, so that we may gain the victory over those things that press us down, over the flesh that so often encumbers us, and over death that seemeth for a moment to win the victory. Thus we, being filled with inward peace, light, and life, may walk all the days of this our mortal life, doing our work as the business of our Father, glorifying it because it is thy will, knowing that what thou givest thou givest in love. Bestow upon us the greatest and last blessing, that we, being in thy presence, may be like unto thee for evermore.—George Dawson.

EVENING SERVICE

Topic: Is Church Membership Necessary?

TEXT: Ps. 34:3.

There are many compelling reasons why Christians should be responsible members of a company who meet to profess Jesus Christ.

I. Jesus had a high estimate of the church. (a) He instituted the church, commissioned the disciples to baptize peoples from all nations into it, and stated that "the powers of death shall not prevail against it" (Matt. 16:18). (See also v. 19.)

(b) Paul speaks of the supremacy of Christ over all authorities and then asserts that this authority is given to Christ. God "made him the head over all things for the church, which is his body" (Eph. 1:22–23).

(c) Those who accept Christ's teachings in the sermon on the mount or who pray the Lord's Prayer need to be consistent and appreciate what Jesus Christ taught about discipleship and the church.

II. Christians have a need for togetherness. (a) As families are motivated to come together for special events, so Christians are motivated to meet together for worship, fellowship, and service. This is innate. There is no solitary religion. The church is a natural expression of the need to celebrate together.

(b) Most of the Bible is addressed to a corporate group of believers, not just to individuals. The Bible does not know separatism from the body of believers as most non-church members state it today. Biblically, you are either for the group of believers or you are against it.

(c) To believe in Christ is to belong to his body—the church. No matter how small or insignificant a Christian you may be, scripture teaches that you have a vital contribution to make to the corporate group.

III. Church membership is in keeping with a realistic concept of life and service.

(a) Christianity is not to be equated with mysticism. Christ's way requires study, discussion, sharing, and work. As belonging to a business, industry, or club requires certain disciplines and responsibilities, so does being a Christian.

(b) Believers should be involved responsibly together in ministry to the world. Christ taught his people that those irresponsibly attached to his church are as dead branches.

IV. The church accomplishes much good in the world. (a) Who would deny the influence of the church through the centuries? Hospitals, educational institutions, and many of our social and welfare causes were initiated or prompted by the church.

(b) A Christian can feel satisfaction in knowing that his or her few gifts and abilities will be multiplied thousands of times around the world through the mission of the church. Committed Christians are the incarnation of Christ in today's world.

V. Is church membership necessary? I would not limit God by saying that one must be a member of the church to be a Christian. God works outside the church. Yet if one understands that the church is an institution committed to belief in God's grace and forgiveness, that it is entrusted with the work and mission of Jesus Christ, and that all who believe are of the same family, then every Christian should want to be a responsible member of God's people. Those believers who have a case against the church should stay with it to make the church what it should be. Dropping out is copping out.—Bert Van Soest.

SUNDAY: MAY THIRD

MORNING SERVICE

Topic: Discovering the Church as a Family (National Family Week)

TEXT: Eph. 2:18 (TEV).

I. A successful family is one where love has become a living reality in human relationships—as natural as breathing, eating, and sleeping.

(a) Such love lasts through conflict, turmoil, turbulence, trouble, poverty, and prosperity. These are outward circumstances which can beat against a life but before which that life can stand masterfully if there is love within the home.

(b) The church is a family with a similar function. We have gathered as a family because we love the Lord. We are brought into a meaningful fellowship through our common love of the God revealed in Jesus. If there is one place where love should be the dominant virtue and spirit, it is in the family of God which we call the church.

(c) In our common love of Christ we come to love each other. One must follow the other or it has no meaning.

(1) Jesus said the essence of the Christian religion is to love God and to love our neighbors as we love ourselves. There are different forms of love. The love you have for your spouse is unique as is your love of your parents. This is a kind of love which develops with the long-term intimacies of daily living in the family. The same spirit of loving and being loved should be manifest in the family of God—the church. It is not divorced from sentiment, but it will be faulty if it is only sentimental.

(2) The command to love you is "an undiscourageable willing of only the good for you." If you know that as a member of this Christian fellowship I love you with this kind of abiding goodwill and I know that you have a similar feeling toward me, we have discovered the church as a family. We are mutually strengthened in our faith. We love because God first loved.

II. Within the home children grow in the pattern of their parents.

(a) The example parents set by their attitudes and actions are determinative of what that child will be fifteen or twenty years from now. It is an awesome responsibility we parents carry. That responsibility begins with a genuine agape form of divine love in the human scene. This means an unconditional love, and we will never stop loving him however unlovable our child may prove to be and will never reject that child however unacceptable he may prove to be.

(b) The child acquires more than physical resemblance by being born into a particular family.

(1) He grows up with the same politics as his parents. His attitude toward school is often parentally determined. His social personality develops or fails to develop on the basis of the social personality of his parents. Certainly his value system begins within the family circle. Though he may deviate from that in later years, he still bears within himself the marks of the family's value system.

(2) In the spiritual realm he learns about spiritual values—for good or for ill—from the spiritual values which govern the lives of his parents. The church becomes important to him or unimportant depending on how his parents feel about it. His practice of religious faith in large measure will be determined by what the practices are within the home. Is the Bible a family book that is read? Is prayer a part of the family rituals? Is involvement in the church life assumed as a normal family practice? Children grow spiritually only when that growth is encouraged and abetted by loving parents within the home.

(c) The church is a family where we learn how to grow more like Jesus. We pattern our lives after his. We seek, as he did, to learn God's will and purpose for our lives. We seek to find, as he did, the strength to do what God calls us to do.

(d) Because we feel the need to keep growing in the faith, we gather as a congregation in worship to renew our dedication, to tighten the tent pegs of our faith, and to share in the corporate praise of God in thanksgiving for his divine love which through Christ has redeemed us.

III. The church as a family calls forth the unique gifts in every member. It is not unlike the home in this.

(a) The home makes possible the development of the talents and aptitudes of its members. Some are musically inclined, others are sharp in classroom studies, and others are gifted in some line of sports. When love controls the family circle, each member is given the opportunity within the limitations of finance and geography to develop those God-given talents and aptitudes.

(b) The church is a family which gives opportunity for its members to grow in the spiritual gifts of God's grace. The church does not give the gifts of God's grace. God does. But God has brought us together in a church family so that we may grow and develop those gifts which strengthen the life of our fellowship.

(c) The church can be a dynamic family of Christian love only as we all share our time, our talents and abilities, and our money to make possible the ministry of Christ among us. We need to keep always before us the charter of our Christian community: "It is through Christ that all of us are able to come in the one Spirit into the presence of the Father."

(d) The church must exist as a family outside these walls. We gather only to scatter. We come here to worship God, to praise him with thanksgiving, to confess our sins, and to find forgiveness through his love. We need this time apart for renewing our faith and regaining our strength. We gather to go out in this familial spirit of love to live our faith in our homes and community, to witness to God's love and redemption, and to serve others in God's holy name.—Hoover Rupert.

Illustrations

TWO FAMILIES. Max Jukes, who lived in the state of New York, did not believe in Christian training and married a girl of like character. From this union 1,026 descendants have been studied. Three hundred were sent to the penitentiary for an average of 13 years each. One hundred and ninety became public prostitutes, and there were 100 drunkards. On today's economic scale, the family cost the state over $6 million. There is no record that they made any positive contribution to society.

Jonathan Edwards, who resided in the same state, believed in Christian training and married a woman of like mind. From this union 729 descendants have been studied. Three hundred became preachers of the gospel. There were 65 college professors, 13 university presidents, 60 authors of good books, three United States congressmen, and one vice-president of the United States. It is impossible to underestimate the contributions this family made to the state of New York and to the country. The Edwards family is a sterling example of the biblical principle: "Train up a child in the way he should go: and when he is old, he will not depart from it" (Prov. 22:6).—Tim and Bev LaHaye.

FOR LITTLE STEPS. Hans Christian Andersen, the Danish writer who enriched the world with his fairy tales, had been ambitious to write important works for adults, but he finally became reconciled to the fact that his most important work was the fairy stories which he had written for children. During his last illness he wrote down instructions for his funeral. One direction read: "Most of those who will follow me at my funeral will be little children. Have the beat of the music keep time to little steps."

Sermon Suggestions

GOOD NEWS FOR THE STRONG. Scripture: Luke 19:1–10. Many Christians have an easier time reaching out to someone who's down and out than someone on their own level or above. (1) You can help such persons to see that Christianity is more than health and wealth. (2) You can help such persons to recognize their need to appreciate what they do have and recognize and acknowledge the one from whom their blessings come. (3) You can help strong persons by assisting them to see that God isn't interested in the slightest in how their performance measures up to others. (4) The most important element in helping the person who seems to have it all together is to build a relationship of mutual trust and respect, the context in which these other ways of helping can happen.—Arthur McPhee.

THE HOME'S SEVEN C'S.   Text: Ps. 16:6 (1) Commitment. (2) Communication. (3) Consistency. (4) Caring. (5) Comradeship. (6) Christian love. (7) Christ-centered.— Charles L. Copenhaver.

Worship Aids

CALL TO WORSHIP.   "Ye shall know truth, and the truth shall make you free. God is a Spirit: and they that worship him must worship him in spirit and in truth." John 8:32; 4:24.

INVOCATION.   Almighty and everlasting God, in whom we live and move and have our being, who hast created us for thyself so that we can find rest only in thee: grant unto us purity of heart and strength of purpose so that no selfish passion may hinder us from knowing thy will and no weakness sway us from doing it and that in thy light we may see life clearly and in thy service find perfect freedom.

OFFERTORY SENTENCE.   "Take heed what ye hear: with what measure ye mete, it shall be measured to you: and unto you that hear shall more be given." Mark 4:24.

OFFERTORY PRAYER.   Dear God, help us to become unobstructed channels that thy love may flow through us to others and our gifts may be used for the proclamation to all men of thy saving goodness.

PRAYER.   Eternal God, who hast shown us in the life of Christ the kind of lives thou wouldst have us live, we bring before thee this day the homes of our church and those who live therein.

We rejoice for those homes where love for thee binds the members of the family in a deeper love for one another. Grant that the abiding faith of these families may be made even stronger as the years go by,

so that the things which threaten to destroy the home may have little effect upon this fortress of thy kingdom.

We pray for the parents of our congregation. May they be given the strength, patience, and ability to rear their children wisely. Especially do we ask that we, as parents, may come to realize that we are the priests of God and that our homes are a church—for it is there that we perform those duties that indicate our concern for the souls of our children.

We pray for the children of our congregation. May they find in our homes love and security. Give to them a realization that we, as their parents, are people, too— people whose added years have given added experience.

May the homes of our church, O God, be bound together in a bond that is stronger than blood or kinship, and may that bond be a higher love to the creator of life and love and homes.—W. H. Kirby.

EVENING SERVICE

Topic: Shadows of Influence (National Family Week)

TEXT: Matt. 26:74.

I. Have you ever watched a group of little children "playing house" and noticed how the "father" betrayed his relationship with his own father, and how the "mother" said things to her "children" that her own mother sometimes said to her? Both of them—the "father" and the "mother"—were acting out their ideas of what parents ought to be like, which is why they were trying to imitate the parents they knew best—their own.

II. All of us are influenced by those we see around us. We are imbued with the spirit of our family, take on the mannerisms of our favorite teacher, and try to walk the way our most important hero walks. Our relationships with other people play a big part in determining the kind of people we are. We get our personalities through our contacts with other persons and assimilate their values and attitudes and outlook on life and make them our own.

III. When Peter tried to deny his Lord

MORNING SERVICE

Topic: When You Say Mother You Say a Lot About God (Mother's Day)

TEXT: Deut. 32:18.

I. When you say mother, you say a lot about God's creativity. (a) Moses said God is the one "who gave you birth." There is something of awe in the presence of a mother giving birth. She is participating with God in the act of creation.

(b) When I was a boy, medical science had not advanced to the point where it has today, and many mothers died in childbirth. The preachers would wax eloquent as they appealed to an appreciation of motherhood on the basis of how mother descended into the very "shadow of the valley of death" that we might be born. It was and is true.

(c) When we say mother, we say a lot about God for that is what God did that we might be born anew. God descended into the valley of death in Jesus on the cross, and by the mighty act of creation we are made new creatures in Christ.

(d) In the early church baptismal fonts were designed in the shape of a pregnant woman for in baptism one was born into a new life. Motherhood speaks to us of physical and spiritual creativity.

II. When you say mother, you say a lot about God's nurture. (a) In this song of Moses from which our text comes is also the image of God as the mother eagle "that stirs up its nest . . . spreading out its wings, catching them." This is a picture of little eaglets whose time has come to leave the nest, and the mother is pushing them out. First she stirs up the nest. With her mighty claw she reaches down through the fluffy down and pulls up the thorns which are part of the structure of the nest, making it very uncomfortable. Then she pushes her young out of the nest, and they fall toward the ground, fluttering, unable to fly. She swoops under them and catches their fall and repeats this until they are able to fly on their own.

(b) A good mother doesn't want her young to go on being dependent on her, and so she prepares them for a life of independency. Nurturing the young, teaching them by precept and example, and training them in the affairs of life is what parenting is all about.

(c) God is like a mother, the mother eagle, who wants those eaglets to be independent and to get on with life. To be sure, we will never come to be independent of God for life depends on God. But we can grow into mature human beings and live responsible lives. God is like our mother who nurtures us for this purpose.

"on the night in which he was betrayed," he was found out. He had spent so much time with our Lord and his other disciples that his denial didn't ring true—a fact that caused a young girl to blurt out to him, "Surely thou also art one of them; for thy speech betrayeth thee." Something of our Lord—something of the awe and love that the band of disciples had for Jesus—was visible to the girl, and Peter couldn't hide it.

(a) A person who has "been with the Lord" doesn't have to fold his hands in an attitude of prayer and wear a pious look. But his speech, his love, his attitude toward life, and his concern for those around him should cause people to say,

"Surely thou also art one of them."

(b) Too often we think a Christian has to do extraordinary things. But a Christian is a person who merely does ordinary things in an extraordinary way, does little things with a touch of love, humility, and quietness, and possesses qualities that are embodied in sainthood.

(c) It is through such people—sacramental people who are vehicles of God's grace—that our lives are drawn to the Lord and our personalities formed in his likeness. We learn about the Lord through our relationships with his servants and then find it possible for his spirit to dwell in us.—Gilbert Runkel in *The Living Church.*

SUNDAY: MAY TENTH

MORNING SERVICE

Topic: When You Say Mother You Say a Lot About God (Mother's Day)

TEXT: Deut. 32:18.

I. When you say mother, you say a lot about God's creativity. (a) Moses said God is the one "who gave you birth." There is something of awe in the presence of a mother giving birth. She is participating with God in the act of creation.

(b) When I was a boy, medical science had not advanced to the point where it has today, and many mothers died in childbirth. The preachers would wax eloquent as they appealed to an appreciation of motherhood on the basis of how mother descended into the very "shadow of the valley of death" that we might be born. It was and is true.

(c) When we say mother, we say a lot about God for that is what God did that we might be born anew. God descended into the valley of death in Jesus on the cross, and by the mighty act of creation we are made new creatures in Christ.

(d) In the early church baptismal fonts were designed in the shape of a pregnant woman for in baptism one was born into a new life. Motherhood speaks to us of physical and spiritual creativity.

II. When you say mother, you say a lot

about God's nurture. (a) In this song of Moses from which our text comes is also the image of God as the mother eagle "that stirs up its nest . . . spreading out its wings, catching them." This is a picture of little eaglets whose time has come to leave the nest, and the mother is pushing them out. First she stirs up the nest. With her mighty claw she reaches down through the fluffy down and pulls up the thorns which are part of the structure of the nest, making it very uncomfortable. Then she pushes her young out of the nest, and they fall toward the ground, fluttering, unable to fly. She swoops under them and catches their fall and repeats this until they are able to fly on their own.

(b) A good mother doesn't want her young to go on being dependent on her, and so she prepares them for a life of independency. Nurturing the young, teaching them by precept and example, and training them in the affairs of life is what parenting is all about.

(c) God is like a mother, the mother eagle, who wants those eaglets to be independent and to get on with life. To be sure, we will never come to be independent of God for life depends on God. But we can grow into mature human beings and live responsible lives. God is like our mother who nurtures us for this purpose.

III. When you say mother, you say a lot about God's tenderness.

(a) This is not true to the Deuteronomy text. Moses said that "because of the provocation of the sons and daughters the Lord spurned them." He said that they had stirred God to jealousy with their idols. "A fire is kindled by my anger, and it burns to the depth of sheol." There is the austere side of God's judgment.

(b) Jesus gives us another side of God when divine grace is spurned. It is that of a mother hen. To Jerusalem, who stoned the prophets and now was ready to kill Jesus, the heart of God cries, "O Jerusalem, Jerusalem, how often would I have gathered your children together as a hen gathers her brood under her wings, and you would not" (Matt. 23:37).

IV. When you say mother, you say a lot about God's reassurance. "God could not be everywhere, so God made mothers." We have trouble with this saying for it denies the omnipresence of God. God can be everywhere. But mothers as an extension of God is good theology. God does work and express a caring nature through people, and mothers represent God in a marvelous way. God has put into every little home the potential of divine presence, a touch of influence through the person of a mother.—James L. Sanders.

Illustrations

LOST IN A CROWD.   In a crowded city a little boy lost his mother. He went in and out of stores and saw ladies carrying packages, but none was his mother. He went to the end of the block where there was a policeman and, pointing to the passing crowd, asked, "Mister, did you happen to see a lady going by without me?"—John R. Brokhoff.

FOOTPRINTS.   One night a man had a dream that he was walking along a beach with his Lord. Through his mind flashed scenes from his past life. In each scene he noticed two sets of footprints in the sand —one belonging to him and the other to the Lord. Occasionally there was only one set of footprints. This seemed to be true whenever he recalled some sad or low point in his life. He wondered why and asked the Lord. "Lord," he said, "you said that once I decided to follow you, you would walk all the way with me. But during the most troublesome times of my life there was only one set of footprints. I don't understand why. During the times I needed you most, you apparently deserted me." Then the Lord answered: "My child, I love you and would never leave you. The reason you see only one set of footprints during your sad times of trials and suffering is that during these times I carried you."—Charles E. Ferrell.

Sermon Suggestion

THE MOTHER OF US ALL.   Texts: Ps. 87:5; Gal. 4:26. Everything that Jerusalem once meant to the Jew she now means to the church. Jerusalem is the mother of us all. (1) The gospel is for the whole man. Jerusalem stands not only for an earthly city but also for a spiritual relationship with God who is concerned about our bodies and our souls, our relationship with our fellows and with him, and about time and eternity. (2) The gospel is for all men. The gospel is not only for Jews but also for Gentiles. (3) The gospel is for each man. God patiently seeks us as individuals, and each must respond for himself.—S. Robert Weaver.

Worship Aids

CALL TO WORSHIP.   "Know therefore that the Lord thy God, he is God, the faithful God, which keepeth covenant and mercy with them that love him and keep his commandments to a thousand generations." Deut. 7:9.

INVOCATION.   O heavenly Father, who hast given us a true faith and a sure hope: help us to live as those who believe and trust in the communion of saints, the forgiveness of sins, and the resurrection to life everlasting; and strengthen this faith and hope in us all the days of our life.

OFFERTORY SENTENCE. "Therefore, my beloved brethren, be ye steadfast, unmoveable, always abounding in the work of the Lord, forasmuch as ye know that your labor is not in vain in the Lord." I Cor. 15:58.

OFFERTORY PRAYER. Our Father, we thank thee that thou art so generous to us. All that we have is a gift from thee. Help us to serve one another so that we may reflect thy spirit and goodness.

PRAYER. Eternal God, through whose wisdom the solitary are gathered into families, we come before thee now with thanksgiving for every Christian home that brightens our land. Through the ministry thereof each of us is made better and every good institution is strengthened. For hallowed memories of a mother's love, a father's devotion, or the company of brother or sister, we are grateful unto thee. In obedience to thee, our heavenly Father, we would honor our earthly parents and provide for our children examples whereof they need feel no shame.

Forbid that in pride of family we should worship our ancestors or our offspring rather than thee. Remind us that he who loves father or mother, wife or husband, sister or brother more than thee is not worthy of thee. Help us in our homes to lose ourselves in thy service that we may find ourselves in thee. Purge us of vanity and of every form of indulgence. Help us to find ways of expressing our affection for one another in our families. And in mutual affection may we find security sufficient to turn us to the needs of others. Deliver us from pampering our prejudices and from childish conceits and selfish gratification. Weld our homes into instruments for thy service.

Help us to be ever grateful for Jesus Christ, mindful that he set the family on a firm foundation and showed to women and children a new respect. As in every gracious home we see his spirit, may our devotion be increased. May his love be ours that whatever of trouble or distress be our lot it may prove but a sacrament of his grace to us. So strengthen, purify, and enlighten us in our family groups to serve thee well, our Father, from birth through death unto life everlasting, which is in Christ Jesus our Lord.—Marion C. Allen.

EVENING SERVICE

Topic: The Ideal Woman
SCRIPTURE: Prov. 31:10–31.

I. The ideal woman maintains her personal attractiveness (vv. 31:21–22, 25–26). The woman described here knows how to clothe herself elegantly. She made her own clothing, but it was the most attractive and fashionable of the day. She also maintained a spiritual and intellectual attractiveness. The inner beauty of the woman is spoken of in Ps. 45:13: "The king's daughter is all glorious within." The latter half of the verse speaks of the external attractiveness she cultivates. "Her clothing is of wrought gold," the psalmist declares.

II. The ideal woman sustains constant industriousness (vv. 31:12–22, 24). The writer of this hymn in praise of the ideal woman pictures her as one who provides food and clothing for her family, develops business ability, and makes wise investments. She does not hesitate to work. Her family benefits from her desire to provide the necessities for them.

III. The ideal woman enables family success (vv. 31:21–27). The children of this woman felt the security of having adequate provision for their physical needs. Her business success helped secure their future. They benefited from her wise words, personal kindness, and knowledge of God's law. Her careful oversight of the family's needs included every area of their needs. (See v. 31:27 in several translations.)

IV. The ideal woman achieves lasting blessedness (vv. 31:28–31). Verse 31 indicates that the ideal woman will profit from the works of her hands. The expression, "Let her own works praise her in the fates," very likely means that the greatness of a woman like this will make her a legend. Her story will be repeated to the young women met for conversation at the city gate. Both the husband and children of this woman will praise her (v. 28).— Richard B. Douglass in *Proclaim.*

SUNDAY: MAY SEVENTEENTH

MORNING SERVICE

Topic: Am I Really a Christian?
SCRIPTURE: I Pet. 2:19–29.

I. Christians are persons who have found themselves. They are no longer wandering aimlessly to and fro, from one thing to another. They no longer live purposeless, meaningless, and untoward lives. They have discovered purpose and meaning in their life because they have now found a shepherd who will lead them to the life they should live.

(a) You can call this "discovering yourself" or coming to your "true self." In traditional religious language it is called "being born again." William James defined being so born as the process, either gradual or sudden, by which a divided self becomes a whole self. Today in psychology it's called the "integrated personality." In popular language it's called "getting it all together in your life." First Peter says it's like ending a period in your life when you have been wandering around purposelessly, aimlessly, and meaninglessly and at last finding a purpose and a meaning for your life in the guide of all life.

(b) We believe that this experience can come in any number of ways. It can come suddenly and dramatically, or it can come gradually and cumulatively. It will happen to you in a very personal way. It will happen to you according to the way you are. Nobody else can predict that experience for you. Nobody else can tell you that you must have the same kind of experience he had had before you can become a Christian. God will come to you the way you are.

(c) Religion is the most intimate and personal experience of life.

(1) For some it will be a dramatic experience with weeping and a kind of joy that cannot be repressed—an irresistible enthusiasm in their life. But for others it will be very quiet.

(2) It will probably happen to you according to the personality God has given

you. The test is not in the experience itself. The test is whether your life now has direction, purpose, and meaning. "You were straying like sheep, but you have now returned to the shepherd."

(d) This implies commitment. The Christian stands for something. The Christian has principles. We need to remember that in this age of expediency.

(1) Christians live by principles, not by expediency. There are ways of living that they simply cannot condone and still follow Jesus as their shepherd. If Christians say yes to Christ, they have to say no to other things.

(2) The Bible makes it clear that the quality of our lives will be determined by the quality of decisions we make in this life. "Choose ye this day life or death, blessing or curse."

II. Christians are persons who are ready to give themselves. (a) The church has always been plagued by heresy, a half-truth blown up to be the whole truth. Christian heresy is taking a part of the Christian message and forgetting the rest.

(1) In the early church the first heresy focused on the doctrine of Christ. The doctrine of Christ said Jesus was fully God and fully man, both God and man at the same time. But there were preachers in those days who said he was only God, and others who said he was merely a man. Both were condemned as heretics because they preached only half the truth. The whole truth was that he was fully God and fully man.

(2) There is a heresy in the church in our day. It focuses on the doctrine of salvation. The Christian teaching about salvation says that Christ has come to give us life so that we will give to others, Christ has come to set us free so we will be the servants of others, and Christ has died on the cross for us so that we will take up crosses for others.

(b) The heresy in our time takes half of that teaching about salvation—the half that says what Christ has done for us and forgets the half that deals with what Christ asks us to do for others.

(1) It's a heresy which sees Jesus as a help in attaining the goals we have set for our lives, never asking if the goals we have set for our lives are the goals Jesus wants us to have—seeing Jesus simply as our partner in business or as the one who helps us win the beauty contest or the athletic contest.

(2) Christ has come to give you new life, but he has also come to challenge you to give your life to something beyond yourself. If you have not realized that, you have not realized what it means really to be Christian.—Mark Trotter.

Illustrations

THESES. The Christian theses of human worth and dignity, of human dependency, of man's free will, of man's proneness to sin, of man's need for purpose and meaning in his life, of man's absolute need for love, of man's need for a sense of ultimate destiny, of man's need for absolute moral precepts, of man's need for surcease from the pangs of guilt, and of man's desire for ultimate acceptance—all these are ways in which the Christian faith frees men and women to fulfill their glorious potential as human beings made in the image of God.—M. N. Beck in *Christianity Today.*

PROPER PERSPECTIVE. Ralph W. Sockman told of a practice he followed during his ministry. In the room where he put on his vestments before a service of worship, there were two objects hanging on the wall. One was a mirror, necessary for seeing that his hair was properly combed and his tie straight. The other was an artist's conception of Jesus Christ. Thus after he had taken care of his personal appearance, he turned to concentrate his thoughts and feelings on Jesus Christ before stepping into his pulpit.—Charles L. Copenhaver.

Sermon Suggestions

A CHRISTIAN'S CREDENTIALS. Text: Acts 19:1 (NEB). (1) Sincerity about Christ. (2) Experience in Christ. (3) Reflecting the character of Christ. (4) Transformed through Christ and directed by him.— Daniel D. Walker.

LIFE IS TOO SHORT FOR THAT! Text: Job 14:1–2. (1) Life is too short to pursue wealth and wordly possessions. (2) Life is too short to invest it in unworthy causes. (3) Life is too short for living with the wrong spirit or attitude toward life. (4) Life is too short to be without Christ.— John R. Brokoff.

Worship Aids

CALL TO WORSHIP. "Let us search and try our ways, and turn again to the Lord. Let us lift up our heart with our hands unto God in the heavens." Lam. 3:40–41.

INVOCATION. Eternal and ever-blessed God, grant this day light to the minds that hunger for the truth and peace to the hearts which yearn for rest. Grant strength to those who have hard tasks to do and power to those who have sore temptations to face. Grant unto us within this place to find the secret of thy presence and to go forth from it in the strength of the Lord.

OFFERTORY SENTENCE. "Every one of us shall give account of himself to God." Rom. 14:12.

OFFERTORY PRAYER. Almighty God, whose loving hand hath given us all that we possess: grant us grace that we may honor thee with our substance, and remembering the account which we must one day give, may be faithful stewards of thy bounty.

PRAYER. Why is it so hard for us to be quiet, Lord? You know that, when we are quiet in your presence, we feel uncomfortable and self-conscious. This feeling is magnified a thousandfold when we are in the presence of one another. We are so conditioned by noise and tension, sound and fury, that silence bewilders us. We don't seem to know what to do, Lord, when we are quiet. We become frightened and terrified, especially when we are alone. Yet we remember that, when you mingled with us on earth, you said that we should pray in quietness and in secret and that we are never alone because you are always with us.

Why is it that we have made life so hectic, Lord, and allowed it to be filled with the busyness of trivia and escape? Why have we shied away from that which gives it depth and meaning? Why have we elevated the empty and the hollow, while chipping away at those values for which you lived and died? What is the trouble with us, Lord, that we have mixed up our values and gotten them out of focus?

Where are we heading, Lord? If you know, Lord, and we are certain that you do, won't you please tell us? Help us to find ourselves that we may find you, discover one another, and come to know each other again. Lord, help us to become part of your family, part of one another, knit together and bound together by ties of Christian love.

From the quietness that heals and from the searching that reveals guide us into channels of faithful service that will aid us in binding up the wounds of the broken, the disinherited, and the rejected, that will bring in the day of brotherly love, and that will unite us as persons, holy and acceptable in your sight and in the sight of one another. Grant that we may always celebrate life in all its myriad aspects and that we may never lose our zeal in working to make this good earth into a place of peace where the celebration of life will not be difficult.—Chester E. Hodgson.

EVENING SERVICE

Topic: Forgive Us Our Syndromes
TEXT: I Cor. 7:7.

It is our syndromes rather than our sins that should concern us. "A syndrome," according to dictionaries, "is a set of symptoms or signs typical of a disease, disturbance, or condition in animals or plants." As branches of the living vine or, if you prefer, members of the body of Christ, these symptoms should concern us. They indicate weaknesses rather than wicked-ness. They are not sins but syndromes.

I. One of the most common is the *bigger is better* syndrome.

(a) It begins innocently enough, since our commission is to make disciples of all nations. This means our numbers should increase, as indeed they will. The disease shows its first signs when we begin to focus our thoughts more and more upon larger numbers and less and less upon the persons these numbers represent. It becomes more important to us how many are in attendance than who is present.

(b) The *bigger is better* syndrome becomes more complicated as the disease spreads.

(1) The victim becomes increasingly preoccupied with quantity and less concerned with quality. Size is all-important and must be realized at any cost. Where once it seemed sufficient to be larger than last year, now it becomes vital to be larger than anybody else.

(2) Questionable methods are employed if they bring results. The whip is used more often, and the sheep are driven relentlessly on. Occasionally—although this symptom is a very rare complication—the numbers are padded through clever or careless methods of counting. The statistics are there, larger than life, but they do not accurately reflect real size.

(3) Worst of all, a pastor who is afflicted with this malady can begin to believe that he did it all. His congregation is larger, his building more prestigious, and his salary more comfortable because he possesses skills and abilities that ordinary men lack. He forgets Christ's words: "Upon this rock I will build my church" (Matt. 16:18). If the disease is allowed to spread, debilitating effects upon humility, compassion, and spirituality can take a frightful toll. The pastor feels it and so do his people.

II. The *money can buy it* syndrome is more subtle but no less destructive.

(a) It is easier, as a rule, to contribute money than to give time and energy. But buying a bus alone will not produce a bus ministry. It takes more than hiring another associate to bring growth.

(b) Any successful pastor will testify that dedicated, tireless, and persistent efforts must be invested along with money. Spending money does not solve problems.

(c) Money is the most overrated commodity on today's market of values. It can buy a house, but it cannot make a home. It can pay for medicine, but it cannot purchase health. It can acquire things, but things do not satisfy the soul. If anyone should know this, it should be the preacher whose master has challenged him to "go and sell that thou hast, and give to the poor, and thou shalt have treasure in heaven: and come and follow me" (Matt. 19:21).

III. *The map is the territory* syndrome makes people more concerned with their "maps"—that is, the feelings, thoughts, suppositions, beliefs, and theories "inside" their skins—than with the "territories"—the facts and realities maps only represent.

(a) We can be guided primarily, if not exclusively, by our "maps" rather than our "territories."

(b) Trouble, confusion, and danger are likely to occur when the map inadequately represents the territory and when the individual is unaware that he is dealing with the map rather than the territory.—James McGraw.

SUNDAY: MAY TWENTY-FOURTH

MORNING SERVICE

Topic: Roots and Fruits (Rural Life Sunday)

SCRIPTURE: Matt. 7:15–23.

Jesus said that the world outside is changed when it is changed on the inside and when men's minds and hearts are focused toward peace, goodwill, love, and service. We find him talking about individuals who have missed the way and who would lead others to miss it. They are prophets or those who parade as prophets, but they are not so. They are wolves in prophets' clothing. He went on to urge that people know others by their fruits, and this led to a discourse on spiritual growth and development. The good tree bears good fruit and an evil tree bears evil fruit. What makes a sound tree?

I. *Location.*

(a) This can be argued when we recall that one poet wrote of a flower in a crannied wall—a tiny bit of life that can grow in the most inconspicuous and most unlikely place. A cactus can bloom even in an arid desert. But most things grow where there is a likelihood for their development.

(b) Ps. 1 refers to the good man in this manner: "He is like a tree planted by streams of water, that yields its fruit in its season, and its leaf does not wither. In all he does, he prospers." Here is the planting, the locating, and the sinking of the roots in soil which gives life.

(c) Growth is up from roots. A flower in a pot is wilted, the petals are falling off, and the branches are droopy. What do you do? Prop up the branches and stick the petals back on? You put water around the roots. You feed the plant with some sort of soil food. And because it's fed at the roots, life springs forth in the branches. The flowers grow. That's basically what Jesus was saying. Life must be lived out of rootage.

II. *Cultivation.*

(a) The most fruitful trees demand the most cultivation. Ask any peach or apple grower. The highest type of person demands the same. That's why the church plants children in the soil of God's love to be cultivated in what we call Christian nurture. There are no great Christians without this.

(b) Nobody outgrows this. An old tree still needs fertilization. It still needs the help that we can give it if it is to bear fruit. I've seen old apple trees discarded in the mountains of North Georgia and North Carolina. Insects and borers have done their worst because the trees were discarded and neglected. More attention would have given them added life. It is the business of the church to restore, to heal, to cultivate, and to make grow—and this for all people of all ages and all kinds.

III. *Pruning.*

(a) This need was demonstrated by Jesus at the Last Supper. When the meal was over, he turned to his disciples and said: "I am the true vine, and my Father is the vinedresser. Every branch of mine that bears no fruit he takes away, and every branch that bears fruit he prunes, that it may bear more fruit." Every branch that bears fruit must be pruned.

(b) Pruning brings pain. You cut a tree and the sap flows. That's its blood.

(1) Often the wounded serve best. People who have been hurt make our best helpers. Yet it's hard to have sin cut out of our lives or to bear trouble. But we have to be purged and cleansed of our impurities and must learn to bear a heavy load if we are to bear fruit for God.

(2) How painful it is to confess our sins. And how much more painful it is to leave our sins. We do not like to be disciplined. Our children do not like to be disciplined. The whole world reacts against it. But it is the pruning knife which provides us with the fruitful life.

(c) F. B. Meyer spoke about circumcision of the heart—the new covenant that God made with us. It was not circumcision of the flesh in the ancient Hebrew term but circumcision of the heart—the cutting away of sin. He said, "There can be no spiritual fruitfulness which has not been preceded by the use of the sharp knife." What this means is that all of our evil or sin against God and our hate and selfishness in the presence of our brothers and sisters in Christ must be ruthlessly dealt with. We must confess these things to God and walk away from them. Then we become fit subjects for God's use in the world.

(d) We wonder sometimes why our lives don't amount to more, why we have so little influence upon other people, or why nothing good seems to come from what we do. It may well be that we have not really planted ourselves near the river of God, we have not yielded ourselves to the cultivating spirit which is all about us, and we have been unwilling to prune away the unnecessary and the evil in our lives in order that the necessary and the good might emerge.—Thomas A. Whiting.

Illustrations

PERSONAL EXAMPLE. When Harry Emerson Fosdick was a student, he was disturbed and uncertain about his beliefs. Looking out the window in those days, Fosdick said his doubt was immediately allayed when he saw Professor William Newton Clarke walking across the campus. For, as Fosdick put it, Clarke was a person who embodied the realities of the Christian theology which he taught, and that was sufficient assurance for the troubled student. That is one of the supreme powers of Jesus. His personal example demonstrates and substantiates his sayings and wins belief.—*The Methodist Christian Advocate.*

ONE-TENTH AT A TIME. In Michigan a Quaker decided to try out the matter of tithing. He began with a cubic inch of wheat which he planted in a patch of ground 4 by 8 feet. When that wheat matured, he took out one-tenth and planted it in a plot of ground 24 by 60 feet. Continuing to repeat the process, the third year the amount of wheat required a full acre of ground. The fourth year required 16 acres; the fifth, 230 acres; the sixth, 2,500. The ninth year would have covered all of the state of West Virginia; the tenth year would have covered the United States; the thirteenth year would have covered the globe.—*Sunshine Magazine.*

Sermon Suggestion

WHAT IS THE CHURCH? Text: Eph. 5:25. (1) A fellowship of believers. (2) A fellowship of those who have not arrived but are on the way. (3) A fellowship of people who love one another as Christ has loved them. (4) A fellowship of those who have a sense of purpose and who give themselves to a cause that is greater than they.—Ivan B. Bell.

Worship Aids

CALL TO WORSHIP. "Trust in [God] at all times; ye people, pour out your heart before him: God is a refuge for us." Ps. 62:8.

INVOCATION. O God, in glory exalted and in mercy ever blessed, we magnify thee, we praise thee, and we give thanks unto thee for thy bountiful providence, for all the blessings of this present life, and for all the hopes of a better life to come. Let the memory of thy goodness, we beseech thee, fill our hearts with joy and thankfulness.

OFFERTORY SENTENCE. "For ye know the grace of our Lord Jesus Christ, that though he was rich, yet for your sakes he became poor, that ye through his poverty might be rich." II Cor. 8:9.

OFFERTORY PRAYER. Our heavenly Father, help us to remember that though Christ does offer his companionship, yet to us belongs the decision as to whether or not we will follow him. May we through these gifts and our witness share with all the world the blessedness that comes to us through thy grace.

PRAYER. O God, who remainest the same though all else fades, who changest not with our changing moods, and who leavest us not when we leave thee, we thank thee that, when we lose faith in thee, sooner or later we come to faith in something that leads us back again with firmer trust and more security. Even if we wander into the far country we take ourselves with us—ourselves who are set toward—thee as rivers to the sea. If we turn to foolishness, our hearts grow faint and weary, our path is set with thorns, the night overtakes us, and we find we have strayed from light and life.

Grant us a clearer vision of the light which shows no shade of turning, so that we stray not in folly away; incline our hearts to love the truth alone, so that we miss thee not at last; give us to realize of what spirit we are, so that we cleave ever to thee, who alone canst give us rest and joy.—W. E. Orchard.

EVENING SERVICE

Topic: What's Going On in Church?
TEXT: Eph. 1:23.

I. People are having their lives put back together in church. The people who go to church are people whose lives need repair. They are in bad shape, they need attention, and they get the attention they need in the church which is the body of Christ.

(a) If you decide to attend church once, you will probably never suspect that the people who are sitting there with you are people with a great many problems, troubles, and sins.

(b) Usually when people come to church, they wear some of their better clothing, and they are on their best behavior. They are polite to one another. There is a special air about them. The church may have a choir, and when they all stand and sing so beautifully, one almost expects to see angel wings tucked somewhere in the folds of their clothing.

(c) If one doesn't know anything about a church, he is apt to get the impression that the church is comprised of people who have been specially laundered and sanitized and have miraculously escaped the contamination of the world. Those of us who are a part of the church know how untrue this impression really is.

(d) The wonderful thing about the church is that we meet to confess that outside of Jesus we are nothing, but because of Jesus we can have hope and peace. One of the great things that happens in church is that people's lives are being put back together. And that's the truth. The church is called the body of Christ in the Bible because it is so very closely connected with him. It is in the church that the full effect of Jesus' perfect sacrifice is applied to the lives of his children.

II. People are going to Calvary, and their sins are being forgiven.

(a) The church, the body of Christ, is so closely identified with him that it is called his body. All the glorious, cleansing power of the forgiveness Jesus earned with his broken body and shed blood is experienced in church.

(b) If you need forgiveness and cleansing, you'd better not stay outside the church of Jesus. Come and sit beside us, and rejoice with us that Jesus can put lives like ours back together again.

III. Believers are given the equipment they need to live new lives in Jesus' power. The same Jesus who forgives them through his sacrifice on Calvary's cross gives them the equipment they need to fight against sin and to begin to live obediently before God.

(a) In church the people of God are equipped to live as the people of God.

And those who are a part of the church of Jesus can testify that they gradually begin to experience a new obedience to Jesus Christ.

(b) In church God equips his people to have Christian families where parental authority is recognized and where God is honored in family worship and love.

(c) The church equips its people to express their obedience to God in connection with their ordinary work. People who are a part of the church don't amount to very much in themselves, but when Jesus gets hold of them in church he helps them change. He makes them useful in his great work in our world.—Joel Nederhood.

SUNDAY: MAY THIRTY-FIRST

MORNING SERVICE

Topic: Christ Ascended and Accessible (Ascension Sunday)

TEXT: Heb. 4:14–16.

I. We have an expanding Christian faith. Our Lord has a continuing ministry. This is what he meant when he said at his ascension, "Lo, I am with you always, even unto the end of age." It may be difficult for each of us to formulate our religious experience of this truth, but our lives can become an adventure in discovering the present ministry of Christ. Our faith can go beyond the high points of historic Christmas and Easter festivals and seek to comprehend what the contemporary Christ is doing.

II. I believe in the ascension of Christ because I am forced to by the historical evidence.

(a) Ask yourself what happened after the Easter resurrection. Is Christ still dead in a tomb? No, of course not. Did he linger for a week or a month and then vanish? If so, where? Did he die again alone in some inn by a dusty road or did he wander off into the hills to perish as a calcium skeleton sprawled on some forested slope? No. It is much easier to believe just what the Bible records of his ascension. He who rose again from the dead still lives in that realm just beyond the reach of our fingertips.

(b) We all know there is a field of reality beyond our senses. Partially we know it in the fields of black light such as ultraviolet and infrared. And there is also a wealth of sound that vibrates beyond and below the decibel range of our ears. He lives and labors there as the ascended Lord in that larger reality which exists beyond the narrow canyon of our own verifiable experience.

(c) Think what dimension this truth adds to the comfort of historical Christianity. We not only have the significant episodes of the past when the ascended Christ converted Paul the Apostle from being an angry skeptic, but we have the new chapters of Christian history which are now being written within our own family circles and churches.

III. There are at least four things which follow from the teaching of our ascended Lord.

(a) He continues to present himself to the whole world rather than to the narrow limits of Judea and Galilee.

(b) He treats his disciples as mature and responsible friends who are growing in effectiveness.

(c) He has established the spiritual body of the church to be the effective means of implementing his ministry today.

(d) He is even now actively engaged in the continuing spiritual work of redeeming mankind.

IV. Today Christ is the man of all the world by his ascension. He ministers beyond the provincialism of Bethlehem and Capernaum. He now presents himself in universal terms which all men can understand whether they be North Americans, Asiatics, or Eskimos. If this were not so, one would be hard pressed to explain the wide appeal of Jesus' words to hungry hearts in modern cultures and in the intervening past centuries. He is more than the Christ of Palestine. He is the savior of the world.

V. The ascension set the disciples free to perform their responsible service for the master.

(a) Do you remember Easter morning at the tomb? Mary was overjoyed to see the risen Christ. She wanted to grasp his hand in eager love. But Jesus said gently, "Touch me not but go tell my brethren I go before them into Galilee." He had no objection to her touching him because he later offered the scarred hand for doubting Thomas to handle and see. But Jesus wanted Mary to know that a new level of fellowship was developing where the disciples would have to move out into deeper maturity and be less dependent on him for direct answers and insights.

(b) Something more than the maturation of individual Christians has come through the years. The whole mission of the church as the witnessing body of Christ has gone out into the world.

VI. Should you and I be content with anything less than full power from the ascended Christ? Dare we think passively that, though he is risen, he is far from us? He is even now ministering to us. He calls on the faithfulness of your heart right where you are to be a partner with him in the redemption of the world. He promises to you his abiding love and presence. He is faithful to minister to and through you from that ascended life which lies just beyond the tiptoe of our sight and the reach of our fingertips. We need to ask, "What are you and I doing this very day for Christ, who is carrying on his present ministry to the world and seeks our partnership?"—Bryant M. Kirkland.

Illustrations

CHURCH WITHOUT DOORS.   Ernest Gordon in *Through the Valley of the Kwai* describes a church at one of the prison camps as a clearing in the jungle to which there were no doors. "One could enter at any point. It was all door. It was hard to know when one was in church and when one was not." There needs to be something of that quality about our religion. What goes on in our everyday life is as much a part of our religious expression as what we sing or say in church on Sunday. Our attitude on the job, our actions and participation in block clubs, community organizations, social and fraternal groups, our so-called private life is far more an indication of our religion than the words we say or the prayers we offer inside the walls. God simply will not be enclosed.—Carl Price.

HUSHED WINDS.   In the White Mountains of New Hampshire, at Crawford Notch, there is a pool formed by the waters of the Saco River. Usually the surface of that pool is ruffled by the winds that rush through the opening of the notch. But there are times when the winds are hushed and the waters become a perfect mirror of the towering cliffs of nearby Mount Webster and the infinite blue of the sky above. It is needful for us to have those moments when the winds of the world that blow across our lives are hushed. Then we will reflect the beauty of the Infinite. Solitude and quiet are thus necessary growing conditions for the soul.—Henry Gariepy.

Sermon Suggestions

THE CERTAINTY OF HOPE.   Text: Heb. 11:1. (1) Faith is a hope that is absolutely certain that what it believes is true and that what it expects will come. (2) It is not the hope which looks forward with wistful longing; it is the hope which looks forward with utter certainty. (3) It is not the hope which takes refuge in a perhaps; it is hope which is founded on a condition. (4) The Christian hope is more than hope; it is a hope that through faith has turned to certainty. (5) This Christian hope is such that it dictates all a person's conduct. It dominates his actions. He lives in this hope and he dies in this hope, and it is the possession of this hope which makes him act as he does.—William Barclay.

FLOWERS FOR THE LIVING.　Text: Mark 14:8–9. (1) There is a need for an expressed and vocal appreciation for the little kindnesses that are often taken for granted. (2) There are people who are discouraged and need the bracing word we might offer. (3) There are those who are obsessed with a feeling of uselessness and need to be encouraged.—Aaron N. Meckel.

Worship Aids

CALL TO WORSHIP.　"How beautiful upon the mountain are the feet of him that bringeth good tidings, that publisheth peace; that publisheth salvation; that saith unto Zion, thy God reigneth!" Isa. 52:7.

INVOCATION.　Lord God Almighty, holy and eternal Father, who dwellest in the high and lofty place, with him also that is of a humble and contrite spirit: we come before thee, beseeching thee to cleanse us by the grace of thy Holy Spirit, that we may give praise to thee, now and forever.

OFFERTORY SENTENCE.　"What shall I render unto the Lord for all his benefits toward me? I will pay my vows unto the Lord now in the presence of all his people." Ps. 116:12–14.

OFFERTORY PRAYER.　O thou who art the Father of all, may we live as thy children and brothers of all whom thou hast made to dwell upon the face of the earth that thy kindness may be born in our hearts.

BACCALAUREATE PRAYER.　We thank thee for hours of insight when the spirit's true endowments stand out clearly from the false ones and when we see life in its true perspective—the big things big and the small things small.

We commend to thy guidance our fellow students everywhere, all who seek to know the truth that makes men free. These are the salt of the earth. If the salt loses its savor, how can it be restored? Save them from the lusts that defile and the jealousies that stain our human brotherhood. Give them a deepening awareness of things unseen.

Unite us in a fellowship of light but, above all, in a deep desire to help heal the hurt of mankind. As knowledge grows from more to more, may more of reverence in us dwell.

We commend to thy guidance this school—all who have built their lives into it and all who are building their lives into it now. May teacher and taught alike be taught by thee, O thou who art the seer's vision, the sage's wisdom, and the poet's tongue. Here may true piety and sound learning go hand in hand that together they may be the salvation of our republic and the stability of our time.

As class after class goes forth from these walls, may they do with their might what their hands find to do, rendering thee sincerest praise of work well chosen and well done. So may this school be like a beacon set upon a hill, a tree of life whose leaves are for the healing of the nations.—Frank Halliday Ferris.

EVENING SERVICE

Topic: Memories: Resource for Great Living

TEXT: Deut. 32:7.

I. The people to whom those words first were spoken were not celebrating an anniversary. They were not resting back upon the glory of past achievements. They were facing their supreme test—an issue of life or death.

(a) Behind them were forty years of struggle for survival in the bleak, pitiless wilderness of Paran which stretched between Egypt and Canaan. Back of that were four hundred years of slavery in Egypt.

(b) Before them was the vision of their destiny. They dared to believe God had called them to be his chosen people, founders of the most important nation in the world, and the special instrument for his purpose.

(c) They were standing upon the threshold of fulfillment. In that time of crisis their great leader Moses had to keep his rendezvous with death. He knew they had to go on without him. So in one of the most dramatic moments of history Moses stood with Joshua, the newly-appointed leader, and gave his final words of counsel to the people he had led from slavery. He said, "Use your memories."

(d) To think of the service given by memories is to be reminded that, like all things precious, they must be given care.

II. Consider the power of memories to awaken our sleeping strength. Each of us is a slumbering giant. Most of our ability remains dormant.

(a) The great difference in people rests not so much in variation of native ability but in the degree to which they use what they have been given. Memories can be a key to unlock and release powers that sleep in us.

(b) To all appearances that ragged, seedy-looking band of refugees were no match for the task before them. They were pitifully outnumbered. Their material resources were pathetically inadequate. But the children of Israel went forward from that time and place and achieved the impossible armed with little more than memories. Memories awakened and released through them giant strength of flesh and spirit. So they captured the promised land.

(c) We, like the followers of Moses, have memories which can awaken and harness our sleeping strength. We have memories which can equip us to take our promised land.

III. See how memories can be a resource for great living as they help us maintain confidence and courage.

(a) Moses and the people who gathered to hear his last words of counsel had spent forty miserable years of dreary wandering in the wilderness because once they had lacked confidence and courage. Moses bid them use their memories lest such a calamity strike again.

(b) Everyone knows someone who through God's grace has mastered a grievous physical handicap, risen above some bitter disappointment, won strength from some sorrow, or wrought music out of life's discords. When caught in some dark night of trouble, it helps to remember someone has been there ahead of us and has won the victory. Such a memory builds confidence and courage. It is a resource for great living.—Everett W. Palmer.

SUNDAY: JUNE SEVENTH

MORNING SERVICE

Topic: Why Pentecost?

TEXT: John 20:22.

The apostles were not really spiritually helpless, for Christ had already given them a special inbreathing. Why was it necessary for Pentecost to happen before they began their ministry?

I. Pentecost provided a visual (fire) and auditory (wind) impression of the Holy Spirit, so that this somewhat obscure person of the trinity might be more real in the minds of believers.

(a) Pentecost provides us with graphic symbols of the Spirit that can help our poor mortal minds comprehend just a bit more of the incomprehensible. The tongues hovering over the disciples represent powerful communication, and their fiery nature communicates both the glow of God's presence and the fury of his judgment. The sound of mighty, rushing wind implies a veritable hurricane of the breath of God.

(b) As the church can look back to the advent of the Son—even though he was present from eternity—so now the church can look back to the advent of the Spirit—

even though he also was present from eternity. As the word became flesh at Christmas, so the Spirit became "flesh" at Pentecost.

II. Pentecost provided confidence for the early Christians. Despite the joyous surprise of the resurrection, the disciples were a hesitant, unsure, and confused group.

(a) On one occasion, for lack of anything more definite to do, they went fishing (John 21:3). For three years Jesus had been their sole authority, and now he was gone. He had left no handbook, no rules of order, no constitution, no organizational structure, no plan of action, and no written records of any kind.

(b) Before he died, Jesus had said, "It is to your advantage that I go away, for if I do not go away, the counselor will not come to you; but if I go, I will send him to you" (John 16:7). With the experience of Pentecost, they knew that Jesus had kept his promise. They were not alone. They had the evidence of the divine presence. They knew they could proceed to build the church, even though they didn't have all the details of the blueprint. Their confidence was not in themselves but in the Spirit of God within them—a truth that has deep implications for us as well.

III. Pentecost provided power for communicating the gospel. Its most significant immediate result was the conversion of 3,000 people.

(a) The communication of the gospel took place in two steps. The first was communication in tongues. This unusual phenomenon caught their attention and prompted them to inquire into these mysterious happenings. It aroused them to the fact that something supernatural was going on.

(b) Then came the second step of the communication: Peter's sermon (vss. 14–36). Tongues were set aside, and the message was proclaimed in one language. In that message the Holy Spirit was so powerful that 3,000 responded in faith. Here is the greatest vocal miracle of Pentecost —the straightforward, understandable sermon which saves souls.

IV. At Pentecost the Holy Spirit came to the whole church, the entire believing community.

(a) Previous references to the Spirit in both the Old and New Testaments emphasized the special outpourings upon certain individuals but did not explicitly say that the Spirit is the possession of all believers. Now there is a definite promise to that effect: "Repent, and be baptized every one of you in the name of Jesus Christ for the forgiveness of your sins; and you shall receive the gift of the Holy Spirit" (Acts 2:-38).

(b) The Holy Spirit is promised unconditionally to brand-new converts and is contingent only on repentance and faith. —LeRoy Koopman in *The Church Herald.*

Illustration

MEMORIAL COMPLEX. We Christians seem to have developed a kind of memorial complex. All some of us can manage is a pleasant historical mood. I grow just a bit weary of anniversaries. Religion is like marriage in this. It can fall away until it becomes little more than a celebration of anniversaries. It never seems to occur to some people that they can do more than remember that they were happy once. Is Pentecost just a subject for research or can it happen again?—Paul Sherer.

Sermon Suggestions

THE EARLY CHURCH AT PRAYER. Text: Acts 1:14. (1) They prayed for God's power and presence. (2) They prayed through their problems. (3) They prayed for greater enlightenment. (4) They prayed in thanksgiving.—Jackson Wilcox.

MEET THE HOLY SPIRIT. Text: John 14: 16, 26. (1) He has the attributes of a divine person. (2) He does the work of a divine person. (3) He must be approached as a divine person.—Paul P. Fryhling.

Worship Aids

CALL TO WORSHIP. "We are laborers together with God: ye are God's husbandry, ye are God's building. Let every man take heed how he buildeth. For other foundation can no man lay than that which is laid, which is Jesus Christ." I Cor. 3:-9–11.

INVOCATION.   Almighty God, regard, we beseech thee, thy church, set amid the perplexities of a changing order and face to face with new tasks. Fill us afresh with thy spirit that we may bear witness boldly to the coming of thy kingdom and hasten the time when the knowledge of thyself shall encircle the earth as the waters cover the sea.

OFFERTORY SENTENCE.   "Offer the sacrifices of righteousness, and put your trust in the Lord." Ps. 4:5.

OFFERTORY PRAYER.   God of our fathers, dearly do we cherish the blessings which thy church brings to us and dearly do we covet the privilege of sharing through these gifts the proclaiming of thy word until all of the earth shall praise thee.

PRAYER.   God, we come out of a world of anxiety, tears, friction, disturbance, and chaos to cleanse our spirits. We would be stripped clean of that which stains the soul. We have been bitter, overworried, and intolerant. And now, O God, we would cast off those cloaks and be made new by fellowship with thee. Our lips are unclean, our souls sordid, and our hearts heavy. Cleanse us, O God of mercy.

God, we come to bulwark our faith in mankind. Once we accepted the goodness of our fellow man and saw only his godlikeness, but now we have been hurt by his evil. Strengthen our faith in our brother. Grant us another view of him through the eyes of our master.

God, we come to catch some ray of hope. The lights which once brightened the paths have gone out. Hold up some tangible means of believing in the everlasting hope. We are enveloped in darkness and seek new paths. Send us out from here knowing in whom and in what we believe.

God, we come to renew our convictions. The pagan world draws us too much with its allurements. Stand us upon Christian faith. Help us to detect the evil and choose the good. We are a weak generation. O God, make us strong. We are too easily led by the world. Help us to follow thee. Convict us mightily, O God, of the great Christian lessons.—Fred E. Luchs.

EVENING SERVICE

Topic: The Expectations of Worship
TEXT: Ps. 27:4.

What do you expect to find when you attend a worship service? Are you looking for comfort, a challenge, an opportunity for repentance and commitment, intellectual stimulation, problem solving, an experience of God's presence, or an esthetic life? Do you believe that your expectation will have a very definite effect upon your experience?

I. Expectancy brings persons to church and opens their minds and hearts to experience God. Many people go to church expecting something to happen, and indeed it does. They go looking for God to speak a word which relates to their situation, and because they are sensitive God speaks to them. Most of us look forward to the joy which is experienced when the people of God come together for worship. This joy is reflected in our very being and is expressed in the manner in which we join together in singing the great hymns of the church.

II. We go to the church expecting to be empowered by God to return to our homes, communities, and jobs so that we might be more effective in our witness to his action in Jesus Christ. We seek the power of the Holy Spirit to accompany us as we attempt to live out our faith in the world.

III. We go to church seeking to be served. We realize that we must continue to reaffirm our commitments to almighty God if we are to continue to grow in our spiritual life. Here we get the assurance that we are never alone in life but that God is always with us.

IV. The psalmist tells that in the sanctuary the beauty of the Lord is revealed. He is stating that there is so much within the sanctuary which has the capacity to show the beauty of the Lord. Among these are such things as the stained glass windows which depict meaningful events, wood carvings, music, scripture, prayer, and the people of God.

V. Those who enter the sanctuary expecting something to happen discover that indeed it does. Those who expect nothing often go away from the worship service complaining about one thing or another.—Charles L. Johnson.

SUNDAY: JUNE FOURTEENTH

MORNING SERVICE

Topic: Is One Religion as Good as Another? (Trinity Sunday)

TEXT: Acts 4:12.

I. How often have you heard the remarks: "It doesn't make any difference what you believe. The important thing is that you live up to your beliefs."

(a) Peter would angrily reject such talk. He boldly preached Jesus Christ in Jerusalem during the days after Pentecost. The rulers of the Jews heard of his success among the people and were annoyed. Peter and John, who was with him, were arrested and brought before the Sanhedrin. Questioned about the mighty works they performed among the people, they were asked by what power and by what name they accomplished such feats. Peter replied that it was by the power of the name of Jesus Christ of Nazareth. "And there is salvation in no one else, for there is no other name under heaven given among men by which we must be saved." No other name. Not Moses. Not Buddha. Not Zoroaster. Not Mohammed. Only Jesus.

(b) Could Peter really have known what he was talking about? He was a common man from a small region of Palestine. He had not traveled around the world. He had not studied philosophy and literature from India or Northern Africa. Perhaps we ought to dismiss this claim of Peter as not informative for us today.

(c) What are we to think about the claim that Christianity is a unique revelation or disclosure of God's nature and will? Is one religion as good as another or is Christianity blessed with more truth?

II. There are attitudes and beliefs in modern society which make the claim that Christianity is unique hard to accept or at least hard to understand. Those outside the church are not alone in having reservations about this bold claim of Peter. Many inside our churches secretly wonder if Jesus is the only name.

(a) Doubts creep in from our own Christian teaching. The ten commandments make it clear that there is only one God. Aren't all religions worshiping the one and same God? Harris Franklin Rall said: "As God is one, so truth is one and righteousness is one. Wherever they are found, there men may see God." If God and truth and righteousness are one, surely we can't downgrade the prayers of the Moslem and elevate the worship of the Christian. So goes the argument.

(b) The similarity that we find between the great religions of the world adds power of persuasion to this argument. Arnold Toynbee wrote, "We ought to try to purge our Christianity of the traditional Christian belief that Christianity is unique." Why? Because all religions believe in some spiritual power that is greater than mankind.

(1) This power is always thought of as being spiritual. All religions believe that this power is available to the believer through prayer and worship. All religions believe in right and wrong. All religions believe in fundamental virtues of life like unselfishness, courage, honesty, and self-control. The founder of no religion encourages selfishness, cowardice, or dishonesty. All agree that "a man's life consists not in the abundance of the things he possesses."

(2) When we think of these similarities between world religions, we are reminded of Paul's remark that God has not left any nation without his witnesses. If God is one

and truth is one, we all worship the same God.

(c) If we think that the one God is the same God of all the world religions, we suspect that all truth is relative. Christianity may be true for us, but Buddhism is true for another culture. Relativity is the keystone of modern thought. Why not conclude that religion also is relative? Christianity is one religion among many religions, but it is not any better than other religions.

III. There is still a claim to be made for the uniqueness of Christianity, and Peter's declaration that Jesus is the only name by which humankind can find salvation is true for us today even as it was true in Peter's day. I am not advocating a narrow-minded and bigoted spirit of antagonism to people who believe differently than I do, but my study of the world religions shows me that Christianity has three distinctive teachings.

(a) The Christian believes in one God. To believe in one God is to believe that ultimate reality, which stands behind the created universe, is alone holy and worthy of our worship. Our Jewish brothers and sisters share this belief, but most of the people of the world do not believe in or worship one God.

(b) Christians believe in Jesus Christ as the center of knowledge and worship of God. When we say that Jesus is the son of God we are not talking about his parentage, but we are saying that Jesus is the window through which we see God. What we see through that window is agape love. "God is love," says I John. There is no other religion where God is taught to be a God of self-giving love.

(c) Christians believe that religion is not man seeking God but God seeking man. Other religions have different formulas for reaching God.

(1) Buddha set forth the eight-fold path to truth. In essence Buddha taught that life is suffering. The eight steps in his teachings are steps to escape the circle of suffering—man reaching God, man working his way up the ladder to salvation, and man seeking Nirvana.

(2) In Christianity God has found humankind. He is searching us. He is the hound of heaven that won't let us rest until he catches us. The theological meaning of grace is this fact of God acting to bridge the gulf that separates humankind and divinity.

(3) Religious observances for the Christian are a response to God's acts. We worship because God has first put a yearning in our hearts. We pray because God's spirit is moving within our inner beings. We serve our fellow man not to earn merits for salvation but to express gratitude for what God has done for us.

(d) After we've acknowledged the similarities between the religions of the world, we can't remain ignorant of the distinctive teachings of Christianity. All of these teachings are summed up in the life of him whom we call Christ. That's why we say with Peter there is no other name under heaven by which men can be saved.
—R. Ralph Nichols.

Illustration

TWO PLUS TWO.   A preacher was standing at the rear of the auditorium greeting the people. A young university senior came by and said, "Sir, I did not appreciate your message." "What did you not like about it?" replied the pastor. "Sir, did you not say that Jesus is the way and the truth and the life and that no man can come unto the Father except by him?" "No, I didn't say that. The Bible says that," said the pastor. "That is undoubtedly the most narrowminded, dogmatic, and bigoted statement I have heard," commented the student. "Son, what is your major?" "Mathematics." "Well, I am going to ask you a question that may seem silly. If I asked you how much two plus two is, what would you say?" "Why, it is four," replied the student. "How about three?" "No, four." "Five?" "No, four." "Son, that is one of the most narrow-minded, dogmatic, and bigoted statements I have ever heard," said the preacher. "However, I think I know why you are so certain that two plus two equals four. As you get into more complex problems in mathematics, if you have not arrived at the correct sum

THE MINISTERS MANUAL FOR 1981

150

of two and two, your ultimate answers will be wrong. And for this same reason I say to you that Jesus Christ is the only way, the only truth, and the only life because in my experience I know that unless I have come to this conclusion, then all the ultimate answers in life are going to come up wrong."—Frank Pollard.

Sermon Suggestions

THE CHRISTIAN'S ROLE.   Text: Eph. 5: 30. A member of the congregation is (1) growing (Eph. 4:11–16), (2) supportive (Eph. 4:1–2), (3) talented (Eph. 4:11–12), (4) worshipful (Eph. 4:23–24), (5) a witness (Eph. 4:17, 20), (6) a steward (Rom. 12:1), and (7) a difference-maker (Rom. 12:11–12).—Jerry Redus.

FINDING MEANING IN LIFE.   Text: Luke 12:31. (1) We find meaning in life as we seek to discover that which will bring abiding joy. (2) Meaning comes through work worth doing to which we give our best. (3) Meaning is found as we develop skills adequate for the tasks at hand. (4) Meaning is a result of finding a purpose that is in harmony with the spirit of love and goodwill as found in Jesus Christ and that will unify our lives and bring a quality that can know no end.—Nenien C. McPherson.

Worship Aids

CALL TO WORSHIP.   "Both young men and maidens, old men and children: let them praise the name of the Lord: for his name alone is excellent; his glory is above the earth and heaven." Ps. 148: 12–13.

INVOCATION.   Teach us, good Lord, in our days of rest to put our worship and prayer first, and may we never let the services of the church be crowded out of our lives. Keep before us the vision of thy dear son Jesus Christ, who in his boyhood days worshiped with his family, and may that vision inspire us and all men to unite as members of the church universal in witness, in worship, and in love.

OFFERTORY SENTENCE.   "Go, and sell that thou hast, and give to the poor, and thou shalt have treasure in heaven: and come and follow me." Matt. 19:21.

OFFERTORY PRAYER.   O living Christ, help us to know the ecstasy of thine everlasting lordship that we may more perfectly become cheerful givers.

PRAYER.   O God of love, we come to this holy place, each of us with his own needs and hopes. So we come seeking your comfort and guidance concerning our individual needs.

We come also aware of the hopes and turmoils of groups of people and of our nations today. So we come here, with Christ as our example, as we seek to know how he would have us to serve him and our fellow brothers and sisters in this spectacular but troublesome day.

We pray that all who have sorrows or pains or troubles may believe in your love and feel your concern and guidance for them and for all of humanity.—Gene N. Branson.

EVENING SERVICE

Topic: Life's Four Tasks (Baccalaureate)
TEXT: Eccl. 9:10.

Life has certain basic tasks that every one must perform. No one can escape them. The question is whether or not we do them well.

I. *To learn.*

(a) This begins almost at birth and is one of the developmental tasks psychologists talk about. An infant has no information, skills, or experience, but he has the capacity to learn.

(b) One of the most important learning experiences is acquiring a language. Anyone who has learned another language knows how difficult it is. Yet the infant must do this with no other language to base it on. Then comes reading, discovering that the strange markings we call letters and words have meaning and contain ideas. So he or she continues through school. Then comes the test! For many all learning ceases; for others it is a lifelong experience.

(c) Not all learning is contained in books or imparted in classrooms. We learn by experience, meditation, and observation. Not all learning consists of knowing facts; it also includes learning to be patient, humble, and kind.

II. *To love.*

(a) The infant is the center of his or her world. Others feed babies, care for them, and protect them. Gradually they begin to distinguish those around them—mother, father, brothers, and sisters. As the years go by, friends, relatives, playmates, teachers, neighbors, and innumerable others are added to the people within their experience.

(b) They no longer hold center stage but must find a place for themselves in this world of people. How well they are able to find that place will go a long way in determining their happiness and satisfaction in life. One of the most important tasks of all is to learn to love.

(c) Psychology underlines the fact that only one who can love and be loved is emotionally mature. Only one who loves finds life's deepest satisfactions. Love is not easy. It takes honest effort to put ourselves in another's place and to feel as others feel.

III. *To serve.*

(a) An infant cannot do things for others. A child, moving from infancy to youth to adulthood, gradually accepts responsibility until he or she is completely independent.

(b) A person can be seemingly independent and still be self-centered. One who accepts the Christian teaching goes beyond this to the point where he or she lives not for self but to serve. This is also true psychologically. Those who find the greatest satisfactions are those who have forgotten self.

IV. *To trust.*

(a) We need to believe in something. We have to have faith. The infant has no experience and no knowledge on which to base a faith. This is why parenthood is so sacred. To a large extent a child takes over the family faith. It is received more by contagion than by direct teaching.

(b) As the child grows older he or she may attend a college or university, where faith must be related to the findings of science, psychology, philosophy, and sociology. This isn't easy, but it is important.

(c) Faith is not only a matter of learning. Ultimately it is an act of commitment in which one goes as far as he or she can intellectually and then makes an adventure of faith and finds that it is real.— Charles F. Kemp in *The Disciple.*

SUNDAY: JUNE TWENTY-FIRST

MORNING SERVICE

Topic: A Christian Father's Role (Father's Day)

Text: Ezra 7:27.

I. With fatherhood comes the responsibility of being the best provider a father can be. A good father will do all in his power to provide adequately for his wife and children.

II. A good father will be deeply concerned for the future of his children. His desire will be to prepare them for the future by providing educational opportunities and training. To do this many fathers sacrifice and work over-

time. Some even secure additional jobs.

III. A good father will strive to be a worthy example for his children. He will never allow occasions to develop where his children may suspect that he is not being honest. He will be certain that, while he wants to be successful in life, he will not set an example of getting ahead by using questionable methods.

IV. A good father will be considerate of his children and will not intentionally do anything to embarrass them. He will be big enough to say, "I am sorry," when occasion calls for him to do so. He will always show interest in his children and in their work. This may cause him to delay doing something he wants to do. A father who is kind and considerate of his children, who will take time to show interest in them and their activities, is a father who will receive his children's respect without having to demand it.

V. A good father is one who will take time to do things with his children. Often when the father is busy the children and the mother find it necessary to do things alone. No matter what the mother and children do, it is always more enjoyable for them when the father is along.

VI. A good father will be a church-going father. God has made fathers the head of the family. The father is to be the family leader. A loved and respected father will usually be successful in persuading his family to go with him to church.

VII. A good father will be a Christian father. He cannot love his children as he ought to love them without first loving God. A Christian father has special benefits. He can pray and ask God for guidance in rearing his children. He can commit his children to God's care, knowing that God is faithful to those who serve him.

VIII. A good father will be a praying father. He will lead his family in devotions. He will teach his children the importance of prayer. When children observe their father seeking God for guidance and when they detect, through listening to him pray, that he depends upon God to supply his daily needs, they too will learn how to trust God.

IX. A good father will be a model church member. He will never do anything or say anything that would weaken his children's appreciation for the church or for the pastor. He will participate in and support the church's program to the best of his ability. He will do everything he can to build respect in the hearts of his children for God, for God's house, and for God's work.—O. W. Polen in *Church of God Evangel.*

Illustrations

HOMECOMING.   While traveling by train on one occasion, from my train window I saw a man pushing a loaded wheelbarrow up an incline toward what must have been his home. It was late in the afternoon, and to me, as I assessed the situation, he appeared to be a dispirited person. I would have said, as I looked at him, that life had beaten him with the heavy end of a stick. Then suddenly around the corner of the house two children burst into view, cleanly dressed and their faces laughing, and in the highest of exuberant spirits shouting to their father, they ran and jumped into the already loaded wheelbarrow. Instantly that man was transformed right before my very eyes. Immediately his bent form straightened, his tiredness left him, and an elasticity came into his step and a new light into his eyes, for now his burden had been transformed into his joy.—John E. Hines.

HOW TO RAISE YOUR PARENTS.   (1) Do not be afraid to speak their language. Try to use strange-sounding phrases like "I'll help with the dishes" and "Yes." (2) Try to understand their music. Play Andy Williams' "Moon River" on the stereo until you are accustomed to the sound. (3) Be patient with underachievers. When you catch your dieting mom sneaking salted peanuts, do not show your disapproval. Tell her you like fat mothers. (4) Encourage your parents to talk about their problems. Try to keep in mind that to them things like earning a living and paying off the mortgage seem important. (5) Be tolerant of their appearance. When your dad gets a haircut, don't feel personally humiliated. It's important to him to look like his peers. (6) If they do something you consider wrong, let them know it's their behavior you dislike, not themselves.—Bruce Larson.

Sermon Suggestions

OUR DAILY BREAD.   Text: Matt. 6:11. (1) God will give what we need. (2) Man must earn what he obtains. To earn something means that one deserves to have it. We must be worthy of what we receive. (3) We are to share this bread. Man ministers to his fellow man. We help God answer our brother's prayer for bread. God's goodness demands man's goodness expressed in help to his neighbor.—Phillips Packer Elliott.

LIVING WITH DIGNITY.   Text: I John 2: 28. (1) To live with dignity is to be possessed of an inner confidence in God which keeps us from being bowled over by sudden shifts of circumstance. (2) To live with dignity is to face the crises of life and death with poise. (3) To live with dignity is to live with a certain reserve which is born of self-respect. (4) To live with dignity is to keep one's head when others are losing theirs and blaming it on you. (5) To live with dignity is to live as children of God who crowned us with glory and honor and made us to have dominion over the earth, the sea, and the air—yes, and over our own bodies and minds.—Ralph W. Sockman.

Worship Aids

CALL TO WORSHIP.   "Let all those that put their trust in thee rejoice: let them ever shout for joy because thou defendest them; let them also that love thy name be joyful in thee." Ps. 5:11.

INVOCATION.   Almighty God, our heavenly Father, who reignest over all things in thy wisdom, power, and love: we adore thee for thy glory and majesty, and we praise thee for thy grace and truth to us in thy son our savior. Grant us the help of thy Holy Spirit, we beseech thee, that we may worship thee in spirit and in truth.

OFFERTORY SENTENCE.   "Seek ye first the kingdom of God, and his righteousness, and all these things shall be added unto you." Matt. 6:33.

OFFERTORY PRAYER.   Almighty God, may we trust more and more in thy kind providence, and may our submission to thy will be revealed in the deep devotion expressed through these gifts we offer in Christ's name.

LITANY.   Let us thank God for all of his blessings.

For the wonders of your creation; for the beauty of the earth; for the order you did bring out of chaos; for life itself:
We thank you, O Lord.
That within the created order and for your own purpose you did ordain and establish the sacred order of marriage and the family:
We thank you, O Lord.
That as we have been loved by your son and have been instructed by your spirit in the ways of love, both human and divine:
So perpetuate your love within our hearts that we may love you fully and that we may love one another freely and sincerely.
That our homes may be built upon our trust in you; that our marriages may be strengthened by bonds eternal; and that our children may be brought up to know you and to love you:
We beseech you to hear us, good Lord.
That within our homes your word may be heard with reverence and appreciation; that your son may reside with us; and that your Holy Spirit may dwell within our hearts:
We beseech you to hear us, good Lord.
From coldness of heart; from idle talk and gossip; from lack of kindness and sympathy for others; and from the withholding of love:
Good Lord, deliver us this day, we pray.
From the pursuit of that which is to perish; from selfishness and avarice; from self-seeking and vainglory; from preoccupation with the temporal and the trivial:
Good Lord, deliver us this day, we pray.
From provincialism and narrowness; from a shallow tolerance and a lack of studied conviction; and from poverty of thought and spirit:
Good Lord, deliver us this day, we pray.
That our homes may be happy and that therein our children may find security, understanding, patience, joy, gentleness, self-control, godliness, and the infinite riches of your grace:
Be our strength and guide, good Lord.
That as husbands and wives may we be as one with our mates; that we may encourage each other in faith and discipleship; and that we may share the dreams,

hopes, nobility, and the excitement and adventure of the Christian pilgrimage:

Be our strength and guide, good Lord.

That as sons and daughters may we honor, obey, and revere our parents; that we may build upon the foundations they have laid for us; and that we may never willingly cause them grief or distress but that we may ever be to them means of joy and grace:

Be our strength and guide, good Lord. —William M. Everhart.

EVENING SERVICE

Topic: Above the Clouds

Text: Rom. 8:18.

The Bible has a great deal to say about clouds, for they sometime symbolize the spiritual forces which obscure the face of God. The Bible indicates that clouds are given to us for a purpose and that there is glory in the clouds and that every cloud has a silver lining.

I. *The cloud of suffering.* The Bible teaches that human suffering is inescapable. We must accept it as an integral part of life. Job said, "Man that is born of woman is of a few days, and full of trouble" (Job 14:1). Life has its beginning in suffering. Life's span is marked by pain, suffering, tragedy, and disappointment, and our lives terminate with the enemy called death. The person who expects to escape the pangs of suffering and disappointment simply has no knowledge of the Bible, of history, or of life.

II. *The cloud of discouragement.* Many of the great Bible characters became discouraged. Discouragement is no new device. It is as old as the history of man. Discouragement is the very opposite of faith. The Bible says, "Wait on the Lord; be of good courage, and he shall strengthen thine heart: wait I say, on the Lord" (Ps. 27:14).

III. *The cloud of disappointment.* There have been times during disappointments that I felt life seemed no longer worth living. But we are called according to God's purpose, and if we love God, all things do work together for good. The psalmist said, "He guided them by the skillfulness of his hands" (Ps. 78:72).—Larry K. Salter.

SUNDAY: JUNE TWENTY-EIGHTH

MORNING SERVICE

Topic: Back to Basics

Text: Matt. 28:18–20.

There is no passage in scripture that will take us back to basics more than the closing words of Matt. 28. Jesus Christ gave us here three basics.

I. He gives us a *claim.* "All authority in heaven and in earth has been given to me" (v. 18).

(a) Many of us, when we use that word authority, think of someone trying to impose something on us. We think of someone trying to jam something down our throats. But Jesus wasn't like that. Jesus wasn't someone who went around saying: "Hey, I'm the authority. You had better do what I say." He had strength, and he made fantastic claims. But Jesus didn't impose his authority. Rather he exposed it.

(b) There was a gentleness, beauty, poise, and a real strength about Jesus Christ. In effect he said, "This is the way it was meant to be." People looked at him and said: "Yes, there is an inner authority that Jesus has. He speaks the truth, and he lives the truth. Now we will put that truth on the cross. We will crucify that authority." But God raised him up from the dead again and said, "All authority in heaven and in earth is given to Jesus Christ."

II. Jesus gives the *command.* "Go, therefore, and make disciples of all nations."

(a) That is the most basic task of the church of Jesus Christ. Jesus didn't say, "Go and have conventions." Jesus didn't say, "Go and have crusades." Jesus didn't say, "Go and make speeches." Jesus didn't say, "Go and have programs." Jesus didn't say, "Go and build buildings." All of these things are proper and necessary at certain times.

But what he said was, "Go and make disciples."

(b) The real question is, how many of those people become disciples? Jesus said we are to become identified with him and with the community of his church. Then he says we are to teach them to observe all things that he has commanded us. He wants disciples who will glorify God by reflecting his character in their lives.

(c) When Jesus said "Go," that is not really an imperative. The way that actually should be translated is "As you go, make disciples." Jesus isn't simply saying, "Go to India, go to Japan, and go to Brazil." He is saying, "Jack, John, Bill, Jane, Mary, as you go through the normal traffic patterns of your life, make disciples."

(d) Jesus Christ didn't very often go out of his way to reach people. He did sometimes. But Jesus was so sensitive to people that even when he was on his way to the cross he saw a blind man beside the road and a little twisted tax collector up in the tree. He saw people along the traffic pattern of his life who were hungry for God, and he reached out to them, loved them, spoke to them, won them, and discipled them. Jesus Christ is saying to each one of us: as you travel the normal traffic patterns of your life, make disciples. Every one of us can do that.

III. Jesus says, "I am with you always." (a) This is his promise. It is the basic need of our lives and the basic need of our world. People everywhere are saying, "Do you know God?" Laymen are saying to us who are pastors: "Do you know God? Can you help me to know him?" Our friends and neighbors are saying: "Do you know God? Can you introduce him to me?"

(b) "Lo, I am with you always, even to the end of the world." We need that renewing, refreshing time in the presence of the Lord. Some of us need to say that what we need and what our church needs more than anything else is renewal. We need that sense of God's living presence in our lives so that we will begin to seek first his kingdom.—Leighton Ford.

Illustrations

INVENTORY.   Prayer is probably least effective when performed in public. Jesus seemed to believe that prayer's requirements were that it be very personal and very honest. Prayer is the quiet inventory of you. Prayer is the setting the lens of your soul on time-exposure.—James O. Gilliom.

ACCORDING TO YOUR FAITH.   Faith says yes to our yes and no to our no. The sailor must hoist his sail if he is to catch the wind. The miner must sink his shaft if he is to discover the gold. The engineer must swing his bridge if he is to harness the river. The aviator must spread his wings if he is to search the sky. The financier must make his investment if he is to find his fortune. The Christian must prepare the way if the living God is to appear.—Hugh T. Kerr.

Sermon Suggestions

BREAKING THE WORRY HABIT.   Text: Luke 10:41. (1) Examine your worries carefully and realistically. (2) Do not dwell on your own troubles. (3) Replace your worrying thought with some other thought that will interest you and stimulate you. (4) Replace your doubting, restless, distrustful, and worrying attitudes with a trustful and confident faith in God. —David J. Davis.

WHERE DO YOU LIVE?   Text: I Pet. 2:5. The house of life has three stories and also a basement as Freud reminded us. (1) On the first floor we live by instinct, impulse, and force. There life is a struggle, and the fittest survive. Desire, not duty, is a rule. (2) On the second floor we live by obligation, moral law, and the beginnings of reason. We begin to live by moral judgment and realize that selfishness is self-defeating. (3) On the third floor we live by insight which is based on faith. There we consider not merely desire but the common good.—Myron J. Taylor.

Worship Aids

CALL TO WORSHIP. "They that wait upon the Lord shall renew their strength; they shall mount up with wings as eagles; they shall run, and not be weary; and they shall walk, and not faint." Isa. 40:31.

INVOCATION. Out of our darkness we are come to thee for light; out of our sorrows we are come to thee for joy; out of our doubts we are come to thee for certainty; out of our anxieties we are come to thee for peace; out of our sinning we are come to thee for thy forgiving love. Open thou thine hand this day and satisfy our every need. This we ask for thy love's sake.

OFFERTORY SENTENCE. "I will freely sacrifice unto thee: I will praise thy name, O Lord; for it is good." Ps. 54:6.

OFFERTORY PRAYER. Our Father, open our eyes, we pray, to the glorious opportunities of sharing with others our blessed experiences of fellowship with one another and with thee.

PRAYER. We come to thy house this day, our Father, to open our hearts to thee, to thank thee for thy loving kindness to the children of men, and to acknowledge our deep dependence upon thee. We confess that we have not always loved thee with all our heart, soul, strength, and mind. We have made the little concerns of this earthly life so important that we have neglected thy will for us. We have concentrated so intensely on schemes to get our own way that we have forgotten thy ways. We have allowed desire to lead us where we should have been led only by thee. Forgive our blindness and our willingness to be drawn away from the highest that we know. Renew a right spirit within us, O God, that we may be released to continue the building of thy kingdom among men.

Come close to us, O God. Teach us the greatness of thy presence. Bless those who fight on beds of pain. Sustain the spirit of those who know that they are close to heaven's door. Quicken the spirits of those who must make the decisions for many people. Break the hardness of heart of those who have turned from thee. Slaughter unrighteousness in the heart of every man that the kingdoms of this world might become the kingdom of thy son, Jesus Christ.—Ray C. Hollis, Jr.

EVENING SERVICE

Topic: Growing as Christians
TEXT: Eph. 4:15.

Would you like to move into the center of the life of faith? Are you bored with sitting on the non-productive edges where Christianity seems trivial instead of triumphant? Then let me suggest three rungs of a ladder of growth. There are levels to conversion. It is not all a level plateau.

I. A person gets converted from his self-centered sinfulness to Christ as savior.

II. Then he gets converted—and this is usually at a later date—to the idea of the church as the body of Christ. He realizes that solitary salvation is only the beginning. As a hand needs an arm and an arm needs a body, so the believer needs the nourishment and support of a congregation of like-minded disciples of Christ.

III. A person is saved to serve Christ and not just to sit around waiting for heaven. Musicians don't make violins to hang on the walls for decoration. They carve them to tuck under the chin and reverbrate the laughter and sorrows of the soul as vibrated by the finger and bow. Likewise Christ saves us to grow and fulfill ourselves in his contemporary program of redemptive mission and service.

IV. When a growing Christian moves up along these lines of maturity, he senses he is part of the communion of saints. The church is more than a parish hall; it is a family house. The members are more than a ticket-holding audience; they are kinsfolk of faith. Salvation is more than a redeemable bond twenty or forty years away; it is a bid to serve now in the present ministry of the loving Christ who is still alive and at work.—Bryant M. Kirkland.

SUNDAY: JULY FIFTH

MORNING SERVICE

Topic: The Christian as Patriot (Independence Sunday)

TEXT: Ps. 137:5.

How can we as American Christians reconcile our fundamentally unchanged love of country with our self-consciousness about that love? What guidelines do the scriptures offer? And how can these guidelines be translated into responsible patriotism?

I. One guideline can be found in the radical monotheism of the Bible: "I am the Lord thy God . . . Thou shalt have no other gods before me . . . Thou shalt not make unto thee any . . . image," whether of engraved stone or colored cloth, to worship in God's place. The nation has always been the most tempting of idols. While the great prophets worried about the frequent relapses of their people into the old ways of the fertility cults, they worried far more about their people's self-worship—about the way the chosen people would forget that it was God who had chosen them and that he had chosen them not for special favor but for a special mission.

II. Another biblical guideline is found in Jesus' cryptic saying, "Render to Caesar the things that are Caesar's and to God the things that are God's." This saying has been bent and twisted by both radical right and radical left.

(a) The saying belongs in the radical middle. Jesus insists that loyalty to God must transcend loyalty to country, to family, and to career. But this is what makes the demand for civic loyalty and for patriotism remarkable. For what Jesus is saying is that loyalty to country, indeed to the government that both governs and symbolizes the country at a given time, is an ordinary religious responsibility, and that only extraordinary circumstances can justify our rejecting this responsibility.

(b) Jesus rebukes nationalism with its "my country, right or wrong" mind-set; but he blesses the patriot who prays, "God mend thine every flaw."

III. The Bible offers a third guideline. In biblical perspective, history has a beginning and an end, and both beginning and end repose securely in the hands of God.

(a) The Bible is hard on both the superpatriot, who makes an idol of some mirage of the nation's golden past, and the hypercritic, who makes an idol of some mirage of the world's golden future.

(b) What both superpatriot and hypercritic lack is the Bible's perspective in which God, the Lord of history, rules over a changing, evolving kingdom that can never be identified with any nation, any social order, or any human utopia—future or past.

IV. How can these guidelines be applied to the problem of patriotism that we confront as Christian Americans? What are some of the practical requirements of a responsible, biblically-grounded patriotism in this year of our Lord?

(a) Such patriotism requires of us an identification with our nation that is neither ambivalent nor apologetic. The battle of the pronouns is always with us.

(1) When our athletes win gold medals at the Olympics or when our astronauts land on the moon, we respond in the first person plural. We have brought home all those medals. We have landed with all that hardware in crater X. But when our taxes go up, it is they who are robbing us, they who are interferring with our life plans, and they who are squandering our money on nuclear arms.

(2) What we need to get through our heads is that we are they. We are America. We are the United States, both governors and governed, and our system of government provides channels for the resolution of all of our conflicts because it also provides channels for changing the channels. Responsible, biblically-grounded patriotism mandates us to work at reforming our institutions through whatever channels may be available, exclusive of violence, and to seek new channels when the old ones seem hopelessly clogged.

(b) Responsible, biblically-grounded patriotism demands that we love all other Americans with Christian love.

(1) This sounds like a platitude until we recall that Christian love is a special kind of love for which the New Testament has a separate word—agape. This love has nothing to do with liking and everything to do with justice.

(2) As American Christians we are expected to agitate for impartial justice for all Americans, regardless of how we may feel about them. God does not expect us to have everybody in for dinner. He does expect us to make sure that everybody can afford a decent dinner.

(c) Patriotism demands that we be able to visualize this world without these United States.

(1) We are a struggling, amazing giant of a nation and, like all nations, a mortal nation. As American Christians, we are responsible for making our country worthy to survive and deserving of survival in the eyes of a righteous God. Christians have survived the rise and fall of other empires and will survive the fall of this empire, if and when that fall is fated to occur.

(2) Only a lover of a country can see beyond the country's self-interest and beyond the country itself. Few people loved their people more than did Amos or Jeremiah. Their quarrels with their nation were lover's quarrels. No one loved God's people, the Jews, more than Jesus did. His quarrel with his country and with its political and religious leaders, was precisely that they were not living up to the ideals and the vision of the prophets, not acting like leaders of the people God had chosen to demonstrate and mediate his love for the human race.

(d) Christian patriotism is critical patriotism. Mature love is not blind. Neither is mature love of country. Mature love has keen, critical eyes. Jesus loved people critically because he saw them not just as they were but as they might be, as God intended them to be. Jesus loved his country critically because he knew it not just as it was but as it was

destined to be in God's design.—John Bodo in *A.D.*

Illustrations

FOLLOWERS AND LEADERS.   Under our Constitution the people are the leader. The phrase used by the founding fathers was "the people are king." And their will, expressed through the electoral process, is sovereign.

Our system was designed to produce followers in government, not leaders—faithful representatives of the people and obedient servants of "the king." Fortunately, for most of the 200 years of our history, the American people have not needed strong leaders.

The need for a leader is created when the people, although certain of their goals, are uncertain, confused, or divided about how to reach them. If the Israelites had preferred the fleshpots of Egypt, Moses could not have led them to the promised land. Nor would they have needed Moses if the way had been open and easy.

For most of our nation's life the people knew where they wanted to go, the way was open, and the Constitution permitted them to get there on their own steam.—Clare Booth Luce.

BRILLIANT TAPESTRY.   The story and meaning of America is unique in the annals of man—a brilliant tapestry of people, land, cities, ideas, machines, triumphs, failures, peace, sacrifice, and most of all, spirit. Our nation is a vast land of millions of people scattered across limitless miles of high mountains and fertile plains, of barren deserts and rich farmlands. It is made up of a polyglot citizenry, speaking in many tongues and heir to a multitude of traditions. It is remarkable that, in spite of our varied backgrounds, we are occasionally able to merge ourselves into a single identity—sometimes in a song, in devotion to a man we revere, in compassion for the misfortune of an individual, and most curious of all, in a holiday.—Henry N. Ferguson.

Sermon Suggestions

THE FAITH OF OUR FATHERS.   Text: Gen. 12:1–3. (1) Their bed-rock belief in the sovereignty of God. (2) Their respect for the dignity of the individual. (3) Their spirit of conciliation. (4) Their concept of serving all mankind.

LIVING WITH DANGER.   Text: Matt. 27:1. (1) God gives clarity of vision to see danger. (2) God gives us courage to confront danger. (3) God gives preparation for handling danger when it comes.

Worship Aids

CALL TO WORSHIP.   "We have thought of thy lovingkindness, O God, in the midst of thy temple. According to thy name, O God, so is thy praise unto the ends of the earth." Ps. 48:9–10.

INVOCATION.   Our Father, we give thanks for Jesus Christ our savior. Help us to receive the fullness of thy salvation. Grant us grace to live joyful, obedient, and triumphant lives as thy children in this world. May the spirit of peace reign within our hearts and invade the nations of the world.

OFFERTORY SENTENCE.   "Of every man that giveth willingly with his heart ye shall take my offering [saith the Lord]." Exod. 25:2.

OFFERTORY PRAYER.   We thank thee, O God, for another anniversary of our nation's independence and pray that this rich gift may be an opportunity to serve one another in love.

PRAYER.   Eternal God, thou who watchest over the destiny of men and nations, in these moments of worship, we celebrate thy presence in the midst of our common life. We come before thee in awesome reverence, for we acknowledge that the ground on which we stand is holy ground, hallowed by the blood, sweat, and tears of men and women of this and previous generations who have supremely sacrificed for the freedom that we enjoy today.

Grant, O Father, that in our generation we may not squander the opportunity which has been so dearly bought or relinquish the ideals for which sacrifice has been so costly made, but may we set ourselves to the unfinished business of freedom as we identify ourselves with the oppressed in our nation and the nations of the world. As is true of all of life's blessings, help us to realize that a freedom that is not shared is soon lost.—John Thompson.

EVENING SERVICE

Topic: Profile of a Patriot

TEXT: Ps. 137:5.

I. It is not enough for the patriot to be solely provincial.

(a) The patriot has to be provincial in many ways. The psalmist said, "If I forget the old Jerusalem let my right hand forget her cunning." A local and provincial loyalty was part of the strength of the psalmist's life. He was able to endure the exile of Babylonia because there was some place he called his homeland. This origin gave him strength.

(b) The patriot has local loyalties. Theodore Parker Ferris said: "You'll never find a man who loves the world in general who does not love some little spot of the world in particular. You'll never find a person who loves family life in general who is not committed to some one family for which he would gladly die. You'll never find a man who is interested in world politics who is not interested in the political life and social life of his own town. A man becomes universal to the degree to which he is willing to be provincial." Local and provincial loyalties are the cradle in which the larger loyalties grow.

(c) Shakespeare never left the shores of England. His mature life was bounded by the city limits of London, the walls of the Globe Theatre, and some time spent at Stratford. Yet he revealed the heights and depths of human nature to people all over the globe. It was rightfully named the Globe Theatre because he spoke a universal language. It was the intensity of his local commitment that produced the extensiveness of his world-wide influence.

(d) I don't want to get rid of provincialism altogether. Perhaps this is not where patriots should end, but it's the place where patriots should at least begin. I would not want to live in a world where everything was uniform. I like things to be differentiated. In a sense I wouldn't want one world. I like for people to be unique. I wouldn't want all the world to be like America. Diversity enriches human life.

II. Patriotism is not enough when it just wants to preserve the past.

(a) The true patriot wants to preserve the best in the past. Sometimes we moderns don't realize the price that has been paid for some of the great qualities that are ours. We're sometimes flippant in our attitude toward great institutions and traditions.

(b) The patriot realizes that the best part of our history has come because we fought hard for principles which make the purpose of the state to serve the causes of the individual. When you think of Franklin, Washington, John Adams, Jefferson, and Madison, only a partial list, their work was to preserve the relationship of the individual citizen to the nation. These men believed in the independence of the nation and in self-government not as an obstruction or as an end in itself but as a specific way of protecting individual man and assuring his right to participate in the shaping of his society. The patriot wants to preserve this truth.

(c) The patriot believes that we can correct our errors. We don't have a perfect history. There are times in our national history that are embarrassing to read about. Our treatment of the Indians, our treatment of the Negroes and slaves, and our imperialistic attitudes toward foreign countries are blemishes on our record. The patriot doesn't think that everything about America is best.

(d) Preserving the best doesn't mean going back somewhere into the past and staying there. It means taking the best in our history and the best in our heritage and cleansing the present and changing it to fulfill the true dream of America.

III. The patriotism that is enough is the one that loves peace.

(a) The peacemaker longs for the day when armament will not be necessary, when we will be delivered not by the sword but from the sword, when the sword will be beaten into plowshares, and when money spent on nuclear arms and bombers will be used for food, housing, and the fighting of disease. That's the ultimate hope of the peacemaker.

(b) Arnold Toynbee expressed the hope that our age may be remembered not for its horrifying crimes nor for its astonishing inventions but chiefly for its having been the first age in which people dared to think it practicable to make the benefits of civilization available for the whole human race.

(c) There are a lot of patriots who do not march with flags or the sound of beating drums, but they are working for justice and they're working for equality and righteousness and goodwill within the nation. Patriots want our nation to be strong within.—C. A. McClain, Jr.

SUNDAY: JULY TWELFTH

MORNING SERVICE

Topic: The Conditions for Forgiveness
Text: Matt. 6:12.
I. We need to realize our need of forgiveness.

(a) Jesus spoke of debts and debts are actually sins. But while intellectually most of us will concede that we sin, a lot of people never come to believe that their sins are anything more than minor blemishes that can be corrected by living a little better. They don't really understand the character and depth of sin.

(b) Originally the New Testament was written in Greek. There were five words which described the various manifestations of sin.

(1) The first word literally meant to miss the mark. It had to do with falling short of God's expectations for us.

(2) The second word visualized a line—one side of which was legal, the other side of which was illegal. Sin, according to that word, was stepping over the line from the legal side to the illegal side. An example of that manifestation of sin would be the twisting or distorting of the truth.

(3) The third word suggested a slipping backward. A modern analogy might go like this. You're driving your car and hit an icy spot, and the car slips off the road. So, if we are not careful, we may lose control of our lives, slip, and do some wrong thing.

(4) The fourth word described deliberate willful sinning—doing what we know full well is wrong.

(5) The fifth, the one Jesus used in the text, meant to incur a debt you could not pay.

(c) When we reflect on the various forms that sin can take, we must realize that there is not one of us who is not guilty before God. We all sin, we all fall short of his glory, and we all miss the mark, the standard he has set for us. We do so overtly, and we do so subtly.

II. We need to want forgiveness. (a) Jesus said that we ought to come to God and ask him for forgiveness. This illustrates that forgiveness is not something which is forced upon us. It is something we desire, and it is something God gives us when we are diligently seeking it.

(b) Many people fail to ask God for the forgiveness they so badly need because they may not recognize the depth of their sin and they may let pride get in the way. Because of their fear of embarrassment and because they are afraid they will be humiliated, many people are content to live lives in which there is no peace because there has been no forgiveness.

III. The third condition for forgiveness is the practice of forgiveness.

(a) Jesus said that unless we are willing to forgive others God will not be willing to forgive us. Why does God say that the practice of forgiveness is a condition for receiving it? Forgiveness is the only proper response to the forgiveness we have already received. It was a very difficult thing for God to forgive us. It was difficult because God took sin seriously and not at all lightly. That meant his having to step into human history and make that long shameful journey all the way to the cross.

(b) The forgiveness we want is the forgiveness we must give. If we fail to reach out in love and mercy to others, how can we possibly expect that God is going to reach out with his forgiveness to us?—Arthur McPhee.

Illustrations

SINS FORGIVEN. The purpose of forgiveness of sins as a principle of life is the continual removal of fear and the isolation that springs from fear. The sense of guilt isolates a man from his fellows because it carries with it the feeling that his fellows have a right to punish him. The forgiveness of sin expresses a social attitude which restores self-confidence and maintains a consciousness which overcomes any sense of isolation.—John Macmurray.

REDEMPTIVE LOVE. When Gandhi was a young man in the south of India, he went on a journey. When he came back to the camp of which he was in charge, he found that an eighteen-year-old fellow had done a great and grievous wrong. Gandhi began to think: "How can I right this wrong? I can punish him, but punishment doesn't prove to be redemptive. I can just overlook it, in which case the young man will use it as license for doing worse. Or I can do this, and this I will do." He called the young man in and said: "In my absence you have done a very great and grievous wrong. The reason for your failure is that I have failed you. I, your teacher and example, have not been to you what I ought to have been or you would not have fallen. Because I have failed you, I am going on a two-week fast." The sullen young man left the room. Every time he sat down to eat in the next room, he knew that Ghandi was not eating. Every time he put a spoonful of food into his mouth, he knew that Gandhi was starving. After three days the young man fell down on the floor and said, "Sir, forgive me." Gandhi said, "There is no forgiveness necessary, but if you feel the need of it, I grant it to you." The young man said, "Well, then, will you stop your fast?" "If I stopped my fast, I would be using it as an instrument to get you to do what is right. I am fasting because I failed you. As your teacher and as your example I must complete the fast." So for the remainder of the two weeks he did not take food of any kind. Every time the young man sat down to eat he was conscious that for him Gandhi was starving. The young man knew that Gandhi loved him so much that he was willing to enter into his sin and failure and take his shortcomings as his own.—Walter L. Dosch.

Sermon Suggestions

HOW TO DEAL WITH HOSTILITY IN OTHERS. Text: Rom. 12:17–18. (1) We can keep open the door of goodwill. "Bless those who persecute you." (2) We can go through the door in some action of goodwill. Never avenge yourself, says Paul. Leave that to God. Your duty is to repay evil with good. (3) We can give ourselves to the noblest action of goodwill. We can pray for our enemies. "Pray for your enemies," commands Jesus.—Everett W. Palmer.

THE RELIGION OF A HEALTHY MIND. Text: Rom. 8:6. (1) Turns our eyes toward God. (2) Takes us out of the center of our world. (3) Makes love our habitual way of responding. (4) Gives us a proper sense of humility. (5) Causes us to have a faith in ourselves because God has the right of way in our lives and we know he desires our best always.—Nenien C. McPherson, Jr.

Worship Aids

CALL TO WORSHIP. "I will lift up mine eyes unto the hills, from whence cometh my help. My help cometh from the Lord, which made heaven and earth." Ps. 121: 1–2.

INVOCATION. O God, whose name is great, whose goodness is inexhaustible, who art worshiped and served by all the hosts of heaven: touch our hearts, search out our consciences, and cast out of us every evil thought and base desire; all envy, wrath, and remembrance of injuries; and every motion of flesh and spirit that is contrary to thy holy will.

OFFERTORY SENTENCE. "If there be first a willing mind, it is accepted according to that which a man hath, and not according to that which he hath not." II Cor. 8:12.

OFFERTORY PRAYER. O heavenly Father, we pray that thy blessings, which are as countless as the stars, may be so used as to bring light and love to thy children everywhere.

PRAYER. Eternal God, in whom the mystery of existence is made known and is given meaning, enter our waiting hearts and lift us above the noise and crowding of life. Transport us from the realm of the spontaneous. Break the chains of dulling routine, and free us to move creatively with the rhyme and rhythm of life.

Father, we confess that there is much in our lives that needs renewal and change. There are still pockets of greed, selfishness, prejudice, ignorance, and faultfinding, and these prevent our best response to thee and to thy will.

Too often the sour notes of life's music win our attention. We become so engrossed in these that the great melodies of life escape us. The sparkle of false values, degrading experiences, and worthless philosophies blind our senses. The creative, life-giving virtues—the things of the spirit—often seem dull and listless by our comparison.

Spirit of the living God, come into our waiting hearts and direct us to those paths that will take us through the swamp and quicksand of the lowlands and place us upon the rocky but firm highlands.

Help us, Father, this week to know that in thy presence fear becomes strength, worry becomes peace, loneliness becomes companionship, illness becomes health, hate becomes love, and doubt becomes knowledge.

Forgive us for foolish ways. Strengthen us to respond to thy prompting today in love and service to thee and to others.—Jack F. Belton.

EVENING SERVICE

Topic: Those Early Churches
TEXT: I Cor. 3:16–17.

I. The most fundamental thing in the New Testament churches was their ascription of absolute lordship to Jesus Christ. "Our Lord Jesus Christ" and similar expressions constantly meet us throughout the New Testament writings. The recognition of Christ as lord on whom alone salvation depends called for absolute obedience. The spirit of obedience was not slavish but loving. "If ye love me, keep my commandments," said the Lord Christ.

II. The second feature is a regenerate church membership. New Testament churches were made up exclusively of those who professed faith in Christ and were ready to devote themselves wholly to his service. The life of the early churches was below the ideal. Impurity existed, but it was recognized by the early Christians as abnormal. "Know ye not that ye are God's temple and the spirit of God dwells in you, for the temple of God is holy, which temple ye are" (I Cor. 3:16–17).

III. Another leading characteristic was that of each local church's entire independence. Each church was self-governing, the only authority recognized being the will of Christ as it was known through the Holy Spirit. There was a fellowship of the churches but no organic union. This element of strength at times became a weakness. The New Testament churches depended upon voluntary cooperation.

IV. A fourth leading feature was recognition of the equality in rank and privilege of all members. Paul said, "As all the parts of the body are one flesh and blood and each part has its function, so each member has an important function of his own." All ministered to the whole, and each member ministered to every other member.

V. New Testament churches chose out of their ranks individuals for special functions. Officers were chosen not to rule but to serve. New Testament churches believed that Christianity was to accomplish its mission by bringing individuals to yield themselves in obedience to Jesus Christ.

VI. New Testament churches were characterized by the regular observance of certain ordinances instituted by Christ—baptism and the Lord's Supper. The subjects of baptism were believers. Baptism was practiced only in connection with repentance for sin and faith in the Lord Jesus Christ. The Lord's Supper was observed to commemorate the incarnation and the death of the Lord Jesus Christ, and it was also a communion of believers with Christ. Those participating in the ordinance were baptized believers.—James H. Landes in *Baptist Standard.*

SUNDAY: JULY NINETEENTH

MORNING SERVICE

Topic: Two Kinds of Theology
TEXT: II Cor. 13:5.

There is a temptation for evangelical Christians to depart from a full biblical theology and to settle for something less. By proclaiming only the love of God and the comfort that comes to one who belongs to him in Christ, there is danger of lapsing into "therapy theology." The temptation of therapy theology follows from its apparent success. The world is so full of people needing love, comfort, reassurance, relief from loneliness, deliverance from despair, and healing for physical and spiritual illness that any declaration of the availability of these blessings is certain to be popular. The catch is that the preaching of deliverance and healing only is not the preaching of biblical Christian faith.

I. Biblical theology calls upon me to serve God because of who he is. It recognizes God as creator, redeemer, sustainer, and judge. Therapy theology calls upon me to accept God because of what he will do for me. God is pictured as a bountiful giver in return for my faith. If I will accept him, then he will pour out his blessings upon me.

II. Biblical theology calls me to responsibility as a disciple of Christ. Out of this responsible discipleship, certain blessings flow. The Bible places obedience to Christ and love for one another as the marks of Christian discipleship. My first call is to be obedient to Christ because I belong to him. Therapy theology calls me not to pass up a good deal. A divine bounty awaits anyone who is willing to reach out and take it.

III. Biblical theology stresses costly grace. Salvation is by grace through faith, but that grace cost the son of God his life. It costs the Christian his life as well, for he has been put to death with Christ so that he might live with him. Therapy theology stresses cheap grace. Healing and comfort are available without claims and without strings, freely provided to anyone who will lay hold on the benefits without the need for counting the cost.

IV. Biblical theology promises that Christ will never leave us but will be with us no matter what happens. Christ does not promise his disciples success or freedom from suffering. He promises us persecution, and he promises that he will be with us through it all. Therapy theology promises that nothing can really happen to us. If we accept the bounty held out to us, then we are safely delivered from all subsequent pain and trial.

V. Biblical theology recognizes that Christians will yet be sick, sad, depressed, lonely, and doubting. Saints are still sinners, and we who belong to Christ are still being sanctified. Therapy theology offers total, smiling, victorious living as the only possibility for a spiritual Christian. Since all that therapy theology has to offer is comfort and release from suffering, the existence of uncomforted or suffering Christians is an affront.

VI. Biblical theology calls a Christian to be salt and light in the world. The inner strength of a relationship with Christ is to flow outward for personal compassion and social justice. Therapy theology calls a Christian to feel better. Its emphasis is on delivery of the self from trials and tribulations.

VII. Biblical theology emphasizes a Christian's calling. Being a disciple of Christ is a responsibility and an opportunity that embraces all of life. Therapy theology emphasizes a Christian's needs and wants. It promises to satisfy all the personal shortcomings of life with victory and successful living.

VIII. Biblical theology extends outward to social righteousness. It seeks to translate the individual relationship of freedom in Christ outward into the society around, even when this society is not yet Christian. Therapy theology emphasizes individual peace and security almost exclusively. It exhausts its concern with the deliverance of the individual from physical and psychological afflictions.

IX. Biblical theology drives "disciples" away. Like the warnings that Jesus gave to those who would be his disciples but were not ready to fully commit themselves, so biblical theology drives away those who are not really willing to surrender their lives to Christ. Therapy theology welcomes "non-disciples." Even those who have no intention of committing their lives to God in Christ are welcomed with promises of blessings.

X. Biblical theology sees Jesus Christ as the lord of the cosmos. As he is the creator by whom all things were made, so he is the one for whom all things were made and to whom all things are intended. No aspect of life lies outside the domain of his lordship. Therapy theology sees Jesus Christ as the great healer. It is to him that we bring our weaknesses, failures, sickness, and despair, and he dispenses healing.

XI. Biblical theology builds Christians. Growth in Christian experience arises from obedience to Christ. It is through obedience that faith grows. Therapy theology encourages addicts. People gather for their "shot" of spiritual strength so that they can go one step further.

XII. Biblical theology embraces the whole word of God. It presents the comfort and the cost, the peace and the persecution, the helplessness and the healing, and the suffering and the salvation. It presents God as loving and holy, merciful and just. It shows God as the lord of the universe, not simply the spiritual influence on human souls. Since it presents the whole word of God, it bequeaths the whole power of God. Therapy theology has difficulty distinguishing itself from other therapy approaches. Is such religious therapy really different from secular therapies? Does it work because it's Christian, or does it mislead people into believing they are Christians because it seems to work? Therapy theology is both true and false. It is true in affirming that God does love his children and has provided for them unmeasured resources of strength and blessing. But in affirming this without recognizing the total context of Christian relationship and commitment, therapy theology is really false.

XIII. Biblical theology leads to a sure faith even when all evidence fails. Therapy theology crumbles when it fails to work.—Richard H. Bube.

Illustrations

SUBSTITUTES. One of the failures, one of the sins, of the human race has always been the natural tendency to try to match wits with God and try to figure out substitutes that are just as good as what God said.—John McBain.

BOUNDLESS LOVE. Jesus did not say, "Peter must first be changed and become another man before I can love him." He did the very opposite. He said: "Peter is Peter, and I love him. My love, if it amounts to anything, will precisely help him to become another man."—Soren Kierkegaard.

Sermon Suggestions

THE GOSPEL: A RELEVANT MESSAGE. Text: Rom. 1:16. (1) A message of hope. (See Matt. 4:16–17.) (2) A message of peace. (See Matt. 11:28.) (3) A message of warning. (See Luke 13:2–3.)—Jake Harms.

PARADOXES OF PRAYER. Text: I Cor. 14:15. (1) God knows what we need before we ask him, but we need to ask him. (2) God is omnipotent and almighty, but he cannot do anything in some situations until we enable him to do it. (3) God to whom we pray also prays. Paul spoke of God's Spirit interceding for us with sounds too deep for articulate utterance. —Charles L. Seasholes.

Worship Aids

CALL TO WORSHIP. "The Lord is exalted; for he dwelleth on high: he hath filled Zion with judgment and righteousness. And wisdom and knowledge shall be the stability of thy times, and strength of salvation: the fear of the Lord is his treasure." Isa. 33:5–6.

INVOCATION. Father God, we come to this place to ask for a new vision of your presence and a resurrected spirit of life within history and beyond history. We come as humble pilgrims, none of us possessing all faith and knowledge but all of us seeking your truth as it lives in our midst. Be with us now, we pray, that we may be aware of you in a special way and, being thus aware, that as we live in the world we may be aflame with your joy.— Richard D. Bausman.

OFFERTORY SENTENCE. "To do good and to communicate forget not: for with such sacrifices God is well pleased." Heb. 13:16.

OFFERTORY PRAYER. Dear Lord and Savior of us all, may we become obedient to thy will both in the dedication of our tithes and of our talents.

PRAYER. O God, our Father, we are grateful for thy providence which has attended our lives and for thy grace which has been extended to us.

Keep us, Father, from letting the luxury of thy blessing dim our concerns. May we be ever conscious of needs about us, and may we lend ourselves and our means to bring help and healing to the stricken people and places of our neighborhoods.

Make us uneasy in our comforts when we ignore the less fortunate. Create a holy disturbance among us that involves us in the troubled areas of our community. Help us to realize that we have no claim to thy goodness when we are not channels for that goodness to flow to others. May we learn that no abundance will satisfy that is not shared.

Guide us through thy Holy Spirit that we may know how and where to give of ourselves for thy kingdom's good.—C. Neil Strait.

EVENING SERVICE

Topic: Suffering—An Invitation to Growth

SCRIPTURE: Mark 1:29–39.

Suffering—whether physical or mental—is a fact of life. Complaining will neither eliminate it nor alleviate it. What is the solution?

I. We need to accept the reality and then begin to deal with it. Denial will not help because the ache will still hurt. Pretending that it doesn't cause us pain or inconvenience is being less than honest. Acceptance is the key.

(a) Jesus accepted suffering in others and in himself, and thus he was able to heal. When the sick came to Jesus for a cure, he faced their illnesses squarely and helped them to do the same. And then he cured them.

(b) In times past the church appeared to almost glorify pain and suffering to the level of virtues. But that was a poor theology of suffering. Through Jesus we learn that suffering is an evil to be avoided and overcome, not sought out. At the same time, suffering is an opportunity to learn some valuable lessons about ourselves, about other people, and about God.

II. Suffering comes to everyone, regardless of age or social status or intelligence. Each person has only two options in the face of suffering—bitterness or growth.

(a) Some react in a way which puts God on trial. "Why has God done this to me? How could he do this?" Such a person forgets that most of our suffering is the result of sin in the world rather than God's activity. This person will learn nothing and will simply become more and more resentful.

(b) The second reaction is not only more Christian but is also more profitable—even from a purely human standpoint. This person knows that bitterness accomplishes nothing, and so he is concerned with making the most out of the situation. Like Jesus, he will seek a cure. But if a cure is not possible, he will attempt to discover the divine purpose in all things, unite his sufferings to those of Christ, and hope to merit a deeper appreciation of life here on earth and a share in the risen life of heaven.—Peter Stravinskas in *Pastoral Life.*

SUNDAY: JULY TWENTY-SIXTH

MORNING SERVICE

Topic: On Growing Old

TEXT: Ps. 37:25.

I. To grow old gracefully requires acceptance of the terms life imposes—terms that are not subject to change.

(a) Emerson pointed out that life operates in a medium of opposites. We have our sunshine and our shadows, our joys and our tears, our triumphs and our tragedies, and our youth and old age. The winds of God are not always tail winds, but this is not without its blessings. If life consisted only of moonlight and roses, it would become boring.

(b) We must have problems to challenge us to achievement, one of the main avenues to happiness. Spring is spawned in winter, roses in dirt, and success and happiness in accomplishments. Thomas Jefferson said that deity does not promise us happiness all the time.

(c) When properly conceived, the morning of life is made for preparation, the afternoon for achievement, and the evening for reward. The true goal of life is to accomplish as much as one's ability will permit. When this is done, the evening of our existence will become more pleasing.

II. How well we accept the terms of our earthly demands is determined largely by our spiritual and intellectual philosophy.

(a) This fact is painted by some of our living sages. (1) Eric Hoffer says that to grow old is to grow common. Old age, he notes, is an equalizer. We are aware that what is happening to us has happened to untold numbers from the beginning of time.

(2) John Wheelock said: "As life goes on it becomes more intense. Our associates increase and many we loved are gone. It is like living in two societies—the living and the dead—and you live with both."

(b) To adapt to the "inaudible and noiseless foot of time" requires work as well as faith. It would be fatal to follow the example of the man who had been unemployed for years. He took the position that if the Lord wanted him to work, then the Lord would find him a job.

(c) The Lord gave us a mind and a will, and we are expected to use them to supplement faith. We are advised to take the golden years standing up rather than sitting down.

(1) One lady said she was too busy to grow old. Another was observed planting a peach tree. When asked why she was planting a tree at the age of 86, she replied, "Because I like peaches."

(2) President Theodore Roosevelt's prescription for growing old was to stay busy and maintain a passionate state of mind.

(d) There is no old age as long as mind and intellect keep growing. Too many ride off into the sunset long before their time. Bishop Sheen said that when he gets to heaven he would rest for a day or two and then ask the good Lord to send him back.

III. People who adapt best to life live by a simple faith. (a) Presidents Truman and Eisenhower expressed confidence in life beyond, and both believed that the path to that realm could be found in the ten commandments and the sermon on the mount.

(b) Charles Lindbergh anchored his belief in a passage of scripture that served him both in life and death: "If I take the wings of the morning and dwell in the uttermost parts of the sea, he will be there also." He carried this verse with him on that historic flight across the Atlantic in 1927, and at his request, it was inscribed on the marker at his grave in the South Pacific.

(c) Ethel Waters found faith in the words of the song, "His eye is on the sparrow and I know he watches me."

(d) Archibald Rutledge, a great lover of nature, took delight in watching the flocks of birds as they winged their way south in fall and north in spring. Just before his death he penned the following: "The migration of the birds ends in finding their haven. Why should we doubt the end of our migration? When the time comes for us to migrate to a land unknown, through misty darkness, God will not desert us. In this flight we shall know what it means by the everlasting arm."—Houston Cole.

Illustrations

LORD, I AM GROWING OLDER.   Lord, thou knowest better than I know myself that I am growing older and will some day be old.

Keep me from getting talkative and particularly from the fatal habit of thinking I must say something on every subject and on every occasion.

Release me from craving to try to straighten out everybody's affairs.

Keep my mind free from the recital of endless detail. Give me wings to get to the point.

I ask for grace enough to listen to the tales of others' pains. Help me to endure them with patience.

But seal my lips on my own aches and pains. They are increasing, and my love of rehearsing them is becoming sweeter as the years go by.

Teach me the glorious lesson that occasionally it is possible that I may be mistaken.

VICTORIOUS.   It was clear to the lonely prophet on the Island of Patmos that the spirit of God, brooding in the heart of a man, could keep him spiritually on his feet despite disaster and death. Robert Louis Stevenson was fond of the book of Revelation and for good reason. The portrait of him propped up in bed and writing his inimitable stories or playing his flute while illness ravaged his body is an unforgettable one. If he asked, "How long, O Lord, how long?" it was not in despair. It was rather a creative question. How long would he have to write all the stories that were bursting in his fertile mind? His was a struggle of the spirit against the weakness of his body, and the spirit was victorious.—Harold Blake Walker.

Sermon Suggestions

SOLDIERS OF CHRIST, ARISE! Text: Ezek. 2:1. Consider three particular situations for which this rallying word of God is intended. (1) We need to hear it when in our religion we have been leaning on others, content with a mainly inherited, traditional set of beliefs instead of shouldering our responsibility to discover a faith of our own. (2) We need to hear this word when we have been knocked out by some blow at the hands of life. (3) We need to hear this word when, beaten by the tempter, we have stumbled into sin.—James S. Stewart.

I WILL NEVER WALK ALONE. Scripture: Ps. 23. (1) My divine companion. (2) My divine provider. (3) My divine leader. (4) My divine comforter. (5) My divine assurance.—W. R. Robinson.

Worship Aids

CALL TO WORSHIP. "Lift up your heads in the sanctuary, and bless the Lord. The Lord that made heaven and earth bless thee out of Zion." Ps. 134:2–3.

INVOCATION. Most gracious Father, who withholdest no good thing from thy children and in thy providence hast brought us to this day of rest and of the renewal of the soul: we give thee humble and hearty thanks for the world which thou hast prepared and furnished for our dwelling place, for the steadfast righteousness which suffers no evil thing to gain the mastery, for the lives and examples of those who were strangers and pilgrims and found a better inheritance in peace of soul and joy in the Holy Spirit, and above all, for the life, teaching, and sacrifice of Jesus Christ.

OFFERTORY SENTENCE. "As we have therefore opportunity, let us do good unto all men, especially unto them who are of the household of faith." Gal. 6:10.

OFFERTORY PRAYER. Dear Father, help us to be ever concerned to find thy way for our lives, and may we never be satisfied to give thee our second best in return for thy great gift of love.

PRAYER. Our Father, if words alone could accomplish your will, we should have a heaven on earth, for most of us are very full of words. If complaints were negotiable, we would have money to spare, for we are very able and earnest at complaints.

Dear Lord, if spiritual inactivity and Christian unconcern were tools of the faith, your kingdom would have already come, because we are slow to follow you and not very anxious to become sensitive to the needs of our neighbors.

Dear Lord, help us to look again at the images we see in the mirror. The persons looking back at us may not be all we think or all the holy Father wants. Help us to want what you want, Lord, that our lives may count for something in your cause.

We cannot hide what we are from your searching spirit, so let us put away our falseness and give ourselves to seek honestly your will, knowing with certainty that you are calling us to a new day and a new commitment. Don't let us succumb to fear and weakness. Strengthen us with power from your heart.—D. W. McCasland.

EVENING SERVICE

Topic: What Do You Expect from Religion?

TEXT: Jude 1:3.

I. What we ought not to expect from religion.

(a) Religion is not a miraculous way of getting what we want in life. To try to control God's power for our own selfish ends is magic, whereas religion is bending our will to God's will.

(b) Religion is not a shield from disease, trouble, or disaster. To be sure, there are diseases, troubles, and disasters from which real religion frees a person. Trust and faith in God do bring to us health, joy, and peace. But religion is no insurance policy against trouble. Religion is not a shield but that which teaches us how to deal with life.

(c) Religion is no substitute for thinking. It does not solve our intellectual problems. Genuine religion has never overlooked the need for brains in religion.

(d) Religion does not keep us always in a state of happiness or of high feelings. To be sure, happiness and inner peace are by-products of a radiant religion. Real religion does give a person a sense of freedom from worry and a real joy in living. But it does not keep a person in high states of deep emotion.

II. What we ought to expect from religion.

(a) Real religion helps a man gain a right relationship with God, with the world, and with man. It brings an understanding and an adjustment to life. It involves a release from sin and a program of overcoming evil with good. This relationship with God is primary.

(b) Religion gives us greater power to do good and greater strength to deal with trouble. It is not a program of avoiding evil or explaining it but of dealing with it and overcoming it with good. It makes of us better persons.

(c) Religion offers us a program for living and supports us in it. It gives to us keener minds, freeing us from fear and worry. It offers us a great cause to live for. Being lost in such a cause, men really find themselves.—Adapted from John K. Benton.

SUNDAY: AUGUST SECOND

MORNING SERVICE

Topic: The Blessing of the Dew

TEXT: Hos. 14:5.

I. Only as we read these words in light of the geography of the Holy Land do we receive their full import. For this is a desert country. For more than half of the year it receives no rain at all.

(a) During the long, hot summer, it never rains, so how does life go on? The answer is the dew. On-shore winds bring moisture from the Mediterranean which condenses to form dew on blades of grass and little plants, and this literally means the difference between life and death.

(b) It is a second best. One would prefer a soaking rain. Yet in the hot, arid months when there are no soaking rains, the dew sustains life in the most unlikely places. No place on earth appears more barren and sun-scorched in summer than the wilderness of Judea. Yet in this death-dealing desert, life goes on. The blessing of the dew is the hope of the land.

II. When the greater blessings are withheld, we can trust the lesser mercies. We do not always receive the best, yet there is enough if we have the wisdom to trust God's promises. While we ask for what we want, God often responds by giving us what we need. His blessings are not always large or dramatic. They may be like the dew—not the best yet enough to sustain us and discipline us with the power of going on.

III. How very personal is God's promise, "I will be as the dew."

(a) The providence of God touches us individually in such form as we can receive. Gaius Glenn Atkins wrote, "Like the dew of Palestinian hills, the ocean of

God's providence comes to us in such ways as even a grass blade can take and grow by."

(b) It may very well be that God's providence would overwhelm us were it not stepped down in the blessing of the dew that we can safely receive. Jesus found the providence of God so overwhelming in Gethsemane that he cried, "Let this cup pass from me."

(c) When God brings us the blessing of the dew, he respects our frailty even while his goodness is enough for us to live by and grow on. He gives us what we need, not what we want, the blessing of the dew if not the blessing of the rain, and his grace is sufficient for our needs.

IV. How quietly climactic is this promise.

(a) When God spoke to the people through Hosea, he gathered up all their life in his providence—past, present, and future.

(1) "I will heal their backsliding" is the wonderful release given sinful men by a merciful God.

(2) "I will love them freely" assures us of the great companion to hearten us on life's way.

(3) "I will be as the dew to Israel" lights the morrow with hope. Though the night be dark, in the morning look for the blessing of the dew.

(b) The life-giving touch of God makes our life a growing experience, says Hosea, like the vine, the corn, the cedars of Lebanon, the fir trees, and the cypress, and life springs in the midst of desert death because of the touch of the living God in the blessing of the dew.—Lowell M. Atkinson.

Illustration

TOWARD THE LIGHT.   Few paintings of Raphael Santi so faithfully interpret the scriptures as "The Transfiguration." The first impression made upon the beholder is that of sharp contrasts. On the mountain above is intensely luminous light and in the valley below dark and menacing shadows. Above are graceful lines and curves all leading to the glorified Christ and below are sharp angles and discordant colors. The artist has sought to present unforgettably the glory of the mount of transfiguration and the contrasting misery and seeming hopelessness of the plain. Below is stark human need and above is divine help and healing. Below is hell-tortured misery and above is the calm serenity of available power. Here concentrated on a single canvas is the long story of humanity—the procession of the generations slowly and painfully struggling toward the light.—John Sutherland Bonnell.

Sermon Suggestions

THINGS YOU CAN GET FOR NOTHING. Text: Isa. 35:1. (1) The privilege of life. (2) Love cannot be purchased. (3) Salvation is a totally free gift of God.—John R. Brokhoff.

WHY BE A CHRISTIAN?   Text: Deut. 33: 29. (1) The Christian life is happier than any other. (2) The Christian life is harder than any other. (3) The Christian life is holier than any other. (4) The Christian life is more hopeful than any other.— James S. Stewart.

Worship Aids

CALL TO WORSHIP.   "Sing unto the Lord, sing psalms unto him. Glory ye in his holy name: let the heart of them rejoice that seek the Lord." Ps. 105:2–3.

INVOCATION.   O Lord Jesus Christ, who art the truth incarnate and the teacher of the faithful: let thy spirit overshadow us as we meditate on thy word and conform our thoughts to thy revelation that, learning of thee with honest hearts, we may be rooted and built up in thee, who livest and reignest with the Father and the Holy Spirit, ever one God, world without end.—William Bright.

OFFERTORY SENTENCE.   "Offer unto God thanksgiving; and pay thy vows unto the most High." Ps. 50:14.

OFFERTORY PRAYER.   Help us, dear Father, to be cheerful givers of our time, means, talents, and self to the Master that he may use us in the upbuilding of his kingdom.

LITANY.   O God, forgive us for the faults that make us difficult to live with. If we behave as if we were the only people for whom life is difficult, if we behave as if we were far harder worked than anyone else, if we behave as if we were the only people who were ever disappointed or the only people who ever got a raw deal, and if we are far too self-centered and far too full of self-pity:
Forgive us, O God.

If we are too impatient to finish the work we have begun, if we are too impatient to listen to someone who wants to talk to us or to give someone a helping hand, if we think that other people are fools and make no attempt to conceal our contempt for them:
Forgive us, O God.

If we too often rub people the wrong way, if we spoil a good case by trying to ram it down someone's throat, if we do things that get on people's nerves and go on doing them even when we are asked not to:
Forgive us, O God.

Help us to take the selfishness and the ugliness out of life and to do better in the days to come.—William Barclay.

EVENING SERVICE

Topic: Listen to Him! (The Transfiguration)

SCRIPTURE: Mark 9:2–9.

The transfiguration event provides scope for seeing, understanding, and responding to life's deepest truths. It takes us literally and figuratively upon the mountain where there is vision, range, and purpose.

I. The transfiguration is like a telescope, enabling us to view life from long range in such a way that the present becomes more meaningful in the light of the future.

(a) The disciples, caught in the perplexing reality of their Lord's announcement of his impending suffering and death, were engulfed with the present problem until this glimpse of future triumph and glory transformed it with hope.

(b) Peter reacted typically to the ecstatic experience: "Master, it is well that we are here; let us make three booths, one for you and one for Moses and one for Elijah." Peter would quick-freeze the thrilling moment and permatize it. He would settle in on the mountaintop with its ready access to the law and the prophets—hence, not much need for faith and trust—and live in present triumph and glory. But God thought otherwise. "This is my beloved son; listen to him." The words Jesus had last spoken to them, according to all three synoptic gospels, were these: "If any man would come after me, let him deny himself and take up his cross and follow me. For whoever would save his life will lose it; and whoever loses his life for my sake and the gospel's will save it."

(c) Life in a fallen world calls for the risk of loving service that is always vulnerable to crucifixion and yet is God's way to redemption and final victory. Peter, missing the true meaning of the transfigured Christ, wishes to make tabernacles to memorialize the event rather than to see it as a way to view all events.

(d) Let us see it as a telescope through which present events, however grim or joyful, are transformed with hope and promise. Jesus Christ is the great explorer and adventurer who sees life steadily and sees it whole. To listen to him is better than a telescope for he has been there and he knows.

II. The transfiguration event is like a stethoscope, enabling us to listen to the inner pulse of life and know its vital functions.

(a) So many go through life with a hearing aid tuned only to the surface sounds of the culture and activity around them. They are impressed with the aggressive self-seeking that constitutes life lived with "gusto," the crass self-indulgence that poses as "really living," and the desperate reliance upon money and creature-comforts that so brazenly offers security and "something to believe in." The voice of God says, "This is my beloved son; listen to him." And the words he has last spoken are these: "What shall it profit a man if he gain the whole world and lose his own soul? Or what shall a man give in exchange for his soul?"

(b) Jesus Christ is the great physician who has laid his stethoscope upon the very breast of life and heard its heartbeat and listened to its breathing. To listen to him is to listen to one who has heard the pulse of life that is healthy and true. "For this is life: to know thee, the only true God, and Jesus Christ whom thou hast sent."

III. The transfiguration event is like a gyroscope, enabling us to have stability and inflexible direction for life.

(a) The great ocean liners and mighty warships of the deep are equipped with gyroscopes that prevent undue rolling, yawing, and pitching that throw everything off-balance and keep those aboard upset. They also have directional gyroscopes that offset the diverting and misleading influence of magnetic fields about

them. With this equipment they may move with poise and stability toward their intended destination.

(b) There are so many upsetting events and experiences in life as to keep us all off-balance and upset—from the personal frustrations that nag at us each day to the massive tragedies and bewildering madness that we learn about so frequently through the news media. There are all the distracting influences and misleading forces that beset us on every hand. One wonders anyone manages stability and direction on such a sea.

(c) Jesus Christ equips those who listen to him with something like a gyroscope that provides stability and sure direction. He says: "Trust in God. Seek first his kingdom and his righteousness and all things needful will be yours as well. Fear not, little flock, for it is your Father's good pleasure to give you the kingdom."—Marshall F. Mouney.

SUNDAY: AUGUST NINTH

MORNING SERVICE

Topic: Escaping the World's Corruption
TEXT: II Pet. 1:4 (BARCLAY).

Escaping the world's corruption is a problem which demands constant effort, constant vigilance, and constant fellowship with Christ.

I. This is an either-or problem.

(a) Either we are producing the fruit of the Spirit or we are producing the works of the flesh. There are some things in life where we can straddle the fence. One day we can be happy, optimistic, and enthusiastic, and the next day we can be down in the dumps, pessimistic and apathetic. When it comes to Spirit and flesh, we cannot be both or neither. We must be one or the other.

(b) Let us not deceive ourselves by thinking that we can be a little worldly and still virtuous. Either we are producing the fruit of the Spirit, or we are producing the works of the flesh.

II. Even when we are producing the

fruit of the Spirit, we are not perfect.

(a) Peter talks about becoming and growing. The unarguable fact about our Christian experience is this: none of us has arrived, none of us has reached perfection, and none of us has grown to the fullness of Christ. I am not what I ought to be and what I could be, and I doubt if any of you would claim to have reached perfection.

(b) While none of us has arrived, all of us are on our way to becoming more and more like our master. An uneducated woman who testified at a prayer meeting said, "I ain't what I ought to be, I ain't what I'm goin' to be, but I'm better than I was." Either we are growing and becoming more like Christ or we are withering and becoming more like the world.

III. The power to live an effective and productive life is a gift.

(a) Peter speaks of this several times. "For his divine power has gifted us with everything necessary for life and godliness . . . ." It was through the excellence of his glory that we received the precious and very great gifts he promised to us. Through these gifts you are enabled to escape the world's corruption.

(b) Often men talk as if they are responsible for their growth and their Christian accomplishments as if it is all our doing. We do have our part to play, but it is God who works for growth in us.

(c) The Christians in Corinth were boasting of their allegiance to Apollos and Paul, but Paul reminded them that while he had planted the seed and Apollos had watered it, it was God who had given the increase.

IV. We have been called and chosen for life and godliness.

(a) Everything in the world exists for a purpose. God has made it perfectly plain why he created us. We have been made to experience life that is abundant, full, victorious, and Godlike. We are to become like him in order that his kingdom might be established on the earth.

(b) Karl Marx described religion as an opiate, an escape from reality. He was right when he said that religion is an escape but wrong in his description of the goal. Christianity is not an escape from reality but an escape from the unreal world of material values and sensual pleasures. It is an escape to life that is real, enduring, and in harmony with the God who created life, sustains it, and guides it, so that the Christian moves along with the flow of life instead of swimming against the current.

V. God is a generous God who provides for all our needs.

(a) After Peter identifies himself in the opening verse, he prays: "May God's grace and every blessing be given ever more richly to you, and may you enter more and more deeply into the knowledge of God and of Jesus our Lord. This I can pray with confidence, for his divine power has gifted us with everything necessary for life and godliness."

(b) God is not stingy but generous and giving beyond our understanding. This impressed the writers of the New Testament. Paul wrote to the Ephesians: "Now to him who can do for us far more than our lips can ask or our minds conceive through the power of his which is at work in us." (3:20, BARCLAY). For the Colossians Paul made this prayer: "We pray that in God's glorious strength you will receive power to cope with anything, a power which will enable you gladly to meet life with fortitude and patience" (1:11).—John C. Middlekauff.

Illustration

PRISON LESSON. Ewald von Kleist died in the horrors of a concentration camp. Shortly before he was to depart this life, he wrote a letter to his family: "My mood has often vacillated between hope and the most gloomy anticipation. But on one point my state of mind has remained constant, serene, and firm. I have resigned myself unconditionally to the will of God. Despite some very gloomy hours, despair has remained far from me. Strange as it may sound, I have learned one thing in prison: to be joyful!"

Sermon Suggestions

TESTED THROUGH TEMPTATION. Texts: Matt. 6:13; Jas. 1:13 (NIV). How do we deal with the contradiction we sense in this petition from the Lord's Prayer? (1) God does not allow us to be tempted or tried in any circumstance when we do not have the strength to overcome the temptation. (2) These temptations equip us to handle even greater challenges that come along. (3) Temptations help us to know where we stand and how yielded we really are to the spirit of God and to Christ's control of our lives.—Arthur McPhee.

LIVING IN A WORLD YOU DON'T UNDERSTAND. Text: John 12:16. (1) Decide to go forward. (2) Decide to express some enthusiastic hope. (3) Decide to live in confidence.—Joe A. Harding.

FINDING PEACE OF MIND. Text: Job 23:3. (1) By coming to terms with our own selves. (2) By coming to terms with others. (3) By coming to terms with God.

Worship Aids

CALL TO WORSHIP.   "Blessed is the man that trusteth in the Lord, and whose hope the Lord is." Jer. 17:7.

INVOCATION.   O God, we thank you for leading us until this hour. Direct us in the days ahead through the difficult places of decision. When the call seems clouded and the road is in poor repair, grant the boldness to face the future in faith and to fortify ourselves in truth. Help us to be ready to recognize our own inadequacy and your sufficiency.—John M. Drescher.

OFFERTORY SENTENCE.   "Give unto the Lord the glory due unto his name: bring an offering, and come before him: worship the Lord in the beauty of holiness." I Chron. 16:29.

OFFERTORY PRAYER.   Our Father, take us with all of our failures and develop us after thine own heart. Give us more of the mind of the master, more of his spirit of compassion, and more of his sacrificial and loving heart.

PRAYER.   Thou who art always coming into our world and into our lives, breathe once more upon this dust, blow away the ashes of our apathy and our cold indifference to thy comings.

Fan the small spark of our awareness into a glad flame of response and gratitude and obedience. Burn the trash of our lives with which we surround ourselves and in which we hide from thee. Light our way to thy presence that we may be still and know that thou art God.

Thou hast called us through thy son, Jesus Christ, and sent us out into life—not for cheap things and not for self but to announce peace—to bring healing and to glorify thy name in the family of man.

We pray now for courage that we may keep our commitment to follow Jesus all the way. We ask not for easy tasks but for strength equal to the work at hand. We ask not for wealth or fortune but only thy blessing upon the loaves we break with our brothers. We ask not for shelter from the storms of life but for the assurance of thy presence in our small boat.

We pray for thy benediction upon our lives—not that we may be powerful and great or that our storehouses may be full —but that we may see thy will and do it, that we may find our brother and love him, and that we may have a vision of thy kingdom and proclaim it from the housetops.

Thou who art always coming to us, help us to come to thee.—Ernst E. Klein.

EVENING SERVICE

Topic: The Grounds of Our Hope
TEXT: Col. 1:15–19.

I. Christ is "the image of the invisible God" (v. 15), which means, among other things, that God is like Jesus with a father's love for all mankind. We are not orphans in an indifferent world but sons and daughters in our father's house—an unfinished house not yet completed according to the designer's plan. But it is God's house in which we live with him and seek to make it a more harmonious home for the whole family of man.

II. Christ is the end of the world. "All things were created through him and for him" (v. 16). "As all things passed out from him, so does all converge again toward him." It will find its completion and its fulfillment in him. The conditions of existence are so ordered that without Christ it cannot obtain its perfection. The God who controls our destinies, who makes the wrath of men to praise him, and who determines the goal that mankind shall reach is the God who became incarnate in Jesus Christ. However far the world may be from him today, in the end he shall reign supreme because he is both the beginning and the end, the source from which all its forces have been derived, and the goal toward which they inexorably tend.

III. Christ is the preserver of the world. As Paul writes, "He is before all things and in him all things hold together" (v. 17). Any individual, any institution, or any nation or international organization which sets itself against the moral law of the universe as revealed in Christ tends to disintegrate and to fall apart.

IV. God is working in the church for the redemption of the world (v. 18). We may wonder at first why the church should be mentioned alongside Christ who is the beginning and the end of creation. But the church draws its life, its energy, and its power from him who is its head, but at the same time it is the agency through which Christ is working to reconcile individuals to God and to one another.—Ernest Trice Thompson.

SUNDAY: AUGUST SIXTEENTH

MORNING SERVICE

Topic: Components of Conversion
SCRIPTURE: John 4:5–30.
I. *Condemnation.* That's where we've got to begin.

(a) The Lord Jesus had an appointment from all eternity at the well in Sychar, a lonely, desolate place in Samaria. Jesus was there. He sent his disciples to town so they would not obtrude, as characteristically they might, into his meeting with the woman. There at high noon she came.

(b) The gospel of Christ is for us sinners, and it necessarily begins in our lives with a recognition of our sinfulness and of our need. Jesus said to her, "Go, call your husband." "Oh, I don't have a husband," she said. "How true. You have had five and the man you are now living with is not your husband." Now we are facing it.

(c) Until we recognize our own incompleteness and sinfulness, we are not ready for the gospel. We have got to face the bad news before we are going to be very receptive to the good news.

II. *Confrontation.* Jesus was at that well. Marcus Dobbs put it so well—it was an unsurpassed situation of delicacy.

(a) There was a racial barrier. She was a Samaritan and he was a Jew. There was a social barrier. She was a woman and he was a man. Familiar conversation at the well with a stranger? There was a moral problem. She had quite a reputation. How would it appear to an onlooker or spectator to see him talking to her?

(b) Jesus spoke to her. He began right where she was with the subject uppermost in her mind. He said, "Would you please give me a drink of water?" He then sought so skillfully and so beautifully to lead her from the water dripping from the bucket in the well to living water and to the deepest need in her heart and life—that deepseated, profound thirst and longing and that unslaked craving. He said: "I have living water. And if you will only let me give you this living water, you will never thirst again."

(c) It was difficult for her to break loose from her bondage to the temporal, the actual, and the physical. Isn't that the problem with which modern man wrestles all the time—to move from the level of the natural to a consideration of the spiritual? And deftly and carefully Jesus steered clear of all the theological red herrings and the traditional arguments, and he brought her to a confrontation with himself.

(d) Conversion must move from condemnation to confrontation with the living Christ. Christianity is not a philosophy. It is not a system of ethical teaching. Christianity is the eternal crashing into time. It is God become flesh, bone of our bone, and flesh of our flesh. It is God coming to us, reaching out to us, speaking to us, and addressing us in his son, Jesus Christ.

III. *A new creation.* This dear woman was converted.

(a) That word in both the Old Testament and the New Testament means to turn, to turn around, to turn back, to return, to make anew, and to be different. She was converted. James Denny said, "It is the essence of Christianity to make bad people into good people, to begin with us in our sinfulness, our waywardness, and to change us, to transform us into new creations."

(b) We don't have to be what we have been. We don't have to remain as we are in such an unsatisfactory situation and circumstance. We can be converted. The gospel has a life-changing power. This woman demonstrates this immediately. Religion is an entirely different and new thing for her. It is no longer, "Now our fathers worshiped on this mountain and your fathers worshiped in Jerusalem, and let's talk now about where we really ought to worship." All of that becomes subordinated and secondary. "I have met him. I have found him."

(c) There is a whole new relationship. (1) The woman doesn't begin to suspect how drastic a revision has been made in her whole statement of faith and belief. Thank God we don't need to know all of that to be converted. I don't need to know a great deal about the physics of electricity to turn the switch. I don't need to have made a chemical analysis of milk to benefit from a cool glass of milk. When we come sensing we can't make it on our own and things aren't going as they ought to go and we have offended a holy God, and we come through Christ the mediator, Jesus the savior, the sin bearer, we may receive him as our own personal savior.

(2) She had a new relationship with the community. She had been in a kind of solitary self-pity for who knows how long, and that changed. I can see this woman as she runs lickety brindle back into town, and there is a new look on her face. She is saying, "I have met him, and he has told me everything I've ever done." That is something to confess. "Will you come out to see him? Come on, something has happened to me!" My friends, she was converted. She was turned around.

(d) Profound changes in character are not conventional. How are we really shaped? The gospel says there is something which can be so much more decisive than nature or nurture, than heredity or environment, than the sum total of all the influences which have molded and formed and shaped us to be what we are. And that decisive influence can be the power of the living Christ to change our lives.—David L. Larsen.

Illustrations

DIVINE TOUCH.   With thy calling and shouting, my deafness was broken; by thy flashing and shining my blindness was put to flight. I drew in my breath and panted for thee. Thou hast touched me, and I am on fire with thy peace.—St. Augustine.

GREATEST DESIRE.   Buddha commanded a would-be disciple to follow him to the river. The man, thinking of ritual purification, eagerly waded in after him until suddenly he found himself pushed under and held down. Only with a desperate wrench was he able to break clear of the water. Whereupon Buddha asked him, "When you thought you were going to be drowned, what did you desire most?" "Air!" shouted the man. "Then," said Buddha, "when you want salvation as much as you wanted air, you will get it."—John H. Townsend.

Sermon Suggestions

THE PRAYER OF FAITH.   Scripture: Ps. 4. (1) The prayer of requesting faith (v. 1). (2) The prayer of rebuking faith (vv. 2, 6). (3) The prayer of rejoicing faith (vv. 7–8). —Stephen F. Olford.

A CRISIS OF FAITH.   Scripture: Ps. 137: 4–6; Jer. 29:1–14. (1) The prophet Jeremiah tells the forlorn captives in Babylon to begin serving God where they are with what they have (vv. 5–7). (2) He tells them that they will never be able to sing the Lord's song until they replace bitterness and hatred with kindness and love. (3) He tells them that God has something better for them than the faith they thought they had lost—faith in the temple, the covenant, and the law (vv. 10–14).—Blake Smith.

Worship Aids

CALL TO WORSHIP.   "Delight thyself also in the Lord; and he shall give thee the desires of thine heart. Commit thy way unto the Lord; trust also in him; and he shall bring it to pass." Ps. 37:4–5.

INVOCATION. Father God, open our eyes that we may see with an inner vision, open our hearts that we may feel with a deep conviction, and open our minds that we might know with a certain understanding. We believe that you are what we confess you to be. Help thou our unbelief! We believe that you are present to us now. Help thou our awareness! We believe that you are acting in the world. Help thou our devotion!—Richard D. Bausman.

OFFERTORY SENTENCE. "Every man according as he purposeth in his heart, so let him give; not grudgingly, or of necessity; for God loveth a cheerful giver." II Cor. 9:7.

OFFERTORY PRAYER. Dear Lord, as we travel the highways of life give us a generous and sympathetic spirit for all people in all circumstances of life.

PRAYER. Eternal God, our Father, creator, author of redemption, giver of meaning, and holder of our eternal destiny, we thank thee for thy great love out of which, through endless time, thou didst prepare by all the processes of creation, evolution, and redemption for the coming of man—one species of living capable of fellowship with thee. We thank thee that, through the infinite past, thou didst cause the earth's separation from other particles of the universe, its cooling, and the coming forth of all manner of plant and animal life from the simplest to the most complex forms from the beginning until now. We praise thee that long ago thou didst give intelligence and freedom of choice to man, thy chosen, by which gifts many civilizations of great power and beauty have been born. Most of all, O Father, we thank thee that, seeing man's struggle with original sin—our inner conflict, our lonely emptiness, and our self-destructive imperfections by which we are so prone to evil—thou didst give thine only begotten son to redeem our life and to show us the way.

We thank thee, O Holy Spirit, not only for the infinite past and for thy gift of salvation but also for the infinite flaming present meaning thy salvation gives to our otherwise dim and so tragic existence. We thank thee for the fresh vitality and motivation that comes with forgiveness, for the whole new sense of meaning that comes when we learn in the depths of our being that we can trust thy power and justice and love, for the new direction a true sense of our stewardship gives to our aimless and meandering path and the value it gives to all our possessions, for the ability to love born of the discovery in Christ that thou didst first love us, and for thy truth, for all truth is thine and is the basis of every form of growth and healing. We thank thee for faith that our lives can mean so much to thee by their commitment, faith that our homes can be made truly happy by thy presence, and faith that these powers for good and for usefulness which thou hast put within us and which sometimes by our feelings of inferiority are made to seem so small are part of thine own infinite life within us. Help us daily to live by this faith and this redemption, we pray.—Winfield S. Haycock.

EVENING SERVICE

Topic: What the Holy Spirit Offers
TEXT: Ps. 51:11.

What does the Holy Spirit do and offer which is so everlastingly essential? The Bible makes it clear. One day all else will fail and disappoint you—your job, your wealth, your need of glory, your mastery of self, and your mastery of others—in the one journey which each must make alone. One day you will turn for home and, according to Christ, on that day, as on so many others, these are the things the Spirit offers.

I. He will lead you into all truth. All the secret mysteries will be explained in full. He will be your guide and teacher all your days to lead you into truth.

II. He will bring your remembrance—Jesus of Nazareth is speaking—of all the things which I have spoken unto you. Not part of them and not selected out to make the point of my denomination or my prior statement of belief—all the things which I forget or set aside to soften Christ's command. He will bring them all to your remembrance and mine.

III. He will confort you and hold your hand in every darkness. Just when you can stand it not a minute longer—the loneliness is heartbreaking and soul destroying —the Spirit comforts you and reaches out within your agony and illness. "I will send the comforter," Jesus promised, and he will comfort you.

IV. He will strengthen you. The coward will be made brave, the weak will be strong, and the tempted will prevail. Those who are afraid of the dark will not be. Strength you will have through all the years and decades yet to come.

V. He will speak for you. The first meaning and duty of the Spirit is to be an advocate in behalf of those whom Christ has chosen. At the moment when they bring you to trial, Mark says, do not be anxious. Simply say what is given to you in that hour, for it is not you who will speak but the Holy Spirit will speak in your behalf. And Paul says, much more quietly, "The Spirit himself will intercede for us, will aid us in our weakness, in sighs too deep for words."—Richard M. Cromie.

SUNDAY: AUGUST TWENTY-THIRD

MORNING SERVICE *RRc,*

Topic: What Kind of a Church? *$o/ /$1*

TEXT: Eph. 2:19–22.

What kind of building are we to be? If we are a building in which God dwells, what does this dwelling look like? Though there may be many models which have been adopted by churches, either consciously or unconsciously, four particular ones come to my mind. The first three offer very inadequate pictures of the church. Only the fourth suggests the kind of structure through which we can become what God wants us to be.

I. The first building which unfortunately represents the shape of some churches is a *mausoleum.*

(a) A little boy asked his nine-year-old brother what a mausoleum was. Wanting to demonstrate his wide vocabulary but not having all the words he needed to describe it, his brother replied, "A mausoleum is a place where dead people live." Some churches are places where dead people live. In his message to the church in Sardis found in Rev. 3, Jesus spoke of that congregation as being dead. "I know you have a reputation for being a live and active church," he said, "but you are dead" (LB).

(b) A church is a mausoleum when its people have never "put off the old manner of life," as Paul spoke of it, and "put on the new nature, created in God's likeness." Paul reminded one group of Christians that they had in the past been "dead in their trespasses and sins." Archaic as those terms may seem today, they still describe the condition of those who, either through indifference or rebellion, do not accept for themselves Jesus Christ, in whom is found God's gift of forgiveness and life.

II. The second building that sometimes serves as a model for the church is a *museum.*

(a) If a mausoleum is a place where the dead live, a museum is a place where the living come to preserve as though alive something that is dead. A museum's purpose is to keep alive the memory of what used to be—to bring the past into the present.

(b) In Mark 9 we read the familiar story of the transfiguration. Peter, James, and John watched as Jesus was transformed before their eyes and as he talked with Elijah and Moses. Do you remember Peter's response after things were back to normal? He said: "Lord, this has been a tremendous experience! Let's build three temples right here to commemorate it— one for you, one for Moses, and one for Elijah." Lord, we don't ever want to forget this, so let's build a museum to preserve it!

(c) I wonder how many churches, as their real purpose, maintain the outward form of a life that used to be. They are different from the mausoleum. In the museum church the people are at least alive, but they are bound to maintaining the past as it has always been. The museum church tries to squeeze God tightly into a box because they feel he is safe there.

III. The third kind of structure is a *colosseum*.

(a) A colosseum is a place where a large group of the living come as spectators to observe a small group of the living participate in the game. This colosseum is the home of our great spectator sports. That is where we go to see baseball, or football. It is better than the mausoleum because people are at least alive. It is better than the museum because something new and relevant is actually happening. But it falls down as a model for the church because it involves a small minority in the real action.

(b) A lot of churches fall squarely into this category. Only a few people, the "paid religious professionals" and a few extra-dedicated lay people, provide the real action. The rest pay their money in varying degrees to watch the participants do their thing. As spectators they vicariously derive a sense of having been involved though they never get out of the pew.

IV. The fourth building is an *academy*.

(a) The church is to be a community in which we grow together toward Christian maturity, so that we will be equipped for the work which God calls each of us as Christians to do. We need to keep in mind that the church is a body, an organism. It is a body of people who are individually and collectively indwelt by Jesus Christ. As a body, each member is intimately connected to the others, so that we depend upon one another.

(b) Why are we joined together as believers? The answer is found in Eph. 4:13. Paul tells us that the central purpose of the church is to bring believers to spiritual maturity and that this is accomplished by believers using their spiritual gifts to build one another up in the faith. The primary purpose of the church is to provide the quality of environment in which believers can be transformed into the kind of people God intends for them to be. In Rom. 8:29, Paul makes it plain that God's design for the individual Christian is that he

be "conformed to the image of Christ."

(c) Consequently the church's primary task is to create and maintain a transforming environment so that the believers can come to the changes God intends in their lives through their interrelationships within the body of Christ. That is not to diminish the Spirit's role in spiritual growth but to clarify that much of his work is mediated through other believers.—Richard W. McClain.

Illustrations

WHO IS THE PROPHET?   The prophet stands uneasily in the permissive society of his day, a part of it, yet critical of it.

In the midst of piety he calls for justice and mercy.

In historical crisis he remembers the past, but even more he looks to the future.

In a land of plenty and luxury he warns of famine and poverty.

To a nation politically self-satisfied he points to possible threats from the North and from the South.

When people want to sleep, he blows a trumpet.

When they want to build a wall to surround their isolation, he points to the world outside.

When they seek sanctuary in liturgy, he thunders a sermon at them.

When they expose their ignorance, he instructs them.

The prophetic voice is frequently invoked in these days, but it is too seldom heard in our churches, in our seminaries, and from our ecclesiastical and theological leaders.

Perhaps—as has often happened in the past—new occasions will teach new duties. The violatile movements in national and international affairs may of themselves provoke the prophetic note in the church. —*Theology Today.*

THESE THREE.   Love is God's love coming to us in Christ, faith is our surrender to that love, and hope is the expectation that the God who has given us so much will in the end give us all things or at least all the things we need to fulfill our humanity.—Colin Morris.

Sermon Suggestions

DELIVERANCE FROM EVIL. Text: Matt. 6:13. (1) God often delivers us from evil, sometimes by a strange or unexpected turn of events. (2) We should not make our faith and faithfulness contingent upon God's delivering us. (3) There may be factors on God's part that preclude deliverance just when and how we ask for it.—Charles L. Seasholes.

OUR FATHER. Text: Matt. 6:9. (1) When we say "Our Father," we recognize that we really are his sons and daughters. (2) When we say "Our Father," we recognize that we are not the only ones to have been redeemed by Jesus Christ. (3) When we say "Our Father," we identify ourselves with the whole human race. (4) When we say "Our Father," we identify ourselves with God.—Oswald C. J. Hoffman.

Worship Aids

CALL TO WORSHIP. "I will bless the Lord at all times: his praise shall continually be in my mouth. O magnify the Lord with me, and let us exalt his name together." Ps. 34:1, 3.

INVOCATION. O God our Father, who dost dwell in the high and holy place, with him also that is of a humble and contrite heart: grant that, through this time of worship in thy presence, we may be made the more sure that our true home is with thee in the realm of spiritual things and that thou art ever with us in the midst of our common walk and daily duties, so that the vision of the eternal may ever give meaning and beauty to this earthly and outward life.

OFFERTORY SENTENCE. "If thou draw out thy soul to the hungry, and satisfy the afflicted soul; then shall thy light rise in obscurity, and thy darkness be as the noonday." Isa. 58:10.

OFFERTORY PRAYER. Dear Father, may we ever give thee a definite, consistent, and heartfelt service.

PRAYER. At times, O God, we wonder about thee, whether thou really knowest all things, whether thou canst see peace coming on earth in the midst of wars and armament races, and whether thou canst tell what we will do tomorrow or a minute from now when we don't even know ourselves. We want desperately to believe that thou hast the whole world in thy hand and that thy eye is on the sparrow and on us, but we are not always sure. Forgive our stubborn lack of faith; take our skepticism and sanctify it.

What gives us trouble, Lord, is our imaginations, for we can see the world and ourselves evaporated by a bomb and can imagine some accident or some madman ending in a moment what thou hast taken eons to make and all that we have come to love. Or we can imagine our lives going on and on in the same old rut, boring us to death from here to eternity. But we would not blank out our imagination, even if we could, for it keeps us dreaming and praying that the world will get better and ourselves along with it.

Sometimes, Lord, we wish we were not so sensitive to the little hurts that spoil our days and to the ugliness and evil we can't help seeing on every side. Never let us get to the place where we stop feeling pain lest we become so anesthetized we can't even feel joy. Never let us blind ourselves to outrageous wrong lest we fail to see the astonishing beauty of goodness.

And bless us, Lord, with concentration that keeps us from being the prisoner of our alternating moods of hope and despair, of joy and sadness. Let us hope and despair, and let us rejoice and weep, but let us do them at the right times and for the right reasons and always in the firm knowledge that the final triumph of righteousness is assured and eternal life is ours through Jesus Christ our Lord.—Harry W. Adams.

EVENING SERVICE

Topic: Temptations That Are Good

TEXT: Mark 10:28–30 (GNB).

Temptation is usually—indeed almost exclusively—associated with evil. But that overlooks the obvious fact that goodness also has its appeal. It also has powerful incentives. There are attractive temptations to right living. These may be considered valuable inducements to faithful Christian living.

I. *Personal health and happiness.* Jesus made a direct promise to his disciples: "I have come in order that you might have life—life in all its fullness" (John 10:10). Physical vitality and inner serenity combine to make an attractive incentive to accept and follow the Christian faith.

II. *A supportive church fellowship.* The Christian life affords one enriching friendships in the church. The Christian doesn't go it alone through life. Through its social, educational, and worship experiences, the church provides the individual believer a valuable supportive fellowship. In joy and sorrow, in success and failure, and in sickness and health church members find a caring and sharing experience.

III. *Meaningful community involvement.*

(a) Some Christians, like some churches, are individualistic and do not wish to get involved. But there is a growing awareness of critical social needs. Individuals feel inadequate to tackle any one of them on their own.

(b) The church is able to organize and train people to participate meaningfully in some community enterprises of an educational, health, welfare, and cultural nature.

(c) To be a working part of an active and aggressive fellowship adds to a person's sense of worth. It is a strong temptation to work together for goodness' sake.

IV. *A partnership with God.*

(a) The central concern of Jesus' message was the kingdom of God. This is the rule of God in the hearts and lives of people in which the will and love of God are a way of living. Jesus called on people to "repent and enter the kingdom" (Matt. 4:17). He invited them to become citizens of this spiritual government. In recognition of this St. Paul exclaims, "We are workers together with God!" (II Cor. 6:1).

(b) Nothing exalts a person's life as much as when he becomes a working partner of God. It gives meaning and dignity to life to think that our finite efforts can be directly related to the infinite resources of the almighty. Surely this is a powerful inducement to choose and follow the good life.—Emil Kontz.

SUNDAY: AUGUST THIRTIETH

MORNING SERVICE

Topic: Helping Someone Who Hurts

TEXT: Matt. 25:40.

What do you do when you want to help someone who hurts?

I. Step number one is to communicate your concern. There are two levels of communication.

(a) The first is prayer. (1) When we care for another person or group of persons, our first agenda item is prayer. We begin by responding to our Lord's invitation, "Ask and it will be given you, seek and you will find, knock and it will be opened to you."

(2) The form of our prayer is very important. It must be positive, not negative. It must be accompanied by faith, not unbelief. Jesus said, "And whatever you ask in prayer, you will receive, if you have faith" (Matt. 21:22). When we pray for someone, we visualize clearly a new situation free from the illness, the problem, and the difficulty.

(3) There is tremendous power in this prayer of faith. Prayer gives God an opportunity, and he never misses an opportunity to bless and enrich our lives.

(b) We need to express our concern as quickly as possible to the hurting person. It can be very simple. There are many ways of saying "I care." For some people it is a sharing of food, and for others it is a note or a card. Children and young people carry an immense capacity to communicate this in their hand-drawn pictures and messages. Some people send flowers, and others use the telephone. There is an infinite variety. The point is the caring must be communicated or it is lost. Caring needs to become visible.

II. Step number two is to accept the other person's need to be involved in the helping process.

(a) It is easy for some of us to become too helpful. We begin to control and dominate the other person, leaving him dependent and resentful.

(b) People who hurt don't want our pity. The biggest problem of the handicapped is not the handicap. It is the attitude of society—a blend of ignorance, cruelty, and unwanted pity.

(c) Some of us try too hard to reform, lead, or control other people. There is resistance that confuses us. People do not respond like a piece of machinery that can be quickly repaired and put back in running order. When people don't respond like machines, many of us, particularly those of us trained to value orderliness, precision, and predictability, get terribly frustrated.

(d) To help a person who hurts, we must respect the other person's need for privacy, solitude, or involvement in the solution process. We avoid being problem possessive in trying to solve other peoples' problems by our logic or suggestions.

(e) Listening is always helpful. Be willing to listen without judgment or advice. When advice is sought, we can serve as a consultant who gives the best counsel he or she has. There is no nagging, no checking up, and no manipulation by guilt. There is simply sharing and then silence.

(f) The most difficult step for those who are motivated to help is a willingness to accept our own limitations and a realization that we don't have to do it all and a willingness to take the long look and to trust the operation of God's grace in the other person's life. If Christ didn't immediately help everyone, neither will we.

III. A third step is to join hands with other people who also care. Human needs are so great today and the issues are so complex that we need each other working together to make a difference.

IV. The fourth step is to be a community of genuine faith and love and hope.

(a) When we worship God, we experience anew the people of healing hope and love. When we come forward to kneel at the altar rail and receive the signs of God's personal love for us, we join in an atmosphere of openness to God's transforming power.

(b) If you want to help hurting people, be loyal and faithful to the body of Christ, the church.

(1) It is here that we ourselves are healed, helped, and given hope.

(2) It is here God enables us to feel good about ourselves. This enables us to reach out and care genuinely and helpfully for others.

(3) It is here that we dream the dreams, share the plans, and do the work of ministry on behalf of Christ.

(4) It is here we are reminded that our prayers and actions do matter.

(5) It is here we are saved from neurotic domination of needful persons.

(6) It is here we join hands to do things greater than we can do alone.

(7) It is here we lift up the light of hope and faith and love.—Joe A. Harding.

Illustrations

BEYOND DEFINING.   I have given no definition of love. This is impossible because there is no higher principle by which it could be defined.—Paul Tillich.

THE BLIND GIRL'S QUESTION.   During President Eisenhower's administration a young girl, who had been blind since birth, was taken by a national organization to meet Mrs. Eisenhower and launch a fund drive. The first lady was never enthusiastic about public appearances, but this was a good cause. "Are we ready?" Mrs. Eisenhower asked, as the entourage walked into the garden. The girl was listening intently, bubbling over with spontaneous feelings. As the president's wife appeared, the blind girl's mother leaned over her daughter and explained that the president's wife was approaching. "Oh, mamma," asked the excited youngster, "am I smiling?"—James M. Dodson.

Sermon Suggestions

HEALING A BROKEN HEART.   Text: Luke 4:18–19. (1) A broken heart can lead you to accept life. (2) A broken heart can become an open heart, and that is an experience in healing. (3) A broken heart can be healed through the necessity of putting your life in the hands of God.—Charles L. Copenhaver.

RELIGION IN THE DAILY ROUND.   Text: Eccl. 1:3. (1) Our Judaeo-Christian faith should give meaning and purpose to the daily round. (2) Our religious faith should give endurance and satisfaction in our work. (3) Our religious faith should give aspiration beyond our work.

Worship Aids

CALL TO WORSHIP.   "The Lord is great in Zion; and he is high above all the people. Exalt the Lord our God, and worship at his holy hill; for the Lord our God is holy." Ps. 99:2, 9.

INVOCATION.   As we begin another day, most gracious Father, make us to know that we never drift beyond thy love and care. Faces may change and conditions may alter, but thou art never so near to us as when we need thee most.

OFFERTORY SENTENCE.   "The end of the commandment is charity out of a pure heart." I Tim. 1:5.

OFFERTORY PRAYER.   God of all good, who hath rewarded our labors, we acknowledge thankfully thy favor and do now dedicate a share of our material gains to the even more satisfying ministries of the spirit.

PRAYER.   Our Father, who hast set a restlessness in our hearts and made us all seekers after that which we can never fully find, forbid us to be satisfied with what we make of life. Draw us from base content, and set our eyes on far-off goals. Keep us at tasks too hard for us that we may be driven to thee for strength. Deliver us from fretfulness and self-pity. Make us sure of the goal we cannot see and of the hidden good in the world. Open our eyes to simple beauty all around us and our hearts to the loveliness men hide from us because we do not try enough to understand them. Save us from ourselves, and show us a vision of a world made new. May thy spirit of peace and illumination so enlighten our minds that all life shall glow with new meaning and new purpose.—Charles C. Albertson.

EVENING SERVICE

Topic: Face to Face
    TEXT: John 20:23.
    Thomas is described as one of the most loyal and courageous disciples of Christ. He is so courageous that he even questions Jesus. At the point we meet Thomas in this passage, his life is in crisis. Jesus has been crucified, tortured, and killed. Thomas' beloved lord is dead. Then the other disciples tell Thomas that while he was off somewhere, Jesus came again and has been present right there among them. But Thomas, not one to accept things easily, said to them, "Unless I see for myself, I won't believe." Eight days later Jesus appeared again before the disciples, and this time Thomas was there. When Thomas saw that Jesus was alive and saw him face to face, Thomas responded, "My Lord, and my God."
    I. Thomas shows us that it is right, normal, and human to have doubts and questions, to need reassurance from God, and to need to see the face of God. Some people think that once we are Christian, have begun our religious pilgrimage, and been converted and belong to the Christian faith, we will no longer have doubts and questions, but there are many times when we may face a situation in which we really need reassurance from God.
    II. The second thing that we see in these

scriptures is that as God is able and comes to us at our point of need, and we meet him face to face.

(a) When Thomas was doubting, God came to him in the risen Christ so Thomas could look at him and say, "My Lord and my God." But how is it that God comes to us?

(b) For all the millions of starving, sick, and poor people of the world, to say that God comes to all of them at their point of need and heals them or feeds them is not faith. It's absurd. To say that God has come, does come, and will come and do whatever he is able to do with the means at hand is true, even if what God does is only to suffer along with those who suffer.

(c) There is here a mystery overshadowed only by the mystery of the cross. How is it that God could allow his own son to be arrested, abandoned by friends, tortured, and killed on a cross?

(1) In the garden of Gethsemane he went to pray, saying, "Father, if possible, let this cup pass from me, but not my will, but thine, be done." I imagine what God might have said to Jesus as he answered him in that prayer: "My son, I love you so much I wish you did not have to suffer and die as you must. But we want the people to know how much we love them, to know that their sins are forgiven, to know that they may live free with dignity, to know that they need not hide nor feel far away from our love, to know that I will care for them, and to know that they need not fear death. There is no other way, my son, for them to really know this. They won't believe it if there are only words. Going to prison for this wouldn't be enough. My son, this great gift that we want them to have can only be bought with your life. Only this will convince them that what you have said is really true. Only this will show them that they may be truly free. It's a price we have to pay, my son, and I will be suffering with you on that cross. But on the third day I will raise you from the dead, and the people will see that the victory is ours. They will see that the price was paid, the gift given, and death overcome."

(2) In this gift God has come face to face with every single one of us, showing us his love, so that if we have the eyes of faith to see, we know God's love in the cross of Christ.

III. A third thing we see in these scriptures is that God would have our face to be his face to other people.

(a) Thomas was a twin. We don't know to whom he was a twin, but in a sense Thomas is a twin to every single one of us, for just like Thomas, there have been moments in our lives when we have felt "unless I see, I won't believe." We have needed a concrete, living, flesh-and-blood human being to care for us in a way that, when we received that love and care, we could look into that person's face and say, "My Lord, and my God."

(b) God needs each of us to be the one who brings his love to this world. And the more of us who are willing to do so, the more hungry who will be fed, the more sick who will be healed, and the more suffering will be ministered unto. For they will see in our face the face of God.—Edward J. Hansen.

SUNDAY: SEPTEMBER SIXTH

MORNING SERVICE

Topic: The God Who Knows Us
Text: Ps. 139:2.

I. The Bible's message concerning God's knowledge of our lives is enormously reassuring and supportive.

(a) We exist in the universe along with the God who has made all things. And that is only part of the story. The rest of the story is that God, who exists with us in the universe, is a God who visits us and who knows us.

(b) You can be sure that the God who has made all things knows about you too. There are so many people in the world. Is it really true that God knows all of these people by name? It is true not because we can understand it or somehow construct a model for it but because this is the message of the Bible. "Such knowledge is too wonderful for me; it is high, I cannot attain it" (v. 6).

(c) This can help you keep your sanity and give you courage when you are terrifically discouraged. Often when people go through deep trouble, they feel abandoned and deserted not only by their friends but also by God. We should not feel deserted. We can go nowhere where God will not meet us. He is close to us, and he knows us perfectly.

II. Another advantage is that it can help us to be more moral and to be better people. What about a man who is cheating on his wife? If he really understood that God was watching him, might he change? What about the person who is engaging in fraudulent activity which he has succeeded in covering up? Might he change if he felt that God was watching him? According to what we have learned from the Bible, God is watching us all, and we must remember that in regard to our conduct.

III. The biggest advantage is that the God who knows us so well is the God who is able to make our lives better than they are.

(a) Ps. 139 concludes with the psalmist's great confession of God's nearness: "Search me, O God, and know my heart! Try me and know my thoughts! And see if there be any wicked way in me, and lead me in the way everlasting!" (vv. 23–24). He acknowledged that he could not escape God and that God knew him perfectly, but he asked God to probe deeper and deeper and learn more and more about him so that God's great repair, God's great renewal, could be applied to his life.

(b) The Bible gives us the picture of God who knows the needs of his people perfectly and who consequently supplies these needs out of his fullness. Wherever we go, we meet God, and we meet him nowadays when we look into the face of the Lord Jesus Christ who has lived, died, and risen again so that his people may be strengthened with abundant life.

IV. It's true that there must be awe in

our consciousness because we are aware of the presence of God. But there must also be a joy-filled dependence upon the resources which God provides people like us who need him so very much. God, who knows our needs, has accomplished a work of salvation that is absolutely astonishing and that is absolutely sufficient.

(a) The God who knows his people perfectly has sent his only begotten son Jesus into our world so that through his perfect sacrifice, offered on Calvary's cross, human sin could be paid for and the way opened for the presence of the Holy Spirit in our lives.

(b) This means that the God who knows us perfectly is also ready to help us become the kind of people we want so very much to be. This is why we can pray: "Search me, O God, and know my heart! Try me and know my thoughts! And see if there be any wicked way in me, and lead me in the way everlasting!"—Joel Nederhood.

Illustration

CONFLICTING INSTINCTS. The military man in me wants to have a strong military and be able to show the world that I will not be pushed around, and the peacemaker in me says maybe the military ought to be cut back. The sexual person in me wants to see R-rated movies, and the moral person in me says that there ought to be self-censorship. One person in me resents the struggle of others to get what I have and to enjoy the kind of life I do, and my other person says it isn't fair and that changes ought to be made.—Carl Baskin.

Sermon Suggestions

THE HIDDEN GOD. Text: Isa. 45:15. (1) We must remember what God is. He is, in the majestic symbolism of the Old Testament, the high and lofty one who inhabiteth eternity, dwelling in light unapproachable. Could we bear the fullness of his presence? God is perfect holiness. We —even the best of us—have sinned against the light. (2) God hides himself because of his respect for human personality. He cannot thrust himself upon us without undoing his own work in making us as we are and without taking from us the most precious thing that he has given to us—our freedom of choice and will. (3) God hides himself in order that man may develop his own powers and so grow. If he hides himself when we suffer, it is only that through pain we may come to maturity, that patience and fortitude may be born, and that we may become strong.—Raymond Abba.

HOW DOES JESUS LOVE US?   Text: John 13:1. (1) Jesus is our *companion.* (2) Jesus *cares* for us. (3) Jesus has *compassion* on us. (4) Jesus is *close* to us. (5) Jesus *communicates* with us. (6) Jesus *communes* with us.— Robert McEniry in *Pastoral Life.*

Worship Aids

CALL TO WORSHIP.   "Come unto me, all ye that labor and are heavy laden, and I will give you rest. Take my yoke upon you, and learn of me; for I am meek and lowly in heart: and ye shall find rest unto your souls." Matt. 11:28–29.

INVOCATION.   Grant, O Lord our God, we beseech thee, that now and every time we come before thee in worship and in prayer we may be vividly aware of thy presence, become conscious of thy power and a sense of thy protection, and know in our hearts and minds and souls the wonder and the grace of thy peace.

OFFERTORY SENTENCE.   "God is not so unrighteous as to forget your work and labor of love, which ye have showed toward his name, in that ye have ministered to the saints, and continue to minister." Heb. 6:10.

OFFERTORY PRAYER.   O Lord Jesus Christ, who hast taught us that to whomsoever much is given, of him shall much be required: grant that we, whose lot is cast in this Christian heritage, may strive more earnestly by our prayers and tithes, by sympathy and study to hasten the coming of thy kingdom among all peoples of the earth, that as we have entered into the labors of others, so others may enter into ours, to thy honor and glory.

PRAYER.   O God our Father, who hast endowed man with the gift of creativity and set him upon the earth to labor in a common venture, we thank thee for the opportunities that are ours in the daily round to be of service. Enable us to stand fast against the influence that would corrupt this potential—employment that sees no further than financial return, work that is meaningless, and tasks that are ignoble. Empower us to resist apathy and slovenliness and the temptation to give less than our best. Speak to us as thou didst to men of old until we know that the place where we stand is holy ground and the most ordinary routine has been sanctified by thy presence. Lift us above the press of busyness until we are captured by the call of thy business. Grant that we might have a visionary faith which realizes that, in the midst of the roar of the factory, the efficiency of the office, and the big noise of small change in the marketplace, thou art working. Teach us thy ways that we might combine our work with the good works of thy kingdom. To this end may we so participate in the richness of thy grace that our labor may be marked by integrity in effort, steadfastness in purpose, and faithfulness in service until at last all our work becomes good works.—Carl F. Schultz, Jr.

EVENING SERVICE

Topic: My Father Worketh (Labor Sunday)

TEXT: John 5:17.

I. We live in a world where work abounds. All around us men are working —building houses, making roads, and inventing machines. But where is God, and what is he doing: Is he interested? Does he care? Is God at work in our world?

II. Some people think God speaks only in the sacred language of the Bible. They make a distinction between the sacred and the secular. Perhaps there is a distinction but not a separation—except in that which is unquestionably evil. To such people

God is shut up in a book and does not make his presence felt in our everyday world.

(a) Jesus said, "My Father worketh." God is still at work in the midst of life. Does not the Bible say God finished his work in six days and rested on the seventh? Has God been resting ever since? Surely not, according to the thinking of Jesus.

(1) The divine work continues. God continues to pack the earth's storehouses with raw materials to be worked upon and fashioned by man. The atmosphere around us radiates with power. The earth beneath us pulsates with life. We live in a universe which is vitally alive. Electricity and atomic power have been here from the beginning. All the discoveries of modern science and medical research have been here from the beginning of time, and the end is not yet. We do not feel the pull of the moon on the tides or the working, life-giving transforming rays of the sun. We do not feel the power of the sun as it lifts thirteen cubic miles of water off the surface of the earth every twenty-four hours.

(2) God is at work and has endowed man with a mind, and with this mind man thinks God's thoughts after him and thus continuously shares in the creative work of God.

(b) Jesus was the greatest evidence of a working God. The incarnation of God in Christ must be thought of as God's greatest work. The divine worker moved heaven and earth to reveal his heart in terms of human life and understanding. The initiative in redemptive work has always been with God. It has been man's privilege and responsiblity to respond. It has ever been true that God's attitude toward man is reflected in the words, "If any man hear my voice and open the door, I will come in."

III. We believe in the redemptive sovereign grace of God.

(a) We believe that within that grace God has made room for our cooperation. Without the help of man God does create scenes of grandeur and beauty. But in the field and the garden there are weeds and pests which must be overcome before we can grow food for the body and flowers of beauty to satisfy our aesthetic nature.

(b) In the realm of character there are weeds that spoil and mar God's intention for our lives. We readily take the weeds from our gardens, but God must take the weeds from our hearts. Most of us cooperate with God in the field and garden. He calls us to cooperate with him in our hearts. There is no limit to what can be done when God and man work together.— Ernest Edward Smith.

SUNDAY: SEPTEMBER THIRTEENTH

MORNING SERVICE

Topic: Train Up a Child (Rally Day)
TEXT: Prov. 22:6.

How can those of us who are parents become more sensitive to the importance of our responsibility? And how do we go about creatively and successfully nurturing the sensitive mechanism of a child's response?

I. We need to begin with ourselves. Proverbs teaches us to "train up a child." The word "train" suggests education by example as well as instruction. That means we need to practice what we teach. It means that it is not enough to merely explain our convictions. Honesty, integrity, and concern for others must be demonstrated.

II. We need to learn that each child is a unique individual with his or her own very special needs. The rest of that verse from Proverbs is in its original Hebrew form, "Train up a child in his own way and when he is old he will not depart from it."

III. Time is the third essential for the effective training of a child. Parenting is a full-time responsibility. Moonlighters are rarely the most efficient producers, and that is especially true with respect to imparting to a child those qualities which will make him a whole person—a person of faith, integrity, and compassion.

IV. A fourth requirement is good communication. Training cannot really take place apart from dialogue. Convictions and commitment arise largely out of clarity and understanding. That means that questions need to be aired and answered. Dialogue is essential to the child's development of the ability to express himself—his needs, his dilemmas, his uncertainties, and his questions.

V. Training implies discipline. There need to be limits. That is important for us all. Discipline must always be administered in love. Discipline is never punitive but always redemptive. It is to be applied consistently and whenever needed, but unless it hurts the parent as much as the child, it is probably not good discipline.

VI. A sixth requirement is to have some goals. We have to know what we want our children to learn. That means deciding upon certain things we definitely want to see developed in our families—things like respect for authority, learning responsibility, learning self-discipline, giving without expecting something in return, and coming to know Jesus Christ as lord and savior.—Arthur McPhee.

Illustrations

REVERENT SPIRIT.   All of us, men and women, rich and poor, white and non-white, and laity and clergy, are to walk before God in the same wise and reverent spirit, in the same denial of all vain tempers, and in the same discipline and care of each other not only because we all have the same rational nature and are servants of the same God but also because we all want the same holiness to make us fit for the same joy to which we are called. It is necessary for Christians to consider themselves as persons who are devoted to holiness and so order their common life by such rules of reason and piety as may turn it into continual service to the glory of almighty God.—William Law.

STRANGE GRACE.   For thirty-eight years W. H. Lax was a Methodist minister in the East End of London. He learned that an old man was gravely ill and called on him. It was at once made plain that he was an unwelcome visitor, for as soon as the sick man caught sight of Lax's clerical collar he turned his head and refused to utter a word. While trying to sustain a conversation, Lax noted the dreariness of the room, the pitifully small fire, and suspected that provisions had run low. When he left he went to a butcher shop and had two lamb chops sent to the house. He called again a few days later, and though the old man was still far from talkative he was disposed to be friendly. On the way home another order was left with the butcher. By the third visit there was a pronounced change in the patient. He was congenial and even expansive, and before taking leave of him Lax read from the scripture and prayed. A preaching engagement took him out of London for some days. When he got back he was informed that the old man had died and had left a message for him. Just at the last when he could barely speak he made a sign that he wanted to say something. "Tell Mr. Lax," he gasped, "it's all right . . . I'm going to God . . . but be sure to . . . tell him . . . that it wasn't . . . his preaching that changed me . . . it was . . . those lamb chops."—Robert J. McCracken.

Sermon Suggestions

STANDING IN OUR OWN WAY.   Text: Gen. 32:24. In October 1842 Emerson entered in his journal the following sentence: "Henry Thoreau made last night the fine remark that as long as a man stands in his own way, everything seems to be in his way —government, society, and even the sun, moon, and stars, as astrology may testify." One of the tragic blunders of living is to blame others for blocking our path when in reality we are standing in our own way. (1) Losing sight of self aids in the discovery of the real self not only because it breaks the vicious and blinding circle of self-centeredness but also because it reveals those deeper needs which mere meditation leaves hidden. (2) We must get out of our own way in order to get to others. (3) We must get out of our own way in order to get to God.—Ralph W. Sockman.

GATEWAYS TO GOD.   Text: Matt. 14:23. (1) The gateway of gratitude. (2) The gateway of love. (3) The gateway of growth. (4) The gateway of union.—Roy A. Burkhart.

Worship Aids

CALL TO WORSHIP.   "If a man love me [saith Jesus] he will keep my words: and my Father will love him, and we will come unto him, and make our abode with him." John 14:23.

INVOCATION.   Almighty God, fountain of all good, kindle in us insight and aspiration that this hour of prayer may be a moment of time lived in eternity. Open our ears that we may hear. Soften our hearts that we may receive thy truth. Reveal thyself to us here that we may learn to find thee everywhere.

OFFERTORY SENTENCE.   "He that hath a bountiful eye shall be blessed; for he giveth of his bread to the poor." Prov. 22:9.

OFFERTORY PRAYER.   Our Father, enable all Christians to know that their lives may be lived with Christ in God and that their gifts are means by which thy love in Christ may reach into the lives of wayward and needy persons everywhere.

PRAYER.   Our Father, in whose patient hands the mighty seasons move with quiet beauty, we would pray for those whom we love. On this day the prayer is for our children and youth. The glory of creation breaks fresh each day into their inquiring minds. The knowledge they acquire is a part of the universal truth given by you to all persons who would diligently seek it out. Let the knowledge which they grasp lead them tenderly through this maze of life and death. Let such information strengthen them as they confront growing responsibilities. There is a discipline by which life alone can be successfully lived

and character achieved. Move their minds to discover it. You have committed to the church the care and nurture of your children and youth. Enlighten us who teach, lest the darkness of our time hide the providences of your spirit. Keep alive in us the grace of your spirit, lest we lose the birthright of that image we find in you.— Kenneth Watson.

EVENING SERVICE

Topic: Qualities of Leadership
TEXT: Neh. 2:18.

Nehemiah must have been an amazing leader. Many of those people had been around there for thirty years, but it did not appear that anything had been done to restore the walls of the city. Nehemiah came along and in thirty minutes or so got the whole project off the ground and moving. What made Nehemiah a leader? When we first saw him he had a responsible position, but he was not really a leader. What makes a good leader? Let's look at some of the qualities that we find in Nehemiah.

I. Nehemiah became aware of a real need. There were some bad problems in Jerusalem, and there did not seem to be anyone on the scene who could handle them. These problems took hold of his heartstrings, and he could not let them go.

II. Nehemiah made the situation a matter of prayer and fasting. He took the problem to God. He felt the need of the guidance and help which God alone could supply. This calmed any fears which he had about approaching the king. A door was opened that made it possible for him to get the consent of the king to undertake this important task.

III. Nehemiah determined the work that was to be done. He surveyed the situation and formed a plan in his mind as to how it could be done.

IV. He succeeded in winning the confidence of the people. He could not do the job without their cooperation. They believed in him and were willing to follow his leadership. He inspired them to get started.

V. Nehemiah was not be discouraged or

defeated by his detractors. No doubt there were some who felt that the job could not be done. There were some who did not want it done. There were plenty of people who felt that the job could be done, and they were willing to put their backs under the load and accomplish the task.—A. Ray Adams.

SUNDAY: SEPTEMBER TWENTIETH

MORNING SERVICE

Topic: Those Who Don't Go to Church
Text: Neh. 13:11.

I. *The anti-institutionalists.* This category includes those persons who are defectors from the church on the basis of what they see as the church's preoccupation with its own self-maintenance. That is, unnecessarily preoccupied with leadership, organization, money raising, and the like. They look at the proliferation of all kinds of churches in the community and simply say that if the churches can't make up their minds what is truth they'd better settle their own differences before they start talking to us on the outside.

II. *The boxed-in.* These are persons who have once been church members and have left the church. When they were inside they felt overly confined, constrained, and thwarted. Their independence was put in a straitjacket. They didn't have room to breathe.

III. *The burned-out.* These are those who feel that their energies have been utterly consumed by the church. They've been on the inside and they've been faithful, active participants in the work of the church, but they feel that the church has depleted their resources, their talents, and their time.

IV. *The floaters.* These are people who were never really committed to the church. These persons tend to lack any deep feelings toward the church. One might speak of them as apathetic people who say, "I could really care less."

V. *The hedonists.* These are the people who find the fulfillment of their purpose in life in momentary pleasures.

VI. *The locked-out.* These are the unchurched people who feel the churches have simply closed their doors against them. They feel rejected, neglected, or in some cases overtly discriminated against by the church. These folks are ones who perhaps more than any others express real hostility toward churches.

VII. *The nomads.* These are the increasing number of people who wander from place to place in American society. They're so much on the move that they seldom stay in one place long enough to call it a home.

VIII. *The pilgrims.* These are very honest people searching for satisfying meanings and values in life. Many of them are among the youth who simply say, "I'm not going to make up my mind too soon." But some others are middle-aged or older people who are still waiting for the last bit of evidence that will convince them that the teachings of the church are correct. They're persons who would refuse to call themselves unbelievers. They just haven't found what they want to believe.

IX. *The publicans.* These are the people who perceive the church to be primarily populated by Pharisees. They call them hypocrites, phonies, fakers, people living double lives, and people whose behavior simply doesn't square with what they say they believe.

X. *The true unbelievers* such as the classical type of the athiest, the agnostic, the humanist, and the secularist. Few persons acknowledge themselves to be complete unbelievers. They appear to be more of the pilgrim class who are not finally decided on unbelief. They're hoping that somebody will give them an answer to their question. But they haven't found it yet.

XI. *The uncertains.* These are people who say very frankly: "I don't know why I'm not a member of the church. I just don't think about it that often. I get up on a Sunday morning, and it never occurs to me that other people are going to church. I don't know why I don't go."—J. Russell Hale in *The Unchurched.*

Illustrations

ODD NUMBER.   A real Christian is an odd number. He feels supreme love for one whom he has never seen. He talks familiarly every day to someone he cannot see. He expects to go to heaven on the virtue of another. He empties himself in order that he might be full. He admits he is wrong so he can be declared right. He goes down in order to get up. He is strongest when he is poorest and happiest when he feels worst. He dies so he can live, forsakes in order to have, gives away so he can keep, sees the invisible, hears the inaudible, and knows that which passeth knowledge.—A. W. Tozer.

UNUSED BOOK.   A little boy took the Bible from the center table, turned its dusty pages, and said to his mother, "Mother, is this God's book?" The mother said, "Certainly it is God's book." Then came the reply from the little boy, "Well, I think we'd better send it back to God for we don't use it here."—William R. Taylor.

Sermon Suggestions

ON BEING USEFUL TO GOD.   Text: Ps. 11:3. (1) God can use you and me as instruments of his purpose. (2) He can use mothers to lay foundations of character in the generation coming on. (3) He can use fathers to build ideals of integrity and honor in youngsters growing toward maturity. (4) He can use all of us to stand for the enduring values of our Christian heritage in an era of flux and uncertainty. (5) He can use us to speak a word for Jesus Christ in a world that increasingly depends on force and is skeptical of love and goodwill. (6) He can use our voices to challenge what is wrong and to speak as critics of the status quo.—Harold Blake Walker.

THE CHURCH'S CALLING.   Text: II Thess. 1:11. The church is a called people. (1) Called out from the ways of rebellion, alienation, and sin. (2) Called into a vital relationship with God. (3) Called to active involvement with God in what he is doing in the world.—R. Eugene Sterner.

Worship Aids

CALL TO WORSHIP.   "It is good for me to draw near to God: I have put my trust in the Lord God . . . God is the strength of my heart, and my portion for ever." Ps. 73:28, 26.

INVOCATION.   Mysterious God of creation, we are forever awed by the wonder of life here and now, beyond and forever. The more we learn of nature and existence the more we ponder the puzzle of your conceptions. Through science and technology we have conquered boundaries unimaginable to our father's father. Yet every answer leaves unknown, though sharper in its reality, the inexpressible nature of your word. The more we discover of the discernible the more we anticipate our need of the eternal.—Richard D. Bausman.

OFFERTORY SENTENCE.   "Seeing ye have purified your souls in obeying the truth through the Spirit unto unfeigned love of the brethren, see that ye love one another with a pure heart fervently." I Pet. 1:22.

OFFERTORY PRAYER.   Eternal God, give us a vision of thy glory that no sacrifice may seem too great, and strengthen us in every step we take from selfishness to generosity.

PRAYER.   O God, overlook our words and hear our thoughts this morning. In these moments of pondering and in our search for significance, we bow our heads but we raise our hopes to thee, O God.

We do not always recognize the riches that we receive—a body that functions without pain and a mind that moves out beyond time and space. We have enjoyed advantages that we did not work for and advances that we did not make—the warmth of the sunshine, the nourishment of the rain, the music of creative Christians, and the wonder drugs that heal bodies.

We are puzzled by our nature because we have such potential for creating life and yet we seem bent on destroying it. We are blessed with ever-increasing knowledge and yet we do not know how to live at peace either with ourselves or with each other.

Maybe that is the reason we are here today, O God. We need forgiveness for doing what we knew was wrong, and we need forgiveness for not doing what we honestly believed was right. Guilt is a heavy load, and we need a reprieve. We need to be moved and motivated by thy spirit, O God, because the facts of division and distrust and of hate and hostility have been quite plain to us, and we still did not move into action.

Sometimes, O God, we cannot even recognize a truth. Our antenna for ideas seems disconnected. May this new week not be identified by our weakness but by our strength, and may our strength, like that of Jesus Christ, bless life and not curse it.—Earl F. Lindsay.

EVENING SERVICE

Topic: Sunday Christianity
TEXT: Luke 18:8.

I. One of the great problems which continues to plague Christianity is the problem of Sunday Christianity. This doesn't mean that there is a problem in the fact that Sunday has become the day par excellence for Christians to assemble and celebrate the resurrection of their Lord but rather that Sunday has virtually become the only day when this crucial identity is recognized either by the watching world or the community of believers.

II. This problem is vastly complicated, having as many implications of a weakened witness as it has symptoms of a fatigued faith. One simple indication of just how problematic Sunday Christianity has become is seen in the fact that practically everyone, Christians included, associates the concept of church with a building.

(a) The early church could never have been characterized by a building, no matter how stunning the architecture or how scripture filled its stained glass.

(b) Part of our problem is that we think of going to church as a means of fulfilling religious obligations rather than the church as gathering itself together to generate energy and to collect and coordinate its resources for a dynamic existence in a world of dissipating influences.

III. If you have ever wondered what Jesus could have been implying when he asked his disciples if the son of man would find faith on the earth at his coming, look to Sunday Christianity and ask if his worst fears might not find realization there. For a faith that limits itself to expression merely one day a week, or sometimes doesn't even go that far, is not a faith that adequately expresses a hope so dynamic and charged with vibrancy that it presents a clear alternative to the multiple but illusory hopes clutched at by our desperate world. A living faith is a way of life.—Randal Lee Cummings.

SUNDAY: SEPTEMBER TWENTY-SEVENTH

MORNING SERVICE

Topic: Where Faith Falls Short
SCRIPTURE: Mark 9:14–29 (NEB).

I. "I have faith."

(a) We believe in the fact of God. The reality of God seems obvious. For that reason the Bible everywhere assumes that God exists and nowhere argues for his existence. (See Rom. 1:20, TEV.)

(b) We believe that God has done great things for his people. God's deliverance of his chosen people from slavery in Egypt never ceases to thrill us. God's answer to Elijah's prayer, which put the prophets of Baal to shame and glorified the eternal God, is exciting, amusing, and satisfying. God's providential deliverance of Simon Peter from prison, when his angel came in the darkness and released Peter, confirms our belief that God has indeed done great things in the days past. And there is evidence that God does such things today.

(c) But can God help us? That is our big question. Will he help us? That may be the bigger question. Yet we do come to God. That indicates that we have faith. There is the ghost of a chance, we suspect, that he might do something for us and that he might answer our prayers.

II. We are prisoners of unbelief. "Help me," we cry, "where faith falls short."

(a) Our troubles may be that we do not feel worthy of God's help and blessing.

(1) Any sensitive person knows that he has sinned.

(2) We know that some wrongdoing has irreversible consequences. Certain physical and social consequences of sin are as permanent as the amputation of a leg or an arm. In such cases our sin is ever before us.

(3) Some wrongdoing does not do permanent or unmendable damage, but the feeling of guilt may be deep and unyielding, even while the Lord is saying, "People can be forgiven any sin and any evil thing they say" (Matt. 12:31, TEV.).

(b) Our trouble may be that we feel that we are destined to fail for some strange reason. It is more a matter of fatalism. We do not feel unworthy, but a series of bad experiences causes us to decide that our destiny must be written in the stars. One man remarked, "It seems that there's always something to keep a man down." He was afflicted with the bitter feeling that life is unfair. To hope for some good gift or blessing from God may seem too much. (See Isa. 43:2, TEV.)

III. God does help us whether we deserve it or not and whether everything seems to deny it or not. But we cannot dictate the way God is to help us.

(a) God helps us simply by letting us come to him with our questions. The father of the sick boy showed a lot of nerve by saying to Jesus, "Have pity on us and help us, if you possibly can" (v. 22, TEV).

(1) Many of the Old Testament heroes poured out their bitter complaints to God with such boldness as would make some tender-minded saints tremble and prepare for a bolt of lightning from heaven. Jeremiah, Habakkuk, and Job all had their

"beef" with God, but their honest, ruthless showdowns led to stronger faith, firmer hope, and deeper love for God. Even Jesus went into the garden of Gethsemane and wrestled with God, wanting desperately to avoid the cross if it were possible but finally willing to accept it.

(2) Nothing can be gained for our faith by letting our doubts, our fears, or our bitterness fester in sullen silence. It is an act of faith to confess our doubts, fears, and bitterness. We may have to bear God's telling us how wrong we are and how immature. No matter. A two-way talk with God is the way to knowledge and growth.

(b) God sometimes helps us by answering our prayers clearly and literally. Not only in the case of the afflicted boy in our text but also in many other stories in the gospels, we find a happy ending. No doubt you can look back among your own experiences and point to blessed answers to prayer. Experience has often confirmed the words of Jesus in Matt. 7:11.

(c) God's help may seem anything but that!

(1) When Joseph Parker's wife died, this great preacher was crushed. "In that dark hour I became almost an athiest. For God had set his foot upon my prayers and treated my petitions with contempt. If I had seen a dog in such agony as mine, I would have pitied and helped the dumb beast, yet God spat upon me and cast me out as an offense—out into the waste wilderness and the night black and starless." This was the first time in his sixty-eight years that Parker had ever questioned anything vital to his faith. But in the days that followed God helped him by causing him to remember the faith by which he had lived and the faith he had preached to others. The faith that came from the crucible was more real, more sympathetic, and more deeply rooted in God's love.

(2) What makes the difference—if indeed anything can make a difference? Nothing has quite the power to enable us to accept the unacceptable or to transform tragedy as does the fact of Jesus' resurrection. Help for the shortfall of faith is present when we commit ourselves to the God who raised Jesus from the dead.

(3) God is infinitely resourceful and can change an impossible situation. Even if Jesus had not healed the boy in the text, he would have done something else. Sometimes our faith is helped most when our request, per se, is denied. We might paraphrase the words of the risen Lord: "Twentieth-century Christian, because you have seen clear answers to your prayers, you have believed. Blessed are those who have not seen their prayers answered and yet have believed."—James W. Cox.

Illustration

HE CARED.   When William Booth died, his funeral was held in a vast exhibition hall in London, and 40,000 people attended. Among the crowd were thieves, tramps, harlots, and the lost and outcast to whom Booth had given his heart and for whom he genuinely cared. Unknown to most, royalty was there too. Far to the rear of the hall sat Britain's Queen Mary, a staunch admirer of Booth. Beside her on the aisle was a shabby but neatly-dressed woman who confessed her secret to the queen. Once she had been a prostitute, and the Salvation Army claimed her for Christ. The woman had come early to claim an aisle seat, she said, guessing that the casket would pass within feet of her. As it did she reached out and placed three faded carnations on the lid, and all through the service they were the only flowers on the casket. Queen Mary was deeply moved when the woman turned to her and said simply, in words which could stand as William Booth's epitaph: "He cared for the likes of us."—Carl J. Sanders.

Sermon Suggestions

OUR COMMON LONGINGS.   Text: John 20:31. (1) The longing for God. (2) The longing for significance. (3) The longing for forgiveness. (4) The longing for hope. —Joseph R. Sizoo.

HOW TO BECOME A PEACEMAKER.   Text: Matt. 5:9. (1) Begin by disarming yourself. (2) Embrace the suffering of your fellow human beings. (3) Learn to recognize the stranger as your brother.—Clarence J. Forsberg.

Worship Aids

CALL TO WORSHIP.   "O come, let us sing unto the Lord: let us make a joyful noise to the rock of our salvation. Let us come before his presence with thanksgiving, and make a joyful noise unto him with psalms." Ps. 95:1–2.

INVOCATION.   Heavenly Father, we come before thee in trembling because we are conscious of our many sins and yet boldly because we know that thou dost love us. Forgive us our sins, and help us to become more worthy of thy goodness and love. May we gain that strength from communion with thee which will enable us to walk humbly and righteously before thee and uprightly before the world, manifesting in life's every experience that faith and courage which befit thy children.

OFFERTORY SENTENCE.   "Verily, verily, I say unto you, he that believeth on me, the works that I do shall he do also; and greater works than these shall he do. And whatsoever ye shall ask in my name, that will I do, that the Father may be glorified in the Son." John 14:12–13.

OFFERTORY PRAYER.   We pray thee, O God, to give us sight to see the Christ, the insight to choose him, the steadfastness to follow him, and the stewardship of loyalty represented in these gifts offered in his name.

PRAYER.   Thou who art greater than all our thoughts of thee, whom we worship with stumbling praise and broken prayer, make thou a sanctuary within our hearts by thy presence there and humble us to kneel in the very company of our inmost thoughts. If there be a church above us, deepen its invisible foundations in us. If we inherit the memory of a redeeming fellowship with Christ, then open our own gates of trust and love. Dispel our fears and pride until the radiance of an abundant communion with one another illumines the darkness and loneliness of this world with joy and peace. If the church seems like a forgotten word or a vain dream, take the mask from the face of life that we may see the dim arches of thy providence looming above the concerns of our day, thy wondrous glory hidden in the turning furrows of time, and the image of thy hope in men struggling to do thy will. We worship at the altar of all these things by which thou hast spoken to us and await thee, for in thee is our hope and our salvation.—Samuel H. Miller.

EVENING SERVICE

Topic: House to House Visiting
TEXT: Luke 10:1–9, 16.

I. Look who's going—not you but Christ (v. 1). (a) You are not going on your own initiative. It is not your idea. "The Lord appointed . . . and sent them . . . into every town and place where he himself was about to come." Christ called you to go to the unchurched in his place and as his representative. Christ seeks the lost in and through you. God says, "I will seek the lost and I will bring back the strayed" (Ezek. 34:16). You are the means of his doing that.

(b) Note the urgency in going. The harvest is plentiful and the workers are few. So much is to be done and so few to do it. When the harvest is ready, there is no time to lose. "Salute no one on the road" (v. 4). Don't take time even to pass the time of day. Don't delay. Seize the opportunity to save a soul. Tomorrow may be too late.

(c) It is not you who are making the calls. It is Christ in you, using you. This gives you a sense of importance as an ambassador of the king. You go with confidence and joy.

II. Look who's helping—not you but Christ, (vv. 5, 9). (a) Christ told the seventy to be a blessing to those visited. Upon entering a home, they were to give it peace —"Peace be to this house!" They were to heal the sick in that home (v. 9). You do not bring peace and healing, for who are you to do it? Who is able? It is not you but Christ in you, using you to do some good to those you visit.

(b) Callers on the unchurched do not go primarily to get members for the church. According to our text, they call to see if they can be of any service regardless of whether they join the church or not. Church visitors are sent to see if they can do any good. They inquire about the welfare of the household. They show they are genuinely interested in the welfare of each member of the family. They ask not, "Are you saved?" but "What are your needs?" or "Are you hurting?" or "Can we be of any help to you?"

III. Look who's talking—not you but Christ (v. 9). Jesus told the seventy what to say: "The kingdom of God has come near to you." This is not your message but Jesus' words. The kingdom of God comes near those you visit because you bring the king and his blessings to them. The king comes in the person of you and through you blesses the home you visit.—John R. Brokhoff.

SUNDAY: OCTOBER FOURTH

MORNING SERVICE

Topic: Come (World Communion Sunday)

I. "Come" is a word for everyone. It applies to all those who have never come to Jesus and need to come to Jesus for the first time. They are people, maybe some of you here, who are far from Christ in the storm of life. You see Jesus miraculously walking on stormy waters, but he is so far from you. To you he says, "Come."

(a) Jesus says "Come" because he wants you and considers you a person of worth. You are acceptable to him. "Come" is Jesus' invitation to be with him. It is a sign of his love and regard for you. He wants you and calls for you.

(b) This invitation implies that your coming in voluntary. Jesus does not believe in force. He does not want to make you a Christian. He does not scare you nor threaten you so that you are frightened into coming. No pressure is used. You can come or stay away, accept or reject, consider the invitation an honor or despise it.

(c) When Jesus says "Come," he implies that it is not as easy to come as it may appear on the surface. It is not a simple matter of getting out of the pew and walking down the center aisle and shaking the hand of a minister and saying, "I want to be a Christian." Look at the danger and difficulty Peter faced when Jesus said "Come." Jesus said he should come to him by walking on the water. Could you do that? Coming to Jesus may seem impossible.

(d) What did Jesus say about those who would come to him? "If anyone would come after me, let him deny himself, take up his cross, and follow me." The cost of coming is leaving sin and evil for a new way of life. Like Paul, the past must be considered garbage in contrast to the new life in Christ. It means giving up a wicked and a selfish way of thinking and now living for that which is good and right.

(e) It takes faith to come to Jesus across the deep and troubled waters of life. When Peter came, he lost his faith when he looked at the high waves and realized the danger of drowning. Jesus asked him, "O man of little faith, why did you doubt?" If you can come to Jesus with an unyielding faith, you will be able to walk on the water of all the demands and sacrifices necessary to come to Jesus. By faith you can do it.

II. "Come" applies to those of us who came to Jesus at one time but need to come again. Jesus is saying not only "come" but "come again." We are Christians gathered here for worship. We came to Jesus when we were baptized. We may have come again at a later time. Right now it may be that we need to come to Jesus, for a Christian needs to come to Christ again and again and again. Peter climbed out of the boat and started walking on the water toward Jesus. When he lost faith, he began to sink and yelled, "Lord, save me." Jesus grabbed his hand and pulled him to the top of the water. He had to

make another start in coming to Jesus.

(a) Why do we need to come to Jesus again? Why isn't once enough? Because we Christians are sinners. Each time we sin we sink into the waters, and we get farther away from Christ.

(b) How do we come to Christ again? To come again means to be aware of one's sins, confess them to God in deep humility, and make a change in life. With true repentance and faith, one comes again to Christ for mercy and forgiveness. This absolution is given to us particularly in the Lord's Supper, for when Jesus passed the cup, he said, "Drink all of it; this cup is the New Testament in my blood, which is shed for you and for many, for the remission of sins." That means we can have the complete blotting out of our sins by properly coming to the Lord's table, and we will be restored to the original relationship with Christ.

(c) When we come back, we come just as we are. We have no excuses and no arguments. Jesus takes us with all of our dirtiness. We come to him as sinners. We are not worthy of his forgiveness. "Just as I am without one plea . . . O lamb of God, I come, I come."

III. "Come" applies to all of us because everyone needs to come closer to Christ.

(a) Peter responded when he left the boat. He sank into the water, and Jesus had to raise him up. Now he is closer to Christ than ever. Together they enter the boat, and the storm is over. Now they are close to each other as they sit in their little boat.

(b) We feel this need to get closer to Christ because our lives are not what they should be. We are not getting very far in our Christian life. Progress is very slow because we are not close enough to Christ. Why are you and I not the kind and loving people we want to be? Why are we not doing more good with our lives? It is because we are too far from the source of our power and wisdom, Jesus Christ. The closer we come to Jesus the more we will accomplish for good in the world.

(c) How do we come closer to Christ? The best way is through the Lord's Supper where we come into concrete union with

Christ through the bread and wine which are the body and blood of Christ. When we receive these elements, we are eating and drinking more than physical elements. In, with, and under these forms we experience the true, real, and genuine presence of Christ.—John R. Brokhoff.

Illustrations

GOODNESS. Much of the current belief in the goodness of life is the belief of men who, because they wear shoes, imagine the whole world is carpeted with leather.—John Hunter.

COMMUNICATION. A world community can exist only with world communication which means something more than extensive shortwave facilities scattered about the globe. It means common understanding, a common tradition, common ideas, and common ideals.—Robert M. Hutchins.

Sermon Suggestion

WHAT CHRIST STANDS FOR. Text: Matt. 27:11. (1) He stands for the friendliness of the universe and the fatherhood of God. (2) He stands for the initiative of God in man's salvation and for the significance of human history. (3) He stands for the worth of human personality.—Robert Ferguson.

Worship Aids

CALL TO WORSHIP. "The cup of blessing which we bless, is it not the communion of the blood of Christ? The bread which we break, is it not the communion of the body of Christ? For we being many are one bread, and one body: for we are all partakers of that one bread." I Cor. 10:-16–17.

INVOCATION. Almighty God, who of thy great mercy hast gathered us into thy visible church: grant that we may not swerve from the purity of thy worship, but may so honor thee both in spirit and in outward form that thy name may be glorified in us and that our fellowship may be with all thy saints in earth and in heaven.

OFFERTORY SENTENCE. "Every man shall give as he is able, according to the blessing of the Lord thy God which he hath given thee." Deut. 16:17.

OFFERTORY PRAYER. Our Father, help us to love thee so well that we shall have all thy kingdom's interests and all thy children at heart.

PRAYER. Almighty Father, whose very presence casts out fear, in whose love we find peace and security, and from whose word we discover our need: search us and try our ways as we come to this hour of communion with thee.

The very thought of thee in thy holiness bows us down in humility. We walk each day under thy protection. We use earth's goods as temporary tenants. Thou art our host throughout life, and we have often abused thy hospitality in our selfishness. Forgive us for thinking only of ourselves. Be patient with us in clamoring for our rights rather than seeking to protect the rights of others. Bear with us when in our smallness we are overly sensitive, puffed up with pride, and quick to injure others in a race for recognition. Give us a willingness to turn ourselves over to thee and a faith that is sufficient to drive away feelings of insecurity when we are faced with needed discipline in our lives, our nation, and our Christian fellowship. Lead us in the true and holy way of repentance that we may obtain thy forgiveness.

Grant that we may gladly accept the symbols of thy broken body and poured out life in remembrance of him who endured the meanness of little people carrying large hates, the hostility of those who opposed his message, and death at the hands of those who knew not what they were doing.—James R. Duncan.

EVENING SERVICE

Topic: Time to Remember
TEXT: John 17:21.
I. Ours is a world of hungry people. Few

people have sufficient to eat. Many are passed over. Holy Communion reminds us of Jesus' sacrifice. Our response expressed tangibly with money and other material resources enables the church to feed hungry people. In cooperation with other groups the church is working to alleviate the root causes of malnutrition. A hungry world is God's call to North Americans to live a less consumption-oriented life-style.

II. Ours is a world of haunted people.

(a) Many men and women are partially paralyzed by an unhappy past. They are indifferent to God as the source of life's meaning. Unlike Israelites rejoicing in their past deliverance, these people have forgotten who and whose they are. They are weighed down with bitter memories. Like the Israelites, all of us need deliverance from whatever oppresses us.

(b) Holy Communion reminds us that Christ's sacrifice has delivered us. Our past, however horrible, has been par-doned. Our present, however unpleasant, is accepted. Our future, however uncertain, promises new possibilities. The church remembers Jesus' sacrificial death and gives thanks for deliverance from all oppressors.

III. Ours is a world of hunted people.

(a) Hostility. Hatred. Terrorism. Assassinations. Revolutionaries. Oppressed people are struggling for liberation. The Christian church witnesses to the liberator of the oppressed. We need not search for the one who liberates. God searches until we are found.

(b) Holy Communion reminds us of our Lord's sacrifice for all sorts and conditions of people—children, youth, adults, healthy people, sick people, alcoholic people, drug-dependent people, sober people, whole people, fragmented people, assertive people, dependent people, hopeful people, desperate people, confident people, and troubled people. All of these are God's people.—William H. Likins.

SUNDAY: OCTOBER ELEVENTH

MORNING SERVICE

Topic: Can't Someone Else Do It? (Laity Sunday)

TEXT: Exod. 3:6–10 (NASB).

I. God says, "I will deliver my people" and "I'm going to do it through you." God, who is never embarrassed to call us to do the impossible, reminds Moses that he is to deliver the children of Israel out of Egypt into Canaan.

(a) The problem was that the Egyptians had conquered Canaan. To deliver the nation of Israel out of Egypt into Canaan would be to take them from the frying pan into the fire.

(b) Besides, Moses had to take two and a half million people. If you were to march that many people in a column of fours, the line would stretch for 375 miles. That is a lot of people to feed and protect. The task was impossible. And God said, "Moses, I'm calling you." So it is understandable that Moses would say, "Who am I?"

(c) Interestingly enough, God does not tell Moses who he is. God just says, "I will be with you." That is really all Moses needs. He does not need to know who he is. All he needs to know is that God is with him.

II. Moses' first question is, "Who am I?" and God says, "It doesn't matter; I am with you." Moses' second question is, "Well, then, who are you?"

(a) The question that Moses asks is not, "What is your name?" Moses knew that the name of the Lord, the covenant God of Israel, was Jehovah or Yahweh.

(b) The interrogative pronoun that he uses means, "Explain to me the meaning of the name." So God explains that his name means "I AM." "Whatever you need, that is what I am. Do you need courage? I am courage. Do you need wisdom? That is what I am. Whatever resource you are lacking, that is what I am. Therefore, tell them I AM sent you."

(c) Even though God told Moses he is sufficient to meet his needs, Moses thinks: "The elders won't believe me. Who am I?

They won't believe that I have the credentials to deliver my people." Have you ever felt that way? "I really don't expect anyone to listen. If I had just a little better position in life, a better job, and more education, people would listen to me."

(d) God does not go into Moses' background to remind him that he has the equivalent of a Ph.D. He does something else. He gives him three signs as his affirmation that Moses was the man he called.

(e) Moses has another problem: "Please, Lord, I have never been eloquent, for I am slow of speech and slow of tongue." And the Lord said to him, "Who has made man's mouth? I know you are slow of speech. I made you."

(f) Moses had one final problem: "Please, Lord, now send the message by whomever thou wilt." This sounds pious, but Moses is not volunteering. This is the Hebrew idiom that means "Send somebody else." Verse 14 says, "Then the anger of the Lord burned against Moses."

III. God was not angry when Moses felt weak, when he felt unequipped, when he lacked credentials, and when he felt impotent. That was no problem to God. What tied God's hands was when Moses said: "I'm not available. Send somebody else."

(a) The great thing about this passage is that God does not leave it there. He would send Aaron as Moses' associate, and Aaron would be the spokesman. God would speak through Moses—through Aaron. God did not write Moses off. He did not set him aside.

(b) From the book of Exodus we learn what Moses accomplished. He was the leader of Israel, the one around whom the nation was formed. Where did his power to accomplish those deeds come from? Where did his resources come from? From the God who is.—David H. Roper in *Decision.*

Illustrations

SPIRIT OF RIGHTEOUSNESS. Being religious is not a work apart by itself but a spirit of righteousness flowing into all the enjoyments and intercourse of the world. Not merely the preacher in the pulpit and the saint on his knees may do the work of religion but the mechanic who smites the hammer and drives the wheel, the artist who seeks to realize his pure idea of the beautiful, the mother in the gentle offices of the home, the statesman in the forlorn hope of liberty and justice, and the philosopher whose thoughts tread reverently among the splendid mysteries of the universe.—Frederic Francois Chopin.

SINGLE PURPOSE. Dear Lord, the great healer, I kneel before you. Since every good and perfect gift must come from you, give skill to my hand, clear vision to my mind, kindness and sympathy to my heart. Give me singleness of purpose, strength to lift at least a part of the burden of my suffering fellowman, and a true realization of the privilege that is mine. Take from my heart all guile and worldliness that with the simple faith of a child I may rely on thee.—Mother Teresa.

Sermon Suggestion

DO YOU WANT TO BE RICH? Text: Acts 20:35. (1) Try giving yourself away. (2) Try spending your life for what will outlast it. (3) Try investing yourself in the practice of mercy, the support of justice, the proclamation of truth, the creation of beauty, the service of righteousness, and the ministry of love. (4) Try giving all you can of yourself to the wisdom and work of Jesus Christ through the church.—Everett W. Palmer.

Worship Aids

CALL TO WORSHIP. "Wait on the Lord: be of good courage, and he shall strengthen thine heart: wait, I say, on the Lord." Ps. 27:14.

INVOCATION. Eternal God our Father, who art from everlasting, thou hast made us and not we ourselves. Thou hast sent us never far from thee that we, thy children, may learn the ways of freedom and choose thee with all our hearts. Grant us now thy Holy Spirit that, confident in prayer, we may worship thee with gladness and become as little children before thee.

OFFERTORY SENTENCE.   "Give, and it shall be given unto you; good measure, pressed down, and shaken together, and running over." Luke 6:38.

OFFERTORY PRAYER.   Open our eyes that we may see thy goodness, O Father; our hearts that we may be grateful for thy mercies; our lips that we may show forth thy praise; and our hands that we may give these offerings according to thy wish and desire.

PRAYER.   O God, creator of all worlds, father of all people, as we gather in worship we come with anticipation of seeking and finding you. Just as the men of faith in past generations discovered you in their day, so we today see you in our generation. We see you in the events of our history. We see you in the faces of those who suffer pain or sorrow or injustice. We see you in the lives of people who give of themselves to serve others. We see you wherever truth is taught through our schools and colleges. We see you in the scientific and medical advances of our generation. We see you in the noisy rush of the cities and in the quiet abundance of the countryside.

Our God, make us more responsive to your presence and your purposes through the people and events of our day. So may we serve you through our lives.—Gene N. Branson.

EVENING SERVICE

Topic: Knowing God's Will
SCRIPTURE: Exod. 19:1–8; 20:1–17.

I. *What we want to know.* Too often we assume that God's will is synonymous with knowledge we wish was ours. Probably the Israelites, in transition between the lands of bondage and promise, frequently wished for advance knowledge of the details of their future. Much of what we want to know, however, remains hidden. This leads many to despair of knowing the will of God.

II. *What we need to know.* Someone has said that "God's will means character long before it means career." Surely God is more concerned with revealing what we need to know than what we want to know. Surely he cares more about our knowing how to live today than what will happen tomorrow. God's gift of the law to Israel was the clear revelation of his will. The ten commandments were the fundamental guidelines for life as God wanted it lived. The Father does not hide what we need to know.

III. *What we already know.* The challenge of God's will is less a matter of knowing and more a matter of doing. The challenge is to live in terms of what we already know, and our knowledge of God's will always exceeds our performance. Israel's difficulties were always more problems of the heart than the head. The ten commandments stand to this day as a profound reminder that we already know what we need to know to live in the will of God. Perhaps more light would come if we were obedient to the light we have.—C. David Matthews in *Proclaim.*

SUNDAY: OCTOBER EIGHTEENTH

MORNING SERVICE

Topic: What God Requests
TEXT: Mic. 6:8.

I. Mic. 6 begins with a summons (vv. 1–5). (a) God brings suit against his wayward people, Israel. He calls on the mountains, hills, and foundations of the earth to

bear witness to his charges. God calls attention to his generous provision for Israel.

(1) God brought them up out of Egyptian slavery.

(2) He gave them strong leaders—Moses, Aaron, and Miriam. A people seldom exceed the vision of their leaders.

(3) God provided protection from their desert enemies. He turned the threat of Balak, king of Moab, into a blessing.

(b) What more was there that God could have done for his people? The Israelites respond, "How shall we approach God?" They protest: "We are religious! What does God expect of us?"

(1) "We sacrifice year-old calves, an extravagant offering."

(2) "We bring thousands of rams to the altar of God and pour out 10,000 rivers of oil. We are generous, even lavish, in our offerings."

(3) "What more are we expected to give? Does he require us to sacrifice our firstborn—'the fruit of my body for the sins of my soul'? What does God want, after all?"

(c) Israel was religious, just as they claimed. But they had neglected a matter weightier than the law. They were pious and religious but unethical. The Almighty accused them.

(1) "Scant measure" (v. 10). They used a false-bottomed bushel.

(2) "Wicked balance scales and deceitful weights" (v. 11). They had two sets of weights—a heavy set for use when buying and a light set for use when selling.

(3) The rich men were violent. They added to their ill-gotten wealth by extortion and bribing the judges. The poor were liars who would also cheat if given the chance.

II. What God requires (6:8). This passage certainly represents the ethical high-water mark of the Hebrew faith.

(a) "You know what is good," wrote Micah. People seldom need to be told what is good or bad, right or wrong. It is not that they do not know. But it is one thing to know what is right and another to do what is right.

(b) "God has shown man [Adam] what is right." The Hebrew word used here means mankind. All men have a conscience and know. Israel had no monopoly on moral insight.

III. The message of the eighth-century B.C. prophets is summed up by Micah. Amos preached about justice. Hosea wrote of suffering love. Isaiah pointed out the reality of reverence. Micah brought their prophetic messages together in a single sentence: "To be just and kind and to live in quiet fellowship with your God" (MOFFATT). Mic. 6:8 cites the fundamentals of the faith:

(a) *Justice.*

(1) God expects his children to do what is right and to be fair. No person is above the law, whether president or pauper. While the wheels of justice grind impatiently slow, they grind exceeding small.

(2) To live justly means to live with personal and corporate integrity. We are to keep our promises and live up to our contractual agreements. Jesus said there should be no need for elaborate oaths. The kingdom man's yes should mean yes, and his no mean no.

(3) Micah is calling for basic honesty in all our dealings. To live justly means to refuse to cheat on a school exam or on an income tax form.

(b) *Mercy.*

(1) A special Hebrew word—*chesed*—is used here. It is translated elsewhere as "steadfast love." "The quality of mercy is not strained." It blesses he who gives and he who receives.

(2) To show mercy means to be kind. God is merciful and kind to us. And he wants us to be the same toward others.

(c) *Faith.*

(1) "Walk humbly with God." Faith is not punctilio. Faith is a process. It is continued action. By faith we feed on God's word. By prayer we live in intimate fellowship with God. The set of our lives is to live according to his will. We grow in faith.

(2) Real religion is a balanced experience. It includes both worship and morality, belief and behavior, and character and conduct. A mature faith incorporates both an inward piety and outward expressions of social conscience and action. Real religion embraces both theology and ethics. Consider the demanding ethics of the ten commandments, Jesus' sermon on the mount, and Pauline epistles.

(3) What a trilogy! The first two relate to man whom we have seen. The third relates to God whom we have not seen. Biblical religion is as large as life. It permeates

all of life as heaven a loaf, salt the meat, or light the darkness.—Alton H. McEachern.

Illustrations

VISION OF GOD.   One night Lord Tennyson and a friend got into a discussion concerning what each sought from life. The friend said, "I ask that I should leave the world a better place than I found it." Tennyson responded, "And I that I should have a new and bigger vision of God."—Guy Case.

SMALL ENEMY.   A fallen tree on Long's Peak, Colorado, was found to be over four hundred years old. It was a seedling when Columbus landed at San Salvador. It had been struck fourteen times by lightning. For over four centuries it has withstood avalanches, tempests, and ice. It fell because it could not withstand an attack of beetles, each one so small it could be crushed between the fingers of a man's hand.—S. Robert Weaver.

Sermon Suggestions

HANDLING THE TRUTH.   Text: Mark 4. (1) Receive the truth and you gain the truth: "Unto you that hear shall more be given" (v. 24). (2) Release the truth and you will save the truth: "With what measure ye give, it shall be measured to you" (v. 24). (3) Refuse the truth and you lose the truth: "He that hath not, from him shall be taken even that which he hath" (v. 25).—Stephen F. Olford.

DO YOU WANT TO BE HEALED?   Text: John 5:6 (RSV). One who wants to be healed recognizes some things he can do for himself. (1) Make up his mind about what he really wants. (2) Put forth an effort and try. (3) Find a focal point beyond oneself.—Wesley P. Ford.

Worship Aids

CALL TO WORSHIP.   "O love the Lord, all ye his saints: for the Lord preserveth the faithful. Be of good courage, and he shall strengthen your heart, all ye that hope in the Lord." Ps. 31:23–24.

INVOCATION.   Eternal God, in whom we live and move and have our being, whose face is hidden from us by our sins and whose mercy we forget in the blindness of our hearts: cleanse us, we beseech thee, from all our offenses and deliver us from proud thoughts and vain desires that with lowliness and meekness we may draw near to thee, confessing our faults, confiding in thy grace, and finding in thee our refuge and our strength.

OFFERTORY SENTENCE.   "Lay up for yourselves treasures in heaven: for where your treasure is, there will your heart be also." Matt. 6:20–21.

OFFERTORY PRAYER.   Help us to remember, O Lord, that a life is a more persuasive testimony than words, that deeds are more effective than argument, and that these gifts are only a portion of the loyalty thou dost require of us.

PRAYER.   God our Father, ruler of all the universe, humble us that in these moments of worship we may sense our need of thy direction, humble us that we may put aside the false pride and the preoccupation with self that mar our lives, humble us that we may see clearly that our best fulfillment comes in relationships and responsibilities and not in self-expression or self-indulgence, and humble us that we may know our need of divine forgiveness and redeeming grace.

Then, O Lord, strengthen us to bear the burdens and pains of the day, to do the hard tasks that must be done, to care for our unloved neighbor in his need, to walk on by faith beyond our moment of despair, to try again when we have failed, and to build together a living temple of spirit where love will prevail, where forgiveness will take away all marks of our natural discord, and where the will to serve is greater than the desire to be served.—Ernest O. Norquist.

EVENING SERVICE

Topic: The Essence of Worship
SCRIPTURE: Exod. 33:9–16, 35:29.
I. *An attitude of confidence.*

(a) One of the striking features of the text is the contrast between the response of Israel to the presence of God in the pillar of cloud and the customary response of other peoples to the divine. While Moses talked with God face to face, the pillar of cloud stood at the door of the tent. Upon these occasions the people of Israel would rise up and worship, every man at his tent door. God came as a friend to be recognized and met as a friend.

(b) The Israelite in worship stood in the door of his own tent. He did not crawl with his face to the ground. He did not cut himself with sharp knives to indicate his worthlessness. He did not fearfully approach, afraid to look straight ahead. He did not abase himself in the various ways of the worshipers of other gods. He confidently stood before his worthy friend.

II. *A recognition of distinction.*

(a) Israel found favor in the sight of God. This favor was confirmed by the fact that God went with them. This made Israel distinct. That God went with Israel had significance in that the God of Israel was not bound to some mountain in the wilderness or to any particular locale. Unlike the gods of the Egyptians who could not leave Egypt, the God of Israel went with his people.

(b) Israel's worship was a recognition of this distinction. She knew and affirmed that she was different because her God was different. The God who still goes with his people makes them different too. All the gods of space and time—things, money, success, family, and education—never allow their worshipers any distinction. Locked into space and time, these gods never go anywhere. Their worshipers die in their tracks.

III. *An act of voluntarism.*

(a) Worship was an act of voluntarily responding to the task given by God. In the historical instance of Sinai it consisted in giving an offering by men and women whose hearts told them to give. This offering was their freewill offering to the Lord.

(b) In this account the centrality of giving in worship can be seen. When the complaint is raised that giving is not an appropriate part of worship, the one who makes such a complaint should review the history of the people of God. When one's attention is directed toward the source of many benefits, the response of giving is only natural and commendable.—Don H. Olive.

SUNDAY: OCTOBER TWENTY-FIFTH

MORNING SERVICE

Topic: Power
SCRIPTURE: Luke 4:1–13.
I. Even in the most local sphere of family or work, each of us is bringing some power to bear on others and playing the power game to some degree. And power corrupts by confusing our motivation, creating irresistible pressures on us, and generating fears of powerlessness. Most of all, power corrupts by distorting peoples' vision, especially their vision of themselves and of God.

(a) The antidote to power's corruption is prayer. (1) I don't mean asking God to do things. That may be another trick of the power game. I don't mean prayer for guidance. That can be a form of one-upmanship.

(2) I mean putting myself into the silent presence of God and letting the flow of communion between him and me clarify my distorted vision, purify my motives, countervail the pressures, and set me free from dependence on any other power except that of the love which suffers long, believing and hoping and enduring all things, until in the long term it never fails.

(b) During his interior conflict of those forty days Jesus contemplated three kinds of power—the power of the provider, "Tell these stones to become bread"; the power of the performer, "Throw yourself down from the parapet of the temple"; and the power of the predator, "I will give you all the kingdoms of the world."

II. The power of the provider is the heavenly Father's power. (a) It is the power wielded by father and mother in every family. It is the power of love. "All that I have is yours," says the father to the son in the parable. But that may so easily slips into they who provide for you know what is best for you. "I'll cook the meals you like but not for friends of that sort. If you get into college, I'll pay for that trip to Europe."

(b) The power of the provider is the power of the means of production, which all too often are held by the very few.

(c) The power of the provider is the power of a benign government or of a government glad to tell you that "you never had it so good."

(d) It is the power to come to the rescue of a starving people and to dictate the terms of aid and to tie the strings. You see the corruption that lurks in the power of the provider?

III. There is the power of the performer. (a) Throw yourself down from the pinnacle of the temple. That will make them believe in you. What a performance that could have been! There are many who serve humanity well, who give wise advice, and in whom thousands place their trust who are essentially performers. An audience is their meat and drink, and their greatest gift is a kind of stagecraft.

(b) Jesus had the power of the performer. His parables are masterly performances and miracles there were aplenty and some of them dramatically staged, but always for others, never one performance for the sake of the applause. He saved others; himself he could not save. He saw the latent corruption in the power of the performer.

IV. There was the power of the predator which had to be thought about. It's an ugly word, not neutral like provider or performer because there is a progression in the devilishness of the three temptations in the wilderness. Each time the latent corruption is a bit stronger and more obvious. "I will give you all the kingdoms of the world."

(a) I might have called this form of power the power of the proprietor or of the prince. Ownership in itself is not wrong, nor sovereignity, nor love of one's inheritance. Jesus loved Jerusalem. He loved his nation. He loved the kingdoms of the world.

(b) There is a difference between the man who feels that he belongs to his family estate and the man who feels that his family estate belongs to him. There is a difference between the Christian who feels that he belongs to the church and the one who feels that the church belongs to him. Just below the surface of every instinct of possession lurks the predator.

(c) To see the world as one whole and to relate my own individual interests to the needs of that global family is a Christlike grace and a Godlike attitude, for when the devil shows us the whole world, it is not as a beloved heritage for which to lay down one's life but as a prize to be captured for one's limited personal interests. You see the corruption latent in that power?

(d) Jesus saw it very clearly. "Be gone, Satan, I know now who you are." For it is a Godlike attribute to see the world as a single whole. But who is this who dares to act as though he were God in offering to give this world to anyone? Here, blatantly revealed at last, is the source of power's corruption. It tempts us to play God toward other people.

V. We may exercise the power of the provider as parent or politician as long as we never imagine it gives us the right to play God toward a child or a nation. We may exercise the power of the performer as orator, counselor, or leader so long as we never use it to make anyone place in us the faith they owe to God alone. We may exercise the power of ownership or control so long as we acknowledge God as the owner and ourselves merely as his stewards.—John V. Taylor.

Illustrations

GOD'S POWER. There came a time in my life when I earnestly prayed, "God, I want your power." Time wore on and the power did not come. One day the burden was more than I could bear. "God, why haven't you answered that prayer?" God seemed to whisper back his simple reply. "With plans no bigger than yours, you don't need my power."—Carl Bates.

PREDICAMENT.   The novel *On the Beach* tells a story in which atomic weapons are used to destroy a large portion of the population of our world. The survivors linger only to discover that they too will die in a short while from lethal fallout. Two of the characters are pensively pondering their predicament when one says to the other: "Why did this have to happen to us? We never did anything." The other responds, "Maybe that's the reason—we just never did anything."

Sermon Suggestions

A LOOK AT OUR CHURCH.   Text: II Chron. 5:14. (1) We are a uniting church. (2) We are an acting church. (3) We are a changing church. (4) We are a global church. (5) We are a church with hope.— Wilbur K. Howard.

ESSENCE OF FAITH.   Text: Luke 17:5. (1) Something to know. (2) Something to feel. (3) Something to choose. (4) Something to do. (5) Something to belong to.—A. Victor Murray.

Worship Aids

CALL TO WORSHIP.   "Now in Christ Jesus ye who sometimes were far off are made nigh by the blood of Christ. For he is of our peace, who hath made both one, and hath broken down the middle wall of partition between us. Now therefore ye are no more strangers and foreigners, but fellow citizens with the saints and of the household of God." Eph. 2:13–14, 19.

INVOCATION.   Our Father, we thank thee for thy word and for the eternal truths which guide us day by day. We thank thee most of all for the living word, Jesus Christ, and the sureness of his presence. Teach us how to turn unto thee so that thy thoughts may be our thoughts and thy ways our ways.

OFFERTORY SENTENCE.   "Bring ye all the tithes into the storehouse, saith the Lord, [and I will] open the windows of heaven, and pour you out a blessing." Mal. 3:10.

OFFERTORY PRAYER.   O thou source of all light, open our blind eyes to see the beauty of the world as thy gift, and grant us the will and wisdom to do our part in bringing thy light into dark places.

PRAYER.   Infinite God, our Father, we thank thee that, in an age so filled with anxieties, fears, and mistrust, we may witness to those eternal truths that are central to our Protestant heritage and faith. We express our thankfulness for the traditions and deeper meanings at the heart of the Reformation and for that freedom that makes it possible for us to give expression to them.

Teach us to love one another. May we see the good in every person. We know that in thy sight there are no racial differences and that every person of every race is a beloved child of thine. Forgive us for the barriers we have erected that separate us one from another. Bring us closer together in unity, understanding, and love. Then, our Father, may we be forgiven for the hurts we have inflicted on others as we forgive the hurts that have been ours.

Bless us, our Father, as we witness to the faith that sets us free as it binds us to thee. Accept our Protestant witness growing out of a biblical faith related to thee, to Christ, and to our brothers. Send us forth from the worship of this day committed to serving thee more fully as Christian workers functioning effectively in the life of our church, community, and world.—Chester E. Hodgson.

EVENING SERVICE

Topic: What Kind of a Christian Are You?
TEXT: Acts 26:28.

Four kinds of Christianity are practiced by most of us. These are not static categories. Over a Christian's lifetime, one can move back and forth among these categories to some extent.

I. *Spirit Christianity.* This is the authentic brand of Christian life. Life lived on the level of the spirit means that one's innermost being is touched by God's spirit.

(a) Among the attributes of spirit Christianity is a frequent mood of repentance and therefore humility. This is a person who is aware that if he or she is not on guard a rebellious life style will emerge.

(b) Out of this comes a second attribute —that of commitment and therefore obedience. This means that attitudes, values, and relationships will take on a new dimension each day as this person becomes aware of how God wants him to act in his personal life.

II. *Knowledge Christianity.*

(a) I am being neither antiintellectual nor antitheological when I worry about Christians who begin to reduce their gospel to a series of doctrinal propositions and defenses. Pride mounts as they master their doctrinal axioms, their labyrinth of behavioral laws, and their great data bank of biblical bits.

(b) The basic result of knowledge Christianity is that it becomes increasingly immune to the dynamics of relationships and the larger world which God has given us to enjoy.

III. *System Christianity.*

(a) This level of Christian practice depends upon knowing a right vocabulary of Christian words, mastering the in-house culture of right actions, following the proper church schedule, and being "in" with the right Christian personalities.

(b) Knowledge and system Christianity have a subtle way of neutralizing the effect of a Christian's life. They make the equipping of the believer an end in itself. When Paul wrote to the Ephesians about the saints being equipped, he followed through by saying that the equipping was for the work of ministry. But many knowledge and system Christians stop at the equipping. They spend all their lives being equipped but never being able to perform. Knowledge and system Christianity dull the believer into thinking that simply by knowing and fitting into the system God is pleased. Yet only in spirit Christianity does the forceful insight emerge that one is equipped by God not only to grow but as a result to serve in Christlike love.

IV. *Experience Christianity* which dwells on feeling good.

(a) If some of us are pulled toward a kind of ultrafundamentality which leads to "knowledge" Christianity, others of us are pulled toward a brand of charismatic Christianity which can become experience for experience's sake.

(b) This emerges out of our tendency to push similar conversions, similar speeds of spiritual growth, and similar spiritual objectives. The ultimate result is burnt-out Christians. Having started with a tiny foundation on the level of spirit Christianity, we move quickly with the structure of knowledge and system Christianity. What happens is that people build six-story homes on foundations which are only capable of one-story construction. The split level is left far behind.—Gordon Mac-Donald.

SUNDAY: NOVEMBER FIRST

MORNING SERVICE

Topic: What Is Our Understanding of Ourselves?

TEXT: I Cor. 3:17.

I. Is our understanding of ourselves, our self-image, that of being a monument or a movement?

(a) We may find ourselves chuckling at the play on words when sarcastic reference is made to the church's edifice complex, its obsession with buildings, but the sarcastic thrust is too well-deserved to be casually dismissed.

(1) Too prevalent and pervasive among local congregations is the self-image or understanding of itself as being the maintainer of a monument called the church building. Everyone wants a piece of the church building as a memorial to a de-

ceased relative or friend. Too few want a piece of the action in personal or collective ministry and mission to other persons.

(2) Congregations may feel more threatened by a proposed relocation of a memorialized painting or the moving of a piano than by the plight in the world of suffering persons relocated by flood, war, or famine. The entire energy of a congregation may focus on building projects and maintenance costs.

(b) A congregation may raise to consciousness a self-image which is the antithesis of the monument-maintenance syndrome. The excitement of the spirit moving in personal relationships, the satisfaction of significant involvement in relieving suffering among persons who may never enter their church building, and the joy of commitment to a real state of discipleship beyond concern for institutional real estate can evolve from a new self-image deliberately embraced. But only a congregation aware of itself can make that choice.

II. Is our understanding of ourselves provincial or prophetic?

(a) An inhibiting self-image for local congregations is that best described as provincial.

(1) It commonly is reflected in one of two manifestations. It may express itself in a self-deprecating assessment echoing the sarcasm of Nathaniel's question to Philip: "Can anything good come out of Nazareth?" Occasionally a congregation may have a self-image that constitutes a perpetual put-down, and no great things happen there because of low expectations of what God might do in their midst.

(2) More often the other extreme prevails—a provincial self-image concentrating attention upon itself as though it were the center of the world or at least the only part of the world that truly deserves the attention of God and the resources of its constituency. This kind of consciousness is disturbed by the prophet who, having comforted the afflicted, begins to afflict the comfortable with the consciousness of a way, a world, and a will greater than their own.

(b) An alternative to the provincial self-image is the choice of the prophetic.

(1) A congregation must discover a gutsy kind of courage to be comfortable with this kind of self-image. There is a deceptively similar aspect of self-regard shared by the provincial and the prophetic self-images—both may be self-deprecating—but the prophetic rises above introverted and extroverted self-centeredness by a consciousness symbolized in the statement of John the Baptist: "He must increase, but I must decrease."

(2) It takes courage to choose Christ-centricity over ego-centricity. A congregation may choose to develop a self-image prophetic in the understanding of its role to be that of being overshadowed by its own Christ-consciousness. Its provincialism may be shattered by an awareness of a world beyond its own community, an awareness of moral challenges beyond provincial taboos, an awareness of visions and dreams that find their ultimate consummation in the kingdom of God.

III. Is our understanding of ourselves captive or creative?

(a) A local congregation may consciously or unconsciously develop a self-image captive to outmoded traditions, ideas once fresh that long since their innovation have petrified into ruts within which faithful and well-meaning followers wear themselves away in the frustration and friction of trying harder.

(1) It may be captive to a leadership team resolutely opposed to change.

(2) It may be captive to a general attitude of sophistication that stifles the flow of the spirit and stagnates in emotional retardation or Laodicean dimensions.

(3) It may be captive to prejudices carefully taught about people who are different.

(4) It may be captive to a role in community life no more significant than that of the preacher called upon to bless some secular program or pronounce a benediction after other agents have done their thing.

(b) Receptivity to the leading of the Holy Spirit and a willingness to risk innovation develops a creative self-image with a freshness at the springs and an excitement in the congregation. Commitment to the risk of trying the new—not just for novelty's sake but in discernment of the leading edge of the activity of God's free grace in new events and new relationships —is to become with him creative.

(c) The church is not essentially a building nor an organization but a movement, a fellowship moving in the mainstream of life, a configuration of personal relationships taking significance from Jesus Christ, who founded its movement, exemplifies its prophetic mission, and stands at the head of a new creation.—Clive Dickins.

Illustration

TOLLE, LEGE. One day late in the summer of A.D. 386 as he sat in his home with his friend Alypius, a devout Christian, suddenly in the midst of their discussions, overcome with self-condemnation, Augustine rushed alone into the garden and there heard the voice of a child from a neighboring house repeating the words, "Tolle lege, tolle lege" ("Take, read"). Whether they were spoken as part of a nursery game or not, Augustine applied them to himself, calmly returned to the house, and took up a copy of the epistles of Paul which he and Alypius had been reading. His eager eyes fell on the words from Rom. 13: "Not in rioting and drunkenness, not in chambering and wantonness, not in strife and envying: but put ye on the Lord Jesus Christ, and make not provision for the flesh, to fulfill the lusts thereof." From that moment Augustine's soul was at peace. Never again, so he relates in his *Confessions*, did he lack the divine power to overcome the sins which had hitherto so easily beset him.—F. C. Stifler.

Sermon Suggestion

THE MATERIALISM OF CHRISTIANITY. Texts: Matt. 4:4; 6:11. Materialist Christianity maintains (1) that the material world is the work of God, (2) that the eternal spirit whom we worship created the world of matter and is intimately connected with

it, and (3) that while God made man in the divine image with spirit, reason, and freedom, he rooted man's life in nature and fitted him with a bodily organism sympathetic with natural forces and acting in unison with them.—Robert J. McCracken.

Worship Aids

CALL TO WORSHIP. "Whatsoever things are true, whatsoever things are honest, whatsoever things are just, whatsoever things are pure, whatsoever things are lovely, whatsoever things are of good report; if there be any virtue, and if there be any praise, think on these things." Phil. 4:8.

INVOCATION. Father God, you are known to us through loving persons who affirm the faith. May we be loving too. Father God, you are known to us through trusting acts which proclaim the truth. May we be trusting too. Father God, you are known to us through the joyous story which celebrates your son. May we be joyous too. For we are here to affirm, to proclaim, and to celebrate. We believe! Help thou our unbelief! Amen!

OFFERTORY SENTENCE. "Unto whomsoever much is given, of him shall be much required: and to whom men have committed much, of him they will ask the more." Luke 12:48.

OFFERTORY PRAYER. We give thee thanks, O Father, that through our tithes and offerings thou dost give us an opportunity to illuminate the dimness of the future and to glorify our present life with the word of him who is the light of the world.

PRAYER. Almighty God, creator of the universe and ground of our being, help us to understand who you are, what you are like, and how you speak to us today.

From scripture we remember the burning bush, the voice from the cloud, and other strange and traumatic manifestations of yourself, and sometimes we have felt cheated because we were not Moses or one of the early disciples or apostles.

Mostly we feel that you do not speak to us because we have never heard you speak in the unusual and unreal ways in which we have come to expect you to speak. How do you speak to us today, O God? How are you communicating with us in this modern age in which we live?

Are you speaking to us through the church, especially when we hear a voice or an opinion with which we do not agree?

Are you speaking to us through young people, our own and others, whom we find hard to understand?

Are you speaking to us through the poor and dispossessed as they seek to gain power so that their voices can be heard?

Are you speaking to us through efforts for peace?

Are you speaking to us through other events and happenings in our day?

How do you speak to us today, O God? Help us to hear your voice—Lyle V. Newman.

EVENING SERVICE

Topic: Our Need for Community (World Community Day)
TEXT: Acts 4:32.

I. We need a community of persons we can trust. I don't mean a community we would trust with our most intimate thoughts and lives. That is for special individuals within the community. What I mean by trust is that we know we can be ourselves within the community and not be ostracized for it, not be laughed at or made to feel ridiculous.

II. We need a community that will nurture our inner life which we have to set time aside for—that life which we neglect unless we are reminded and that inner life which is like water to a thirsty mountain climber or love to a lonely soul. And yet we mostly ignore it. We need a community that practically shouts to us that our life inside—our thoughts, our feelings, our fears, and our hopes—is deeply important and profoundly life-giving.

III. We need a community that will form a basis for ministry—yours and mine. Whatever it is that calls so many of us to outreach calls us first to community in order to do it. We gather groups around our concerns, we seek dialogue with honest critics, and we yearn for honest and open conversation about the issues of the world. No one that any of us has ever met has all the answers. We need to find the courage through community to try things that help the city, the state, and the world, no matter how difficult or dreamy such attempts may seem.

IV. An ideal community is the goal of Christian life. We are pulled toward it, not pushed into it. But in such a community we can trust each other. How could we mistrust when we own nothing? In such a community we are nurtured to deepen and broaden our inner life, discovering and rediscovering the spirit within. In such a community we are given a base for social action, for ministry in the community, and for individual ministries and the things we can do together because we are the church of God.—Craig Biddle III.

SUNDAY: NOVEMBER EIGHTH

MORNING SERVICE

Topic: The Stewardship of Sharing and Caring (Stewardship Sunday)
TEXT: Acts 2:44–45.

I. The early church understood the stewardship of sharing.

(a) They shared a fellowship. The church is a fellowship. It is a family, a unit. We have one Lord, one message, and one purpose. We are a building fitly joined; Christ is the chief cornerstone. We are individual parts of one body; Christ is the head and God's Holy Spirit is the life principle.

(b) They shared a possession.

(1) All they possessed was converted into usable assets for the kingdom of God. That is the essence of commitment. A commitment means a deposit. It means to lay something down for someone or to place it in trust. They laid down all they

possessed for the work of God. They made the ultimate material commitment.

(2) They had all things common. The Greek word for common is *koinoo* or *koinos,* and it literally means "belonging equally to several or to all." Surely it is this fact— this unseen connection between present deeds and future glory—that prompted Christ to note that to feed the hungry is to feed him, to visit the sick is to visit him, to comfort a man in prison is to comfort Christ, and to give even so much as a glass of water in his name is to give to him personally.

(c) They shared an attitude. That attitude pervaded the church. "Freely ye have received, freely give" (Matt. 10:8). We see in this passage believers who gave freely and willingly. They were not forced to give, not pressured, not conned or tricked. They shared with gladness and singleness of heart, and they went everywhere convinced that they were to live for the glory of God and the work of his kingdom.

II. The early church understood the stewardship of caring.

(a) The object of their caring—"all men." Their concern was unlimited. They considered every man to be worthy of their message. They believed in their responsibility to care for all men by sharing the grace of God. This ability to care for all people is only possible when we see them as Jesus saw them, feel about them as Jesus felt about them, and do for them what Jesus would do for them.

(b) The extent of their caring—"as every man had need." These believers had a fixed formula for their giving. They gave to every man "according to his need." At the gate called Beautiful, Peter and John ministered to a lame man "according to his need." It would have been easy to flip him a coin and easy to pass on with a pious, "God bless you." But that wasn't what the man needed.

(c) The cost of their caring.

(1) There was a cross to carry. Jesus said, "If anyone wants to follow in my footsteps, he must give up all right to himself, take up his cross and follow me" (Mark 8:34, PHILLIPS). Jesus had in mind a place of execution. We must distinguish between the cross and the inescapable burdens and hardships of life in general. Burdens and hardships are the common lot. They visit the righteous and the wicked alike.

(2) The cross is something one may escape if he chooses. It involves a certain price of self-denial and self-surrender. It asks one to make Christ's sacrificial death the gateway to a new life of total commitment. He who will carry Christ's cross will find it far more than a pattern by which he is to live. He will find it a power by which he is made fit to live.—Cecil B. Knight.

Illustrations

FELLOWSHIP.　　Everyone has a great, often unknown, gift to care, to be compassionate, to become present to the other, to listen, to hear, and to receive. If that gift would be set free and made available, miracles would take place. Those who can receive bread from a stranger and smile in gratitude can feed many without realizing it. Those who can sit in silence with a friend, not knowing what to say but knowing they should be there, can bring new life in a dying heart. Those who are not afraid to hold a hand in gratitude, to shed tears in grief, and to let a sigh of distress arise straight from the heart can break through paralyzing boundaries and witness the birth of a new fellowship—the fellowship of the broken.—Henri Nouwen in *National Catholic Reporter.*

KICKING THE DEVIL.　　During a conversation on stewardship a man was challenged to defend his belief in tithing. He said: "Christians have so much to be thankful for. I just think that any Christian should be willing to start giving where the best Jew leaves off." He explained that he tithed to his church and other Christian causes and that when special appeals or offerings were announced, he "put in a few extra dollars—just to kick the devil." "I just want the devil to know that he doesn't control the other 90 percent either," he added.—John Stapert in *The Church Herald.*

Sermon Suggestions

WHY TITHE? Text: Lev. 27:32. (1) It teaches me to put God and the kingdom first. (2) It teaches me to recognize and acknowledge God's ownership. (3) It teaches me that God's ratio of giving is the tenth. (4) It teaches me that tithing is an act of worship.

THREE KINDS OF GIVING. Text: Acts 20:35. (1) Grudge giving says, "I have to"; duty giving says, "I ought to"; thanksgiving says, "I want to." (2) The first comes from constraint, the second from a sense of obligation, and the third from a full heart. (3) Little is conveyed in grudge giving since the gift without the giver is bare. Something more happens in duty giving, but there is no song in it. Thanksgiving is an open gate into the love of God.—Robert N. Rodenmayer.

Worship Aids

CALL TO WORSHIP. "God hath exalted him, and given him a name which is above every name: that at the name of Jesus every knee should bow, of things in heaven, and things in earth, and things under the earth; and that every tongue should confess that Jesus Christ is Lord, to the glory of God the Father." Phil. 2:9–11.

INVOCATION. Heavenly Father, we are grateful for this beautiful world thou hast created for us; for the singing birds, the radiant flowers, the blue sky, the soft breeze; for the dark night which gives way to a bright dawn; for the good earth which, when tilled by the plow, shoots forth the wheat, the corn, the beans that our hungry bodies may be fed; for the trees which will fruit and a thousand gifts which come from thy bountiful hand. Help us to share this wealth, this treasure, with all who are in need.

OFFERTORY SENTENCE. "Upon the first day of the week let every one of you lay by him in store, as God hath prospered him." I Cor. 16:2.

OFFERTORY PRAYER. O Lord, who hast given us the privilege of life, help us to magnify eternal values and to show forth by our lives and our tithes the Christ, whom to know aright is life eternal.

PRAYER. Heavenly Father, in the busy rush of our lives we urgently need times of renewal, of quiet meditation, and of spiritual rebuilding. Come into our lives, we pray, with the strength and insight we need, that we may reformulate the images by which we live, reexamine the goals we seek, and redefine the purposes we serve. We find it too easy to trust wholly in our own resources, to blame our troubles on someone else, to think that all the world is out of step except us, and to live unconcerned about the frustrations and hardships of those whom we do not see.

Grant us, we pray, a full measure of the compassion of Christ, whose name we profess. Involve us in the needs of our fellow man so that we cannot be complacent or self-centered. Show us our responsibility for what goes on in our world so that we cannot be self-righteous. Commit us to the church so that we come to know the fullness of life and all its potential in the very roots of our being.

Our Father, we would be sensitive now to those around us whose lives know challenge and despair, frustration and defeat. May we reach out with hands and hearts that are understanding and compassionate to enfold our brothers in the assurance that we care what happens to them. May we ever be ready to rejoice with those who rejoice and to weep with those who weep and ever ready to fulfill the scriptures in bringing good news to the poor, release to the captives, recovering of sight to the blind, and liberty to the oppressed.—Madison L. Sheely.

EVENING SERVICE

Topic: I Don't Tithe Because—
TEXT: Mal. 3:10; Matt. 6:33.
I. "I didn't know we had to tithe. I thought we were saved by grace." We are saved by grace and not by works. How grateful we should be and how gladly we

should contribute our time, energy, and possessions to help share this glorious gospel of grace to the ends of the earth. The most meaningful demonstration of our love we can show is in freely giving tithes and offerings. Paul pleaded with the Corinthian Christians to prove the sincerity of their love by their gracious giving.

II. "Tithing was intended for Jews, not Christians." The ten commandments, the law, the prophets, and the psalms were also all intended primarily for Jews, but according to Paul they were also written for our instruction. (See Rom. 15:4; II Tim. 3:16.) Just as the Old Testament writings have proved helpful to Christians, so will the practice of the tithe be.

III. "The tithe is not one of the ten commandments." Many important duties are not listed in the ten commandments. Prayer, love, forgiveness, and benevolence are not in the ten commandments. Lev. 27:34 says, "These are the commandments, which the Lord commanded Moses for the children of Israel in Mount Sinai." It is interesting that at the same place and through the same man the law of the tithe was given.

IV. "In the New Testament we do not have a definite command to pay a tithe." Neither do we have instructions forbidding it. This commonly observed part of ancient worship was taken for granted in New Testament times. The Pharisees were commended for observing it (Matt. 23: 23). A Christian ought to do more as an expression of his religious faith than a Jew would do for his.

V. "Since Jesus taught his followers to go the second mile, I don't want to restrict my giving to the tithe." This is great, but how can we go the second mile until we have gone the first mile? Tithing is the first mile. Some of our members haven't gone the first hundred yards. Certainly the tithe should be a minimum and not the maximum in Christian giving.—John Alexander.

SUNDAY: NOVEMBER FIFTEENTH

MORNING SERVICE

Topic: Survival of the Word (Bible Sunday)

TEXT: II Tim. 2:9.

I. The word of God has successfully withstood every attempt to destroy it physically.

(a) About 600 B.C. Jehoiakim, king of Judah, attempted to destroy the word of God and failed. He was angered at the message which the scroll of Jeremiah contained, cut it to pieces, and threw them into the fire. But the word did not burn— just the paper on which it was written. The writing was reproduced at the command of God. We have it today in the book of Jeremiah. The efforts of men and devils to annihilate the word have brought about its sure increase. The ashes of its burning are the seeds of reproduction.

(b) In A.D. 303 the Roman emperor Diocletian instigated the most terrific onslaught against the Bible the world has ever known.

(1) Every manuscript found was destroyed. Every copy of any portion of the Bible located was burned. Thousands upon thousands of persons who possessed copies—and even their families—were martyred. After two years of ruthless slaughter and destruction, a column of victory was erected over the embers of a Bible and inscribed "Extinct is the name of Christians."

(2) Less than ten years later the emperor Constantine had the Bible enthroned as the infallible word of truth. Desiring to place copies of the New Testament in all the churches of his empire, Constantine offered a reward to anyone who could discover and deliver to his officers the holy book. Within four hours fifty copies were brought out of hiding and presented to the emperor.

II. The enemies of the word have tried to keep it from the hands of the people. Martin Luther said, "I was a grown man and had never seen a Bible." The Bible was written in Hebrew and Greek. When the prophets of the Old Testament and the apostles of the New Testament lived, no one had ever heard of English. Every time we read an English Bible we ought to be supremely grateful for all the sacrifice involved. Circumstances surrounding the first English translation of the scriptures form an exciting chapter in the history of the Bible.

(a) In A.D. 405 Jerome completed a Latin translation of the Bible from Greek and Hebrew. For this great work he was bitterly assailed by the bishops of his time, accused of tampering with the word of God and of promoting his own ideas—a reward similar to that which many translators have received since his day. But Jerome's version lived through the Dark Ages as the Bible of Europe.

(b) In 1379 John Wycliffe gathered about him a group of Oxford scholars and with them began the translation of the Latin Bible into English.

(1) Fierce opposition by the church and state arose immediately, for both were violently opposed to giving the word of God to the people. Wycliffe and his associates were threatened, maligned, and hauled into court again and again. He was finally forced to resign his beloved professorships at Oxford University.

(2) Relentlessly he continued the work of translation. As each portion of the Bible was completed, hundreds of handwritten copies were made by the Oxford scholars and poor priests who rallied to the cause. These were circulated among the people who could read, and by 1383 thousands of copies of the Bible were in the hands of the English.

(3) So determined was the effort to stamp out the new English Bible that those who possessed it were hunted down like wild animals and burned at the stake with their scriptures about their necks, but Wycliffe's Bible could not be stopped. In spite of the law forbidding this Bible and its wholesale destruction over a period of years, 170 copies of Wycliffe's priceless handwritten translations still exist.

(c) One hundred and fifty years after Wycliffe's death and 75 years after the invention of the printing press, there was still no printed English Bible. The Wycliffe manuscripts which had survived were available to only a few and could be read only by scholars because the language had changed substantially through the years.

(1) In 1524 William Tyndale resolved to put the Bible into the English of his time and to disseminate it throughout the nation. His purpose was contrary to English law, and because it appeared impossible to do the work in England, Tyndale resorted to the continent of Europe. In extreme poverty and constant peril, he secretly made his translation of the New Testament from the original Greek. This translation is so excellent it is retained in large measure in our English versions today.

(2) Printing of the manuscript was begun in Cologne, but before the gospel of Matthew was off the press, the secret was divulged by a careless workman and authorities were alerted. Tyndale managed to escape with his manuscript and printed portion, went to Worms, and there completed the publication of the New Testament. Three thousand copies were smuggled into England in barrels of flour, bales of cloth, and other disguises before the stratagem was discovered. In spite of every attempt to stop the flow, they continued to enter the country in increasing numbers. Thousands of copies were seized and burned, but other thousands took their places.

(3) Through the treachery of a supposed friend, Tyndale was finally apprehended and imprisoned. During sixteen months of confinement in a cold, dark jail in Belgium, he worked secretly on a translation of the Old Testament, aided by his guards, but it was never completed. He was strangled and burned at the stake in 1536 for the crime of translation and disseminating the New Testament. His last words were, "Lord, open the king of England's eyes."

(4) His prayer was speedily answered. In less than three years Henry VIII authorized the publication of the Great Bible. It combined the work of Tyndale and Miles Coverdale, whose translation appeared in 1535. At least one copy was chained in

every parish church in England so that all of the people might read.

III. Another attack that has been leveled against the word of God through the ages is an intellectual attack.

(a) Such an onslaught was made by the French philosopher, Voltaire, and it illustrates the vain intellectual attempts to overthrow the word of God.

(1) Voltaire dared to predict that within 100 years the Bible would be a forgotten book. These are his words: "One hundred years from my day there will not be a Bible in the earth except one that is looked upon by an antiquarian curiosity seeker."

(2) Before the century was up, his home was owned and used by the Geneva Bible Society, from which millions of Bibles have gone around the world.

(3) One hundred years after Voltaire's prediction, a first edition of Voltaire's work sold in the market in Paris for eleven cents, and later the British government paid the Soviet Union $500,-000 for the Codex Sinaiticus, a copy of the Bible.

(b) Robert Ingersol, an American agnostic of the nineteenth century, held a Bible high in his hand and declared, "In fifteen years I will have this book in the morgue." In fifteen years Ingersol was in the morgue. The Bible was as much alive as ever.

(c) "Heaven and earth will pass away," said our Lord, "but my words will never pass away." The Bible is God's word to you and me. He has kept it for us. He expects us to know it and obey it.—Frank Pollard.

Illustrations

HEARING WHAT WE WISH.   There is always the danger that we will find in the Bible only what we take with us to it. We use it to confirm what we already think. We hear only what we want to hear. Because they already hated Jews before they read the Bible, some German Christians found in the Bible justification for slaughtering millions of Jews. Because they wanted to keep their human property, some American Christians argued from the Bible that it is right to buy and sell human beings as if they were animals. Have you noticed that mean people usually find a mean God in the Bible? And that superficial people usually find a superficial God. Comfortable, powerful men usually find that the Bible supports political conservatism, and poor, exploited people usually find that it supports social and political reform.—Shirley Guthrie.

CHICKEN THIEF'S VERSION.   A member was brought before the church for disciplinary action for stealing chickens. The accused defended his crime on the basis of Eph. 4:28, which reads: "Let him that stole steal no more: but rather let him labor, working with his hands the thing which is good, that he may have to give to him that needeth." By dropping five words and changing some punctuation, the ingenious culprit came up with the following translation: "Let him that stole steal. No more let him labor, working with his hands is good, that he may have to give to him that needeth." —Jack Gulledge in *Proclaim*.

Sermon Suggestions

THE RIGHT BOOK.   Text: Ps. 12:6.
(1) The Bible has the right questions. (2) The Bible has the right answers. (3) The Bible gives us the right vision.—Gerald Kennedy.

WHY READ THE BIBLE?   Text: Isa. 40:8. The Bible (1) sinews up the intellect, (2) clarifies the perception, (3) enlarges the view, (4) purifies the heart, (5) quickens the imagination, (6) strengthens the understanding, and (7) educates the heart.—Theodore Cuyler Speers.

Worship Aids

CALL TO WORSHIP.   "Thy word is a lamp unto my feet, and a light unto my path. I have sworn, and I will perform it, that I will keep thy righteous judgments. Quicken me, O Lord, according unto thy word." Ps. 119:105–107.

INVOCATION. O Lord God, who hast left unto us thy holy word to be a lamp unto our feet and a light unto our path: give unto us thy Holy Spirit, we humbly pray thee, that out of the same word we may learn what is thy blessed will and frame our lives in holy obedience to the same, to thine honor and glory and the increase of our faith.

OFFERTORY SENTENCE. Every man hath his proper gift of God, one after this manner, and another after that." I Cor. 7:7.

OFFERTORY PRAYER. Our Father, may we who have seen thy providential hand in all the experiences of our lives seek to possess such greatness of mind and spirit that we shall be enabled to offer these gifts with an unselfish joyfulness.

PRAYER. Thou hast promised that, if with all our hearts we truly seek thee, we shall ever surely find thee. With all our hearts we seek thee now, O thou who art ever seeking us.

We thank thee for thy goodness to us. May we try more consistently to deserve it. We thank thee for treating us better than we deserve. Help us to treat each other in the same way.

We need thy forgiveness. We have done things we ought not to have done. We cannot plead ignorance. We knew what was right and did what we knew was wrong. When we contrast our moral shabbiness with thy holiness, we are ashamed. Create in us a clean mind and a clean imagination. What in us is dark, illumine; what is low, raise and support.

We need thy reinforcement. We do not ask to escape the sorrows which are part of man's lot. We ask only assurance that in thy divine economy nothing good is lost and that what is excellent as God lives is permanent. We do not ask to be relieved of our share of life's burdens. We ask for strength to bear them without faltering or failing. We do not ask exemption from exacting tasks. We ask for wisdom and skill to do them aright.

We need thy peace. In a troubled, strife-torn world we need a peace that the world cannot bestow. We know that all peace comes from thee and that we cannot find it until we first find thee. But we should not be seeking thee unless thou hadst already found us. What is our prayer but an answer to thy call and a response to the intimations of thy presence around us and within? May the benediction of thy peace enfold us, calm, compose, and quiet us as we lift our prayer to thee in Jesus' name. —Frank Halliday Ferris.

EVENING SERVICE

Topic: Those Feelings of Guilt
TEXT: John 8:9.

I. Consider the problem of the undernourished sense of guilt or the extreme situation when a person is wholly amoral and is incapable of feeling guilty.

(a) There are the more sophisticated manifestations of guilt-free lives in the wheelers and dealers and the rip-off artists who take advantage of innocent and trusting people without any compunction at all. They are a sorry lot, having no sense of guilt in spite of their miserable vulture existence.

(b) A much larger group in our society are those who live irresponsibly and without serious involvement or sincere commitment. These are the get-while-the-getting-is-good and the do-what-you-want-to-do-when-you-want-to-do-it kind of people who are our secular hedonists. Someone called them "our pleasing pagans." They see nothing wrong in their self-serving without self-giving relationships, taking what they can get permissively without any inhibiting sense of guilt.

(c) For all these there is an urgent need for a healthy sense of guilt. A good dose of hell fire and brimstone would be appropriate. A genuine sense of regret and remorse needs to be created within them.

II. There is another kind of guilt feeling that is neither wholesome nor useful. It is found in those people who harbor hyperactive consciences and who put themselves under the punishing and fiendish whip of self-condemnation. In this kind of person the guilt feeling is punitive, setting a person on a self-destructive course. I do not mean suicide. I mean rather the death-wish syndrome in which a person says things and does things counter to reason and to his own best interests. It is a subtle and unsatisfactory way of doing penance in response to the demands of an abnormal and excessive guilt feeling.

III. The one extreme is the numbing of a proper guilt feeling or else its complete obliteration, while the other extreme is an unwholesome and tyranically punitive sense of guilt which can enslave a person. Either extreme needs attention and some kind of treatment. In both instances the Christian religion functions helpfully.

(a) It believes that there are rights and wrongs, moral laws, and when they are broken there are correcting consequences. It holds that conscience is a reality which a person must accept and attend to or else there is trouble. To be a Christian is to be a moral being.

(b) Our religion believes that the confession of sin to God is answered by a compassionate God's forgiveness. In this the person chained by guilt knows release, the contrite heart is restored to health by God's healing love, and the awesome burdens of regret and remorse, induced by guilt, are lifted.—Charles L. Copenhaver.

SUNDAY: NOVEMBER TWENTY-SECOND

MORNING SERVICE

Topic: A Lesson in Thanksgiving (Thanksgiving Sunday)

Scripture: Luke 17:11–19.

I. Ten lepers congregated on the border between Galilee and Samaria, an outpost for lepers, for leprosy, being a very contagious and incurable disease, had no means or methods of treatment other than quarantine. Nine of the lepers were Jewish, and one was a Samaritan, but a common need broke down all racial and national barriers. It was into that community of separation that Jesus entered one day, much to the chagrin and protests of his friends who feared for his own health. He loved those people, heard their cries, and responded to their physical problems by promising them health. He told them to go and show themselves to the priest, a necessary legal thing if they were to reenter the life of society. They did as Jesus requested, and the priest pronounced all ten of them as healed. The Samaritan returned to thank Jesus for what he had done for him. The others never came back.

II. Suppose we were to conduct an interrogation of the nine men who did not return and ask each why he had not done so. We would get a varying degree of responses with each echoing some modern counterpart.

(a) The first leper responded by asking:

"Did he expect me to return? That is his profession, isn't it? Isn't that what we pay him to do?" There are many people who feel that because they pay a fee for a benefit received, somehow their obligation is evened. But can you adequately pay with money for some of life's richest blessings?

(b) The second leper said: "I'm the quiet, reserved type, rather timid, you know. I'm not good at speech-making." He went on to explain: "That's not my thing. Some can and some can't." Isn't it interesting how a tongue-tied person cannot utter one syllable of praise, but suddenly he waxes very eloquent in condemnation of someone who violated his rights? Had Jesus taken away health instead of giving it, the victim would have found no lack of words in criticism and faultfinding.

(c) The third responded that he was not certain that a thank-you was even necessary and if it was, to whom must it be expressed? "He told me to show myself to the priest. On the way I was healed. How do I know that this was not just a coincidence?" For this type of person, luck, fate, chance, and other such expressions characterize their lives and thinking. It's easier that way for they don't have to feel gratitude to God or anyone.

(d) The fourth respondent said: "Why should I thank him? Actually his image got as much out of this as I did." It is the attitude that, because someone seems to enjoy doing what he does for others, he should never be told of one's appreciation. That is the sin we commit against our parents, our companions, and even our children. It is the sin of silence when a word fitly spoken could have helped make many burdens much lighter.

(e) The fifth leper said, "When I began thinking about all I needed to do to get back into the swing of things, I just didn't take the time to go back." Isn't that interesting? Whenever we do not have our health, whenever things are going poorly for us, or whenever we feel helpless and somewhat hopeless, we think of the intrinsic values and even make our promises to God about what we're going to do when our circumstances change. But upon the occurrence of that change we forget those death-bed promises. The pressures of one's daily routines often exact from him all of his time and energy, and there's no time to go back to say, "I'm grateful." Many sincere promises made in troubled times are forgotten when the rain ceases.

(f) "Don't get too involved with controversial people, I've been advised," said the sixth healed leper. "This Jesus, well, you know he's not the best-loved man in Galilee. People are divided in their opinions. Some think he ought to be king, and some think he ought to be crucified. I've even heard that they're not fond of him down at the temple because of his association with sinners." It is a way of saying that religion is good and we need it, but we don't want too much of it. "Don't get me wrong. I do appreciate the fact that I'm healthy again and that God had mercy on me, but I don't want to overdo the religion bit. I'm a Christian and I'm glad, but I don't want to be too closely identified with Christ. Someone might call me a fanatic." What a travesty! But it happens all the time.

(g) The seventh said, "I just hate to feel obligated to anyone." He expressed the fear that had he gone back to this man Jesus, he might have felt an obligation to do something for him. "My motto is," he said, "never give people the idea that you owe them anything, and then you are free to do your own thing."

(h) The eighth leper said, "I didn't want to be healed anyway." Some people literally resent the help they have been given. Some have sick minds that delight in having ready excuses or reasons for the lack of acceptance of responsibility. They are spiritual invalids who, if they had the abundant life, might feel obligated to share it. E. E. Cummings described many Christians as "undead." It is not that they or we are dead, but we are not enough alive to matter a great deal to God or anyone else.

(i) The ninth man said: "I didn't think." When you don't think, you don't thank. When you think of the beauty of creation and the providential care of God, you thank. When you think of the contribution that others are making to your life, you thank.

III. Jesus asked, "Were there not ten of you? and where are the nine?" But to the one he said: "Go thy way. Thy faith hath made thee whole." God's grace and mercy were shown to ten alike. Physically he blessed all ten, but only one of the ten received the healing of the soul, the cleansing of sin, and the forgiveness that makes eternal life possible.—Jerry Hayner.

Illustrations

GRUMBLING. A tourist was watching some women in Mexico who were washing their clothes at a spot where hot and cold springs bubbled side by side. They boiled their garments in the hot springs and rinsed them in the cold. The tourist said to his guide, "I suppose the people here think Mother Nature is generous to them, do they not?" "No, senor," was the reply, "just the opposite. There is grumbling because she does not supply soap."

LEGEND. *Springs in the Valley* tells us of a legend of a man who found the barn where Satan kept his seeds ready to be sown in the human heart. On finding the seeds of discouragement more numerous than others, he learned that those seeds could be made to grow almost anywhere. When questioned, Satan reluctantly admitted there was one place he could never thrive. "Where is that?" asked the man. Satan replied sadly, "In the heart of a grateful man."

Sermon Suggestion

A CALL TO CELEBRATION.   Text: Num. 10:10. (1) We have a heritage of growth to celebrate. (2) We have a heritage of outreach to celebrate. (3) We have a heritage of sacrificial service to celebrate. (4) We have a heritage of challenge to celebrate. —Hoover Rupert.

Worship Aids

CALL TO WORSHIP.   "Make a joyful noise unto the Lord, all ye lands. Serve the Lord with gladness: come before his presence with singing. Enter into his gates with thanksgiving, and into his courts with praise: be thankful unto him, and bless his name." Ps. 100:2,4.

INVOCATION.   O God our Father, giver of all good things, we are grateful for the Thanksgiving season when we come with gratitude for bountiful harvests filling granary and bin. Give us such a spirit of thankfulness that every day and every season and all thy continuing gifts may be occasions for thanksgiving and all the year be blessed with an ever-continuing gratitude. As thy mercies are new every morning, so may our praise rise to thee each day and hour.

OFFERTORY SENTENCE.   "And whatsoever ye do in word and deed, do all in the name of the Lord Jesus, giving thanks to God and the Father by him." Col. 3:17.

OFFERTORY PRAYER.   Cleanse and accept these our gifts, O God, and may they be used according to thy will to redeem, restore, and renew the ministries within thy kingdom.

PRAYER.   O thou great horn of plenty, source from whence flow every good and perfect gift, we give thanks for thy ceaseless procession of colorful fruits. Field, valley, and mountainside are clothed with thy beauty. Thus is thy beauty and affection declared. Thy divine promise of an ancient day is ever new with the rising of the sun and fulfilled with its setting. Seedtime and harvest, cold and heat, summer and winter, day and night continue by thy faithful providence and care.

We are especially grateful, O God, for the fruits of the spirit which have their sacred origin in thee and their enduring continuation as blessings in our lives. For the harvest of the spiritual manna of love, joy, peace, patience, kindness, goodness, faithfulness, gentleness, and self-control, we thank thee. Our longing hearts and souls find satisfaction in thy divine gifts only as we become fountains of prayer pouring forth thankfully what thou hast given to us.—Harold A. Schulz.

EVENING SERVICE

Topic: God's Provisions
TEXT: Phil. 4:19.
I. *The surety of the provisions.* Paul did not say, "My God might supply" or "My God could supply" or "My God ought to supply." He said, "My God will supply all your needs."

(a) When days were dark for Israel captives in a foreign land, God promised that there would be a time when they would be returned from Babylonian captivity. And the day came when the walls of Jerusalem were rebuilt and the nation was reestablished.

(b) When their hopes did not materialize, God promised Israel that his messiah would come and establish the new kingdom of God. There are 333 promises about the messiah to come made in the Old Testament and fulfilled in the New Testament, and every one is a testimony to the faithfulness of God.

(c) To the disciples of the first century Jesus promised power when the Holy Spirit came upon them. (See Acts 1:8.) And who can read again the exciting story of the early church without recognizing the fulfillment of that promise?

(d) To the disciples of every century he promised his continuous presence. "Lo, I am with you always, even to the end of the age" (Matt. 28:20). Who here today cannot share an experience in your life when, though all else seemed to fail you, the presence of God was nevertheless powerfully felt?

II. *The sufficiency of God's provisions.* Paul says, "My God shall supply all your needs." The Amplified Bible reads, "And my God will liberally supply and fill to the full every need." What is your need?

(a) Do you need forgiveness? God promises to provide for that in I John 1:9.

(b) Do you need fellowship with God? God promises to meet that need in John 14:23.

(c) Are you burdened by the weight of your load? God provides for that in Matt. 11:28.

(d) Do you need to overcome temptation? The provisions of God are promised in I Cor. 10:13.

(e) Do you need help with worry? Read again the promises in Phil. 4:6–7.

(f) Do you need a purpose for living? Jesus said, "Follow me, and I will make you fishers of men" (Matt. 4:19).

(g) Do you need hope for tomorrow? Then hear the great truth in James 1:12.

III. *The source of these provisions.* The provision promised in v. 19 is sufficient because of its source. Paul says, "And my God shall supply all your needs according to his riches in glory."

(a) In vv. 15–18 Paul had been talking about the provisions made for him through an offering the Philippian Christians had sent to him. He then contrasts this with the provisions of God. Paul is saying: "You met one need that I have, but my God will meet all of your needs. You gave out of your poverty, but God will supply your need out of his riches in glory."

(b) Someone has said that God has four accounts that are mentioned in scripture. There are the riches of his goodness (Rom. 2:4), the riches of his wisdom (Rom. 11:33), the riches of his grace (Eph. 1:7), and the riches of his glory (Eph. 1:-18). It is out of the latter account that God will supply all of our needs, and the implication is that this source is incomparable, infinite, and inexhaustible.—Brian L. Harbour.

SUNDAY: NOVEMBER TWENTY-NINTH

MORNING SERVICE

Topic: What Do You Expect? (Advent)
Text: Matt. 11:3.

I. Eugene O'Neill based his play *Lazarus Laughed* on the familiar biblical story. Lazarus was much loved by Jesus. Sudden illness overtook him and he died. The gospel of John describes Jesus' own grief. Four days after Lazarus' death Jesus arrived at the tomb and—in defiance of all known phenomena—called Lazarus forth. This man, dead and entombed, was alive again.

(a) The O'Neill play focuses on intriguing questions. How did Lazarus, who was raised from the dead by Jesus, respond to his new earthly life after four days in eternity? Did that interval in the eternal world make any difference to Lazarus in his view of the importance of things in this world?

(b) The conclusion is that it made a tremendous difference.

(1) Having seen the things which count in eternity, Lazarus measured the things of this world by a new standard. He had no fear. Very often, looking at his world, he gave a low, musical laugh. Hence the play's title.

(2) He would see people straining every nerve to amass piles of money. He laughed at that. He saw the pretensions of the Emperor Tiberius of Rome and laughed at such vain display. When the emperor threatened to put him to death, he merely laughed all the more. He knew that no one could destroy an immortal soul.

(3) Because Lazarus had seen eternity, he knew what counted in the long run or forever. He could laugh, not in derision but in confidence, having perceived things

on a scale of values different from others around him.

(c) This imaginative drama offers a lesson in identifying priorities and marking out life's truly important concerns. Vicariously we enter Lazarus' experience and get a glimpse of what it means to view all actions under the aspect of eternity. Such a view, however limited, is chastening and instructive to us in many ways.

II. We are pressed to review our own values and priorities and our sense of what truly is important.

(a) That is a consideration which Jesus emphasized in an encounter with followers of John the Baptist sometime after Jesus' public ministry had begun and John's had ended because of imprisonment. John sent his friends to evaluate Jesus' work and to gain a feeling for what was going on. Those men bluntly asked, "Are you he who is to come, or shall we look for another?"

(1) Their question was based on certain expectations—those things they held to be most important. The Jews of Jesus' day were looking for a messiah—a leader, a king, a person of power and authority who could inaugurate a new and better day for an oppressed people. This was what they wanted and deemed of primary importance. At that time, Jesus' ministry was an enigma. The question, they felt, had to be raised.

(2) The answer they got was both yes and no. Yes, Jesus was fulfilling ancient scriptural mandates by preaching good news to the poor, but no, he was not leading a political revolution. Jesus said: "Go and tell John what you see and hear: the blind receive their sight and the lame walk, lepers are cleansed and the deaf hear, and the dead are raised up, and the poor have good news preached to them. And blessed is he who takes no offense in me." Do these expectations identify your true priorities? What things matter most with you?

(b) It becomes necessary for you and me periodically to take stock as well. We need to answer Jesus' question about himself and about our world, "What do you expect?" We begin to name priorities and items of importance, we spell out our hopes and deepest yearnings, and we begin to see our expectations for what they are.

III. Jesus asks not only what we expect of him but proceeds also to describe what he expects of us.

(a) When William Carey wrote, "Expect great things of God," he immediately went on to say, "Attempt great things for God." And Carey was right. The street goes both ways. We have our hopes and dreams, but God has his for us as well. Great expectations are found in each direction. Only if these begin to coincide can there be inner peace, happiness, and ultimate satisfaction.

(b) What are the divine expectations? A careful reading of the gospels will tell us. A serious look at Jesus' own life and service will make it plain. There is no better explanation than that offered centuries ago by the prophet Micah. Micah was talking about expectations when he said, "What does the Lord require of you but to do justice, and to show constant love, and to walk humbly with your God?"

(c) Goethe said: "If you speak to a man as he is, he will remain what he is. If you address him as he might be, he will grow to that level." That is why it is important to talk about expectations. We believe that we may expect great things of God, but we also must believe that such things are realized only as his expectations for us are allowed to shape our days and direct our lives. We will grow to the level of our dominant desires, be they low or high. "Come up higher," says our lord, and so we must. —John H. Townsend.

Illustrations

LIGHT WITHOUT SHADOWS. In *The Violence Within*, Paul Tournier tells about his days in the military service when light without shadow was needed in the hospital operating room. He helped to construct what is called a scialytic lamp which illuminates the operating area without casting shadows because of a large circular mirror which reflects the central light source in all directions. What a perfect picture of the light source of life, Jesus Christ! There are no shadows where his light comes into a life. And exposure brings healing.—Kenneth A. Wotherspoon.

DIVINE HIDDENNESS. God has chosen to make himself known in the person of his son, Jesus of Nazareth. We refer to this as revelation. When I say revelation, I do not mean that the hidden God has come out of hiding. I could not say that because his hiddenness is not an accident; it is of his essence. God does not come out of hiding. What does he do when he reveals himself? He rehides himself in human history in the person of Jesus of Nazareth. He rehides himself successfully, incognito. Who would have thought to look for God there? I mean, God on the breast of Mary, God in a carpenter shop, God at the back of a fisherman's boat, and God on a cross! The Christian message is a proclamation that strikes the ear of the world with the force of a hint. Some get it. Some do not. And to those who do, it is the power of God unto salvation.—Carl Michalson.

Sermon Suggestions

THE STRENGTHENING SIMPLICITIES OF OUR FAITH. Text: Matt. 11:30. (1) The sufficiency of God's strength. (2) The depth of God's love. (3) The urgency of God's work.—Gene E. Bartlett.

LIGHT FOR AN ADVENT WREATH. Text: Ps. 18:28. Candles signifying Old Testament prophecies: (1) The candle of the covenant (Jer. 31:31–34). (2) The candle of judgment (Mal. 4:1–6). (3) The candle of John the Baptist (Isa. 40:1–8). (4) The candle of Moses (Deut. 18:15–19).

Worship Aids

CALL TO WORSHIP. "And we declare unto you glad tidings, how that the promise which was made unto the fathers, God hath fulfilled the same unto us their children." Acts 13:32–33.

INVOCATION. Almighty God, who in thy providence hath made all ages a preparation for the kingdom of thy son: we beseech thee to make ready our hearts for the brightness of thy glory and the fullness of thy blessing.

OFFERTORY SENTENCE. "Every good gift and every perfect gift is from above, and cometh down from the Father of lights." Jas. 1:17.

OFFERTORY PRAYER. O God, who didst give to us the gift of thy son, stir us with such love toward thee that we may gladly share whatever thou hast entrusted to us for the relief of the world's sorrow and the coming of thy kingdom.

PRAYER. Lord Jesus Christ, who for us men and for our salvation didst become man: be with us now as we prepare to celebrate Christmas that we shall not be so blinded by the artificial glitter that we are unable to behold thee. In common forms thou dost come to us and we, confusing the sensational and spectacular with greatness, see thee not, though thou art near. Few saw thee, the Lord of glory, in the child of the manger or the strange man on the cross. Thou wert in their midst and men knew thee not. Teach us then to look for thee in the simple things and in humble places, lest, even this Christmas, we shall miss thee, the best present of all. Grant us true Christmas joy and give us all the blessings which our hearts will receive. —Gilbert A. Jensen.

EVENING SERVICE

Topic: The Purpose of His Coming (Advent)

SCRIPTURE: John 1:1–5, 14–18.

I. Jesus came to personalize God to man (v. 1). In characterizing God, Jesus demonstrated the concern of God in behalf of sinful man. "For the law was given by Moses, but grace and truth came by Jesus Christ" (John 1:17). "Grace" or divine favor was shown to man when a savior was provided. "Truth" is what Christianity is all about. Jesus said: "I am the way, the truth, and the life: no man cometh unto the Father, but by me" (John 14:6). The glory given of God to his "only begotten" was reflected in Christ's message, miracles, death, resurrection, and ascension.

II. Jesus came to accomplish God's purpose (vv. 2–3).

(a) Because Christ was God, he came to earth with the authority of God. He came to redeem from sin. The promise of Gabriel to Mary was fulfilled in the birth of Jesus. (See Luke 1:32.) Today God rules the universe through Christ.

(b) The beginning of the son's spiritual rule was marked on the day of Pentecost following his resurrection. "Let all the house of Israel know assuredly, that God hath made that same Jesus, whom ye have crucified, both Lord and Christ" (Acts 2:-36).

III. Jesus came to mediate between God and man (v. 4; cf. II Tim. 2:5). No business is ever transacted between God and man except through Christ. With his own blood he provided life for man. Jesus entered into heaven where he applied his blood to the sinner. (See Heb. 9:12.)—Ard Hoven in *The Lookout.*

SUNDAY: DECEMBER SIXTH

MORNING SERVICE

Topic: Where Is Bethlehem? (Advent)
TEXT: Mic. 5:2.

I. Bethlehem is any time and place on life's journey where and when songs of praise to God are sung. We are there when we stand in the shoes of the shepherds to listen to and then to join in the angels' "Glory to God in the highest!" We find ourselves in Bethlehem whenever we truly and joyously worship God rather than simply go through an order of worship when we come together to praise God and seek his presence with others here or elsewhere.

II. Bethlehem is any place in our lives or in the lives of other people when unexpected stars—insights and bright ideas—send us on significant spiritual journeys of the heart and the mind. We are there when the questions are asked that lead us toward a fresh understanding of God's plan for our lives and to a new apprehension of his will, his love, and his reality. We are there when we sit down before scripture and ask ourselves and others, "What are these ancient words really saying to you and to me?"

III. Bethlehem is all the moments in our lives when the challenge of the manger child grown to manhood is heard and responded to. He, beyond all others, lived on the growing edge of humanity's moral and spiritual experience. Because of this he continually beckons us onward, inviting us to live with him in love and hope and trust and challenging us to pass through the world in affirmation, not denial, in faith, not doubt, in integrity and responsive sensitivity to others and to their needs.

IV. Bethlehem comes at the moment in any life when the spirit of the master enters our lives and the world in which we live as the result of our having at long last started to take him seriously. We have arrived at Bethlehem when we begin to realize that light is indeed available—a light which is not our own, a light that scatters our awful feeling of loneliness and helplessness, and a light which reflects "the glory of God in the face of Jesus Christ."

V. Bethlehem is that place and time wherever and whenever gifts are given. When a child opens his present at the foot of the Christmas tree, when food is sent to a hungry family next door or to a starving nation overseas, when welfare is given to and received by the desperate widow who cannot feed and clothe her children, and when ideas are shared, enthusiasms communicated, and the gifts of friendship, sympathy, and appreciation are expressed, we are in Bethlehem.

(a) Christmas is all about gifts including God's great gift of new life under the direction and leadership of that child in the manger grown up.

(b) Halford E. Luccock wrote, "Is our Christmas still only a story about a baby, or is it a deathless story about a person into whom the baby grew, who can redeem the world from its sin, and who calls us into partnership with his great and mighty purposes?"—Edward C. Dahl.

Illustrations

IN HIS PRESENCE. Things change their aspect when we view them in the presence of Jesus. We fret and fume if we feel our proper place is not given to us. We grow hot and jealous about rank and position and the rest of it. But how mean and petty it all looks when we bring it into the presence of Jesus. It would do us good to bring our ambitions and desires and plans constantly into the presence of the lowly Jesus and test them there.—J. D. Jones.

LOST TIME. Do you remember the story of the man whose jet arrived late on the eve of an important speaking engagement in a certain city? Racing through the terminal and into a waiting taxi, he could think of only one thing—somehow he had to make up for lost time. "Step on it, quick!" he blurted to the cab driver. The taxi fifteen minutes later was still racing down streets and skidding around corners. Finally the man asked the driver, "How much farther is it?" And the cabby replied: "I don't know, sir. You haven't told me where you want to go!"—Arthur McPhee.

Sermon Suggestions

ETERNAL LIFE. Text: John 3:16. (1) Eternal life is life in Christ. (2) Eternal life is a life of serving God. (3) Eternal life is a life of goodness. (4) Eternal life is a life of worshiping God.—John R. Brokhoff.

FIVE JOYS OF CHRISTMAS. Text: Luke 2: 10–11. (1) The joy of seeing. (2) The joy of hearing. (3) The joy of fulfillment. (4) The joy of being forgiven. (5) The joy of life eternal.—John W. Rilling.

Worship Aids

CALL TO WORSHIP. "O send out thy light and thy truth: Let them lead me; let them bring me unto thy holy hill and to the tabernacles." Ps. 43:3.

INVOCATION. Our Father, help us during this special season to remember the many ways thou hast pointed out to us the coming of our Lord Jesus Christ. May we be ever mindful that thou wilt not let us sit in darkness, but if we are receptive we will see the light of thy many signs in the prophets, in the lives of our neighbors, and in the eyes of our family.

OFFERTORY SENTENCE. "As every man hath received the gift, even so minister the same one to another, as good stewards of the manifold grace of God." I Pet. 4:10.

OFFERTORY PRAYER. May we find it to be a joyful experience, O Lord, to offer these gifts in the name of Jesus. Grant unto us the wisdom of the men of old who found a token in a star, worshiped the child as a newborn king, and made offerings at his feet.

PRAYER. Blessed and eternal God, whose son, Jesus Christ, did come in due season to grant salvation to all having faith in him, grant us in these holy days to grow in our understanding of the wonder and glory of his first coming, to increase in our openness to the presence of thy Holy Spirit in our lives, and to deepen our commitment to all things in thy created world that are lovely and of good report.

Teach us to tune some loftier song, to phrase some nobler prayer, and to perform some more worthy deed of love and compassion in this day, to the end that we may show forth the joy and gratitude that rise within us when we consider the graciousness of thy forgiveness and the tenderness of thy dealing with the sons of men as thou dost seek to lead us from darkness into light, from fear into trust, from despair into hope, and from doubt into faith.

In this blessed advent season we rejoice

greatly in the greatest of thy gifts, the gift of Jesus Christ which sprang from love for us and love for all men. Teach us that having received great gifts, so must we give. Let us know full well that we cannot give to thee save as we give to men love, service, generosity, compassion, and forgiveness. Teach us that the gift without the giver is bare, and forbid that we should think our duty done to thee or to our neighbor when the cold tithe of charity has been released. Guide us in that same holy way of utter self-giving that our Lord Christ walked before us.—Charles R. Britt.

EVENING SERVICE

Topic: The Grace and Truth of God
Text: John 1:14.

I. Christianity is the religion of the incarnation. What is God like? You see him revealed in his son, full of grace and truth.

(a) The grace of God is the miracle of a stable child become the savior of the world, forgiveness from a cross of pain, and a second chance for those having the humility to accept.

(b) The grace of God is the understanding heart of the universe—the affirmation of the importance of each man, woman, and child, the sacredness of human life, and the infinite worth of the soul.

(c) The grace of God is a love that keeps on loving beyond measure, a faith that keeps on believing undeterred, and the welcome that awaits the prodigal limping home from the far country. It is the constancy that never changes, the stability that undergirds weakness, the strength that offers encouragement amidst struggle, and the compassion that ministers to our needs.

(d) The grace of God is the promise that harvest follows seedtime and that daylight follows darkness, the assurance that eternal life follows death, the end is but the beginning, and in God's house there are many mansions and a place has been prepared for us, a house not made with hands, eternal in the heavens.

(e) The grace of God is the assurance that "God so loved the world, that he gave his only begotten son, that whosoever believeth in him should not perish, but have everlasting life." It is the unfailing covenant and pledge of the almighty that he will not fail nor forsake us. (See Rom. 8: 38–39.)

(f) The grace of God is God seeking people through Christ at Christmas—the shepherd searching for his sheep and the perfect restoring the imperfect.

II. God is truth as well as grace. Truth makes its demands, has its requirements, sets its standards, and holds high expectations.

(a) Truth is righteousness in the wilderness of temptation, unswerving loyalty in the face of compromise, and unyielding conviction above self-interest.

(b) Truth is the unending quest to love God with heart and soul and strength and mind and to love neighbor as self. It is the Samaritan who would have chosen otherwise and the crossbearer who denies self and follows the higher calling.

(1) It is accountability. "To whom much is given, of him shall much be required."

(2) It is dependability. "Well done, good and faithful servant, enter into the joy of your reward."

(3) It is respectability. "You shall know them by their fruits."

(4) It is integrity. "But I do as the Father has commanded me, so that the world may know that I love my Father."

(5) It is responsibility. "Inasmuch as you have done it unto the least of these my brethren, you have done it unto me."

III. We have beheld the glory of one full of grace and truth. The baby became man and is none other than "God of God, light of light, very God of very God."

(a) When he taught people, it was God himself speaking the same creative word by which the heavens were made.

(b) When he was nailed to a Roman cross, it was God in action to reconcile an estranged world to himself.

(c) When he rose from the dead, it was God bringing eternal life to mortal man.

(d) Our life is now linked with God's life. We know God because we know Christ: "His name shall be called Emmanuel, which means 'God with us'."—Allan J. Weenink.

SUNDAY: DECEMBER THIRTEENTH

MORNING SERVICE

Topic: A Man Who Missed Christmas (Advent)

SCRIPTURE: Matt. 2:7–18.

Herod was a man who missed Christmas.

I. *Christmas came before he was prepared for it.*

(a) The shepherds had been alerted by the angels. The wise men were prompted by an unusual star which they saw in the east. Mary and Joseph were spoken to in dreams. In the temple Simeon and Anna recognized the Christ Child when he was brought in for the ceremonial purification rites, and they confessed that now they were ready to die for they had seen the salvation of the Lord. But Herod had no dream, no angel, no star, and no vision. He was left out entirely, and he was the king.

(b) Herod was a bitter man. Bitterness often blinds us to reality. People who are bitter with others, bitter with life, and bitter because of the past have a tendency to miss a lot.

(c) Herod was an unbelieving man. He was not particularly looking for God to do anything unusual. He was so wrapped up in himself, what he was doing, where he was going, and what was going on in his own little world that he had no time for God. People who live like that miss God. They miss the sunsets, the rainbows, and the miracles. They miss the mangers, the swaddling clothes, and the footsteps of God on the sands of time.

(d) Herod was a man with a closed mind. God can never enter a closed mind. Whenever a person is certain that he has it all together, that there is nothing more to be learned, and that God can do no new thing, he will never hear the angels sing or see the star in the East.

II. *He had no inclination to follow the word of God.*

(a) He was a proud man. He would admit to no need, particularly the need of God in his life. Pride kills marriages, it kills relationships, and it even kills souls. Pride keeps people from admitting that there might be some knowledge that they do not know. It keeps them from saying, "I'm sorry," or "Forgive me." Pride is keeping many people out of the kingdom of God.

(b) Amid the festivities of that first Christmas, Herod called the scribes in and asked them about the birth of Christ. They read to him from Micah's prophecy, written 500 years before Herod. Now that he has heard them surely he will not reject God's word, but he did. That verse alone could have led him to Christ, but he had no desire to follow God's instructions.

(c) Many today are missing salvation for the same reason—an unwillingness to follow the word of God. Without Christ, Herod was lost, and so are we.

III. *He would have no one on the throne of his crusty heart except himself.*

(a) At an art gallery in Germany is a picture that is not quite finished. King Frederick the Great is artistically portrayed as talking to his generals. In the center of the painting is a section etched in charcoal outline. It indicates the artist's intentions, but the artist died before the painting was finished. He had painstakingly sketched in oils all the generals and the background material, but the king he had left till last. He died before painting the king. Today his work of art is the contribution of a man who omitted the king.

(b) Anyone who does not receive Christ into his life is one who paints his portrait without the king. Herod did that, and so he missed Christmas.—Jerry Hayner.

Illustrations

LOVING FELLOWSHIP. Somewhere in the world there should be a society consciously and deliberately devoted to the task of seeing how love can be made real and demonstrating love in practice. Unfortunately there is only one candidate for this task. If God, as we believe, is truly revealed in the life of Christ, the most important thing to him is the creation of centers of loving fellowship which in turn infect the world. Whether the world can be redeemed in this way we do not know, but it is at least clear that there is no other way. —Elton Trueblood.

NOT FACELESS. Christianity is not to love in abstraction but to love the individual who stands before me in a person-to-person relationship. He must never be faceless to me or I am denying everything I say I believe. This concept will always involve some cost. It is not a cheap thing. —Francis Schaeffer.

Sermon Suggestion

THE ANGELIC CHORUS. Text: Luke 2:14. (1) The angels sang to persons in a harsh world. (2) The angels sang of God's glory. (3) The angels sang of God's good news. —Hoover Rupert.

Worship Aids

CALL TO WORSHIP. "Lo, the star, which they saw in the east, went before them, till it came and stood over where the young child was. When they saw the star, they rejoiced with exceeding great joy." Matt. 2:9–10.

INVOCATION. Dear Christ, who art the light of the world, shine, we pray thee, so that all who walk in darkness and dwell in the land of the shadow of death may have the light of life. May thy word at this season be for us a lamp unto our feet and a light unto our path.

OFFERTORY SENTENCE. "If ye then, being evil, know how to give good gifts unto your children: how much more shall your heavenly Father give the Holy Spirit to them that ask him?" Luke 11:13.

OFFERTORY PRAYER. O God, thou giver of all good gifts, in gratitude we bring our gifts on this day of joyous worship. Refine them, we pray thee, in the mint of thy divine purpose and use them to the end that thy kingdom may come and thy will be done on earth as it is in heaven.

PRAYER. Eternal God, who on that bright and radiant night long ago sent thy son to be our king, we sing praises to thee and bless thy holy name. We who live in a world of crowns and thrones are humbled by his lowly birth. We had not thought that creation's story could be told from a manger. Yet Christ is crowned with a star and surrounded by heavenly choirs singing, "Peace on earth, good will to men." Christ is bearing kindness and mercy that put our threatenings and slaughter to shame. Thou hast sent thy dayspring from on high to visit us.

Thou, who didst come in Christ to bring peace on earth, bring peace to our troubled souls. We so often lose our faith and wander in darkness when we may follow thee and live in the light. Teach us that the darkness may pass away in the glory that surrounds us. Teach us that the tribulations and sufferings of this present time are not worthy to be compared with the glory that shall be revealed to us.

We worship in thy church, surrounded by symbols of thy royal birth. We seek in this heavenly setting the true direction of our lives. Thou who art our father, fill us with the knowledge of Christ and surround us with thy beauteous heavenly light.—Albert Buckner Coe.

EVENING SERVICE

Topic: The Cliches of Christmas
TEXT: Prov. 15:26.
I. *Christmas is the spirit of giving.*
(a) At Christmas our society places emphasis on giving. The newspapers are full of "holiday gift suggestions." The television screens flutter with countless Christmas trees surrounded by ribbon-wrapped packages, each one promising to hold the best gift of all.
(b) Much of the talk about giving simply spurs feelings for getting. Parents give to their children so that they can get as much as the other kids on the block or in the family. Relatives or co-workers give because they know they must, and they will get something in return. Men give for the smiles, thanks, and satisfaction they get in return.

II. *Christmas brings peace and joy.* For whom? The mad mob of shoppers—crowded, crushed, and consumed by the holiday? The disillusioned, drunken group at the office party, dulling their fears by drowning their minds? The international peacemakers, smiling at the media while lying to each other? Never.

III. *Let's keep Christ in Christmas.* How can we keep what was never there? Most of our society has rejected religion and Christ along with it. They have been confused and disenchanted by the meaningless ritual and ecclesiastical double-talk of most that's called Christianity. They've never known Jesus even if they have become acquainted with the church. They don't know how to make him a part of Christmas because they have no idea of including him in any other day of the year.

IV. When persons know Jesus as the living God and their forgiving savior, they see depth in each of these sentences. Each one becomes exciting and important instead of trite and lifeless.

(a) Giving without thought of getting is at the heart of Christianity. We see it in the example and in the commands of our God. Those who are learning to make him Lord are learning how to give without worrying about the return. And they do it at other times than Christmas.

(b) Peace and joy, while considered unattainable by the world, are guaranteed to the Christian. Christmas may not bring them, but remembering Christ's birth can certainly remind us of their reality.

(c) Keep Christ in Christmas? It's not easy. We must resist the pressures of our peers who keep expecting us to squeeze Christmas into their humanistic molds. Only Christ can wash the cynicism from our materialistic observance. Only Christ can give us a reason to celebrate now and after Christmas. May we do so with an awareness of his presence. And may we recommit ourselves to taking him to those who don't realize how much these cliches can mean.—Mark A. Taylor in *The Lookout.* Reprinted by permission.

SUNDAY: DECEMBER TWENTIETH

MORNING SERVICE

Topic: Where Christ Should Be Born (Advent)

TEXT: Matt. 2:2.

I. The wise men came to Jerusalem asking, "Where is he that is born King of the Jews?"

(a) They quite naturally made their inquiry of Herod, the ruling monarch. He then appropriately turned to the leading religious leaders of the Jewish community for an answer to this question. Searching through their scrolls, they came upon a prophecy made by Micah, a man who had lived in the seventh century. (See Mic. 5: 2.)

(b) The gospel according to Matthew leads us to believe that it was on the basis of that 700-year-old prophecy that the magi were sent to Bethlehem. They were directed by a star to a house where they saw the young child with Mary, his mother.

(c) The gospel according to Luke provides us with another and quite different reason for Bethlehem's being the birthplace of our Lord. Luke says, "It came to pass" that a very short time before the child was to be born, Caesar Augustus sent out a decree that all the world should be taxed and everyone had to go to his own city for this taxing or enrollment. Because Joseph was of the house and lineage of David, he was under the legal necessity of going to David's city—to Bethlehem—for this purpose.

II. We should not be nearly so concerned with why it was that Christ was born in Bethlehem as where he should be born anew this Christmas.

(a) In a very real, as well as in a highly symbolic sense, he must be born anew if he is to have the quality of influence on our lives which he had on the lives of those who knew him in the days of his flesh long ago.

(b) God did not then nor does he now wait for what we might term ideal situations before revealing himself. Even as then, Christ is born in the most unlikely places. He is born wherever God can find room to perform his divine miracle.

III. We may find some clues to the answer to our question as we take note of some of the places where Christ was born during the days of his ministry.

(a) He was born in the hearts of those sturdy fishermen and their kind, who responded to his invitation to leave their accustomed ways of providing for themselves and follow him that he might make them fishers of men.

(1) How vital it is that we often remind ourselves that Jesus chose to insure the perpetuation of his way and truth and life through quite ordinary people—men not greatly unlike ourselves.

(2) That should tell us that right now he is waiting to be born in the hearts of any person—all people—who will respond to his invitation to give him room in their lives.

(b) "Born again" lies at the core of one of the most dramatic stories found in the gospel record—the story of Nicodemus. This ruler in the religious community went to Jesus at night, saying in effect: "I want to know your secret. I want to have what you have. I am not satisfied with what religion is doing to my real life." Jesus said, "Verily, verily, except a man be born again, he cannot see the kingdom of God."

(1) Then follows one of the great lessons which is so important to an understanding of the meaning of the religion of Jesus. It declares that we must allow the spirit of God to enter into the deep places of our lives to make us new creatures. When the spirit of God enters into a human life, the person becomes the dwelling place for the divine life.

(2) When we feel this spirit moving within us, prompting us to do what no man nor legalistic code can require of us and when we gladly give ourselves for love's sake, asking nothing in return but the satisfaction of having made someone else happy and their life more full of meaning, we know that Christ has been born in our hearts.

IV. Where should Christ be born? He should and will gladly be born wherever there is need for his quality of redeeming love. Is that not everywhere?

(a) As in days of old, men should not be surprised if he turns up in the midst of the most abject situations, for that will be where he is needed most. They are the people he came to seek and to save.

(b) That lays a challenge at our feet.

(1) He is waiting to be born in places which prepare him room, and he looks to those of us who dare consider ourselves his disciples to make ready for his coming.

(2) He counts on us to join the angelic chorus in proclaiming, "Glory to God in the highest and on earth peace, good will toward men."

(3) He commissions us to shout the glad tidings of great joy which shall be to all people—the news that unto them is born a savior which is Christ the Lord.—Homer J. R. Elford.

Illustration

GOSPEL FOR SINNERS.   God might have found so many other ways to spread the gospel of the love of God. He might have written his love on the leaves of the trees, and blowing winds would have sent news of deliverance and redemption far and wide. God might have written his love in the skies and in the sun so that men looking upward could have read the message, "God so loved the world." He might have made the ocean sing his love and nightingales to chant. None of these, not even angels, could ever preach and say, "I've been redeemed." So this is a gospel for sinners saved by grace, and only saved sinners can preach.—Gardner C. Taylor.

Sermon Suggestion

THE FIRST CHRISTMAS GIFT.   Text: Luke 2:11. (1) The gift of a baby, and that baby was a gift of love, a gift of a life, and a gift of light. (2) The gift of a savior. (3) The gift of a lord.—S. Robert Weaver.

Worship Aids

CALL TO WORSHIP.   "Behold, I bring
you good tidings of great joy, which shall
be to all people. For unto you is born this
day in the city of David a Savior, which is
Christ the Lord. Glory to God in the highest, and on earth peace, good will toward
men." Luke 2:10–11, 14.

INVOCATION.   Hushed be our hearts, O
God, by the mystery and the wonder of the
birth of the Christ Child. Make us truly
wise with the wisdom of a little child that
once again the highest truth may be born
afresh in our hearts. Let not our souls be
busy inns that have no room for thy son,
but this day throw wide the doors of our
lives to welcome our holy guest.

OFFERTORY SENTENCE.   "When they
were come into the house, they saw the
young child with Mary his mother, and fell
down, and worshiped him. And they presented unto him gifts; gold, and frankin-
cense, and myrrh." Matt. 2:11.

OFFERTORY PRAYER.   Our Lord Jesus
Christ, whose birthday has become a season of benevolence and giving, bless these
our gifts which we offer in thankfulness for
thyself, God's unspeakably precious gift.

PRAYER.   In these sacred moments, our
heavenly Father, wilt thou grant us thy
light and thy peace? Wilt thou illumine
our lives with the glad good news and the
wonderful tidings that a savior has been
born and we need never despair because
we can live in the light of his truth?

Wilt thou give us peace in our hearts so
that, at the very center of all of our vigorous activity, there may be a quiet place
where we are mindful of the sacred birth
of our Lord Jesus and find rest and quiet
for our spirits where the crib becomes an
altar and our hearts gladly bow in reverence?

Wilt thou touch our lives in this time of
holy worship that once again our hearts
may sing with joy that a hope has been
given to all men everywhere that nothing

can take away? Strengthen our spirit of
faith, grant us the power to see the wonder
of thy truth, and give us in our daily life
the power for going forward.

We come into thy presence, our heavenly Father, recognizing our very deep
need of thee. As we confess our selfishness, our wrongheadedness, and our stub-
bornness of spirit, we find our only faith in
the gospel of thy mercy. Take hold of us,
grant us thy cleansing forgiveness, renew
us, hearten us, and set us upon our feet.
Challenge and commission us that our
lives may ever be facing forward. Let us
march with strong confidence as pilgrims
of thy truth.—Lowell M. Atkinson.

EVENING SERVICE

Topic: The Crib and the Cross
TEXT: Matt. 1:23.

I. The symbols of the crib of Bethlehem
and the cross of Golgotha come together
to point to the deep significance of the
Christmas miracle. Born in a stable with
no doctor, the Christ Child was greeted
not only by the adoration of the shepherds
and the wise men but also by the brutal
edict of King Herod that this supposed
contender for his throne should be killed
even if it meant taking the lives of all the
male children of Bethlehem. And it was
the same fearful insecurity of men in high
places and low that led to the cross. The
crib and the cross proclaim that in the very
midst of these depths we encounter the
accepting, forgiving, and life-transforming love of God.

II. In his ministry Jesus gave high priority to touching the lives of those who lived
in the darkest corners of life—persons
who were forgotten, ignored, or actively
shunned. He was not at all ashamed to be
labeled as one who ate with tax collectors,
gluttons, and sinners. To those who knew
from their own experience what the harsh
realities of human life were, Jesus proclaimed the reality of God as loving Father
who accepts us as we are and invites us to
live out our lives trusting his love in the
face of all the harsh realities of human life,
even death. He calls us to reflect his love
in the world by loving our fellowmen.

Jesus was so filled with the eternal reality of God's love that he chose the cross rather than turn aside from his mission of sharing God's love with all that would listen.

III. The crib and the cross point to the miracle of Christmas—God with us. New life, new hope, new directions, and new purposes are possible because God encounters us in the depths of our lives. He encounters us in the world of the little things of our lives, the world of homelessness and refugees, the world where there are lepers, lost sons, poor old ladies, and men and women who are afraid, the world in which men cheat and are cheated, and the world in which men die and are killed.

IV. Crib and cross are the extremes of life's curve, and God in Christ has traveled it all. Emmanuel—God is with us. He is not off in some painless and sanitary heaven. He is with us in the midst of life as we know it and experience it. We do not have to first become godly and noble before we can have a part in him, for there are no depths in our lives where he has not already come to us and no depths to which he has not been able to give meaning by surrounding them with love and making them a place where he encounters us and brings us into his kingdom.—Robert D. Hunter.

SUNDAY: DECEMBER TWENTY-SEVENTH

MORNING SERVICE

Topic: The New and the Old (New Year)
TEXT: Mark 2:21–22.

What message is there for the modern church in Jesus' parable about the new wine and the new patches? Do those words have any relevance for us?

I. They remind us that, however important tradition is, we must allow room for the working of God in the present and the future. Our God is an active God, alive and moving, shaking history, revealing himself in the events which involve mankind, upholding the cause of truth and justice, exercising his unlimited mercy, and always trying to reveal himself and his incomparable love to all persons everywhere.

II. Our God is involved in change. He made a world that is ever changing in every particle of creation. Nothing is static and nothing is stable. Everything is impermanent and transient in nature, and everything is in flux. The eternal truth of earth is always: "Everything nailed down is coming loose." Our God who made a world so mobile in nature is in his own way working in that change and through that change to reveal himself. That is why we hear him saying through the prophet Isaiah, "Behold, I am doing a new thing; now it springs forth, do you not perceive it?"

God never changes, but he changes everything else.

III. It is human nature to resist change. Don't we often wish we could slow it down, even stop it? Someone commented to a ninety-year-old man that he must have seen lots of changes. "Yes," he said, "and I've been against every one of them."

(a) How prone we are to be against change and to settle down in a well-worn rut. Ruts offer us security. We know their boundaries and where we are. Get out of the ruts and we might go into a ditch. Ruts keep us on the straight and narrow and out of trouble. So they can supply us with comfort and certainty.

(b) There is great truth to the old saying that ruts are nothing but a grave with both ends knocked out. Whatever value tradition may have, sometimes it may well be just stupid.

IV. Jesus appreciated the best in his tradition, but he ignored the meaningless and binding and mechanical. He broke meaningless tradition often. To that degree he was revolutionary, even radical and nonconformist.

(a) Jesus enabled those who took him seriously to know that God frequently reveals new truth to mankind. God still reveals new truth in almost every area of life. He allows researchers to discover new scientific truths, new technological truths, new sociological truths, new psychological truths, and so on.

(b) Every new truth means the demise of some old way of thinking which once seemed so lasting. The growth of knowledge is exploding in almost every field one can mention. There is always something more to learn and something new under the sun. God keeps allowing us to discover new truths and new facts and to develop new insights about himself and the world he has made.

V. We are compelled always to question the old order, the old assumptions, and the old traditions. It may turn out that what was good in the past is still good in the present. But when truth and logic demand that we scrap the old, then we must scrap it.

(a) You and I should quit looking longingly backward and become breathtakingly excited about the new ways of understanding our faith, the new Christian music that God is giving us, the new liturgies and creeds being written, and the new ways of worshiping and serving God.

(b) The book of Revelation speaks of believers having a new name (3:12), singing a new song (5:9; 14:3), dwelling in a new Jerusalem (21:2), and pictures God upon his throne saying, "Behold, I make all things new" (21:5).—Charles E. Ferrell.

Illustrations

SPIRITUAL OPPORTUNITY. The new year's chief value to us is its spiritual opportunity. A year from now we may be richer or poorer than we are today; stronger in body or weaker, or more famous or more obscure. Whatever these results may be, they will not interpret the real significance of the year. That will only be revealed by the application of finer tests. If the year makes us more patient and courageous with a purer zeal for righteousness and a consciousness of deeper fellowship with the spirit of Christ, it will have brought us the richest harvest it can bring. Whatever else the new year may mean to us, it surely means the opportunity for spiritual attainment. If we go forth

into it with the full appreciation of that fact and the purpose and prayer to redeem the time, we shall estimate our experiences by a true standard and be certain not to fail to gather the choicest fruitage of the days.
—George E. Horr.

FALLING STARS.   One night, during a veritable shower of stars, a frightened young man encountered an old man who he thought would be terrified by the falling stars. "Aren't you fearful?" asked the young man. "Oh, no," said the other. "Just the little ones are falling. The seven big ones haven't moved an inch."

Sermon Suggestion

THE JOURNEY OF FAITH.   Text: Eph. 4: 13. In Eph. 2 there is a context that spells out the journey of faith. (1) The journey begins in darkness—sin—as mentioned in vv. 1–3 (NIV). From the context three observations may be made about the life of sin. (a) Its destination is death. (b) Its companion is darkness. (c) Its view is despair. (2) The journey of faith continues with discovery. (a) The discovery of freedom through Christ (vv. 4–7). (b) The discovery of faith (vv. 8–9). (c) The discovery of a future (vv. 11, 13). (d) The discovery of the family of God (v. 19). (e) The discovery of a foundation in Christ (vv. 20–22). (3) The journey of faith leads to discipleship (v. 10, LB).—C. Neil Strait.

Worship Aids

CALL TO WORSHIP.   "Arise, shine; for thy light is come, and the glory of the Lord is risen upon thee. Lift up thine eyes round about and see." Isa. 60:1, 4.

INVOCATION.   Eternal God, who committest unto us the swift and solemn trust of life, since we know not what a day may bring forth but only that the hour for serving thee is always present, may we wake to the instant claims of thy holy will, not waiting for tomorrow but yielding today. Consecrate with thy presence the way our feet may go, and the humblest work will shine, and the roughest places be made plain.—James Martineau.

OFFERTORY SENTENCE.   "Thou crownest the year with thy goodness . . . Samuel took a stone, and set it between Mizpeh and Shen, saying, Hitherto hath the Lord helped us." Ps. 65:11; I Sam. 7:12.

OFFERTORY PRAYER.   Our Father, help us who claim to be Christians to bring forth fruit consistent with our profession of faith. May these tithes and offerings be so used that others may hear the glad story of thy redeeming love.

LITANY.   Eternal God, who hast numbered the stars in their courses, set the planets in motion, called time itself into being, mercifully hearken unto us, creatures of the dust, products of a little day, who yet have seen in the face of thy son the light of life eternal. That thou wilt teach us to number our days, learn of thy wisdom, and lay hold on that which passes not away:

We beseech thee to hear us, O God.

That we slaves of the hours and driven servants of the days may become masters of time in the spirit of Jesus, who amid hurrying moments and fleeting years did perfect thy noblest word in the knowledge that thou wouldst finish the mission to which he was ordained:

We beseech thee to hear us, O God.

That when past failures discourage and broken resolutions lay waste our powers, we may not be bound by chains of the past:

Help us to forget.

That unjust treatment, resentment, bitterness, and grudges borne within the bosom may not harden us to thy gracious pardon:

Help us to forgive.

Into thy hands we commend our bodies, minds, and spirits. Unto thee who are able to keep us from falling and make of us a new creation, through the power of Jesus Christ, redeemer and guide, be glory and majesty now and forever.—Marion C. Allen.

EVENING SERVICE

Topic: What Is My Part in the Good News? (Watch Night)

TEXT: Rom. 2:16.

I. *My personal relationships.* List ways in which you fall short of being the loving person Jesus Christ calls you to be in your one-to-one relationships with others.

II. *My group relationships.* How caring and just are the groups to which I belong in the world, and how can I improve them? How caring and just are the groups to which I belong in the church, and how can I improve them?

III. *My public relationships.* Review the roots of the call to justice in the Old and New Testaments. If needed for stimulation, see Ex. 20:13–17. Think through some of the possible responses to situations of human suffering and injustice.

IV. *My role in making Jesus Christ known to those who do not know him.* Discuss what is unique about Jesus Christ that we should wish to share him with others. What guidelines can the congregation offer to guide its members in sharing Jesus Christ with others?

V. *My stewardship of my time, talents, and resources.* What have I learned about giving more of my time and talent to the church, and how did I learn it? What have I learned about giving more of my financial resources to the work of Jesus Christ through his people, the church, and how have I learned it? Which comes first—renewal in mission or responsible stewardship? Or does it vary with the person?

VI. *My inner life with God in Jesus Christ.* The basic resource for living lovingly and justly in our personal, group, and social relationships is our most important relationship of all, our relationship to God in Jesus Christ.—*The Episcopalian.*

SECTION X. *Ideas and Suggestions for Pulpit and Parish*

APOSTOLIC PREACHING. Pastor Harold F. Filbrandt of the First United Methodist Church in Marshall, Michigan, preached a series of sermons, based on extensive research, in which, dressed in the role of each apostle, the story is told of the relationship of each to Jesus. Some apostles appeared more than once. Peter in three sermons told of his early relationship with Christ, his preparations for Jesus' last week, and his thoughts as he stood before the empty tomb on Easter morning.

SILENT REMINDER. Every five minutes during a worship service emphasizing Christian concern for world hunger, a member of the United Church of Christ in Lakewood, Colorado, walked silently to the front of the chancel. The fifteen who had participated in this way during the service represented those who had died of hunger while others were worshiping.

LIST OF THREE. Members of the Cumberland Presbyterian Church in Providence, Kentucky, carry a list of three persons they wish to win for the church and whom they invite to church activities and for whom they pray. Such persons, when they respond, are helped in their growth in the faith, and a new name is added to a member's list which is always kept at three.

PALESTINE REVISITED. Life in a Jewish village at the time of Christ became real for 150 people in the United Methodist Church and five other churches in Williamston, Michigan, who for three days at a retreat center engaged in various household, community, and religious activities that were commonplace during Jesus' boyhood.

ROLL CALL SUNDAY. To celebrate the ongoing ministry, the Jefferson Avenue United Methodist Church in Detroit, Michigan, held a Roll Call Sunday attended by former pastors and members. The Lord's Supper, recognition of longstanding members and church leaders, and a tea following worship were included.

BIBLICAL PREACHING. Charles L. Allen, minister of the First United Methodist Church in Houston, Texas, preached on a text from a different book in the Bible for fifty-two consecutive Sundays, beginning on the first Sunday in January with a text from Genesis.

FRIENDSHIP QUILT. Each family in St. Mark Cumberland Presbyterian Church in Fort Worth, Texas, designed and contributed a square for a friendship quilt.

ACTION SERMONS. Chapel worship for adolescents at Pine Rest Christian Hospital in Grand Rapids, Michigan, includes verbal expositions followed by action sermons. Representative themes and activities: (a) The forgiveness of sins. Worshipers write on pieces of paper something they wish to surrender to Christ and for which they desire to receive his forgiveness. These are crumpled, put in a large container in front of a rude wooden cross, and then burned to symbolize that God forgives and cleanses. (b) Developing a caring fellowship. The Polish ceremony *(apwatki)* is simulated when each person offers a piece of bread to another and says, "I would like to share my bread (or good thoughts or wishes) with you." (c) Being a fellowship of the concerned. The people plunge their hands into a bucket of water and others dry them with paper towels, thereby providing an opportunity to give and receive.

MEMORY CIRCLE.   Several weeks following the death of a beloved church member, friends and associates may meet informally at the church or in a home where in a circle of memory they may recall meaningful experiences, memorable words and deeds, and anecdotes, emphasizing ways by which the life of the deceased might continue to be a living witness and inspiration in the ongoing ministry of the church.

EVEN THINE ALTARS.   A minister climbed a ladder one Saturday night and placed a bird's nest on one of the arms of the cross high above the altar. The next morning one after another of the parishioners spotted it and pointed it out to others. During the following weeks the nest became either a curiosity or an annoyance to the members. Then the minister preached on Ps. 84:3–4, and in this simple way the congregation forever remembered that the house of God was a refuge not only for the bird but also for them and that he whose eye is on the sparrow cares lovingly for each of his children.

CHRIST AND CURRICULUM.   Invite college students in the church to speak, one on each of several successive Sundays, for three or four minutes during the worship service on the relationship between their commitment to Christ and their college majors and career preferences.

COMMUNICATION.   By dialing a telephone number, members of the First Cumberland Presbyterian Church in Austin, Texas, receive a daily summary of news of the church family by recording. The church communication system is called "Dial-a-Concern."

DIAL-A-SPEAKER.   Using a conference phone system, the members of the Boyd Memorial Christian Church in Charleston, West Virginia, each Sunday during the church school assembly time engage in a two-way dialogue for five minutes with a preselected   denominational   church leader, author, or out-of-town pastor.

CHRISTIAN SOLDIER.   Fourth and fifth graders in the First Congregational Church of Emerald Grove (UCC) in Janesville, Wisconsin, researched Roman armor and constructed a suit of armor for their teacher who, standing at attention, wore it when the minister read Eph. 6:10–17 and preached on a topic relating to the Christian soldier.

PROPHETIC VISITORS.   Old Testament prophets including Amos, Hosea, Micah, Jeremiah, and Isaiah visited the Court Street United Methodist Church in Flint, Michigan, and gave autobiographical sermons through their interpreter, biblically-dressed Ralph Janka, pastor of the church.

VETERAN MEMBERS.   On Recognition Sunday long-standing members of the First Baptist Church in Seattle, Washington, are awarded 25 and 50-year membership certificates.

POST SERVICES.   A church having members in the military requests that bulletins from distant and overseas churches or post chapels be sent for a "In Touch with Our Service Personnel" bulletin board in the church vestibule.

PRAYER LIST.   Each Sunday the bulletin of the Clarendon United Methodist Church in Arlington, Virginia, includes in a prayer list the first names of women in the Arlington Detention Center. The church women contribute craft items and money to support the work of church members whose Christian ministry at the center involves a prayer circle, a song fest, listening, counseling, and providing yarn for crocheted articles.

FOUR-FOOT CANDLE.   The young people of the Ocee United Methodist Church in Alpharetta, Georgia, made a four-foot candle out of stubs of altar candles, decorated with a purple cross from the remnants of Advent candles, inscribed it with the words "Alpha" and "Omega," lit it for the Easter service, and thus revived an ancient Christian custom.

PASCHAL CANDLE.   The lighting of the paschal candle for Easter worship at the Augustana Lutheran Church in Denver, Colorado, perpetuates historical Christian tradition in which the unlighted candle symbolizes the death and burial of Jesus and the lighted candle the splendor and glory of his resurrection and the wick his humility. The lighting of other tapers from the pascal candle represents Christ's giving of the Holy Spirit to his disciples. After Easter the candle is lighted each time baptism is celebrated.

WIDER FELLOWSHIP.   To encourage regular church attendance by members away on summer vacations, a large map was put on an easel at the front of the sanctuary of the First Christian Church in Ocala, Florida, and the cities were pinpointed where parishioners worshiped. In a book a record was kept of names, dates, and churches attended.

MOSES AT VBS.   Moses—Bob McAndrews, pastor of youth and education at the First Reformed Church in Portage, Michigan—went each day to the Vacation Bible School where in costume he told the morning story and dramatized such events as the burning bush, the Red Sea crossing, and the receiving of the ten commandments. At various learning centers the children were interviewed for the *Daily Exodus,* prepared passover foods, or constructed a model of the tabernacle.

GALILEAN SERVICE.   Each October the members of the Melrose United Methodist Church in Lottsburg, Virginia, hold a Galilean service at which the pastor preaches from a boat anchored in the Rappahannock River.

CONTINUOUS LIGHT.   "Twenty Centuries of Christ's Light" was the theme of the Christmas worship service of the First Presbyterian Church in Alliance, Ohio. Twenty young and older persons briefly traced the influence of Christ in each century in Christian history. Each in turn lighted a candle from the Christ candle at the center of the Advent wreath. Singing of carols and choral music representing twenty centuries of lyric religion became inspring interludes between the historical interpretations.

ADVENT SERIES.   Names given to the Christ Child was the theme of worship during Advent at the Wesley United Methodist Church in Ishpeming, Michigan. On successive Sundays worship included a sanctuary decorated with the flowers and plants associated with the season, the ringing of bells each member was asked to bring, a scriptural drama written by the pastor, and a drama reenacting the annunciation in which an angel asked teenagers about the coming of him who would be called Jesus. On the Sunday following Advent the baptism of infants recalled the dedication of Jesus in the temple.

INTERGENERATIONAL   EVENT.   Young and old members of the congregation of the Valley Presbyterian Church in Scottsdale, Arizona, are invited to an Advent activity in which they deal with the money changers, participate in Caesar's enrollment, take a pilgrimage to the stable, plant a tree for the future, and share an agape meal.

ADVENT COMMUNION.   On a Sunday in December, members of the First Baptist Church in Redlands, California, gathered around tables at the morning worship hour to share an agape meal and the

Lord's Supper according to the practice in the early church.

DRIVE-THROUGH NATIVITY. Thirty-five costumed young people of the Eastview Christian Church in Bloomington, Illinois, stage each Advent a drive-through nativity in the parking lot of the church. Nine tableaux depict the prophecy preceding Christ, the announcement of his coming to Mary, the birth of Jesus, the baptism of Jesus, Jesus and the children, his miracles, his agony in the garden of Gethsemane, his crucifixion, and the empty tomb. Visitors receive brochures explaining each of the nine scenes and inviting them to Sunday meetings.

LYRICAL PRAISE. "Christmas Around the World," a worship service featuring carols from many nations sung in their original languages, was presented by the chapel choir of the Cumberland Presbyterian Church in Doraville, Georgia.

NATIVITY SCENE. The Christmas Eve worship service of the Rolling Hills Community Center (RCA) in Zellwood, Florida, is held in a local barn lighted by kerosene lanterns and using bales of hay for seating while the Lucan nativity story is reenacted.

PENNY OFFERING. In 1963 an elderly widow, hospitalized at Christmas, sent to the pastor of the Second Presbyterian Church of Waynesboro, Virginia, a box containing pennies she had saved throughout the year for the Christmas offering. When the pastor told his people about her widow's mite, they wished to share in the spirit of her giving, and on the first Sunday in December of each year that followed the members form a procession to the altar where they pour thousands of pennies into a washtub as an act of benevolence and charity. More than 500,000 pennies have been given to date.

CONTINUITY. After Christmas the decorated tree was left in the sanctury of the First Baptist Church in Dearborn, Michigan, until the needles fell. Then the church young people fashioned it into a cross and returned it to the sanctuary for the Good Friday service and left it until Easter when it was decorated with flowers.

SENIOR FELLOWSHIP. Two hundred senior citizens and retired members and friends of the Westminster United Presbyterian Church in Des Moines, Iowa, share lunch on Tuesdays where food and fellowship include devotions, talks on practical topics such as hearing aids, social security, and tax matters, and planning of trips and outings.

NEW YEAR SUGGESTIONS. The Broadway Christian Church in Lexington, Kentucky, begins a new year by making a time and talent stewardship survey and listing church and church-related jobs that need to be done. Commitment forms are provided for members wishing to respond.

The Bay Area Christian Church in Houston, Texas, circulates in January a church calendar which lists under the heading "Live for the Master" thirty-one ideas for developing Christian habits. Typical suggestions: Write at least one encouraging letter. Do something thoughtful for someone you are not particularly fond of. Do something together as a family. Give up a TV program and use the time to do someone else a favor.

The Church of Christ in Fairfield, Ohio, sponsors an outreach program at the beginning of the year in which members make five visits to the homes of the unchurched. Each of the five visits has an individual purpose: (1) Who are you? (2) I want to know you, (3) We want you to know the church, (4) We want you to know Christ, and (5) We want you to accept Christ as your lord and savior.

EUCHARIST FELLOWSHIP. During the past several years nearly 100 members of seventeen denominations in Richmond, Virginia, have met five times annually to celebrate Holy Communion and to come to know and to participate in the Eucharist according to the various traditions represented by those attending.

SECTION XI. *A Little Treasury of Illustrations*

GOD'S ANSWER.   There's a story about St. Theresa of Avila and her relationship with the mother superior of the abbey. Apparently the mother superior, whose power within the abbey was absolute, was being particularly difficult and irksome. Theresa was having a terrible time getting along with her. One evening in her prayers Theresa spoke quite frankly to the Lord. "Lord," she prayed, "if I had my way that woman wouldn't be mother superior here." There was silence. God answered. "Theresa," he said, "if I had my way she wouldn't be either."—Craig Biddle III.

STICKING TOGETHER.   A sailor was fishing with a man who couldn't swim. Late in the afternoon the man who couldn't swim hooked a really big fish. The land lover was so excited about catching this big fish that, as he was reeling it in, he got carried away, leaned too far over, and fell into the water. He was panic-stricken and began to yell, "Help, save me!" So the sailor calmly reached out to grab the man by the hair of the head, pull him over a little closer, and get him into the boat, but as he pulled, the man's toupee came off and he slipped down under again. And he came up again yelling, "Help, save me!" So the sailor reached down again. This time he got an arm. And it came off because it was an artificial limb. The man continued to thrash, sputter, and splash. The sailor grabbed a leg and

pulled it. And it came off. It was a wooden leg. The man continued calling, and the sailor in disgust said, "How can I help you if you won't stick together?"—Joe A. Harding.

JESUS PASSING BY.   When Dick Sheppard left Cambridge around the turn of this century, he went to East London. He described himself as "a rather conceited and bumptious undergraduate" who thought that in a year or so he could do a lot for the working classes. In his zeal to "uplift the masses," as he said, Sheppard began seeing an aged man who lived off Bethnal Green Road in East London—a man whose days often ended in drunkenness. The man's wife was suffering extensively with this burden, and things seemed to be going from bad to worse. As a young theological student, Sheppard talked with this fellow. So did some other student friends. The only result, reported Sheppard, was that "we bored the old gentleman stiff."

Some months later word came that the whole situation was reversed. Drunken degeneration no longer was a problem, and the wife was a happy woman again. The only new element in the picture about which Sheppard knew was the visitation to that household of an elderly clergyman, a Mr. Strickland of Bethnal Green. He was a noticeably unattractive man—at least in Sheppard's mind—and "had no gifts at all" like the young theologians thought they possessed.

Curiosity led Sheppard to call again on the old man who had been unpersuaded by his earlier preachments. Sheppard asked why things were so markedly improved. The answer was simply, "Mr. Strickland used to come round day after day." Sheppard responded, "Mr. Strickland hasn't much to say for himself, has he?" "No," was the reply, "it is quite true he doesn't say much, and sometimes I don't quite know what to say to him, but when he is gone I kind of say to myself that it seems as if Jesus of Nazareth had passed by."—John H. Townsend.

TERRIFIC PITCHER.　A little boy called his dad out into the yard to show the father how far he could hit a baseball. The boy tossed the ball up in the air and took a mighty swing. He missed it completely. "Strike one," he cheerfully called as he retrieved the ball. He tried a second time and missed again. "Strike two!" he called. Once more he tossed it up and swung with all his might. But to no avail. "Strike three. I'm out," he said, with a shrugged shoulder sense of finality. Then, tucking the bat under his arm, he looked up at his Dad and said, "I'm going to be a terrific pitcher!" —Rupert Hoover.

WHAT THE BISHOP SAID.　Handley Moule, an Anglican bishop, was walking down the street one day in his clericals and a little girl, a very zealous Christian no doubt, thought it appropriate to address the bishop. "Bishop," she said, "are you saved?" It's a good question for bishops. And Moule, a godly and kindly man, smiled and said: "My dear friend, might I just inquire a little more exactly as to what it is you are asking me? Are you asking me have I been saved? Or are you asking me shall I yet some day be saved?" That pretty well flustered her. She didn't respond. "Honey," he said, "all three are true. I have been saved, I am being saved, and I shall yet be saved."—David L. Larsen.

MOTHER'S ADVICE.　A little girl had been fighting with her smaller brother all day. When her father came home from work she ran to him, and he picked her up. While hugging her father, she looked over his shoulder at her little brother and stuck out her tongue at him. Watching all this, the mother said, "Honey, you can't love your father and stick out your tongue at your brother!"—Frank Pollard.

ELECTION.　A wise, although not very well-educated, old preacher preached often about predestination and divine election. One day a local politician of some note met him and said to him: "I hear that you preach a lot about predestination and about those who will be the elect to heaven. What about me? Do you think I will be elected to heaven?" To which the preacher replied: "Well, sir, you run for city council, and you got elected. Then you run for mayor, and you got elected to that. Then you run for Congress, and you got elected to that. And now you ask me if I think you might get among the elect for heaven. But I don't see how you can expect to get elected to something that you ain't running for."— Walter Russell Bowie.

PRAYER.　A boy was in an auto accident and prayed, "Dear Lord, may this accident not have happened."

A KNOCK AT THE DOOR.　An old woman was living in dire poverty. She owed more than she could ever pay. Even her rent was overdue. One day there came a knock at the door, but the woman was afraid to answer. The knocking became louder and more urgent. The old woman responded by crawling under the bed in sheer panic. She was afraid it would be the landlord. She was afraid he might dispossess her and that even her bed might be sold to pay her debt.

The knocking persisted, and soon she decided she wouldn't be able to hide forever. So she answered the door. When the old woman opened the door, she stood face to face with a clergyman she knew to be from the parish just down the street. "Hello," the minister said, "I have come to tell you that we heard of your poverty and of your need and found some friends who have paid all of your debt. I have come to give you your receipt and also to offer you assistance any time in the future should you need it."—Arthur McPhee.

SERMON PREPARATION.   After Dwight L. Moody preached a moving sermon on the compassion of Christ, someone asked how he prepared that sermon. Said Moody: "I took up the Bible and began to read it over to find what it said on the compassion of Christ. I prayed over the text as I went along until the thought of his infinite compassion overpowered me, and I could only lie on the floor of my study with my face in my open Bible and cry like a child."

RESCUE.   A World War II aviator was downed in the North Sea in bitter winter weather. Day after day he clung to his safety raft in spite of the winds, the sleet, and the mountain-like waves of that sea of sudden storms and vicious weather. At last he was rescued. When one of his rescuers asked him how he had ever held out for so long under such adverse conditions, he answered, "Well, I could never have done it except for the fact that I knew I was being sought."—Edward C. Dahl.

BUMPER TO BUMPER.   Perhaps many of us feel that our lives are like a steel ball in some giant pinball machine. We get bounced from bumper to bumper, occasionally get in a hole, are ejected, ring a bell here and there, and if we can avoid getting tilted before the game ends we score a few points and then drop harmlessly into the place of all spent steel balls —the grave at the bottom.—Jerry Hayner.

WHY NOT?   The photographer had just taken a picture of an old man on his ninety-eighth birthday. He thanked the old man, saying, "I hope I'll be around to take your picture when you're one hundred." The old man replied: "Why not? You look healthy to me."—*The Cumberland Presbyterian.*

THANKSGIVING.   One stormy Sunday a member of his congregation said, "He'll have nothing to thank God for on a horrible day like this." But when the minister got up, he began his prayer, "We thank thee, O Lord, that it is not always like this."

GIFT OF GOD.   Riches are the least worthy gifts which God can give man, yet men toil for them day and night and take no rest. God frequently gives riches to foolish people to whom he gives nothing else.—Martin Luther.

TWO GAMBLERS.   Two gamblers wanted to break that habit's grip on their lives and are subjected to the temptation to try just one more game. The one man says, "I shall doubtless break down and gamble many times in the future, but tonight I will not." That man will break the habit. The other says, "After tonight I'll never gamble again, but tonight I will gamble for one last time." This man would never kick the habit. He is hopeless.—Søren Kierkegaard.

MELLOWING MOMENTS.   The spectacular rise to artistic prominence and of operatic stardom of a Kansas-born young woman of two or three generations ago— a soprano of unusual talent and promise— followed her debut at the Metropolitan that was almost without parallel in its excitement and its surprise. Her name was Marion Talley. The incomparable Madame Schumann-Heink, though at the end of her own distinguished operatic career, heard that fresh young voice in that memorable debut. When asked by reporters and critics to give her assessment of Miss Talley's triumph and of her operatic potential, Madame Schumann-Heink said: "Miss Talley will be a very great singer after something has happened in her life, something calculated to heighten her sensitivities, broaden her appreciation, and deepen her compassion."—John E. Hines.

INFINITE GRACE.   If we must choose to have vision or merely sight, let us keep our eyes generous for that greatness which once created us and now, if we are willing, will sustain us by nothing less than infinite grace at mountain height or ocean depth. If we have dwelt in the vision of God, then our joy will be an effectual, working power. We will have no orders for the world; no wealth to give it; no rewards to promise it. We have but one thing to give —ourselves; one way to give it—in love; one hope for the giving—that God may be glorified and the world redeemed.—Samuel H. Miller.

SOMEONE TO SING ABOUT.   In the days of the Great Depression, Clarence Darrow, the brilliant attorney, was addressing the members of a black church in Chicago. Most of them were desperately poor, without jobs and without much hope. When Darrow began to speak, he recounted all of their troubles and summed up their woes. Then recalling how they had sung so gloriously, he said: "And yet you sing! No one can sing like you do! What do you have to sing about?" Quick as a flash, a lady in the congregation shouted out, "We've got Jesus to sing about!" One who was there said that Darrow, a nonbeliever, was stopped dead in his tracks. What could he say?—Harold A. Bosley.

INEVITABLE ENCOUNTER.   Legend tells of a strange encounter in the marketplace of Bagdad. The servant of a wealthy merchant was securing provisions for his master when he experienced the most frightening moment of his life. When he raced into the courtyard of his master's house a few minutes later, he was trembling and pale with fright. When the merchant saw his ashen servant, he grabbed him by the shoulders and said, "Tell me quickly, what is wrong?" "Master," said the servant, "I just now have seen Death in the marketplace, and when he saw me, he raised his arm to strike me. Please, master, I am certain he means to take me. Loan me your fastest horse so that I can get away." "But where will you go?" said the merchant. "To Samarra," said the servant. "Death will not find me there." So the merchant gave his servant the fastest horse in the stables, and the servant rode swiftly off to the city of Samarra where he hoped to hide. Then the merchant took up his servant's empty basket and went himself to the marketplace to secure the provisions needed for the household. Sure enough, he too saw Death, so he went to him and said, "Why did you raise your hand to strike my servant here a little while ago?" And Death replied: "Actually I meant him no harm. That was a gesture of surprise. You see, I didn't expect to see him here, for I have an appointment with him tonight in Samarra."—Arthur McPhee.

KNOWING AND LOVING.   We become more human not by producing or consuming but by developing our facilities of knowing and loving. It is normal to suppose that knowledge and love will constitute the essential activities of eternal life. There is no danger that these activities will ever become boring. Those who have experienced authentic love and intellectual achievement know that they can never reach a saturation point. The scientist who consecrates all of his time and energy to research knows that the more he learns the more there is to learn, and the more his appetite for knowledge increases. Likewise those who love truly know that there is no imaginable limit to the growth of their love. And in eternity there will be no obstacles to our appetite for knowledge and love.—Ignace Lepp.

DANGEROUSLY FAITHFUL.   In 1941 a Resistance fighter in France was facing the invasion of his land by Hitler's troops. Tyranny had come, and it looked hopeless for a long time ahead. What should he do? He could come to terms with a tyrant. A good many people were doing that. He could join the underground movement and risk his life. And in that moment he wrote down these words: "This is not a time for me to desert my faith. It is not a time to turn for new images to fit my belief. This is a time for me to be dangerously faithful."—Jerry Hayner.

WHAT NEXT?   It would be better for us to throw away 99 percent of our learning and our tangled philosophy and stick to just one simple thing for our daily life—to keep asking God, "Who needs me next, Father?"—Frank Laubach.

THE RECONCILER.   Her name is Reconciler. She is a rare adhesive owned by the Master Creator-Mender. The Master designed her especially for his most delicate projects. They work side by side creating works of art and mending those masterpieces that are broken in the rush of life.

One day Reconciler became curious about herself and her role in the workshop. "Master," she timidly probed, "why do you always make sure I'm not seen when we mend those china teacups? Don't you think it would be good if others saw me and knew what good work I am doing?"

The Master replied, "I place you where I need you the most. I ask you to do the job you do best. I approve. Isn't that enough reward?"

"O Master, it is! But sometimes I feel so insignificant."

"Reconciler, let me tell you how essential you are to my work. My work of creating and mending could not possibly go on without you. I cannot get in between the broken parts to hold them together except as I place you there to make that bond. Also the jobs where I use you require total self-involvement. I cannot use my other glues which participate half-heartedly. I made you strong so that with you at the center my creations do not fall apart under the stress of everyday use. I don't know what I'd do without you!"—Jeannie Orjala.

HAZARD.   The uninvolved, nonparticipating, and uncommitted life is a hazard to the self and to society. Through involvement, participation, sharing, burdening oneself, communications, and community come health and effectiveness. —Earl Loomis.

WHO MADE THE STARS?   When Napoleon set out on his famous expedition to Egypt, he took along with him a group of scientists, philosophers, and scholars. One night, as they were gathered on the deck of the ship, they looked up at the bright stars in the sky and began a discussion about where the universe came from. Nearly everyone said that natural laws and occurrences alone were enough to account for all that is. There is no need for a creator God, they said. Napoleon had been standing silently nearby. Lifting his hands toward the stars, he said: "Gentlemen, think it over again. Who made these?"—David J. Crawford.

DISCARDED PUTTER.   Before Bobby Jones launched his career as a professional golfer he found an old, abandoned putter. He put it into his golf bag and never gave it another thought. But when he went to Australia for the Australian Golf Tournament his caddy handed it to him as he was about to make a putt. According to the rules a golfer couldn't change clubs after he started to use one. So Jones was stuck with the discard.

He made the putt. And went on to win the tournament with it. He continued to use it while winning the American Invitational and the American Open, the British invitational and the British Open, the Canadian Invitational and the Canadian Open.

The putter can now be seen in a glass case at Georgia Tech next to an editorial from a Georgia newspaper written by Jones entitled, "Be Careful What You Abandon."—Robert Ward in *The Michigan Christian Advocate.*

MEANS OF SERVICE.   Anyone who believes that he has the right to enjoy his wealth as a natural right, simply because it belongs to him according to the law of the land, has no conscience at all. Wealth for the Christian can never be a means of enjoyment but a means of service.—Emil Brunner.

THE WORRY CLUB.   A noted motion picture producer has an interesting way of handling his worries. He decided to do all his worrying on one single day of the week, so he has what he calls his Wednesday Worry Club. If anything worries him on any other day, he writes it down and

puts it in a box to be worried about on
Wednesday. And when he opens the box
on Wednesday, he finds that most of the
things that disturbed him have already
been settled. But a few are still worrisome
—so he puts them back in the box to be
worried about the following Wednesday!
By this whimsical but practical method he
broke his worry habit.—Norman Vincent
Peale.

WORRY FREE.   There are two days in the
week about which I never worry—two
carefree days kept sacredly free from fear
and apprehension. One is yesterday and
the other is tomorrow."—Robert Jones
Burdette.

ACTIVE LISTENING.   Active listening carries its own risk. Something happens to a
person who practices active listening.
When you understand accurately how another person thinks or feels, put yourself
momentarily into the other person's
shoes, see the world as another is seeing it
—you run the risk of having your own
opinions and attitudes changed.—
Thomas Gordon.

ACCEPTANCE.   General Booth wrote a
book that made complacent Englishmen
squirm called *In Darkest England,* in which
he told a story that still disturbs. In London one night a run-away-girl applied for
a night's lodging at a hospice that proclaimed itself a "Home for Fallen
Women." The clerk at the desk took a reg-
istration card and asked the girl's name
and home address, then proceeded to the
next question, "Are you a fallen woman?"
When the girl blushed and looked down at
the floor and explained she wasn't but that
she had no money, the clerk tore up the
card and turned her away saying, "Sorry,
this institution is for fallen women only."
Later she returned and said: "I am now.
Will you take me in now?"—John W. Rilling.

DIALOGUE.   A husband said to his wife,
"I thought you had agreed to forgive and
forget." "Yes," she replied, "but I don't
want you to forget that I have forgiven and
forgotten."

NOT ALONE.   In August of 1914 when
Ernest Shackleton left England on his famous attempt to cross Antarctica, his ship
was crushed in the ice and his whole party
stranded with three small boats. Partly by
sailing and partly by sledding, they
managed to get to Elephant Island at the
mouth of the Weddell Sea. There Shackleton left most of his men with two boats for
shelter while he and two companions
started across nearly 1,000 miles of sea.
His aim was the island of South Georgia
which they managed to hit, though on the
wrong side. Now Shackleton and his companions had to cross an unexplored
mountain range 9,000 feet high. The next
thirty-six hours were terrible. They were
not mountaineers but seamen, yet they
reached the top of the range at the end of
the day. Here they were trapped, for they
could not cut steps down the sheer side of
the cliff. "We'll slide," said Shackleton,
and the three of them sat on their coils of
rope, held fast to each other, and took off
into the darkness. When miraculously they
reached the bottom safely, Shackleton's
only comment was "It's not good to do
that kind of thing too often." Later they
walked into the whaling station they had
been seeking. Shackleton wrote about the
experience and said he had had the curious feeling that there were four men and
not three on the perilous trek. He said
nothing to the other two, but one remarked to him, "Boss, I had the feeling on
the march that there was another person
with us." The third man agreed.—Jack Giguere in *Michigan Christian Advocate.*

CREATIVE FORCE.   Listening is a magnetic and strange thing, a creative force.
The friends who listen to us are the ones
we move toward, and we want to sit in
their radius. When we are listened to, it
creates us and makes us unfold and expand. I discovered this a few years ago.
Before that, when I went to a party, I
would think anxiously: "Now try hard. Be
lively." But now I tell myself to listen with
affection to anyone who talks to me. This

person is showing me his soul. It is a little dry and meager and full of grinding talk just now, but soon he will begin to think. He will show his true self and will be wonderfully alive.—Karl Menninger.

BOUNDARIES.   A farmer was once walking through his fields with a visitor. Spying some thistles in an adjoining field, he crossed the fence and carefully pulled them out. "Is that your field too?" asked the visitor.

"No," answered the farmer. "It belongs to a neighbor."

"Well, then why did you go over and pull his weeds?" the visitor questioned.

"The thistles were about ready to bloom. Once they went to seed, the seed would be blown everywhere. Thistle seeds have no respect for boundary lines," came his reply.—John Wade.

TURNING POINT.   Some years ago Roy Campanella, the baseball player, was left a semi-invalid after an accident. His autobiography tells about a discovery that marked a turning point in his life. He wrote: "The doctors and nurses tried to get me interested in things. They'd turn on the radio and read the sports pages to me. They even bought me a TV set, but I didn't want to watch it. I just lay on my back, my brain full of panic. There were times when I was close to hysterics. I know I cried myself to sleep many a night.

"One day the doctor came in, asked the nurse to leave, and closed the door. I couldn't turn my head. I couldn't see him. But I could tell from the tone of his voice he hadn't come to pass the time of day. He got right to the point. He said he was disappointed in me. He had expected me to put up more of a battle. He told me to stop feeling sorry for myself, that I wasn't the only man who had been hurt. 'Roy,' he said, 'you've got to fight. We can only help you 10 percent. The other 90 percent has got to be your effort.' His lecture shook me up. I had to get hold of myself. All my life whenever I was in trouble, I had turned to God for help. I remembered my Bible and asked the nurse to get it out of the drawer in the night table. I opened it

to the 23rd Psalm: 'Yea, though I walk through the valley of the shadow of death, I will fear no evil; for thou art with me.'

"From that moment on I was on my way back. I knew I was going to make it!"

HEART'S VOICE.   In the early history of Oklahoma when it was still Indian Territory and the painful adjustment of the Indian and the white man was still being worked out, a government agent was addressing a tribal chieftain to arrange a treaty. The official interpreter arose to translate the words to the chief. But the dignified warrior raised his hand for silence and said gruffly, "I shall listen to the man in silence, for my heart can tell whether his heart speaks the truth to match his words."—Bryant Kirkland.

WORTH OF THE CHURCH.   What is it worth to the world to have in it one institution believing in the soul's limitless possibilities, lifting up a challenge and disturbing us with higher dreams, and making us restless and dissatisfied with the life that creeps and crawls?—J. Wallace Hamilton.

COMMITMENT.   It is ever the man who believes in his own idea, who can think and act without a crowd to back him, who is not afraid to stand alone, who is bold, original, and resourceful, who has the courage to go where others have never been, and to do what others have never done that accomplished things that leaves his mark on his time.—Orison S. Marden.

BRIDGE.   A high school student convalescing from serious surgery persisted in asking his mother some difficult and penetrating questions about his future. Seeking to leave the questions open rather than give pessimistic answers or build false hope, the mother often replied, "Well, son, we'll just have to cross that bridge when we get to it." But one day the young man retorted, "But, mother, I want to be sure that the bridge is going to be there when I get to it."—Roy Bassett.

RECITATION.   A famous English actor was being honored with a great banquet at the time of his retirement from public life. After dinner, instead of the usual speeches, he offered to recite any dramatic role that might be requested. There was the usual awkward pause, and an old minister nearby, perhaps to start something, asked him to recite Ps. 23. He thought a moment, and then agreed to do so on one condition that the minister should recite it after him. With some regrets the minister agreed. The actor recited Ps. 23 with all of his power of oratory, and when he had finished there was a great burst of applause. The minister then began slowly, "The Lord is my shepherd; I shall not want." When he finished there was no applause, but the story says that some eyes were moist and some heads were bowed. The actor, quickly sensing the situation, put his hand on the minister's shoulder and said to the crowd: "I appealed to your hearts. I know the Twenty-third Psalm, but this man knows the Shepherd."—J. Walter Malone.

THE   DIFFERENCE.   Two preachers preached the same message in the same church in successive pastorates. Both told their congregations that they were living a life that was leading them straight to hell. One minister encountered stubborn opposition to his preaching while the other was able to help enlist change in the lives of his people. The difference? The one said they were going to hell and it gave him a thrill to be the one to tell them, while the second, in sharing the same message, let it be known that it broke his heart. —George H. Freeman.

ALL PERVADING.   Beauty is all-pervading presence. It unfolds in the numberless flowers of the spring, it waves in the branches of the trees and in the green blades of summer grass, it haunts the depths of the earth and the sea, and it gleams out in the hues of the shell and the precious stone.—William Ellery Channing.

SEPARATED PARTNERS.   Gilbert and Sullivan were two talented Englishmen who wrote delightful light operas, but they both were far too sensitive for their own good. Once Sullivan ordered a new carpet for a theater they had bought. When Gilbert saw the bill, he became outraged. He thought it was far too expensive. One thing led to another until they wound up in court. Consequently they never spoke to one another again. When Sullivan wrote the music for a new production, he mailed it to Gilbert. When Gilbert wrote the words, he mailed them to Sullivan. Once when they had to make a curtain call together, they stood as far apart on the stage as possible.—Charles E. Ferrell.

RESTRAINT.   A seven-year-old boy was sitting on a fence and looking at his neighbor's heavily-laden apple tree. The neighbor came out of his house and called: "Johnny, are you trying to steal one of my apples?" "No, sir," he said, "I'm trying not to."—Frank Pollard.

WHAT LINCOLN SAID.   During the early days of the War Between the States, Dr. Sunderland, who was the pastor of the New York Avenue Presbyterian Church in Washington, advised his congregation one Sunday morning that church would be closed to worship because, he said, it had been commandeered by the government for hospital purposes. President Lincoln was in the congregation that morning. He arose in his place and said: "Dr. Sunderland, that order was issued without my knowledge. I rescind it. We need to keep the churches open to keep the stars shining in our sky."—John E. Hines.

NEAREST THINGS.   The best things are nearest, breath in your nostrils, light in your eyes, flowers at your feet, duties at your hand, the path of God just before you. Then do not grasp at the stars but do life's plain, common work as it comes, certain that daily duties and daily bread are the sweetest things of life.—Robert Louis Stevenson.

DARING.   One must have the adventurous daring to accept oneself as a bundle of possibilities and undertake the most interesting game in the world—making the most of one's best.—Harry Emerson Fosdick.

KNOWING THE COLONEL.   "What is God like?" G.A. Studdert-Kennedy, an English chaplain in World War I, said that after three years in the trenches he had decided that this was life's basic question, the one that matters most. He recalls that when he first went to France, before he had experienced the agony of battle and the horror of war, he went to visit a wounded officer in the base hospital. The conversation turned almost immediately to religion. "What I want to know, Padre, is, 'What is God like?' I never thought about it much before the war. I took the world for granted. I was not religious, though I was confirmed and went to communion sometimes with my wife. But now it is different. I have come to realize that I am a member of the human race with a duty toward it, and that makes me want to know what God is like. When I'm transferred to a new battalion, I want to know what the Colonel is like. He bosses the show, and it makes a lot of difference to me what sort of chap he is. Now I'm in the battalion of humanity. I want to know what the Colonel of this world is like. That is your business, Padre. You ought to know."

KINGDOM SERVICE.   To care for a little child or for one who like a child needs our sympathy, our protection, our guidance, and our help is really to do a great thing, so great indeed that to do so in the name of Christ and for the sake of Christ is really to render the service of Christ. It is even more, if more can be; it is to render a service directly to God, for Jesus adds, "Whoever receives me, receives him that sent me." True greatness in the kingdom of God consists not in attaining the first place in the notice and praise of the world nor in being served by many but in being willing to stoop down to a humble place not for the sake of self-effacement nor in timid diffidence but in order to serve others for the sake of Christ.—Charles R. Erdman.

ABILITY TO SEE.   Children often have the ability to see beauty that escapes us, for they still "dream with their eyes open." After a rain a little girl said to her mother, "Oh, look, mummy, there's a rainbow in the gutter!" "That's not a rainbow, silly," her mother corrected her. "That's a dirty oil slick."—Eileen Mears.

IDEALS.   The power of ideals is incalculable. We see no power in a drop of water. But let it get into a crack in the rock and be turned to ice, and it splits the rock; turned into steam, it drives the pistons of the most powerful engine. Something has happened to it which makes active and effective the power that is latent in it.—Albert Schweitzer.

HEARING AND LISTENING.   Larry Warberg suggests that preachers ought to say to their congregations, "Before I start my message, I want all of you to put a finger in one ear." The idea is to keep what a person hears from escaping through the other ear. Jesus said about the same thing in Luke 8:18, "Take heed therefore how ye hear." This is because a person can hear without understanding. But he also can hear without hearing. "Hearing they hear not" is the way the Bible expresses it. So how do you hear? How do you listen? —Raymond L. Cox in *The War Cry*.

PRAYERS AND ARMIES.   Mary, Queen of Scots, was heard to say she feared the prayers of John Knox more than the armies of England. This may be one of the reasons his parishioners declared: "John Knox can put more spirit into us than 500 trumpets blowing at once."

IN CHURCH.   Here we may be cast down, but we praise God. Here we may be lost in darkness and confusion, but we praise God. We may not know all the answers to all the fears and tragedies that overwhelm us, but we praise God. We stand in the midst of troubled times. We do not know what the morrow will bring forth, for we are not prophets nor the sons of prophets, but we praise God. We have found in our lives mysteries we cannot understand, problems we have not solved, difficulties that irk us and irritate us, but we praise God. We are buffeted about by all kinds of pains of body and mind and spirit, and yet we lift up our souls and we praise God.—Samuel H. Miller.

BEYOND TRADITION.   The crisis of faith in the present time cannot be answered by a servile repetition of the faith and practice of the past. The best service that can be rendered the universal church and the Reformed community is to bring to the task today the same intellectual labor, the same moral integrity, and the same vision and imagination that have served the tradition in the past.—John H. Leith.

TWO WORDS.   A young man came for an interview with a bank president.
   "Tell me, sir, how did you become so successful?"
   "Two words."
   "And what are they, sir?"
   "Right decisions."
   "How do you make right decisions?"
   "One word—experience."
   "And how do you get experience?"
   "Two words."
   "And what are they?"
   "Wrong decisions!"—Biblical Recorder.

SELF-LOVE.   The remarkable thing is that we really love our neighbor as ourselves and do unto others as we do unto ourselves. We hate others when we hate ourselves. We are tolerant toward others when we tolerate ourselves. We forgive others when we forgive ourselves. It is not love of self but hatred of self which is the root of the troubles that afflict our world.—Eric Hoffer.

REVERENT SPEED.   During the London blitz the nave of Westminster Cathedral displayed this sign: "In the event of trouble, parishioners will descend to the crypts with all due reverent speed."—James A. Lollis.

OUT OF DARKNESS.   One day Tchaikovsky wrote to a friend, "My faith in myself is shattered and it seems that my role is ended." He suffered through a loss of confidence in himself. His hypersensitive nature was ready to surrender to all the painful blows that life had inflicted upon him. Out of the darkness that closed in upon him, he recorded musical notes. The ashes of his disappointment became Symphony No. 6, in B Minor, the "Pathetique." This symphony expresses the poignant, soul-searching lament of a wounded spirit, and it could never have been composed had the composer never suffered.—Robert N. DuBose.

NOTHING HAPPENS.   A young man went to Horatio Bonar one day and said, "Dr. Bonar, I love to preach, but nothing happens when I preach." Dr. Bonar is reported to have turned to the young man and said, "But, young man, do you love people?"—Lloyd Perry in Christianity Today.

THE STILL.   In the British Navy when there is a disaster aboard ship, a special signal is sounded. This signal is called "the still."
   "The still" is a whistle which calls the crew to a moment of silence at the time of the crisis. With the sounding of "the still," every man on the ship is to stop for a moment and consider, "What is the wise thing for me to do in this situation."
   Aboard ship, this moment for calm thinking has prevented possible catastrophe and foolish actions.—Lee Prince in Baptist and Reflector.

LOOKING ON.   A dear old preacher labored late one night on a sermon to be given next day to a handful of parishioners. His wife said: "Dear, why do you work so hard on your message? Only a few will hear it." "You forget, my dear," he replied, "how large my audience will be!" Nothing is trivial here if heaven looks on. We shall play a better game if, "seeing we are encompassed," we remember who is in the grandstand!—Vance Havner.

COMMITMENT TO RIGHT. The church's ability to affect public affairs depends less on pronouncements from headquarters than on the Christian understanding of its people and the people's willingness to use their political and economic power as citizens. Unless we know what is right and are committed to it, we cannot act effectively to do the right.—Arnie Sovik.

WARTIME MESSAGE. I have struggled against facts and experience on behalf of belief in the good and the true. At the present time, when violence dominates the world more cruelly than it ever has before, I still remain convinced that truth, love, peaceableness, meekness, and kindness are the strength that can master all violence. The world will be theirs as soon as a sufficient number of persons with purity of heart, with strength and perseverance think and live out the thoughts of truth and love, of mercy and peaceableness.—Albert Schweitzer.

CONDITIONING. Lord Joseph Duveen, American head of the art firm that bore his name, planned in 1915 to send one of his experts to England to examine some ancient pottery. He booked passage on the *Lusitania.* Then the German Embassy issued a warning that the liner might be torpedoed. Duveen wanted to call off the trip. "I can't take the risk of your being killed," he said to his young expert.

"Don't worry," the man replied. "I'm a strong swimmer, and when I read what was happening in the Atlantic, I began hardening myself by spending time every day in a tub of ice water. At first I could stand it only a few minutes, but this morning I stayed in that tub nearly two hours."

Duveen laughed. It sounded preposterous. But his expert sailed; the *Lusitania* was torpedoed. The young man was rescued after nearly five hours in the chilly ocean, still in excellent condition.—Vernon C. Grounds in *Christianity Today.*

THE WAY. An American aviator had to parachute into a jungle in Burma. A Burmese came along, slashing his way through with his machete, trying to get the American airman out. The American was scared to death, afraid he was going to be captured by the guerrillas. And he yelled out: "Where is the way? Where is the road?" And the Burmese, in broken English, turned to him and said: "I'm the way. Follow me." And he got him out.— Billy Graham.

WINDS OF GOD. Above the doorway that leads into the divinity school building at Duke University is a stone carving of a ship's hull sailing on restless waves. The ship's mast, maintaining balance and proportion, is the cross. Mankind today is adrift on perilous seas, and we are not promised favorable winds and a fair voyage. But with the cross as our mast, with a faith to hoist the sails, and with a courage to lose the land we know for greater knowing, I believe the winds of God will blow. —John W. Carlton in *Western Recorder.*

ALMIGHTY'S SHADOW. Once when Martin Luther felt very despondent, he heard a bird singing its evening song. Then he saw it tuck its head under its wings and go to sleep. He remarked: "This little bird has had its supper and now is getting ready to go to sleep, quite content, never troubling itself as to what its food will be or where it will lodge on the morrow. Like David, it abides under the shadow of the Almighty. It sits on its little twig content and lets God care."

SHORT OF HELP. When a man and his wife both passed away, they took different routes to their destiny. The wife got to heaven and immediately called her husband on the telephone.

"How do you like it down there?" she asked.

"Fine," was the husband's reply. "All we have to do is wear a red suit with horns and every now and then shovel coal on the fire. We don't work more than two hours a day. Tell me, how is it up there?"

"My goodness," said the wife, "we have to get up at four in the morning and gather in the stars. Then we have to haul in the moon and hang out the sun. And we roll clouds around all day long."

"How come you have to work so hard?" asked the husband.

"Well, to tell the truth," said the wife, "we're awfully short of help up here."—James N. Criffith.

UNSHAKEN.   To assume that contemporary paganism can succeed in a task in which the worst of Roman emperors and the most corrupt of popes failed is to take ourselves altogether too seriously. The best reason to conclude that the Christian faith will survive the challenges of our generation is that it has survived far harder challenges not for a short period but for centuries.—Elton Trueblood.

4000 SUNDAYS.   Leslie D. Weatherhead told of a dying man who was frightened and sent for him. "When, as tenderly as I could, I tried to talk to him about God and religion and the soul, he said very bitterly and brokenly: 'I have led a very busy life. I have never had time for that sort of thing!' But he'd had 4,000 Sundays."

FEARFUL CROSSING.   During the westward migration of our nation in the nineteenth century a pioneer reached the banks of the mighty Mississippi River in the early winter when ice covered its surface. Because he didn't know how thick the ice was, he hesitated a long time about crossing over. But night was approaching, and he had to reach the other side before dark. Finally, with fear and anxiety, he crept out on his hands and knees to distribute his weight more evenly. When he had crawled about half-way across the river, he heard singing behind him. There in the gathering dark was a man driving a four-horse load of coal across the ice, singing as he went. He knew that the ice was thick enough to support tons of weight.—Marshall F. Mouney.

CHALLENGE.   As I look over the drama of history, I find amid the apparent chaos evidence of law and plan and immense achievement of the human spirit in spite of disasters. I am convinced that the world is not a mere bog in which men and women trample themselves in the mire and die.

Something magnificent is taking place here amid the cruelties and tragedies, and the supreme challenge to intelligence is the challenge to make the noblest and best in our curious heritage to triumph and prevail.—Charles A. Beard.

ALONE.   He was left alone without the slightest pity or understanding on the part of man. Indeed, what a solitude was his at that moment, a loneliness full of grief in the horror of the night! It is noteworthy that at this point the historical record for the first time registers a complaint on the part of Jesus, as if his pain had become too great for him to bear: "My soul is sorrowful, even unto death." For the first time also we see him seeking the companionship and comfort of men, but this is denied him. His disciples continue to sleep.—Emile Cailliet.

DOING GOD'S WILL.   The Christian should not ask the question, "What ought I do?" unless he has first decided that he will do the will of God before he knows what that will is. He must be willing to do God's will whether or not he likes it and whether or not it seems suitable and expedient. Indeed, doing the right thing may be costly, and to the coldly calculating mind it may appear to be the height of foolishness. But the "foolishness" of God is wiser than the wisdom of men, and what does not make sense to the world makes a great deal of sense in the kingdom of God. —Harold Lindsell.

RESPONSE.   When a friend made a trip to Boston, she stayed in an old mansion that had been converted for tourists. When Mary Lou settled her bill, the manager asked, "Did you enjoy your stay?" Mary Lou replied, "Oh, yes, but I didn't expect such warmth and love from people I don't even know." The manager smiled. "Do you know why you found it like that?" Shaking her head, Mary Lou said, "No, why?" "Because," said the manager, "they responded to the love you gave to them." —Gerri Hearn in *Decision.*

WHERE YOU ARE.   A ship-wrecked crew was dying of thirst under a tropical sun. Suddenly another boat was sighted, and the crewman raised their pitiful plea, "Send us water or we die." The reply came back, "Dip down where you are." Thinking they had been misunderstood, the bewildered crew again appealed for water. Once more came the reply, "Dip down where you are." Reluctantly the men let down a pail, fully convinced they were being mocked. But they drew up fresh water! They were at the mouth of the Amazon River and did not know it. Life for them consisted in dipping down into the fresh living waters right where they were. —Arthur Brown.

MOSES AND THE BEGGAR.   An ancient story tells of a beggar who came to Moses and asked for bread.

"Come into my tent," said Moses, "and you shall eat with me."

The beggar entered the tent, and Moses set out food for both of them. Before eating, Moses gave praises to God. The beggar did not do so. He watched in silence while Moses gave thanks.

"Why do you not praise God?" asked Moses.

"Why should I praise God?" asked the beggar. "What has he done for me? Why has he allowed me to be so poor?"

Hearing these words, Moses became very angry. He picked up his staff and beat the beggar, chasing him from the tent without food.

When the beggar had gone, God came to Moses and said, "Moses, why did you not feed the beggar, and why did you beat him?"

"Because he would not praise you, Lord," said Moses, feeling very righteous.

"Moses," said God, "that man has not praised me for twenty years, and he is still alive. He has not praised me because during all that time you have neglected him. He is alive at all only because I am less religious than you are and have not allowed him to perish. And it seems to me, Moses, that if I were as religious as you appear to be, there would be no one left alive on the earth."—Bert Van Soest.

VICIOUS CIRCLE.   When one tries to change institutions without having changed the nature of men, that unchanged nature will soon resurrect those institutions. Here was the old vicious circle; men form institutions, and institutions form men; where could change break into this ring?—Will Durant.

RESPONSIBILITY.   Basically love means that life has no meaning except in terms of responsibility—responsibility toward our family, toward our nation, toward our civilization, and now, by the pressures of history, toward the universe of humankind which includes our enemies.—Reinhold Niebuhr.

FAITHFULNESS.   I cannot find in any of Paul's letters a single word which lays on the churches the task of evangelism. There is never anything remotely resembling a pep talk about their duty to be more vigorous in their efforts to spread the gospel. The emphasis all the time is upon faithfulness to Christ. That is what is required, and by that standard we shall all be judged at the last day. But the final outcome, the triumph of God's reign, is not in the hands of the church. It is entirely in God's hands. On that subject optimism and pessimism would be equally irrelevant.—Lesslie Newbigin.

CHANGED LIFE.   I came to Africa because I wanted my life to be my argument. I didn't want my ideas to become an end in themselves. Those ideas took hold of me and changed my life. To be a follower of Christ may well sweep a person into an entirely new course of life.—Albert Schweitzer.

LETTER TO MOTHER.   At a time of a great family crisis, a little boy of five who was parted from his mother sat quietly coloring a sheet of white paper. "What are you doing?" his grandmother asked. "I am writing a letter to mother," he replied. Not wanting to doubt his skills, she asked, "What are you saying to her?" The boy looked up as if it were perfectly plain. "She'll know," he commented. "It says, 'I love you; I made it for you; I made it myself.' " And with the confident knowledge that that settled it, he asked for an envelope.—Winifred Waltner in *The Upper Room.*

INCREDIBLE LOVE.   In John Gardner's short story, "Pastoral Care," the hero is a free-wheeling minister who has perhaps more courage than he has discretion. At one point he tells his people: "Cheer up, God loves you! Crazy as it seems."

PARTIAL BAPTISM.   Among the Franks whole armies were sometimes given baptism at one stroke, and many warriors went into the water with their right hands held high, so that they did not get wet. Then they could say, "This hand has never been baptized," and they could swing their battle axes just as freely as ever. The modern counterpart is seen in many people who have been baptized—all except their pocketbooks. They hold these high out of the water.—Halford E. Luccock.

RECURRING MOTIF.   To the early Christians the image of the good shepherd was everywhere. Fresco paintings of the good shepherd have been discovered in the catacombs where the early Christians were buried, dating back to the third century. Statues of the good shepherd, like the one in the Vatican Museum, have been unearthed in the fourth and fifth century churches throughout the length and breadth of Italy. Chalices, glassware, and medals embossed with the good shepherd image belonging to the sixth and seventh centuries have been discovered by Christian archeologists. Early Christian mosaics of the good shepherd were created in baptistries from Venice and Ravenna in the north to Naples and Brindisi in the south. They all show the good shepherd, staff in hand, with a lamb nestled on his shoulders.—Robert McEniry in *Pastoral Life.*

SPEAKING OF GOD.   Until the angels come down with a heavenly dictionary, we have no words but human words, picture words, and partial words with which to speak of God. Pity the poor preacher who

has to stand in a pulpit talking to men about God. See the little man with a yardstick trying to measure the horizons.—J. Wallace Hamilton.

STORM CLOUDS.   One day in India an eagle soared overhead, taking advantage of the rising air currents from the warm earth below. Then a strong wind began to blow, the sky grew dark, and in the distance a threatening storm cloud began to make its way across the land. At first the eagle flew away from the storm, as though in fear of it. Suddenly the eagle turned and drove directly toward the storm. Then, arching its wings against the force of the onrushing wind, he was vaulted upward, higher and higher, until at last he could be seen soaring in the calm air above the storm. We cannot escape the storm clouds of life, but we can learn how to face them. We do so not by running from them but by confronting them in the strength of our Lord.—E. Stanley Jones.

VISION OF POSSIBILITIES.   More than 100 years ago, when settlers were making their way across the flat, cactus-covered land which is now the state of Arizona, they came upon the ruins of an ancient civilization. Towering above the plain were the ruins of a building which now bears the name of Casa Grande—the Great Castle. Around it were the adobe foundations of smaller buildings which probably had served as houses for small industries. There were also the outlines of old canals which may have served as irrigation ditches. It was later learned that about the year 600 or 700 A.D. there had been an Indian community in this place. Probably having migrated from Mexico, these people had established what was undoubtedly a thriving community, using water from the nearby mountains to irrigate the soil and grow their food.

Then something happened. We can only speculate about it, but some suggest that these people did not know how to leach the soil and that eventually it became sour and would no longer produce crops. Others say these folk were overtaken by disease, and still others speculate that they were annihilated by enemy tribes. In any case, by the middle of the last century, only the bare outline of their community remained.

Coming upon these ruins, the pioneers caught a vision of the possibilities. They reasoned that if the Indians had once found it possible to live there, they could live there too. Having seen the lush grass springing up wherever the mountain streams overflowed, they determined to make their channels for irrigation that they might make the desert to bloom. They said, "We shall call this place Phoenix, for like the legendary bird which rose from the ashes, we shall bring life from this place of seeming death." Today fruit, grains, and vegetables grow in abundance on the very soil which was once barren desert.—Homer J. R. Elford.

MORNING PRAYER.   Who can tell what a day may bring forth? Cause us therefore, gracious God, to live every day as if it were to be our last, for that we know not but it may be such.—Thomas à Kempis.

HIS LOVE.   Love is Jesus holding little children close to him and saying, "Of such is the kingdom of God."

Love is Jesus standing beside a tomb weeping with Mary and Martha.

Love is Jesus saying to an adulteress, "I do not condemn you, go and sin no more."

Love is Jesus touching a leper and making him clean.

Love is described by Jesus in the story of a Samaritan who crossed over to the other side of the road to help and to heal an injured person.

Love is Jesus going home to dine with a despised tax collector named Zaccheus and by friendship with him transforming him from one mastered by greed to one mastered by grace.

Love is Jesus driving from the temple those who would profane the sacred things of God and take advantage of other persons.

Love is Jesus with a cup and loaf in his hand saying, "This is my body . . . this is my blood."

Love is Jesus praying from the cross, "Father, forgive them."

Love is the resurrected Christ saying to his followers, "Go make disciples . . . and lo, I am with you."—C. P. Minnick, Jr.

GOD'S BUSINESS.   In George Bernard Shaw's play *Saint Joan of Arc*, Charles Dauphin complains to the importunate and mystical Joan: "I don't want to be any of these fine things you all have your heads full of. I want to be just what I am. Why can't you mind your business and let me mind mine?" Joan replies contemptuously: "Minding your own business is like minding your own body—it's the shortest way to make you sick. What is my business? Helping mother at home. What is thine? Patting lap-dogs and sucking sugar sticks. I tell thee it is God's business we are here to do—not our own. I have a message for thee from God; and thou must listen to it, though thy heart break with the terror of it."

FREEDOM IN PRISON.   The dreaded knock on the door came in the middle of the night. Hans Lilje knew quite well what it must be. He rose, dressed, and said a quick, tearful goodbye to his wife. Then he accompanied the Gestapo to prison. The only "crime" of this Lutheran pastor was that he had preached the gospel in ways the implications of which had been strongly displeasing to Hitler.

For months he was in prison. He was repeatedly interrogated, harassed, beaten, and tortured. As the bombings by the allies grew more and more frequent and severe, the hatred of his Nazi guards became more and more evident.

Yet, Lilje later wrote, he realized that in a larger sense he, not his guards, had freedom. High above them the war was being fought, and their leader was losing. Higher yet, he knew, God was sure to win in the cosmic battle. In the fullest sense Lilje was secure. But these frightened Nazis were bound by terror and hatred. And he wrote, "Even chained hands can pray."—William M. Ramsay.

COME FURTHER. One morning Alexander Whyte noticed a celebrated Scottish scientist sitting in the congregation. He got quite a thrill when the great scientist appeared again the following Sunday. Dr. Whyte thought he would take advantage of this new and distinguished listener, so he prepared six sermons on "Religion and Science," thinking to himself, "These may win him to membership." Dr. Whyte worked carefully through the sermons, proving conclusively that there was no real conflict between sound science and true religion, and the great scientist came Sunday after Sunday and heard them all. Nothing could have exceeded Dr. Whyte's delight when the scientist said, "I want to join your church." Said Dr. Whyte: "I am glad about this. Will you please tell me which of my sermons it was that brought you finally to the point of seeking membership?" "Oh," said the scientist, "it wasn't one of your sermons at all." Dr. Whyte's face fell. "Well, what has happened?" he asked. "One snowy morning," said the scientist, "I was leaving the church and walking down the steps when a dear old lady put her hand on my arm and said, 'Would you please help me down the steps? I find them a little treacherous in this weather.' When we reached the bottom of the steps, she said, 'I expect you are a follower of Jesus Christ, aren't you?' I replied, 'Well, I am interested.' Then," said the scientist, "the old lady looked up into my face and smiled a lovely, radiant smile and said: 'Oh, do come in further than that. Jesus Christ means everything to me.' Then," added the scientist, "I realized that I should never find the way through your arguments, sound as they are, but that I could find the way through experience. When I saw the light in her face, I knew that she was living in a different world from me."—Leslie D. Weatherhead.

DEEPEST FAITH. I do not know where this truth hits you, but for myself, now in my elder years, I bear witness. My deepest faith in God springs not so much from my Galilees where "God clothed the lilies so that Solomon in all his glory was not arrayed like one of them" but from the times when "the rains came down, the floods rose, and the wind blew."—Harry Emerson Fosdick.

HOLY CALLING. A saint is not so much a man who realizes that he possesses virtue and sanctity as one who is overwhelmed by the sanctity of God. God is holiness. And things are holy in proportion as they share what he is. All creatures are holy insofar as they share in his being, but men are called to be holy in a far superior way—by somehow sharing his transcendence and rising above the level of everything that is not God.—Thomas Merton.

THE MONK'S SURPRISES. A medieval monk said that everyone who gets to heaven will be surprised by three things: First, he will be surprised to see many he did not think would be there. Second, he will be surprised that some are not there whom he had expected to see. Third, he will be surprised that he himself is there. —Gerald Kennedy.

LEGACY. We have not completely fulfilled our responsibility as parents until we bequeath to our children a love of books, a thirst for knowledge, a hunger for righteousness, an awareness of beauty, a memory of kindness, an understanding of loyalty, a vision of greatness, and a good name.—William Arthur Ward.

JESUS ONLY. At a Lenten program a famous minister known for his great presence in the pulpit, for his good voice, and for his clarity of thought rose from his prayers as the sermon was about to end. With robes flowing, he ascended the pulpit stairs and prepared to preach the word of God.

But there was one small thing that no one had told him. This great church had a tradition. Whenever anyone entered the pulpit, the first words the preacher would read were inscribed in bold letters across the lectern: "Sir, we would see Jesus."

The congregation was not interested in seeing a grand person with a great reputation, they were not interested in hearing phrases neatly turned out and skillfully presented, and they were not interested in being wooed from the pulpit. They came to church to see Jesus.—Craig Biddle III.

SPIRITUAL CATCH 22.   A book written some twenty years ago was called *Catch-22*. It ran like this: You can't get out of the army unless you are crazy, but those who are crazy want to stay in and keep killing people. You have to be sane to want to get out, but you have to be crazy to get out. So it was Catch-22. There seems to be a similar catch in Christianity. You must repent and believe, but you cannot believe until you have repented and you cannot repent until you have believed. It is a spiritual Catch-22. How do we let loose jealousy before we have love, self-control, gentleness, and joy? How can we receive the joy and love when our hearts are too full of anger, idolatry, and resentment?—C. Fitz-Simmons Allison.

ALL FOR ALL.   I have said to thee many times before, and yet I say to thee again: Forsake thyself and resign thyself wholly to Me, and thou shalt have great inward peace in Me. Give all for all, and nothing keep to thyself of thine own will, but stand purely and stably in Me and thou shalt be so free in heart and soul that neither darkness of conscience nor thraldom of sin shall ever have power in thee.—Thomas à Kempis.

PRIVATE ENTRY.   In Bruges, Belgium, is a beautiful cathedral, the Church of Our Lady. The guide tells an interesting story about a balcony on one of the walls near the high altar. The balcony was built for the benefit of Louis de Grotehuis, who lived next door in a great mansion. He had a door cut in the wall of the cathedral behind the balcony and then a passageway built to his house. In this way he could secretly enter the church and witness the service from behind a screen. Thus he did not have to have any contact with the common people who worshiped in the nave below.—John Wade.

WE ARE THE CHURCH.   We are called to be the people of God who transcend the centuries, nations, races, and languages of humankind.

We are witnesses to the love of God.

We are called to participate in the creation of a world that promotes justice for all, relieves misery, and reconciles the estranged.

We are a worshiping and celebrating community in the presence of God.

We are a mutual support system.

We are the glue that helps hold a fragmented world together.

We are a reservoir and conserver of the faith.

We are a nurturing community for new generations—for any who are seeking faith.

We are enablers called to assist and strengthen one another to use our differing gifts for others.

We produce prophets, often to our chagrin.

We are an instrument of God for the accomplishment of his will.

We reflect the political, economic, and cultural systems of which we are a part.

We are frequently part of the problem of a given society, but more often we have much to say about the solution.

We have thrived or survived in the midst of every kind of political, economic, and social order devised by men and women.

We are a channel and source of strength to those who gather with us and a witness, conscience, and servant to those who do not.

We are called to be one people so that the world may believe.—Donald O. Newby.

OPEN DOORS.   The church proclaims the world's highest standard of morality and expects its members to uphold this standard. Yet its doors are open wide to men and women who know themselves to be sinners. It is the one fellowship in the world which admits men and women to membership for the one reason that they are needy sinners.—Merrill R. Abbey.

POLITICAL ARENA.   You may say, "Don't let the church get into politics." If you do say that, you are saying: "Don't get the church into the world. Let's be another distraction from reality." This world is political. Politics understood for what it really is today has to do with the decisions men make which determine how they shall live and how they shall die. They are not living very well, and they are not going to die very well either. Politics is now the locale of morality. It is the locale both of evil and good. If you do not get the church into the moral issues of politics, you cannot confront evil and you cannot work for good. You will be a subordinate amusement and a political satrap of whatever is going on. You will be the great Christian joke.—C. Wright Mills.

SYMBOLIC.   During World War II Viscount Halifax wrote from London that before the war St. Paul's Cathedral was hemmed in by offices, shops, and commercial buildings. "But," he said, "all these have crumbled now into dust and ashes under Nazi bombs. However, St. Paul's stands, as it should stand and as its builder wished it to stand—clear, majestic, its great cross of gold above the city, sharp cut against the sky." He added: "Surely there is something symbolic about that. A great deal we thought of value is gone, but we have found again something that is best of all and that matters most." Like a London which was struck down but not destroyed, as we live through trouble, such as sorrow, we can invariably find that which is best of all and which matters most. We may be struck down, but we need not be destroyed.

SUMMARY.   Anatole France has a parable about a king who in his youth desired to possess a survey of the universal history of mankind that he might, as he said at that time, learn its lessons. At the end of twenty years his learned men brought him a dozen camels, each bearing five hundred volumes of their work. But the busy king said, "Kindly abridge," and sent them back to their task. After a long period of time they brought to the king a smaller edition of their work, only to be met with the identical request, "Kindly abridge," until at last his secretary brought to the king only one volume—but still a very formidable one—only to find the king on his deathbed. As the now aged, failing king eyed the massive volume, he sighed and said, "Alas, I shall die without knowing the history of mankind." "Your majesty," said the scholar, "I will summarize it for you in three phrases, 'Men are born, they suffer, and they die.' "—John E. Hines.

QUESTION.   Charlie Brown and Peppermint Patty are seated under a tree when she asks with a sigh, "Do you know any good rules for living, Chuck?" Charlie gives this advice: "Keep the ball low. Don't leave your crayons in the sun. Use dental floss every day. Don't spill the shoe polish. Always knock before entering. Don't let the ants get in the sugar. Always get your first serve in." Mystified, Pattie asks, "Will those rules give me a better life, Chuck?"

CREDO.   As I sit in the study on a beautiful, cool August afternoon, I look back with many thanks. It has been a great run. I wouldn't have missed it for anything. Much could and should have been better, and I have by no means done what I should have done with all that I have been given. But the overall experience of being alive has been a thrilling experience. I believe that death is a doorway to more of it and clearer, cleaner, better with more of the secret opened than locked.—Samuel M. Shoemaker.

THINGS REMEMBERED.   It's interesting when you look back at hundreds of dying patients—young and old. Not one of them has ever told me how many houses she had or how many handbags or sable coats. What they tell you are very tiny, almost insignificant moments in their lives— where they went fishing with a child or they tell of mountain climbing trips in Switzerland. Some brief moments of privacy in an interpersonal relationship. These are the things that keep people going at the end. They remember little moments that they have long forgotten, and they suddenly have a smile on their faces. And they begin to reminisce about little joys that make their whole lives meaningful and worthwhile. I never understood in forty years what the church tried to teach—that there is a meaning in suffering—until I found myself in this situation.—Elisabeth Kübler-Ross.

PRAYER.   O Lord, support us all the day long of this troublous life until the shadows lengthen and the evening comes and the busy world is hushed and the fever of life is over and our work is done. Then, Lord, of thy mercy, grant us a safe lodging and a holy rest and peace at the last.—John Henry Newman.

EPITAPH.   Ruth Graham, the wife of Billy Graham, says that when she dies she would like to have the words of a sign she saw along a stretch of highway where construction was underway to be placed on her tombstone. It read: "End of construction. Thank you for your patience."

INVESTMENT IN HUMANITY.   Leland Stanford lost his only son. It was a crushing blow. "I have nothing to live for," he said mournfully. He thought he might find satisfaction in building himself an expensive new home. It cost a million dollars. But it did not bring much comfort to him. One night he had a dream. He saw his son coming to him and saying: "Father, never say again that you have nothing to live for. Live for humanity. Live for other people's children." That was the message Stanford needed to hear. He built Stanford University at an initial cost of twenty million dollars. He and his wife became servants of the poor and the suffering. They left all of their property to go on doing good for the rising generation.—Charles E. Ferrell.

SURRENDER.   Faith means being seized by a power that is greater than we are, a power that shakes us and turns us and transforms us and heals us. Surrender to that power is called faith.—Paul Tillich.

INTO HISTORY.   If a thousand Christs had been crucified and no one said anything about, what use would that have been? We must draw this deed into history and divulge it to the whole world.—Martin Luther.

TEMPTED.   A little boy was told by his father to remain in the yard. But before long some of the boy's friends came by and enticed him to go with them to a playground several blocks away. Soon the father discovered that he was missing and, cutting a switch, went to find him. After the switch had been appropriately applied, the father asked his son why he disobeyed.

Remembering his Sunday school lesson, he replied, "Dad, I was tempted to disobey by the other boys."

"Well, then," responded the father, "why didn't you turn a deaf ear to the temptation?"

"But, dad," protested the boy, "I don't have a deaf ear!"—John Wade.

ALSABRATES SYNDROME.   We are suffering from a disorder called "Alsabrates syndrome." George Hunter has given an interesting explanation of Alsabrates syndrome. In one of Plato's dialogues a student asks Socrates about a person of some prominence named Alsabrates. He asks: "Alsabrates is rich, influential, educated, and well-traveled. Why is Alsabrates so unhappy?" Socrates answers: "What you say is true. Alsabrates is rich, influential, educated, and well-traveled, and Alsabrates is very unhappy. He is unhappy because everywhere Alsabrates goes he has to take Alsabrates with him."

GOOD AND EVIL.   It was only when I lay there on the rotting straw that I sensed within myself the first stirring of good. Gradually it was disclosed to me that the line separating good and evil passes, not through states, not between classes, nor between political parties either, but right through every human heart and through all human hearts.—Alexandr I. Solzhenitsyn.

FRIEND OF SINNERS.   Every morning St. Peter found in heaven a horde of undesirable aliens whom he was certain he had never admitted at the regular hours. Some had never been baptized; some were ignorant of the Bible; many were soiled and damaged souls who clearly had no right in the celestial precincts. He decided to discover just how this leakage occurred and one night prowled about the ramparts of heaven. At last he discovered a dark corner where a few stones had been removed from the wall since his last inspection an hour before, and a crowd was steadily creeping in. He rushed at them with indignation but was amazed to find the Savior there, helping some of the cripples over the wall. "I'm sorry, Peter,' the Lord said, 'I know it's against the rules. These poor souls aren't all they should be. Some were never baptized. Some of them were not quite orthodox in their opinions about me. All of them were miserable sinners. But they are my special friends, and I want them here."—Frank Harris.

PRAYER OF CONFESSION.   If anyone feels that the language which the church asks him to use is exaggerated—"We do earnestly repent and are heartily sorry for our misdoings; the remembrance of them is grievous unto us; the burden of them is intolerable"—then let him think of slums and sweating and prostitution and war and ask if the remembrance of these is not grievous and if the burden of them ought not to be intolerable. Let him remember that these horrible things are there not because some men are outrageously wicked but because millions of men are as good as we and no better.—William Temple.

FRAMES AND PEOPLE.   Have you ever noticed what usually happens to the many old pictures which are offered for sale at country auctions? It is the frames which are sold, not the pictures. Nobody wants the pictures—the forbidding portrait of great-great-grandfather, the ridiculous likeness of Aunt Ella, the awkward grouping of the father and mother and three or four children. But many people want the frames—the fine walnut ovals, the elaborately gilded rectangles, and the stately mahogany moldings. So the auctioneer sells what the people will buy. "How much am I offered for this lovely frame?" he asks. But God sees man through other eyes. The frames of life are important all right—the earth on which man lives, the mountains and the valleys, the sun and the stars, the fields and the rivers. But far more important is what the frame contains—the human beings, the people, the men and women and children. These are God's kinfolk. They are his sons and daughters. And they are not common. They are holy.—Roy Pearson.

STAR GAZER.   A native skipper on the African shores could not understand the pilots of great ships who guided themselves by the stars. "This foreign going ship," he said, "is a star gazer. I go from headland to headland. I steer by what I know. I keep to terrestrial ground. But he fancies that out of sight of land people can find out what spot they are on by looking at another world through a glass. We are not simple enough to believe that it is from another world that we are gling to learn whether it is here we are or there."—Vere V. Soper.

CONTROLLING SPACE.   Before man learns to control outer space he needs to learn to control the space that lies immediately under his hat. Man has been learning to control guided missiles into outer space, but he has not yet learned how to control himself. He needs to learn to control inner space before he can control outer space. He needs to learn to control his own heart before he controls the heart of the universe. He needs to learn how to get along with his fellow men before he tries to get along with potential men on other planets.—Harold E. Buell.

SELFLESS EMOTION.   To worship is to quicken the conscience by the holiness of God, to feed the mind with the truth of God, to purge the imagination by the beauty of God, to open the heart to the love of God, and to devote the will to the purpose of God. All this is gathered up in that emotion which most cleanses us from selfishness because it is the most selfless of all emotions—adoration.—William Temple.

ONE MAN'S EFFORT.   There is only one way in which one can endure man's inhumanity to man and that is to try in one's own life to exemplify man's humanity to man.—Alan Paton.

SPIRITUAL EMPTINESS.   Why is it true that people are drinking more and more? Is it not because there is an unnamed anxiety springing from a spiritual emptiness? We are trying to be cheerful with cocktails because the truth about us is that we are cheerless. We are trying to exude confidence because deep inside there are fears that gnaw at us. We seek the security of genial companions around the bar because we are so terribly insecure about the things that are really important.—Charles L. Copenhaver.

WESLEY'S ANSWER.   John Wesley began his ministry at a time of religious depression, social evils, political and economic inequalities, at a time when, according to one observer, "the light looked like the evening of the world." But Wesley offered his discouraged generation just one answer. His answer was often recorded in his journal: "I simply offered Jesus Christ to the people." At the Christmas Conference in 1784, when the Methodist Church in America was organized, the following question was placed in the discipline: "What is the best general method of preaching?" The answer: "To offer Christ." Circuit riders in the frontier days of our country's development had only one answer to the question, "What shall I do to be saved?" That was, "Believe in the Lord Jesus."—W. Wallace Fridy.

OVERCOMING DISADVANTAGES. We speak of the advantages of birth and education, but how many have triumphed in the face of tremendous disabilities? Moses had a great chance, being the adopted grandson of Pharaoh, but he sprang from the common stock. Gideon was busy threshing wheat when his call came. David was only a shepherd lad, while that mighty preacher of righteousness, the prophet Amos, was but a simple herdsman. When our master called together the twelve to whom he committed the honor of serving him and carrying on the work of founding the kingdom, he chose men for the most part unlettered and lowly. Zwingli has written his name deep in history, but he was once a shepherd amid Alpine pastures. Melancthon labored in an armorer's shop, while Luther came from the miserable hovel of a miner. Carey, who sought to capture the strongholds of heathenism for his Lord, was only a cobbler, and Robert Morrison, David Livingston, and, perhaps chief of all, Abraham Lincoln, together with a host of others, testify to the power of the man who will hitch his wagon to a star.—J. W. G. Ward.

HARDENED VIRTUE.   When a man has won most of the battles against the world, the flesh, and the devil and when he has made himself a walking embodiment of the ten commandments and is highly disciplined in virtue, he often loses sympathy with those who have failed in the fight. He grows hard toward sinners. His very passion for righteousness makes it hard for him to adopt any attitude which seems to lessen the gravity of sin, and the man, who of all others should be showing tenderness to penitents, seems concerned only to tax them with the enormity of their wrong doing.—W. E. Sangster.

FROM HEAVEN'S HEART.   Inspiration is such a fragile thing—just a fragile thing. Just a breeze, touching the green foliage of a city park. Just a whisper from the soul of a friend. Just a line of verse clipped from some forgotten magazine or a paragraph standing out from among the matter-of-fact chapters of a learned book.

Inspiration—who can say where it is born and why it leaves us? Who can tell of its reasons for being or for not being?

Only this—I think that inspiration comes from the heart of heaven to give the lift of wings and the breath of divine music to those of us who are earthbound.—Margaret E. Sangster in *Guideposts*.

DIVINE LOVER.   The journey which our divine lover took was from heaven to earth to win his bride. In his people he found a bride deep in debt and paid it all; under sentence of death and died in her place; a lost creature, clad in rags, and took of his own royal robes to cover her. To wash her, he shed his blood; to win her, he shed his tears; finding her poor and miserable and naked, he endowed her with all his goods; heir of all things, she was to enjoy everything that he possessed as his Father's son and to share all things with himself—for are not his people "heirs of God and joint heirs with Christ"?—Thomas Guthrie.

MORE THAN ENOUGH.   When I think of my sin, it seems impossible that any atonement should ever be adequate; but when I think of Christ's death, it seems impossible that any sin should ever need such an atonement as that. There is in the death of Christ enough and more than enough. There is not only a sea in which to drown our sins, but the very tops of the mountains of our guilt are covered.—Charles H. Spurgeon.

POWER PLANT.   In Spurgeon's Tabernacle in London, England, one of the members met a stranger at the front of the church and asked him if he would like to see the power plant of the church. He then took the visitor to the basement of the church where the stranger thought he might see the huge equipment which operated the building. When the door opened, there were over 700 people on their knees praying for the services. The man showing him around happened to be Spurgeon himself who said, "This is our power plant."—Jaroy Weber.

TEST OF DISCIPLESHIP.   What is the test of Christian discipleship? What would be the result if in this city every church member should begin to do as Jesus would do? The test would be the same today as then. I believe Jesus would demand as close a following, as much suffering, and as great

self-denial as when he lived in person on the earth and said, "Except a man renounce all that he hath he cannot be my disciple."—Charles M. Sheldon.

STORY OF THREE MEN.   The two men of Lincoln's cabinet who did most to help him sustain the burden and win through to victory—Seward and Stanton—had treated him with contempt and even insult.

Soon after Lincoln's inauguration, Seward wrote him an amazing letter expressing in thinly veiled terms his feeling that Lincoln was incompetent to deal with the great issues confronting the country and offering himself to assume the responsibility of national leadership. Lincoln gently but firmly showed him that that could not be, and they worked together in loyal friendship to the end.

While yet a member of the cabinet, Chase sought to be nominated for the presidency in Lincoln's place, but Lincoln cherished no resentment and soon thereafter appointed him chief justice of the Supreme Court of the United States. Stanton openly insulted Lincoln when they first met at a court of law in Illinois, refused to continue with a case if Lincoln were to be associated with him, and profanely called him a "gawky, long-armed ape." But in time Lincoln said, "The War Department has demonstrated the great necessity for a secretary of Mr. Stanton's great ability, and I have made up my mind to sit down on all my pride—it may be a portion of my self-respect—and appoint him to the place." His trust was justified, and in the end it was Stanton who stood by Lincoln's deathbed and in reverent awe pronounced the solemn verdict: "Now he belongs to the ages."—Luther A. Weigle.

DOING ONE'S BEST.   If I tried to read, much less answer, all the criticisms made of me and all the attacks leveled against me, this office would have to be closed for all other business. I do the best I know how, the very best I can. I mean to keep on doing this down to the very end. If the end brings me out all wrong, no one swearing I'd been right would make any difference.

If the end brings me out all right, then what is said against me now will not amount to anything.—Abraham Lincoln.

LINCOLN AT HIS SIDE.   The Civil War was at its height, but, despite the pressure of affairs, the president made time to visit the wounded in the hospitals. He came one evening to the bed of a boy who was not far from the Valley. Moved to the depth of his being, the president sat beside him and asked if there were anything he could do. The light was fading, or the mists from that same Valley clouded the lad's mind. He did not recognize his visitor. But the kindly tones encouraged him to make a request. Would he write a letter to the boy's mother? Lincoln consented. He took down what the dying soldier wanted to say, although the difficulty of dictation made the task a long one. However, the letter finished, with an effort the youth sat up to sign it. "Please write your name too," he murmured. "I would like her to know how kind you have been." Lincoln signed the letter, and thinking it would please the boy, he showed it to him. "What? You are the president? I wouldn't have asked you if I'd known." Lincoln reassured him and then asked, "Now is there anything else I can do—anything at all?" "Oh, sir, I know I cannot last long. If you would see me through." The president put his arm about the boy's shoulders, supporting his pain-racked body. Ten o'clock came—eleven—twelve—and still this great man, to whom time meant so much, sat on. "If you would see me through" was a plea that no man of his caliber could ignore. With the flush of day the young spirit passed into everlasting arms. Lincoln had seen him through.—J. W. G. Ward.

BOUND TOGETHER.   What Christ is saying always, what he never swerves from saying, what he says a thousand times and in a thousand different ways but always with a central unity of belief, is this: "I am my Father's son and you are my brothers." And the unity that binds us all together, that makes this earth a family and all men brothers and so the sons of God is love.—Thomas Wolfe.

HE THAT HATH EARS.   In an interview of Joan of Arc with the ill-humored Dauphin of France, he complained that he never heard the voices which Joan insisted were guiding her. Joan replied: "They do come to you, but you do not listen. You have not sat in the field in the evening and considered their message. When the angelus rings, you cross yourself and you are done with it; but if you prayed from your heart and listened to the thrilling of the bells in the air, after they stopped ringing you would hear the same voices as I do."

TWO LOVES.   In this life two loves are striving for mastery—love of the world and love of God. The conquering love, whichever it be, puts force upon the lover and draws him after itself.—St. Augustine.

SUPREME GIFT.   Nothing deserves the homage and devotion of the immortal soul except something which itself is immortal. That is why love is supreme above all the gifts. Love never faileth. Love is imperishable. It is never outgrown. It never becomes obsolete. It is never done away with. It is as much at home in heaven as it is here upon the earth. It is the only permanent and abiding wealth of life. Riches, fame, positions, knowledge, tongues, and prophecy—they will all slip from our hands. But the love we practice and cherish we shall keep unto the eternal life.—J. D. Jones.

ALTOGETHER LOVELY.   Christ came from the bosom of the Father to the bosom of a woman. He put on humanity that we might put on divinity. He became a man that we might become the sons of God. In infancy he startled a king; in boyhood he puzzled the doctors; in manhood he ruled the course of nature. He walked upon the billows, hushed the sea to sleep, and healed the multitudes without medicine. He never wrote a book, yet the libraries of the world are filled with volumes that have been written about him. He never penned a musical note, yet he is the theme of more lyrics than any other subject in the world. Great men have come and gone, yet he lives on. Herod could not kill him, Satan could not seduce him, death could not destroy him, and the grave could not hold him. All others have failed in some way but not Jesus. This perfect one is altogether lovely.—*The Free Will Baptist.*

LIFE IN CHRIST. Everything depends on our being right ourselves in Christ. If I want good apples, I must have a good apple tree; and if I care for the health of the apple tree, the apple tree will give me good apples. And it is just so with our Christian life and work. If our life with Christ be right, all will come right. There may be the need of instruction and suggestion and help and training in the different departments of the work; all that has its value. But in the long run the greatest essential is to have the full life in Christ; in other words, to have Christ in us, working through us. I know how much there is often to disturb us or to cause anxious questionings; but the master has such a blessing for every one of us and such perfect peace and rest and such joy and strength, if we can only come into and be kept in the right attitude toward him.— Andrew Murray.

EASY CLIMB. Several years ago two boys were playing in the field near their home in Ohio. They came to an old abandoned oil derrick about 100 feet high. They dared each other to climb to the top. One climbed all the way to the top. Farmers in the field almost fainted as they saw that boy at the top. The other boy would climb a few feet and then stop and look down. Finally he had to come down because he was too frightened to get to the top. He asked his brother, "How did you go all the way to the top?" His brother replied: "It was easy. I never looked down."—W. G. Pinson.

LOVED DEEPLY. Since people don't have the courage to mature unless someone has faith in them, we have to reach those we meet at the level where they stopped developing and where they were given up as hopeless and so withdrew into themselves and began to secrete a protective shell because they thought they were alone and no one cared. They have to feel they're loved very deeply and very boldly before they dare appear humble and kind, affectionate, sincere, and vulnerable.— Louis Evely.

THINGS ETERNAL. When Thoreau, the nature lover, saw the woodman's axe destroying the forest, he exclaimed, "Thank God, they cannot cut down the clouds!" There are some eternal things that the destructive powers of men in all their fury cannot destroy. To think of these things is to achieve an inward quiet and peace even in a wartorn world. The stars still shine. The sun still rises and sets. The mountains are not moved. Birds sing. Little streams dance merrily on their way. Flowers bloom and give off their perfume. The world goes right on being an everlasting, beautiful place. There are the indestructible qualities of the human spirit too. Mother love is immortal and, though cursed to earth, will rise again. Courage and sacrifice glow with a new light in the midst of the blackouts of hope. Faith gallantly rides the whirlwind. You cannot cut down the clouds. The spirit of man cannot be destroyed. The finest things of life are immortal. They will survive.

BEYOND KNOWING. Children need to know what deserves to be emulated and loved and nurtured, but knowing these things is not transmitted through their genes. These things must pass through education from generation to generation. —William J. Bennett.

FAITH'S HARVEST. No ray of sunlight is ever lost, but the green which it wakes into existence needs time to sprout, and it is not always granted to the sower to live to see the harvest. All work that is worth anything is done in faith.—Albert Schweitzer.

GROWTH. The human being cannot live in a condition of emptiness for very long; if he is not growing toward something he does not merely stagnate; the pent-up potentialities turn into morbidity and despair, and eventually into destructive activities and attitudes.—Rollo May in *Love and Will.*

HAPPY PEOPLE.   *The London Tablet* asked this question: Who are the happiest people on earth? These were the four prize-winning answers: a craftsman or artist whistling over a job well done; a little child building sand castles; a mother, after a busy day, bathing her baby; and a doctor who has finished a difficult and dangerous operation and saved a human life.— George F. Riley.

THE FAITH WE DECLARE.   In using the word "faith" we are not thinking of creeds or dogmas. We are speaking of personal religion that to which men come not head first, thinking themselves into it, but heart first; for you will notice that experimental faith precedes assurance. "With the heart man believeth." It is not "He that hath the witness believeth" but "He that believeth hath the witness." Experience comes before explanation and impression before expression, and the great events of spiritual life are not to be negated because there is no rationalistic explanation of them. If faith be lost, life is turned into a naked struggle for the trough where greed prevails and finer things are trampled underfoot. The cynical idea that personal religion is false and unreal undermines life and leaves men forlorn. Without faith, life is a sum that will not come right, a riddle without an answer, a night without a star, a story without a meaning, a journey without a goal.—Albert Orsborn in *The War Cry.*

PARABLE FOR SUNDAY CHRISTIANS. Soren Kierkegaard told a parable about a flock of geese that lived together in a close, harmonious fellowship in the safety of a fine barnyard. Once a week one of their number would climb up on the barnyard fence and tell the other geese about the joys and wonders of flight and how they, like all geese, were made for something more than a barnyard existence. He

would relate to them the adventures of their forefathers who winged their way across the trackless wastes and of their gratitude to God for giving them such talent. And as he preached his hearers often nodded their heads in approval and felt proud of having such a fine preacher in their flock. Once in a while they even flapped their wings as a sign of their agreement. But, said Kierkegaard, "They did not fly because the corn was good and the barnyard safe."—Gilbert Runkel.

FELLOWSHIP IN CHRIST.   We are not, after all, a church so concerned about society that we have forgotten the needs of the individual. Nor are we to become a church so concerned about individuals that we ignore the evils of society. As we cannot be, locally or nationally, a one-class or a one-race church, neither can we be a one-viewpoint church. We can and must differ with one another as our individual consciences dictate, but somehow we must learn better how to find in Christ a unity larger than our disunities. We must, each one, subject our convictions to the judgment of the gospel and also to the judgment of our brothers and sisters in faith. We must learn how to distrust some proposed solutions without having to distrust the motives of those who suggest them. We must learn to disagree without destroying one another. When we do this, we shall discover anew and with power what fellowship in Christ really means and what the nature of the church really is.—William C. Schram.

SECONDARY ROLE.   Perhaps one of the difficulties of discipleship today is due to the fact that we have put church life into the category of leisure time—the weekend. So when it all boils down, discipleship is something quite trivial which competes only with such other trivia as lying in a hammock or sailing or watching television—after we've "slipped into something more comfortable." Discipleship is something to do after the important things in life have been cared for— if we have any time left over.—David V. Yeaworth.

MEN AND METHODS.   We are constantly on a stretch, if not on a strain, to devise new methods, new plans, and new organizations to advance the church and secure enlargement and efficiency for the gospel. This trend of the day has a tendency to lose sight of the man or to sink the man in the plan or organization. God's plan is to make much of the man, far more of him than of anything else. Men are God's method. The church is looking for better methods; God is looking for better men.—E. M. Bounds.

BASIC CHARTER.   If we ever forget our basic charter—"My house is a house of prayer"—we might as well shut the church doors forever. For if we lose that emphasis, all the rest—the dynamic of our corporate witness, the impact on society, the outreach existentially into the lives of men —will soon rot and wither and die.—James S. Stewart.

THE CHURCH BUILDER.   It is not we who build. No man builds the church but Christ alone. Whoever is minded to build the church is surely well on the way to destroying it, for he will build a temple to idols without wishing or knowing it.
We must confess; he builds. We must proclaim; he builds. We must pray to him that he may build. We do not know his plan. We cannot see whether he is building or pulling down. It may be that the times which by human standards are times of collapse are for him the great times of construction. It may be that the times which from a human point of view are great times for the church are times when it is pulled down.
It is a great comfort which Christ gives to his church and you confess, preach, bear witness to me, and I alone will build where it pleases me.—Dietrich Bonhoeffer.

PROPHETIC VOICE.   The prophetic voice which the church is called to speak in our age is more likely to be heard and followed by those in political power when it is spoken by those who in committed pastoral relationships have shown their genuine concern and love.—Mark Hatfield.

FORGIVENESS.   Bryan Green, an English evangelist, was ending a campaign in the United States. At the last service he gave the people an opportunity to share what the campaign had meant to them. A girl rose. She was not eloquent and her speech was broken and halting, but she managed to say, "Through this campaign I have found Christ, and he made me able to forgive theman who murdered my father."—Chevis Horne.

TRANSFORMING EXPERIENCE.   The mark of the Christian interpretation of life is realism. It is a meeting in which God takes the initiative and which becomes for man a transforming experience that changes his life, illumines his thought, and shapes his destiny.—Gerald Kennedy.

COMMENTARY ON MATT. 25:38–40.   A large crowd had gathered to hear the great lecturer. His subject: "How can mere man meet God?" The philosopher, giving his life to ethereal thought, was there. The theologian, currently systematizing great doctrines of God, was there. The charismatic, with recent overwhelming personal experiences, was there. The Sunday school teacher, the choir director, and the deacon were there. So was the architect who had designed the sanctuary so aesthetically that some were certain God spent most of his time in it. All waited eagerly for an oratorical answer to the question, "How can mere man meet God?"
The leader was suggesting that some might have specific questions, the answers to which might be included in the speech. Several carefully worded inquiries emerged. Then an older, slightly stooped, laboring man asked to speak. A little girl, just nine, who had entered with him shyly, was on his mind. Perhaps some would show her compassion. She had been wandering on the street. He had bought her a warm meal, a winter coat, and had gone with her to the local jail where her father was being detained on a vagrancy charge.

Would anyone pray? Could someone spare a few dollars?

Some felt a touch of sympathy. Some would have helped if a receipt had been available. But what did any of this have to do with the momentous subject of the evening? Many were angry with the laboring man for introducing something so utterly irrelevant.

The famous lecturer rose to speak. "Ladies and gentlemen," he began, "the subject tonight is a question, 'How can mere man meet God?' That question has already been answered. I have nothing more to add. Let us close with a passage of scripture on the subject."—Arnold W. Cressman.

RENEWING ACTION. Our message is a message of hope. God is active in his world. The changes which bewilder are not all evil, though all challenge us to find the right human response. God is active in his church, renewing it so that the church may more clearly proclaim its faith to the world, may more effectively discharge its mission of service to the world, and may recover that unity for which our Lord prayed and without which it cannot be truly itself. It is for us to recognize the signs of his renewing action and to welcome them and obey them. It is no time for either despair or doubt. Rather it is a time to remember the Lord's saying: "Be of good cheer: I have overcome the world."—Lambeth Conference.

DIVINE INTENT. Science and religion are not incompatible. While science tries to learn more about the creation, religion tries to learn more about the creator. One cannot be exposed to the order and beauty of the universe without conceding there must be a divine intent behind it. Must we light a candle to see the sun? The more we understand the universe and the intricacies of its operation, the more sense we have to marvel at its creator.—Wernher von Braun.

RELIGION AND SCIENCE. Science has never superseded religion, and it is my expectation that it never will supersede it.

Science has begun to find out how to cure psychic sickness. So far, however, science has shown no signs that it is going to be able to cope with man's most serious problems. It has not been able to do anything to cure man of his sinfulness and his sense of insecurity or to avert the painfulness of failure and the dread of death. Above all, it has not helped him to break out of the prison of his inborn self-centeredness into communion or union with some reality that is greater, more important, more valuable, and more lasting than the individual himself.—Arnold Toynbee.

MORE THAN A DREAM. A discouraged minister had the following strange dream. He thought he was standing on the top of a great granite rock, trying to break it with a pickaxe. Hour after hour he worked with no result. At last he said: "It is useless. I will stop." Suddenly a man stood by him and asked: "Were you not allotted this task? If so, why are you going to abandon it?" "My work is vain. I can make no impression on the granite." Then the stranger solemnly replied: "That is nothing to you. Your duty is to pick, whether the rock yield or no. The work is yours, and the results are in other hands. Work on." In his dream he saw himself setting anew to his labor, and at his first blow the rock flew into hundreds of pieces. This was only a dream, but it proved to be a valuable lesson to the minister and a means of comfort and cheer to his soul.—*Decision.*

WHAT COUNTS. During World War II, a flyer in the South Pacific wrote to his minister, "Since I've been out here, I've learned how few things count in life; but I've learned how much those things count."

FEEBLE RESPONSE. Called to be the moral guardian of the community, the church at times has preserved that which is immoral and unethical. Called to combat social evils, it has remained silent behind stained-glass windows. Called to lead men on the highway of brotherhood and to summon them to rise above the narrow confines of race and class, it has enun-

ciated and practiced racial exclusiveness.
—Martin Luther King, Jr.

ACT OF CONSECRATION. What counted in Jesus' baptism was that it made public his identity and entered him into the crucial phases of his long journey of victorious service and obedience. His life was the expansion of all that was signified and anticipated as he identified himself with the human predicament and chose to take up his task as the anointed righteous servant of the Lord. In the same way the full meaning of that act of consecration which occurs in our baptism becomes apparent in new and different ways as we practice being the Lord's in the bewildering diversity of contemporary living.—The United Presbyterian Church.

EXPLICATION. The word *Christian* in Christian church does not mean that the church is named after the disciples of Christ. Neither does it mean that the church belongs to Christians. The church belongs to Christ, and that is the meaning of the word *Christian* as it is stated in Christian church. We have the word *Christ* and the suffix *ian* which denotes possession. So what we are expressing when we say Christian church is really church of Christ. It is just another way of saying it. The Bible gives a number of other names which actually mean the same church—church of God, church of the saints, church of the first born, the church, etc. The term most often used is "the church." When we are baptized, we are baptized into Christ and become a part of his church—the universal church.—Noble Tribble in *The Lookout.*

BODY AND SOUL. We err when we fail to think of men and women as persons with body and soul. Evangelistic work can fail by forgetting the bodily needs, and social work can fail by forgetting the hunger of the human spirit for God.—Don Crowhurst.

KING'S HIGHWAY. I do not know, Lord, how the road that leads to you can be called narrow. To me it seems not a path but a King's highway. You are always there to raise up those who stumble, and not one fall nor even many falls will make us lose our soul if we have given you our hearts and follow you in the way of humility. We must not despair. He who thinks he is only on the lowest rung of the ladder may in the sight of God have reached the top.—St. Theresa of Avila.

AN IMPATIENT DISCIPLE. No one can tell with certainty what motives influenced Judas to be ay his master. Very likely they were mixed, as impulses are mixed in other lives. But there is certainly a strong appeal in the view that Judas was not the horrible and diabolical man he is often supposed to have been. Very possibly he was a passionate nationalist, who had not learned Jesus' conception of patriotism and who was disappointed by Jesus' refusal to use his divine power to overthrow the foes of his people. His impatience finally became irresistible. He would force Jesus to act. Probably he had no idea that Jesus would allow himself to be put to death. He let Christ down without meaning to because he would not understand. Perhaps that is the explanation of a good many of our sins.—Carl M. Gates.

SOCIAL PRAYER. Even when in solitude an individual is communing with God, he is to say not merely I and my but our. The degree to which this social spirit in prayer will take possession of us depends on the vividness with which we perceive the intimate relationships that bind all men together until each individual is seen not simply as a separate thread but as an inseparable element in the closely woven fabric of human life.—Harry Emerson Fosdick.

BURIED TREASURE. People are prepared for everything except for the fact that beyond the darkness of their blindness there is a great light. They are prepared to go on breaking their backs plowing the same old field until the cows come home, without seeing, until they stub their toes on it, that there is a treasure buried in that field rich enough to buy Texas.—Frederick Buechner.

COMPASS. God speaks to us through the Bible not because we can look up, as in an encyclopedia, what he has said but because, we read and meditate upon the Bible, he speaks to us directly through it. He speaks to us through the words of Jesus Christ, but we cannot without thinking apply these words to our immediate questions. We are given a compass, not a map.—Nathaniel Micklem.

STRONG HAND. Karl Barth spoke of the word of God "as the long strong hand that reaches out after us. What does this hand want of us and what will happen to us in the grip of this hand is none of our business. We only need to know that we are in this hand. He who knows this understands the Bible and the heart of the Bible, Jesus Christ."

BEGINNING. Whatever else the Bible has to say, it makes it quite plain from the outset that life will have neither meaning nor purpose unless we begin with God. The first four words of the story the Bible tells are not "Once upon a ime" but "In the beginning God."—William Neil.

WHAT THE BIBLE CAN DO FOR US TODAY. The Bible shows us God. The Bible teaches moral standards. The Bible sets our human life in its right relations to God and to his government and saves us from the futility and waste of trying to live life as it cannot be rightly and richly lived. The Bible recreates the sense of historic values. The Bible portrays the basic weak-nesses of human life. The Bible portrays the glories of triumphant human character. The Bible points the pathway to the discovery of God. The Bible shows people how to reproduce for and in themselves the great religious discoveries of Christians.—American Bible Society.

WALKING WITH CHRIST. He that seeks to abide in Christ must walk even as he walked. A branch bears fruit of the same sort as the vine to which it belongs. The life of the vine and the branch is so completely identical that the manifestation of that life must be identical too. When the Lord Jesus redeemed us with his blood and presented us to the Father in his righteousness, he did not leave us in our old nature to serve God as best we could. No. In him dwelt eternal life, and every one who is in him receives from him that same eternal life in its holy, heavenly power. So he that abides in him must also walk even as he walked.—Andrew Murray.

EXPECTATION. Today, on the first day of the year, when the thought of the future obtrudes itself upon me, I will not glut my soul with all sorts of expectations nor split it up by imagining all sorts of things. I will collect myself together and, hale and happy, please God, I will go forth to meet the future. Let it bring what it will or may. Many expectations will be disappointed, many fulfilled. That is bound to be, as experience has taught me. But there is one expectation that will not be disappointed—experience has not taught me this but neither has it the power to disavow it—and that is the expectation of faith. And this is victory.—Søren Kierkegaard.

INDEX OF CONTRIBUTORS

Abba, Raymond, 186
Abbey, Merrill R., 253
Adams, A. Ray, 110, 190
Adams, Harry W., 99, 180
Albertson, Charles C., 117, 183
Alcott, Bronson, 8
Alexander, John, 212
Allen, Charles L., 73
Allen, Diogenes, 81
Allen, Marion C., 135, 232
Allison, C. FitzSimmons, 253
Alsobrook, W. Aubrey, 128
American Bible Society, 265
Anglican Digest, The, 39
Aquinas, St. Thomas, 10
Armstrong, Richard S., 52, 67
Atkinson, Lowell M., 57, 60, 104, 170, 229
Atwater, Jeffrey S., 106
Augustine, St., 8, 176, 259

Baillie, John, 9
Bainton, Roland H., 66
Banks, Louis Albert, 73
Barclay, William, 10, 23, 87, 144, 171
Barth, Karl, 8, 10
Bartlett, Gene E., 221
Baskin, Carl, 185
Bassett, Roy, 243
Bates, Carl, 205
Beard, Charles A., 248
Beaven, Albert W., 57
Beck, M. N., 137
Beecher, Henry Ward, 8, 10
Bell, Ivan B., 112, 140
Belton, Jack F., 163
Bennett, William J., 260
Benton, John K., 169
Bergendoff, Conrad, 60
Biblical Recorder, 246
Biddle, Craig III, 71, 77, 124, 209, 237, 253
Bird, Lewis, 22
Bishop, Arthur H., 120
Bishop, John, 37
Blackwood, Andrew W., 92
Blanchard, Roger W., 38, 81
Bodo, John, 158
Bonhoeffer, Dietrich, 8, 52, 262
Bonnell, John Sutherland, 33, 170
Bosley, Harold A., 240
Bounds, E. M., 262
Bowie, Walter Russell, 238
Bradford, James O., Jr., 93

Branson, Gene N., 150, 200
Braun, Wernher von, 263
Britt, Charles R., 224
Brock, Edith, 69
Brokhoff, John R., 24, 49, 54, 63, 89, 134, 137, 170, 195, 197, 223
Broome, C. Richard, 16
Brown, Arthur, 249
Brubaker, Robert C., 76
Brunner, Emil, 241
Bryson, Harold T., 104
Bube, Richard H., 165
Buck, Charles H., Jr., 95
Buechner, Frederick, 264
Buell, Harold E., 256
Bunch, Robert P., 61
Burdette, Robert Jones, 242
Burkhart, Roy A., 189
Burroughs, John, 10
Bushnell, Horace, 10
Butterfield, Herbert, 9
Buttrick, George A., 9, 10, 92
Buxton, Charles, 10

Cabrol, Fernand, 58
Cailliet, Emile, 248
Calvin, John, 39
Camus, Albert, 9
Caperton, Donald, 32
Carlton, John W., 247
Carrel, Alexis, 9
Cartwright, Colbert S., 31, 83, 125
Case, Guy, 45, 202
Cavert, Samuel McCrea, 47
Channing, William Ellery, 244
Chapin, Mervin L., 94
Chesterton, G. K., 9
Chopin, Fréderic François, 199
Christian Century, The, 61
Christian Herald, 44
Churchill, Winston S., 9
Clement of Alexandria, 9
Clinard, Turner N., 18, 22
Coe, Albert Buckner, 226
Coffin, Henry Sloane, 53
Cole, Houston, 167
Collier, Jeremy, 8
Copenhaver, Charles L., 15, 19, 31, 132, 137, 183, 216, 257
Cox, James W., 194
Cox, Raymond L., 78, 245
Crawford, David J., 241

Cressman, Arnold W., 263
Cromie, Richard M., 21, 68, 80, 178
Crowhurst, Don, 264
Crutchfield, Finis A., 64
Cullmann, Oscar, 33
Cumberland Presbyterian, The, 239
Cummings, Randal Lee, 115, 192

Dahl, Edward C., 223, 239
Danziger, Harry K., 44
Davidson, J. A., 83, 107
Davidson, Thomas W., 86
Davies, A. Powell, 8
Davis, Davis J., 155
Dawson, George, 128
de Cervantes, Miguel, 9
Decision, 263
Dennison, A. Dudley, 75
DesAutels, William W., 23
Dickens, Charles, 9
Dickins, Clyde, 208
Dobbs, Eugene H., 18
Dodson, James M., 78, 183
Doidge, Fred R., 24
Dosch, Walter L., 162
Douglas, J. C., 38
Douglass, Richard B., 135
Douglass, Truman B., 113
Drakeford, John W., 20
DuBose, Robert N., 99, 246
Duncan, Bill, 26
Duncan, James R., 197
Durant, Will, 249

Elford, Homer J. R., 42, 122, 228, 251
Eliot, T. S., 59
Elliott, Phillips Packer, 153
Elliott, William M., 98
Emerson, Ralph Waldo, 9
Epictetus, 9
Episcopalian, The, 232
Epp, Frank H., 114
Erdman, Charles R., 245
Erskine, Thomas, 10
Evans, Owen E., 119
Everhart, William M., 154
Evely, Louis, 260
Ewell, Donna Roberts, 70

Fagerburg, Frank B., 111
Farmer, H. H., 52
Farrar, Frederick W., 54
Faulkner, William, 8
Ferguson, Henry N., 158
Ferguson, Robert, 197
Ferrell, Charles E., 134, 231, 244, 255
Ferris, Frank Halliday, 109, 144, 215
Fifield, Harry A., 62
Filson, Floyd V., 54
Forbes, John, 26, 38

Ford, Leighton, 76, 155
Ford, W. Morris, 45
Ford, Wesley P., 202
Foreman, Kenneth, 108
Forsberg, Clarence J., 194
Fosdick, Harry Emerson, 245, 252, 264
Free Will Baptist, The, 260
Freeman, A. Daniel, 71
Freeman, George H., 244
Fridy, W. Wallace, 25, 257
Fromm, Eric, 9
Furfey, Paul Hanly, 8

Gaeddert, John W., 25
Galle, Joseph E. III, 58
Garfield, James A., 10
Gariepy, Henry, 143
Germain, Donald L., 75, 79
Garriott, Christopher, 20
Gates, Carl M., 264
Gibson, Raymond W., Jr., 127
Giguere, Jack, 242
Gilliom, James O., 155
Goethe, J. W. von, 8, 9
Goodrich, Robert E., Jr., 108
Gordon, Thomas, 242
Gospel Herald, 9
Graham, Billy, 247
Grant, Frederick C., 48
Griffith, James N., 248
Grounds, Vernon C., 247
Gulledge, Jack, 214
Guptill, Nathanael M., 111, 123
Guthrie, Shirley, 214
Guthrie, Thomas, 258

Hale, J. Russell, 190
Hamilton, J. Wallace, 243, 250
Hamilton, William, 26
Hansen, Edward J., 184
Harbour, Brian L., 106, 108, 219
Harding, Joe A., 73, 75, 81, 173, 182, 237
Harkness, Georgia, 10, 109
Harris, Frank, 256
Harris, Pierce, 105
Hatfield, Mark, 262
Havner, Vance, 246
Haycock, Winfield S., 127, 177
Hayner, Jerry, 15, 66, 120, 217, 225, 239, 240
Hearn, Gerri, 248
Henderson, Robert, 21
Henry, Matthew, 9
Herald of Holiness, 75
Hines, John E., 152, 239, 244, 254
Hobbs, Herschel H., 51
Hoffer, Eric, 246
Hodgson, Chester E., 138, 205
Hoffman, Oswald C. J., 180
Hollis, Ray C., Jr., 156
Holt, Ivan Lee, 37

Holt, John A., 58
Holt, William M., 27
Hope, Norman Victor, 41
Hopkins, Jerry B., 89
Horne, Chevis, 262
Horr, George E., 231
Hough, Lynn Harold, 111
Hoven, Ard, 222
Howard, Wilbur K., 205
Hubbard, Elbert, 9
Hudson, R. Lofton, 103
Humphrey, Sara, 39
Hunter, A. M., 39
Hunter, John, 197
Hunter, Robert D., 230
Hutchins, Robert M., 197

Jackson, Jesse, 8
Jacobs, Charles F., 44, 103
Jefferson, Thomas, 10
Jensen, Gilbert A., 221
Jerome, St., 10
Johnson, Charles L., 148
Johnson, Gardner A., 29, 38, 41
Jones, E. Stanley, 10, 250
Jones, J. D., 223, 259
Joubert, Joseph, 9
Jowett, John Henry, 40
Jung, Carl, 10

Kaplar, Jameth, 74
Kellems, Jesse R., 17
Keller, Helen, 61
Kemp, Charles F., 102, 151
Kennedy, Gerald, 57, 92, 120, 214, 252, 262
Kennedy, Larry, 43
Kerr, Hugh T., 155
Kierkegaard, Søren, 165, 239, 265
Killinger, John, 10
King, Martin Luther, Jr., 8, 264
Kingsley, Charles, 9
Kirby, W. H., 132
Kirkland, Bryant M., 143, 156, 243
Klein, Ernst E., 174
Knight, Cecile B., 210
Kontz, Emil, 43, 181
Koopman, Leroy, 146
Kordick, F. Gene, 23
Kübler-Ross, Elisabeth, 255

Ladies' Home Journal, 56
LaHaye, Tim and Bev, 131
Laman, Earl A., 21
Landes, James H., 27, 163
Landor, Walter Savage, 8
Lanier, Randolph, 65
Lankler, Ralph Conover, 70, 75, 80
Larsen, David L., 83, 176, 238
Larson, Bruce, 152
Laubach, Frank, 241

Law, William, 188
Leith, John H., 246
Lepp, Ignace, 240
Lester, Donald G., 43
Lewis, C. S., 10, 46, 95
Likins, William H., 198
Lincoln, Abraham, 10, 259
Lindman, Ted, 8
Lindsay, Earl F., 192
Lindsell, Harold, 248
Loane, Marcus L., 125
Loder, Dwight E., 50
Lollis, James A., 246
Loomis, Earl, 241
Luccock, Halford E., 250
Luce, Clare Booth, 10, 158
Luchs, Fred E., 147
Luther, Martin, 10, 239, 255

Macartney, Clarence Edward, 42
MacDonald, Gorden, 206
MacFarlane, W. Norman, 9
Mackay, W. Mackintosh, 122
MacLennan, David A., 20
Macleod, Donald, 49
Macmurray, John, 161
Maeterlinck, Maurice, 9
Maier, Walter A., 59
Malone, J. Walter, 244
Marden, Orison S., 243
Mathew, Thomson K., 15
Matthews, David M., 200
May, Rollo, 261
McBain, John, 165
McCabe, Joseph, 9
McCasland, D. W., 168
McCheyne, Robert Murray, 8
McClain, C. A., Jr., 105, 160
McClain, Richard W., 179
McCracken, Robert J., 60, 188, 208
McEachern, Alton M., 51, 202
McEniry, Robert, 71, 186, 250
McGeachy, Pat, 73
McGraw, James, 139
McGregor, Kermit, 15
McMillan, Christine, 51
McPhee, Arthur, 52, 69, 74, 78, 132, 161, 173, 188, 223, 239, 240
McPherson, Nenien C., Jr., 150, 162
Mears, Eileen, 245
Meckel, Aaron N., 144
Mendell, Taylor, 44
Menninger, Karl, 243
Merton, Thomas, 252
Methodist Christian Advocate, The, 140
Michalson, Carl, 221
Micklem, Nathaniel, 265
Middlekauff, John C., 118, 173
Miller, John, 10
Miller, Roy F., 37

Miller, Samuel H., 195, 240, 246
Mills, C. Wright, 254
Minnick, C. P., Jr., 103, 251
Moody, Dwight L., 10, 73
Morgan, Bill, Jr., 9
Morris, Colin, 180
Morrow, Mic, 68, 76
Morse, Hermann N., 67
Mott, John R., 117
Mouney, Marshall F., 172, 248
Murray, Andrew, 260, 265
Murray, A. Victor, 205

Nance, W. A., 10
Nederhood, Joel, 142, 185
Neil, William, 265
Newbigin, Lesslie, 16, 249
Newby, Donald O., 253
Newman, John Henry, 8, 255
Newman, Lyle V., 126, 209
Newton, Joseph Fort, 57
Nichols, R. Ralph, 149
Niebuhr, Reinhold, 249
Niles, D. T., 64
Norquist, Ernest O., 202
Nouwen, Henri, 210
Nygren, Malcolm, 8

Ogden, Glenn B., 55
Olford, Stephen F., 89, 95, 117, 128, 176, 202
Olive, Don H., 203
Orchard, William E., 141
Orjala, Jeannie, 241
Orsborn, Albert, 261
Owen, Frank, 16, 70

Palmer, Everett W., 18, 145, 162, 199
Paton, Alan, 257
Peale, Norman Vincent, 242
Pearson, Roy, 256
Perry, Lloyd, 246
Pinson, W. G., 260
Polen, O. W., 152
Pollard, Frank, 150, 214, 238, 244
Porter, Boone H., Jr., 29
Prentice, George D., 43
Price, Carl, 143
Prince, Lee, 246
Pulpit Digest, 48

Ramsay, William M., 251
Read, David H. C., 49
Redhead, John A., Jr., 101
Redus, Jerry, 150
Rees, Paul S., 50, 56, 63, 120
Rest, Friedrich, 45
Riley, George F., 261
Rilling, John W., 223, 242
Robertson, Frederick W., 56
Robinson, W. R., 168

Rodenmayer, Robert N., 211
Rollins, J. Metz, Jr., 50
Roper, David H., 199
Rose, Delbert D., 105
Ross, G. A. Johnston, 37
Ross, Helen, 72
Runkel, Gilbert, 69, 133, 261
Rupert, Hoover, 21, 30, 46, 50, 92, 131, 218, 226, 238

Saint-Exupery, Antoine de, 83
Salter, Larry K., 154
Sanders, Carl J., 84, 100, 194
Sanders, J. Oswald, 116
Sanders, James L., 134
Sanford, William C., 23
Sangster, Margaret E., 258
Sangster, W. E., 257
Sayers, Dorothy L., 61
Schaeffer, Francis, 226
Schoenhals, G. Roger, 77
Schram, William C., 261
Schultz, Carl F., Jr., 186
Schulz, Harold A., 218
Schwartz, Delmore, 10
Schweitzer, Albert, 9, 245, 247, 249, 260
Sciratt, James E., 121
Seasholes, Charles L., 55, 165, 180
Sedgwick, Ellery, 89
Seymour, Josephine E., 86
Shaw, Robert, 64
Shedd, Charlie W., 10
Sheely, Madison L., 211
Sheldon, Charles M. 258
Sherer, Paul, 146
Shoemaker, Samuel M., 254
Sizoo, Joseph R., 194
Smith, Blake, 176
Smith, Ernest Edward, 29, 35, 187
Smith, Roy L., 8
Sockman, Ralph W., 9, 10, 117, 153, 189
Soderblom, Nathan, 10
Soest, Bert Van, 129, 249
Solzhenitsyn, Aleksandr, 9, 255
Soper, Vere V., 256
Sovik, Arnie, 247
Speers, Theodore Cuyler, 214
Spieler, David A., 88, 96
Spurgeon, Charles H., 258
St. Andrew Herald, 58
Stapert, John, 210
Sterner, R. Eugene, 191
Sterner, Robert L., 9
Stevenson, Robert Louis, 244
Stewart, James S., 122, 125, 168, 170, 262
Stidger, William L., 59
Stifler, F. C., 14, 208
Stinnette, Charles R., Jr., 53
Stoddard, William S., 10
Stow, Gerald, 26

Strait, C. Neil, 15, 28, 66, 84, 114, 166, 231
Straton, Hillyer H., , 90, 101
Stravinskas, Peter, 17, 166
Suenens, Leo Cardinal, 59
Sunshine Magazine, 76, 78, 140
Sun Yat Sen, 10

Tagore, 8
Taylor, Gardner C., 228
Taylor, J. Randolph, 95
Taylor, John V., 204
Taylor, Mark A., 227
Taylor, Myron J., 20, 27, 36, 90, 100, 155
Taylor, William R., 191
Temple, William, 256, 257
Teresa, Mother, 8, 199
Thackeray, William Makepeace, 10
Theology Today, 179
Theresa of Avila, St., 264
Thomas a Kempis, 9, 251, 253
Thompson, Ernest Trice, 98, 175
Thompson, John, 96, 159
Thurman, Howard, 61
Tillich, Paul, 182
Tonne, Arthur, 38, 65, 72, 80
Tournier, Paul, 9
Townsend, John H., 71, 77, 100, 176, 220, 238
Toynbee, Arnold, 263
Tozer, A. W., 191
Traherne, Thomas, 52
Tribble, Noble, 264
Trotter, Mark, 137
Trueblood, Elton, 9, 226, 248

Ullman, Richard L., 122

Van Dyke, Henry, 9
Van Ens, Jack R., 58

Wade, John, 67, 103, 243, 253, 255
Walker, Alan, 20, 24, 38, 86
Walker, Daniel D., 137
Walker, Harold Blake, 168, 191
Wallace, Eva M., 45
Wallace, Ray W., 8
Waltner, Winifred, 250
Ward, J. W. G., 257
Ward, Robert, 241
Ward, William Arthur, 9, 111, 252
Watson, Kenneth, 114, 189
Weatherhead, Leslie D., 44, 80, 252
Weaver, S. Robert, 28, 46, 98, 134, 202, 228
Webber, George, 39
Weber, Jaroy, 258
Weenink, Allan J., 224
Weigle, Luther A., 258
Wesley, John 33
Whale, John S., 10, 52, 53
Whiting, Thomas A., 140
Wiebe, Bernie, 53
Wilcox, Jackson, 146
Wirt, Sherwood E., 65
Wotherspoon, Kenneth A., 221
Wright, Henry B., 9

Yeaworth, David V., 261

SERMON TITLE INDEX

(Children's stories and sermons are identified cs; *sermon suggestions* ss)

Above the Clouds, 154
Accepting One Another (cs), 69
Am I Really a Christian?, 136
Angelic Chorus, The (ss), 226
Assumptions of Contemporary Culture, The, 20
Attitude Toward Death, An, 41
Authentic Faith, 26

Back to Basics, 154
Beauty Everywhere (cs), 73
Behaving Like Christians (ss), 103
Blessing of the Dew, The, 169
Body of Christ, The (ss), 117
Boy Who Kept Sunday, The (cs), 80
Breaking the Worry Habit (ss), 155
Brother Little (cs), 70
Buried with Christ, 17

Call to Celebration, A (ss), 218
Call to Commitment, 107
Can't Someone Else Do It?, 198
Certainty of Hope, The (ss), 143
Christ Ascended and Accessible, 142
Christ of the Gospels, 48
Christ as Physician, 120
Christ the Physician (ss), 117
Christian as Patriot, The, 157
Christian Citizen, The, 22
Christian Father's Role, A, 151
Christian Loyalty, 17
Christian's Credentials, A (ss), 137
Christian's Leisure Time, The, 24
Christian's Life-Style, A, 26
Christian's Role, The (ss), 150
Christmas Apple, The (cs), 80
Christmas Gift List, 30
Christmas in Greece, A (cs), 81

Christ's Church (ss), 95
Church and Our Families, The, 21
Church in Work and Witness, The, 27
Church on a Mission, The (ss), 89
Church That Makes a Difference, The, 16
Churches as Communities, 21
Church's Calling, The, 96, 191
Clichés of Christmas, The, 226
Close Encounter with God, A, 85
Come, 195
Commissioned Christians, 62
Commitment (cs), 81
Companions (cs), 73
Components of Conversion, 175
Conditions for Forgiveness, The, 160
Consolation of God, The, 57
Credo for the Family, A, 21
Crib and the Cross, The, 229
Crisis in Faith, A (ss), 176
Cross as Judgment, The, 18
Crown Him with Many Crowns (ss), 120
Crucial Hour, The, 48

Dare to Be a Daniel (cs), 70
Day of Contrasts (ss), 122
Day of Decision, 18
Day of God's Visitation, The, 55
Deeper Meanings of Christmas, 56
Deliverance from Evil (ss), 180
Diamonds Where You Are (cs), 78
Difference Easter Makes, The, 50
Dimensions of Palm Sunday, 123
Discovering the Church as a Family, 130
Do You Want to Be Healed? (ss), 202
Do You Want to Be Rich? (ss), 199
Door, The, 104

Early Church at Prayer, The (ss), 146
Easter Candle, An (cs), 72
Easter Blossom of the Poor (cs), 71
Easter Confidence, 50
Echoes in the Old House (ss), 103
Escaping the World's Corruption, 172
Essence of Faith (ss), 205
Eternal Life (ss), 223
Eternal Life: The Christian's Hope, 109
Expectations of Worship, The, 147

Face to Face, 183
Faith That Pleases God, The, 93
Faith of Our Fathers, 159
Falling in Love, 15
Family of God, The, 26
Fear of Failure, The, 25
Finding Meaning in Life (ss), 150
Finding Peace of Mind (ss), 173
First Christmas Gift, The (ss), 228
Five Joys of Christmas (ss), 223
Flowers for the Living (ss), 144
Forgive Us Our Syndromes, 138

Forgiving One Another (cs), 77
Fortunate Misfortune (ss), 98
Forty Martyrs of Sebaste (cs), 76
From Sin to Salvation, 104

Gateways to God, 189
Getting a Rise Out of Resurrection, 49
Gift of Love, A (cs), 70
God's Gift of Peace, 15
God Our Refuge (ss), 86
God's Daily Blessings (cs), 71
God's Peculiar Treasure (ss), 105
God's Provisions, 218
God's Valentine (cs), 69
God Who Knows Us, The, 184
Going to Bed (cs), 78
Going to Church, 94
Good Grief, 42
Good News for the Strong (ss), 131
Gospel: A Relevant Message, The (ss), 165
Gospel We Proclaim, The, 64
Grace and Truth of God, The, 224
Greater Light, The, 40
Grounds of Our Hope, The, 174
Growing as Christians, 156
Guidelines for Boat Rockers, 23
Guidelines for Constructive Criticism, 23

Handling Grief, 41
Handling Jealousy, 24
Handling the Truth (ss), 202
Hands That Break the Bread, 33
He Saved Others (cs), 75
Healing a Broken Heart (ss), 183
Helping Someone Who Hurts, 181
Hidden Beauty, The (cs), 75
Hidden God, The (ss), 185
His Convictions and Ours, 121
His Decision and Ours, 114
His Father's Voice (cs), 77
Holding the Rope (cs), 69
Home's Seven C's, The (ss), 132
Hope of Resurrection (ss), 125
House to House Visiting, 195
How Does God Spend His Time?, 23
How Does Jesus Love Us?, 186
How God Would Finance a Church (ss), 89
How Good Is Good?, 101
How Prayer Changes Things (ss), 111
How to Become a Peacemaker (ss), 194
How to Deal with Hostility in Others (ss), 162
How to Hear the Easter Story, 49
How to Live with Uncongenial Saints, 20

I Don't Tithe Because—, 211
I Will Never Walk Alone (ss), 168
Ideal Woman, The, 135
Image of the Heavenly, The, 42
In God We Trust (cs), 74
In the Direction of Perfection, 87

Inner Struggle, The, 27
Is Church Membership Necessary?, 129
Is One Religion as Good as Another?, 148

Joey's Friend (cs), 68
Journey of Faith, The (ss), 231
Joy of the Lord, The (ss), 95

Keeping Men on Their Feet, 28
Keeping the Sabbath, 102
Knowing God's Will, 200

Late Christmas (cs), 68
Learning Experiences (cs), 74
Lent: A Second Honeymoon, 17
Lenten Emphasis, The, 47
Lesson in Geography, 120
Lesson in Thanksgiving, A, 216
Life Full of New Beginnings, A, 82
Life Is Too Short for That! (ss), 137
Life Triumphant, 40
Life with Father (cs), 74
Lifelong Work, A (cs), 77
Life's Four Tasks, 150
Life's Handbook (cs), 79
Light for an Advent Wreath (ss), 221
Light from Bethlehem's Star, 29
Light of the World, The, 29
Listen to Him!, 171
Living in a World You Don't Understand (ss),
  173
Living with Danger (ss), 159
Living with Dignity (ss), 153
Longest Shadow, The (cs), 76
Look at Our Church, A (ss), 205
Lordship of Jesus, The, 112
Love and Demand, 16
Love and Hostility, 26
Love Letter (cs), 78
Love Never Fails (cs), 80
Luminous Christ, The, 57
Lyric Religion (ss), 128

Man Who Missed Christmas, A, 225
Man Who Wrote "Silent Night," The (cs),
  80
Materialism of Christianity, The (ss), 208
Media of Grace, 32
Meet the Holy Spirit (ss), 146
Memories: Resource for Great Living, 144
Messengers (cs), 72
Mother Hen, The (cs), 73
Mother of Us All, The (ss), 134
Mountain's Complaint, The (cs), 74
Mustard Seed Faith (ss), 108
My Dream for Our Church, 21
My Face (cs), 75
My Father Worketh, 186
Myth of Pornography, 20

New and the Old, The, 230
New Life of Easter, The, 19

On Being Useful to God (ss), 191
On Growing Old, 166
On Loving Oneself, 22
One Day at a Time (ss), 83
One Tick at a Time (cs), 73
Our Common Longings (ss), 194
Our Daily Bread (ss), 152
Our Father (ss), 180
Our Ministry of Reconciliation (ss), 98
Our Need for Community, 209

Paradoxes of Prayer (ss), 165
Part God Made, The (cs), 74
Partnership in Service, 88
Paul's Word for Pastors (ss), 128
Possibilities (cs), 73
Power, 203
Prayer of Faith, The (ss), 176
Praying as Jesus Prayed, 91
Preparers of the Way, 29
Prince and the Fisherman, The (cs), 78
Profile of a Patriot, 159
Prophetic Day, 56
Purpose of His Coming, The, 221

Qualities of Leadership, 189
Questions for Questionables, 24

Reaching Out in Love (cs), 68
Religion in the Daily Round (ss), 183
Religion of a Healthy Mind (ss), 162
Resurrection and the Life, The, 124
Revolutionary Christianity (ss), 113
Right Book, The (ss), 214
Roads We Travel, The (ss), 86
Roots and Fruits, 139

Saying Thanks (cs), 69
Season for Preparing, 55
Seeking and Saving, 63
Self-Examination on Good Friday (ss), 122
Shadows of Influence, 132
Shalom, 99
Shortest Prayer, The (cs), 72
Soldiers of Christ, Arise! (ss), 168
Sources of Joy, The, 177
Spelling Lesson (cs), 78
Standing in Our Own Way (ss), 188
Steps in Prayer, 20
Steps Toward Health of Mind and Spirit, 90
Steward's Temptations, A, 16
Stewardship of Sharing and Caring, The, 209
Straight Line, The (cs), 76
Strengthening Simplicities of Our Faith, The
  (ss), 221
Suddenly It's Easter, 50
Suffering—An Invitation to Growth, 166

Sunday Christianity, 192
Survival of the Word, 212

Temptations That Are Good, 181
Ten Commandments for 1981, 84
Tender Heart for a Tough World, A, 23
Tested Through Temptation (ss), 173
That Helpless Feeling, 15
Their Hymn of Praise, 34
They Knew Jesus (cs), 77
Things You Can Get for Nothing (ss), 170
This Hallowed Season, 55
This Table Talks, 32
Those Early Churches, 163
Those Feelings of Guilt, 215
Those Who Don't Go to Church, 190
Three Great Promises (ss), 114
Three Kinds of Giving (ss), 211
Three Roads of Easter, 126
Time to Remember, 197
Train Up a Child, 187
Two Kinds of Theology, 163
Two Reflections (cs), 76
Two Sacraments of Life, The, 24

Uniqueness of Christ, The, 115

Way, The, 31
Wesley's Counsel, 33
What a Difference!, 63
What Can We Say About Love? (ss), 100
What Christ Stands For (ss), 197
What Do Christians Celebrate?, 20
What Do You Expect?, 219
What Do You Expect from Religion?, 169
What Does God Have to Say?, 14
What Does Prayer Accomplish? (ss), 92
What God Requires, 200
What Happened at Calvary?, 49
What He Left Behind, 77
What Is Brotherhood? (ss), 100

What He Remembered (cs), 71
What Is Christian Education?, 25
What Is Evangelism?, 62
What Is Faith?, 18, 112
What Is Gratitude?, 28
What Is Love? (cs), 71
What Is My Part in the Good News?, 232
What Is Our Understanding of Ourselves?, 206
What Is the Church? (ss), 140
What Kind of a Christian Are You?, 205
What Kind of a Church?, 178
What More Can You Say After the Sermon?, 127
What the Cross Shows, 118
What the Holy Spirit Offers, 177
What's Going On in Church?, 141
When Faith Falls Short, 192
When Faith Takes Hold, 27
When Is Religion Healthy?, 15
When Life Matters Most, 99
When the Shepherds Returned, 57
When Trouble Comes, 97
When You Say Mother You Say a Lot About God, 133
Where All Meet Together, 34
Where Christ Should Be Born, 227
Where Do You Live? (ss), 155
Where Is Bethlehem?, 222
Where the Rainbow Never Fades, 43
Why Are You Here?, 106
Why Be a Christian? (ss), 170
Why Did Jesus Come?, 56
Why Go to Church?, 109
Why Pentecost?, 145
Why the Cross?, 47
Why Tithe? (ss), 211
Why Read the Bible? (ss), 214
Word for the World, The, 14
Wren and the Cowbird, The (cs), 75

Your Church Is What You Make It, 25

SCRIPTURAL INDEX

Genesis 12:1–3. . .159
15:1–11. . .27
32:24. . .188
37:19. . .21

Exodus 3:1–12. . .14
3:6–10. . .198
19:1–8. . .200
20:1–17. . .200
20:8. . .102
33:9–16. . .203

35:29. . .89

Leviticus 27:32. . .211

Numbers 6:24–26. . .99
10:10. . .218

Deuteronomy 32:7. . .144
32:18. . .133
33:27. . .86
33:29. . .170

II Samuel 7:20. . .127

I Kings 19:9. . .106

II Chronicles 5:14. . .205

Ezra 7:27. . .151

Nehemiah 2:18. . .189
6:10. . .109
8:1–10. . .95

13:11. . .190
14:1–2. . .137

Job 15:11. . .57
23:3. . .173
23:10. . .86

Psalms 4. . .176
11:3. . .191
12:6. . .214
16:6. . .132
18:28. . .221
23. . .168
24:3–4. . .20
27:1. . .90
27:4. . .147
30:5. . .97
34:3. . .129
37:25. . .166
51:14. . .177
55:6. . .24
68:6. . .21
71:16. . .84
84:2. . .94
87:5. . .134
88:9. . .20
90:1. . .83
119:71. . .98
137:4–6. . .176
137:5. . .157, 159
139:2. . .184

Proverbs 10:12. . .26
14:30. . .24
15:26. . .226
22:2. . .34
22:6. . .187
31:10–31. . .135

Ecclesiastes 1:3. . .183
3:11. . .14
9:10. . .150

Isaiah 30:21. . .103
35:1. . .170
40:8. . .214
43:18–19. . .82
45:15. . .185

Jeremiah 29:1–14. . .176
29:13. . .99

Lamentations 3:22–23. . .83

Ezekiel 2:1. . .168

Daniel 10:11. . .28

Hosea 2:16–20. . .17

14:5. . .169

Micah 5:2. . .222
6:8. . .200

Malachi 3:16–17. . .105

Matthew 1:21. . .55
1:23. . .229
2:2. . .227
2:7–18. . .225
2:21–22. . .230
3:10. . .211
4:4. . .208
4:25. . .117
5:4. . .41
5:9. . .194
6:9. . .180
6:11. . .152, 208
6:12. . .160
6:13. . .180
6:33. . .211
6:34. . .83
7:15–23. . .139
9:29. . .18
9:36. . .15
11:3. . .219
11:29. . .25
11:30. . .221
14:23. . .189
14:26. . .34
16:18–19. . .95
17:20. . .108
20:18. . .121
20:28. . .48
21:5. . .122
23:8. . .100
25:40. . .181
26:74. . .132
27:11. . .197
28:7. . .19
28:18–20. . .62, 154
28:19–20. . .89
28:20. . .23

Mark 1:29–34. . .120
1:29–39. . .166
4. . .202
6:13. . .173
9:2–9. . .171
9:14–29. . .192
10:28–30. . .181
12:31. . .22
14:8–9. . .144

Luke 1:17. . .55
2:7. . .56
2:10–11. . .223
2:11. . .228

2:14. . .226
2:20. . .57
2:25. . .57
4:1–13. . .203
4:18–19. . .183
5:1–11. . .88
5:31. . .120
9:51. . .18
10:1–9. . .195
10:16. . .195
10:29–37. . .23
10:41. . .155
11:1. . .91
12:49–50. . .113
15:18. . .25
15:32. . .20
17:5. . .205
17:11–19. . .216
18:8. . .192
19:1–10. . .131
19:37–40. . .123
22:19. . .24, 33
22:53. . .48
23:33. . .49, 120

John 1:1–5. . .221
1:9–30. . .56
1:14. . .224
1:14–18. . .221
1:23. . .29
3:16. . .223
4:5–30. . .175
5:6. . .202
5:17. . .186
8:9. . .215
9:39. . .18
10:9. . .104
11:17–27. . .124
11:25. . .40
12:16. . .173
12:46. . .29
13:1. . .186
13:13. . .112, 120
13:14–15. . .24
14:6. . .31
14:8. . .85
14:16. . .146
14:26. . .146
14:27. . .15, 30
17:21. . .197
19:17–18. . .122
20:22. . .145
20:23. . .183
20:24–31. . .124
20:26. . .49
20:31. . .194

Acts 1:14. . .146
2:44–45. . .209

4:12...148
4:32...209
5:20...63
16:30–31...104
19:1...137
20:35...199, 211
26:8...125
26:28...205

Romans 1:16...165
2:16...232
5:5...29
5:8...100
5:10...118
8:6...162
8:18...154
12:3...23
12:17–18...162
12:18...20
14:1–15...103
15...98

I Corinthians 3:16–17...163
3:17...206
4:2...16
7:7...138
10:16...26
11:26...32
12:12–31...117
14:15...128, 165
15:1...62
15:1–2...64
15:1–4...17
15:3...47
15:49...42
15:54–55...41
15:58...50

II Corinthians 4:6...57
13:5...163

Ephesians 1:23...141
2:18...130
2:19–22...178
3:14–15...21
3:17–19...20
4:13...231
4:15...156
5:20...28
5:25...140
5:27...27
5:30...150
6:24...15

Philippians 1:3–11...16
1:19...218
2:4–7...114
2:9...115
3:10...50
3:12...17
3:13–14...47
3:13–16...87

Colossians 1:15–19...174
2:6...26

I Thessalonians 1:5...114
4:13...42
5:21...101

II Thessalonians 1:11...191

I Timothy 3:15...21
4:1–11...107

4:8...49
4:12...128

II Timothy 1:1–7...15
1:10...126
2:9...212

Titus 3:1–2...22

Hebrews 4:14–16...142
11:1...112, 143
11:5...93
11:6...26
13:20–21...24

James 1:13...173
5:16...92

I Peter 2:5...155
2:9...96
2:19–29...136

II Peter 1:4...172

I John 1:5...16
2:28...153
3:2...109

III John 8...23

Jude 1:3...169

Revelation 2:19...25
3:20...111
19:12...120

INDEX OF PRAYERS

Advent, 174, 221, 223, 226, 229

Baccalaureate, 144
Brotherhood Week, 93, 101, 165

Children's Day, 132
Christmas, 221, 226
Communion, 106

Easter, 125

Family Week, 132, 135, 153
Father's Day, 132, 135, 153

Holy Week, 123

Independence Sunday, 101, 159

Labor Sunday, 186
Laity Sunday, 171, 186

Lent, 120

Missionary Day, 90, 186
Mother's Day, 132, 135, 153

New Year's Sunday, 84, 96, 141, 177, 232

Ordination, 114

Palm Sunday, 123
Pentecost, 104, 147, 194

Reformation Sunday, 205
Rural Life Sunday, 153

Thanksgiving Sunday, 87, 117, 218

World Communion Sunday, 197
World Community Sunday, 165

INDEX OF MATERIALS USEFUL AS CHILDREN'S STORIES AND SERMONS NOT INCLUDED IN SECTION VIII

Advent purple, 58

Baseball, 238
Bible, 191, 208, 244
Blindness, 182
Boy and Jesus, 38

Caring, 194
Christmas candle, 59
Christmas star, 58
Christmas tree, 60
Church, 95
Climbing, 260
Communion, 37

Darkness, 98
Diamonds, 66

Enemy, 202

Falling stars, 231
Father, 151, 152
Fear, 238
Forgiveness, 36

Friend of sinners, 256

Good shepherd, 250

Helpfulness, 52, 237

Lamb chops, 188
Lincoln, 259
Lost, 134

Parents, 152
Possibilities, 250

Rescue, 239
Response, 248
Restraint, 244

Stars, 241

Temptation, 255
Testimony, 65
Thankfulness, 217

Weeds, 243

INDEX OF MATERIALS USEFUL FOR SMALL GROUPS

Celebration, 20
Christian, 136, 205
Christian growth, 156
Christmas, 56
Criticism, 23
Church, 25, 109, 141, 178
Church attendance, 190

Evangelism, 62

Failure, 25
Faith, 26, 112
Fatherhood, 151

Grief, 41, 42

Guilt, 215

Healing, 181

Leadership, 189
Leisure time, 24

Mental health, 90

Pornography, 20
Power, 203

Relationships, 232
Religion, 169

INDEX OF SPECIAL DAYS AND SEASONS

Advent, 29, 55–61, 80, 219, 221, 259
All Saints' Day, 156, 252
Ascension Sunday, 142

Baccalaureate, 150
Baptism, 264
Bible Sunday, 14, 79, 92, 191, 202, 212, 214, 265
Brotherhood Week, 44, 69, 75, 99, 100, 166, 180

Children's Day, 21, 131, 132, 133, 187, 245
Christian Education Week, 25, 140, 181, 255
Christmas, 30, 55–61, 68, 80, 81, 222, 223, 225, 226, 227, 228, 229
Commencement, 114, 150, 206
Communion, 24, 32–39, 197

Easter, 19, 47–54, 72, 124, 125, 126

Family Week, 130, 131, 132, 252
Father's Day, 21, 74, 151
Funeral services, 40–46, 97, 109, 240, 246, 250

Good Friday, 47, 48, 49, 50, 53, 118, 120, 122, 247, 248

Independence Sunday, 22, 74, 157, 158, 159

Labor Sunday, 77, 103, 186
Laity Sunday, 25, 28, 94, 108, 127, 189, 195, 198, 210
Lent, 15, 17, 18, 47–54, 70, 71, 72, 107, 115, 252
Lincoln's Birthday, 244, 258, 259

Maundy Thursday, 24, 34, 37
Memorial Day, 144, 146
Missionary Day, 62–67, 68, 88, 89
Mother's Day, 21, 73, 134, 135, 249

New Year's Sunday, 82, 83, 84, 230, 231, 265

Ordination, 128, 137, 189, 237, 246, 257, 263

Palm Sunday, 18, 121, 122, 123
Passion Sunday, 71, 118, 120, 248
Pentecost, 94, 95, 129, 145, 146, 163, 177, 253, 262
Prayer Week, 20, 91, 92, 111, 146, 165, 258, 262

Rally Day, 25, 187
Reformation Sunday, 27, 247
Revival services, 62–67, 104, 175, 238
Rural Life Sunday, 139, 169, 244, 260

Stewardship Sunday, 16, 89, 140, 209, 210, 211, 255

Thanksgiving Sunday, 28, 69, 216, 218
Transfiguration Sunday, 170, 171
Trinity Sunday, 148, 177

Valentine's Day, 69, 100

World Communion Sunday, 26, 34, 36, 77, 195, 197
World Community Sunday, 21, 36, 98, 197, 209
World Temperance Day, 105, 172, 173, 181, 239, 257

TOPICAL INDEX

Abraham, 27
Academy, 179
Acceptance, 70, 75, 242
Action, 125
Advent, 55, 57, 58
Adventure, 112
Advent wreath, 221
Advocate, 51
Amen, 127
America, 158

Angelic chorus, 226
Anxiety, 83
Apple, 80
Ascension, 142
Athiest, 65
Attitude, 210
Attractiveness, 135,
Augustine, St., 208

Baby, 100

Baptism, 17, 32, 41, 250, 264
Beauty, 73, 75, 244, 245
Bed, 78
Beggar, 249
Beginning, 82,
Belief, 19
Believe, 253
Bethlehem, 58, 222
Bible, 14, 79, 191, 208, 212, 214, 265

Bird, 247
Blessedness, 135
Blessing, 169
Body, 264
Body of Christ, 117
Boundary, 243
Brainard, David, 65
Bread, 33, 152
Bridge, 122, 243
Brooks, Phillips, 89
Brotherhood, 100
Brothers, 259
Booth, William, 194
Buoyancy, 45
Burden, 52
Burning bush, 14
Business, 60, 251

Calling, 96, 191
Calm, 250
Calvary, 49, 121
Campanella, Roy, 243
Candle, 59, 72, 221
Captive, 207
Care, 194
Caring, 209
Cathedral, 77
Cause, 19
Celebration, 20, 218
Change, 105, 230, 249
Child, 38, 187
Children, 130, 131, 151, 245
Choice, 46
Christian, 86, 103, 136, 150,
    170, 191, 205, 264
Christian citizenship, 22
Christian education, 25
Christianity, 113, 192, 205
Christmas, 56, 57, 59, 68, 81,
    223, 225, 226
Christmas bells, 61
Christmas tree, 60
Church, 16, 21, 25, 27, 63, 89,
    94, 95, 96, 107, 109, 130,
    140, 141, 143, 146, 163,
    178, 190, 205, 243, 244,
    245, 253, 261, 262, 263
Church builder, 262
Church membership, 129
Circumcision, 140
Citizen, 22
Claim, 154
Climbing, 260
Clock, 73
Cloud, 154, 250, 260
Colosseum, 179
Comfort, 45
Command, 154
Commission, 62

Commitment, 81, 107
Communication, 188, 197
Communion, 32, 37
Communion cup, 37
Communion of saints, 156
Community, 19, 21, 96, 181,
    197, 209
Campanion, 73
Compass, 265
Compassion, 239
Complaint, 74
Concern, 57, 120
Condemnation, 175
Conditioning, 247
Confession, 105, 256
Confidence, 50, 145, 146, 203
Confrontation, 175
Congregation, 207
Conversion, 175
Conscience, 215
Consecreation, 264
Consolation, 57
Contrast, 122
Conversion, 65, 175
Conviction, 121
Conviction of sin, 104
Corruption, 172
Courage, 207
Cowbird, 75
Creative, 207
Creativity, 133
Credo, 254
Criticism, 23, 258
Cross, 18, 34, 47, 52, 53, 118,
    122, 229, 247
Crown, 120
Crucifixion, 50, 51, 53
Cultivation, 139
Culture, 20

Danger, 159, 240
Dangerous, 92
Daniel, 28, 70
Darkness, 44, 98, 246
David, 97
Day, 83
Death, 41, 109, 126, 240, 254
Decision, 18, 65, 114, 246
Demand, 16
Devil, 210
Dew, 169
Diamond, 66, 78
Difference, 16, 63, 244
Dignity, 153
Disadvantage, 257
Disappointment, 154
Disciple, 188
Discipleship, 164, 258, 261
Discouragement, 154, 217

Disobedience, 255
Distinction, 203
Door, 104, 253
Doubt, 126
Dream, 21, 263
Drinking, 257
Duty, 65

Eagle, 250
Ear, 255
Easter, 19, 49, 50, 53, 126
Echo, 103
Education, 260
Eggs, 54
Election, 238
Elijah, 106
Emptiness, 126
Encounter, 240
Encounter with God, 85
Enemy, 202
Enoch, 93
Enthusiasm, 96, 123
Eternal life, 109, 223
Evangelism, 62, 64, 67, 249
Evil, 180, 255
Example, 140
Expectancy, 147
Expectation, 220, 265
Experience, 108, 246

Face, 75, 183
Failure, 15, 25, 52
Faith, 18, 26, 27, 93, 105, 111,
    112, 126, 155, 176, 192,
    201, 205, 221, 231, 260, 261
Faithfulness, 240, 249, 255
Family, 21, 26, 130
Father, 74, 77, 151, 152, 180
Fear, 248
Fearful, 231
Fellowship, 140, 181, 209,
    210, 225, 261
Finance, 89
Fisherman, 78
Flower, 71, 158
Forgiveness, 141, 160, 161,
    262
Forgiving, 77, 242
Frames, 256
Freedom, 251
Friend, 68
Fruit, 139
Funeral, 131

Gambler, 239
Gandhi, 161
Geography, 120
Gift, 58, 172, 228, 239
Gift list, 30

Giving, 211, 226
Goal, 188
Godliness, 173
God's visitation, 56
God's will, 200
Golf, 241
Good, 78, 255
Goodbye, 72
Goodness, 101, 197
Good shepherd, 24, 250
Golden Gate Bridge, 81
Grace, 32, 188, 224, 239
Gratitude, 28
Grief, 41, 42
Growing old, 167
Growth, 156, 260
Grumbling, 217
Guilt, 215
Gyroscope, 172

Habit, 49
Hallelujah, 127
Happiness, 261
Hazard, 241
Healing, 183
Health, 90, 162
Healthy religion, 15
Hearing, 49, 214, 245
Heart, 71, 243
Heaven, 38, 52, 252, 256
Healing, 202
Help, 90
Helplessness, 15
Hen, 73
Herod, 61, 225
Hidden God, 185
Hiddenness, 221
History, 113, 157, 248, 254
Holy, 252
Holy Communion, 198
Holy Spirit, 146, 177
Homing instinct, 43
Honesty, 94
Honeymoon, 17
Hope, 110, 125, 143, 174, 263
Hostility, 26, 162
Humanity, 113, 255, 257
Hymn, 34, 128

Ideal, 245
Immortal, 260
Immortality, 44
Impression, 77
Incarnation, 224
Industriousness, 135
Influence, 132
Inspiration, 257
Instincts, 185

Institutions, 249
Investment, 255

Jealousy, 24
Jerusalem, 134
John the Baptist, 29
Jones, Bobby, 241
Journey, 231
Joy, 95, 117, 223, 227
Judgment, 18, 110
Justice, 201

Keller, Helen, 71
Knowing, 240
Knox, John, 245

Last Supper, 24
Lazarus, 219
Leader, 158
Leadership, 189
Learn, 94
Learning, 74, 150
Leisure, 24, 261
Lent, 17, 47
Leper, 216
Letter, 78
Life, 44, 99, 126, 137, 150
Life-style, 26
Light, 29, 40, 170, 220
Lincoln, 244, 258, 259
Listening, 242, 245
Little, 70
Longing, 194
Lord's Supper, 32, 33, 36
Lordship of Jesus, 112
Love, 15, 16, 22, 26, 56, 70, 71, 80, 100, 130, 151, 161, 179, 226, 246, 250, 251, 259
Loving, 240
Loyalty, 17
Luther, Martin, 247

Martyrs, 76
Materialism, 208
Mausoleum, 178
Meaning, 126, 150
Memories, 144
Mercy, 201
Method, 262
Minister, 128
Ministry, 209
Misfortune, 98
Mission, 65, 89
Missionary, 65, 66, 67, 77, 96
Money, 138
Monument, 206
Moody, Dwight L., 239
Moses, 14, 198, 249
Mother, 73, 133, 249

Movement, 206
Mount Hermon, 74
Museum, 178
Mustard seed, 108

Napoleon, 241
Near, 244
Nehemiah, 189
Neighbor, 246
New, 230
New creation, 175
New year, 83, 231
Nothing, 52
Numismatist, 74
Nurture, 133

Offering, 95
Old age, 166
Old year, 230
Opportunity, 321

Pain, 52
Palm Sunday, 18, 123
Parent, 130, 152, 252
Partner, 244
Partnership, 86, 181
Passerby, 53
Passion everlasting, 72
Past, 82, 160
Patriot, 159
Patriotism, 157
Peace, 15, 100, 160, 227
Peacemaker, 194
Pentecost, 145
People, 256
Perfection, 87
Performer, 204
Physician, 117, 120
Pitcher, 238
Politics, 254
Pony express, 72
Poor, 71
Pornography, 20
Possibility, 73, 250
Possession, 209
Poverty, 238
Power, 57, 203, 204
Praise, 34, 245, 249
Prayer, 20, 91, 92, 111, 128, 146, 155, 165, 176, 181, 203, 262, 264
Praying, 258
Preacher, 246
Predator, 204
Predicament, 205
Preparation, 55, 57
Pride, 225
Prison, 251
Program, 107

Promise, 114
Prophet, 179
Prophetic, 207
Prophetic voice, 262
Provider, 204
Provincial, 207
Provisions, 218
Pruning, 140
Purpose, 199
Purple, 58

Questionables, 24
Quiet, 56

Rainbow, 43
Reassurance, 134
Reconciler, 241
Reconciliation, 98, 119
Reflection, 76
Refuge, 86
Rejoice, 94
Relationship, 99, 232, 254
Relax, 90
Religion, 15, 148, 162, 169, 183, 263
Remember, 197
Renewal, 37, 92
Repent, 253
Repentance, 50, 105
Requirement, 201
Request, 200
Rescue, 239
Response, 248
Responsibility, 90, 249
Restraint, 244
Resurrection, 40, 49, 53, 54, 110, 124, 125
Rich, 199
Right, 247
Righteousness, 199
Road, 86, 126
Root, 139
Rope, 69
Rules, 254

Sabbath, 102, 103
Sacrament, 24, 32, 38
Saint, 20, 252
Salvation, 63, 104, 136, 164, 176
Satisfaction, 104
Saved, 238
Skepticism, 49
Science, 252, 263

Schweitzer, Albert, 92
Scrooge, 60
Scout, 79
Security, 104
Self-acceptance, 47
Self-commitment, 47
Self-examination, 47, 122
Self-image, 206
Self-love, 22, 246
Sermon, 95, 127, 246, 252
Sermon preparation, 239
Service, 88, 241, 245
Shackleton, Ernest, 242
Shadow, 76, 220, 247
Shalom, 99
Sharing, 209
Shepherd, 57, 244
Sheppard, Dick, 237
"Silent Night," 80
Simeon, 60
Simplicity, 56
Sin, 18, 52, 104, 119, 160, 161, 258
Singing, 240
Sinner, 228, 256, 257
Sorrow, 43, 44, 98, 254
Soul, 264
Space, 256
Speed, 246
Spiritual values, 130
Star, 58, 231 241 256
Star of Bethlehem, 29
Step, 83
Stethoscope, 171
Stewardship, 16, 209, 210, 232
Straight line, 76
Strength, 43, 90, 145
Strong, 131
Struggle, 27
Success, 135, 246
Suffering, 154 166, 255
Sunday, 80, 103, 192, 261
Surprise, 252
Sympathy, 257
Syndrome, 138

Tchaikovsky, 246
Telescope, 171
Temptation, 173, 181
Tempted, 255
Ten commandments, 84, 102
Tenderness, 134
Teresa, Mother, 68, 119

Testimony, 65
Thankfulness, 28
Thanksgiving, 69, 127, 216, 239
Theology, 163
Theresa of Avila, St., 237
Tiger, 76
Time, 23, 59, 90
Tithing, 140, 210, 211
Togetherness, 129
Tradition, 38, 230, 246
Transfiguration, 170, 171
Treasure, 105, 264
Tree, 139, 202
Trouble, 97
Trust, 90, 151
Truth, 202, 224

Understanding, 206
Unhappy, 225
Uniqueness of Christ, 115
Uniqueness of Christianity, 149

Value, 254
Virtue, 257
Vision, 202
Voices, 259
Voluntarism, 203

Walking with God, 93
Water, 249
Way, 31, 247
Well, 52
Wesley, John, 257
Whitefield, George, 64
Will of God, 248
Winds, 143, 247
Winter, 59
Wise men, 227
Witness, 27, 93
Woman, 135
Work, 27, 77, 186, 263
World communion, 26
Worry, 155, 241, 242
Worship, 95, 109, 127, 137, 147, 203, 256
Wren, 75

Valentine, 69

Zacchaeus, 63